Developmental Disorders

Developmental Disorders

The Transitional Space in Mental Breakdown and Creative Integration

Peter L. Giovacchini, M.D.

$\mathcal{A}$

Jason Aronson Inc.
Northvale, New Jersey
London

Library of Congress Cataloging in Publication Data

Giovacchini, Peter L.
    Developmental disorders.

    Bibliography: p. 361
    Includes index.
    1. Personality, Disorders of.   2. Psychoanalysis.
I. Title.   [DNLM: 1. Mental Disorders—therapy.
II. Psychoanalysis.   3. Psychoanalytic Therapy.
WM 460 G512d]
RC554.G55   1986   616.89   86-10877
ISBN 0-87668-919-5

Manufactured in the United States of America.

Contents

Preface

Many clinicians, myself included, have repeatedly stressed how necessary it is to modify our conceptual scaffold both to gain understanding and to learn how to treat our patients. Modifications of our viewpoints about psychopathology go hand in hand with modifications in technique.

In this volume I continue to use the structural hypothesis as a basic frame of reference. However, I include various factors that have received little attention in the literature; they have been neither integrated with other elements nor given the particular emphasis they receive here. I have attempted an integration of spatial qualities of the psychic apparatus within a developmental sequence. Special attention has been given to the formation and structuralization of the inner world of the psyche as it differentiates from and structures the external world. The role of the transitional space in this sequence of development is especially important. As we increasingly understand its contribution, the processes of fusion and secondary narcissism recede

viii Developmental Disorders

into the background as developmental impetuses. The concept of the transitional space as initially formulated by Winnicott (1953) has recently gained prominence as clinicians focus on problems caused by blurred ego boundaries. Transitional space is founded on illusion: the patient believes it is part of the self and the outside observer views it as belonging to external reality. According to Winnicott, the subjective space between the inner and outer world houses transitional objects and illusions, and as it develops leads to progressive and creative development or to crippling structural defects.

My thoughts about these issues were stimulated by patients whose misery pervaded the consultation room and who baffled and frustrated me. I did not understand them, and I could not help them by making interpretations. If I developed any ideas they usually turned out wrong or, at best, not particularly helpful. Thinking in terms of psychic structure and early fixations on primitive mental states, although generally useful, did not seem sufficient to explain certain clinical phenomena accompanied by intense emotional pain.

These perplexing patients all had problems in maintaining self-esteem and defects that affected the cohesion and synthesis of their self-representation. This is not an unusual constellation, and it has received considerable attention in recent literature. The more experience we have with such character disorders, the more apparent it becomes that large gaps in our knowledge interfere with our capacity to treat these patients effectively. By gaps I mean lack of details. It is as if our understanding of the patient is macroscopic; to be therapeutically useful, it must move in the direction of the microscopic. Vicissitudes of the development of transitional space are dominant factors in the production of psychopathology. Our continuing appreciation of the role of transitional space in both normal and faulty development widens our clinical horizon providing us with a vantage point of observation and exploration that enables us to better understand the subtle details of structural psychopathology.

The participation of early developmental stages in determining ego functioning, or malfunctioning, is also being increasingly recognized. I recall several patients who defied all my efforts to understand their emotional problems in terms of inner conflict, adaptive failure, and uncontrolled destructive or guilt-producing feelings. Although they appreciated my vain attempts to help them, they would ruefully shake their heads at my misguided efforts. They were trying to tell me that I was intent on making sense of something that did not make sense. As I much later learned, I was formulating their problems in terms of higher psychic levels with psychological content. The difficulties of these patients, however, resided in the earliest developmental stage, which precedes psychological awareness. I was dealing with prementational rather than mentational issues.

These patients felt constantly agitated because they had not been properly soothed as neonates. Although their problems were, indeed complex, and many ego defects were in evidence, their incapacity to effectively soothe themselves was always a prominent feature of their psychopathology. This had to be taken into account as a difficulty that might create obstacles in the treatment setting. The greatest such obstacle would have been the therapist's confusion as occasioned by his clinging to old models exclusively concerned with mentational factors.

Many of the ground rules of psychoanalysis that we have taken for granted must be reexamined in the face of specific treatment dilemmas. Our therapeutic responses should be consistent with our formulations; yet this does not mean that we must abandon our psychoanalytic technical orientation. The extensions of the structural model this book proposes require that we review our principles about psychotherapy in general and the psychoanalytic process in particular. The ultimate test is whether our increased understanding can be used to the patient's advantage. Fortunately, in many instances, it can.

Peter L. Giovacchini, M.D.

Developmental Disorders

Chapter 1

Introduction

Changing Attitudes on the Analytic Interaction

The patients discussed in this book suffer from relatively severe emotional problems. The materials presented here are derived exclusively from the clinical interaction. They are precipitates, so to speak, of the transference–countertransference interaction, the responses of both patient and therapist as feelings from all levels of the psyche of each become intertwined and continue to bring to the surface emotions that have to some extent been buried. Systematic observation of reciprocal interplay and continuous feedback that characterizes the therapeutic process is itself a type of research, as well as the instrument that makes psychoanalytic or psychoanalytically oriented treatment possible. Freud (1909b) suggested as much when he defined psychoanalysis as both a research method and a form of therapy.

I place greater emphasis than Freud did on the mutuality of

the treatment relationship. He placed the analyst at a distant vantage point, making impartial and neutral observations (Freud, 1911–1915). The analyst was cautioned not to let his feelings contaminate the aseptic psychoanalytic field. Countertransference responses were to be eliminated as soon as possible; if necessary, the therapist should seek further analysis for himself. Freud conceptualized psychoanalytic treatment as unidimensional, that is, a process in which the flow of associations moves in one direction only, from patient to analyst, the latter remaining an impassive mirror. In Bertin's report (1982) of Freud's analysis of Marie Bonaparte, as well as in various accounts by Jones (1953), Freud appears as anything but an impassive mirror. He must certainly have been emotionally involved when he took over the treatment of his daughter Anna (Bertin, 1982, p. 159). Still, he advocated an impersonal, objective approach that compared the analyst to a telephone receiver that unscrambles messages.

The transference as a one-way street did seem an apt metaphor to describe the optimal conditions for conducting the psychoanalytic treatment of psychoneurotics, that is, patients whose psychopathology can be explained on the basis of conflicting intrapsychic drives. The psyche was simplified into vectors that clash with one another, leading to symptoms that define the various neuroses. These symptoms indicate a connection between the internal world of the psyche and the external world. In treatment, the analyst resides in that outer world, and the patient's associations are viewed as flowing toward him. The symptoms, as Freud put it, often "join the conversation" (Breuer & Freud 1895, p. 296). Once symptomatic expressions become the means that bind patient to analyst, we are witnessing a relationship based on transference. Symptoms are the outcome of infantile and defensive adaptations.

Today our concepts of psychopathology have broadened, as have our attitudes regarding the therapeutic process. We know that countertransference factors are not always contaminants damaging treatment, but may represent instead a useful tool for understanding current interactions between patient and therapist (as well as for illuminating infantile traumas as they are being reconstructed in the treatment setting). With this recognition, the transference–countertransference axis can become the most important factor promoting the process of working through.

The therapist's role has expanded considerably beyond that of a reflecting mirror. Many clinicians view it in fact as an intrinsic aspect of the treatment modality. The analyst does much more than listen, understand, and interpret. Put briefly, the situation is as follows: The analyst participates in the analytic interaction by processing the patient's associations. As various aspects of the therapist's unconscious are stimulated, they manifest themselves in a variety of ways, and cannot help but influence the patient's flow of associations. The latter, in turn, will have further effects on the analyst's psyche. This reciprocal interaction characterizes the therapeutic process, and the contributions of both analyst and patient must be taken into account. This is a more dynamic view of therapy than Freud took in his initial formulations, in which free association was solely the patient's responsibility. To a much larger extent than previously acknowledged, analytic communication is a shared experience.

The Patient's Influence

I have wondered about the patients Freud and his early followers treated. How accepting of the ground rules were they? At the beginning of this chapter, I stated that Freud did not always practice what he preached. Apparently, he was often very active with his patients; on one occasion, he seems to have fed a patient, the Rat Man (Freud, 1909b), a point of technique that has been actively debated in the analytic literature (Lipton, 1977). As early as 1895, Freud (Breuer & Freud, 1895) describes how he argued with a patient who would not follow his procedure or accept his explanations. After much persuasion and some threats, the patient, Emmy von N. accepted what Freud had said, but when asked why, she replied: "since you insist" (p. 99). Something similar must have happened with his patient Irma, discussed in the famous specimen dream of Irma's injection (Freud, 1900). His anger at her for not having complied with his wishes served as a stimulus to the formation of the dream. The content of the dream suggests that Irma must have defied Freud by resisting some aspect of his method; in his dream she was reluctant to open her mouth for him to examine her throat. Freud's associations displayed resentment over Irma's not wanting to reveal herself; he compared her with a woman friend of hers who would have been more cooperative (p. 110).

Thus, at least some of Freud's patients did not accept the requirements of the analytic method. Freud learned from these experiences and postulated the concept of resistance. Most of his patients' difficulties stemmed from their resistance to free association; Freud actively struggled against the resistance in order to get them to reveal themselves.

Today, although we do encounter concretely oriented, non-psychologically minded patients, we also find many patients not at all reluctant to reveal the innermost, most primitive aspects of the self. From Freud's viewpoint, there is no resistance. Still, because they are much too needy, they do not often adapt themselves to the abstemious setting Freud recommended. Instead, they seek primitive gratification and demand that the analyst supply them what they were deprived of during infancy. The silent analyst would not last beyond the first session.

In a sense, we are faced with an impasse similar to the one Freud faced. There are, however, differences that make it easier for us than it was for Freud to remain analysts and still keep these patients in treatment. Freud was stymied at the most fundamental level. His patients would not let him understand how their minds worked, whereas our patients, or rather a sizable group of them, openly and insistently reveal their mental processes. To learn about the hidden recesses of the mind is a fundamental aim of psychoanalysis. Consequently, from one viewpoint our patients are better adapted to psychoanalysis than were Freud's resistive patients. There are many difficulties in treating any patient, and the patients we see today are particularly difficult, but the problems we encounter are in areas that do not always or necessarily threaten the integrity of the psychoanalytic situation.

Freud believed he was working with psychoneurotic patients who had intrapsychic conflicts. Various levels of the psyche opposed one another, an opposition that became an impediment to free association. Although some clinicians (Reichard, 1956) have questioned whether his patients were in fact classical neurotics, that is nevertheless how Freud viewed them. The phenomenon of a resistance that had to be overcome was central to his therapeutic strivings. By contrast, most of our patients—schizoid personalities, borderline states, and character neuroses (Giovacchini, 1979b)—are formulated in terms of structural defects and are thought of as character disorders.

Ego psychology has become in many clinical circles the predominant approach, pushing id psychology into the background. Our patients' psychopathology is better understood in terms of ego defects and structural factors than as the product of id forces clashing with the ego and superego. Therapeutic approaches have been modified on the basis of our shifting conceptual systems, but, as I emphasize throughout this book, these are modifications and extensions of the analytic method and do not represent its abandonment.

The concept of what constitutes psychoanalysis has to be extended. Our current generation of patients, if not particularly different from the hysterics seen 80 or 90 years ago, have proven either less compliant or less suggestible. This may partially be explained by sociocultural change—an atmosphere that has minimized the revered and authoritative position of the physician and therapist. Patients today are in general not easily swayed, nor will they unquestionably accept interpretations or directions as to how to run their lives.

Developmental Factors

Although Freud did not stress emotional development or dwell particularly on object relations, he nevertheless constructed a developmental scale, a sequence of phases leading to final emotional integration and structuralization (Freud, 1905, 1911, 1914c, 1920, 1923a, 1923b). He also discussed object relations in terms of shifts of psychic energy (Freud, 1914c). We do not ordinarily think of Freud as an object relations theorist, because he paid less attention to the influence of the external world than

to the power of the drives in shaping the psyche and in neurosogenesis.

Freud (1920), however, referred to the impact of the environment from the beginning of psychic life and at the time of
the earliest differentiation of the ego from the id. He viewed
external stimuli as impinging on the psyche, causing its periphery to form a nidus of structure that constitutes the rudimentary ego. Freud went into considerable detail describing this
earliest interaction and the mother's participation in modulating
these stimuli by providing a protective shield, a *Reizschutz*, lest
they become disruptive.

The ego gains further structure as it passes through various
developmental stages. I simply wish to point out what has
received very little notice, and that is how Freud's sequence is
compatible with an ego psychological and object relations perspective. It is not simply a drive theory, although it is drive-
oriented (Giovacchini, 1980).

According to Freud, the ego's first functional mode is auto-
erotic. It does not acknowledge the participation of external
objects in achieving gratification of inner needs. Rather, it supplies its own gratification, although the environment creates a
setting that makes such self-induced pleasure possible. It is in
this context that Freud postulates the development of object
relationships, first a preobject phase of primary narcissism and
then the first contact with the external world by the formation
of narcissistic object cathexes. The latter phase is that of secondary narcissism.

Freud's purpose here was to explain certain phenomena as
variations and shifts in cathexes, an index of his heavy reliance
on psycho-economic principles derived from contemporary de-
velopments in thermodynamics, a science concerned with the
accumulation and discharge of physical energy. Still, Freud did
not entirely ignore the influence of transactions with the infantile environment on both normal development and psychopathology. The role of sexual trauma in the etiology of neurosis is an
early formulation designed to demonstrate how outside events
determine psychic development.

The psychosexual stages Freud postulated were object-
related, though he did not explicitly state that in early develop-

mental phases the psyche relates to *part* objects. Drives during the oral stage, for example, were understood as directed primarily to an external object, but to which the infant relates solely on the basis of the object being able to satisfy the need to be nurtured. Subsequent phases show a similar pattern, inasmuch as significant persons in the surrounding environment are important only by virtue of their ability to gratify progressively structured drives. Persons are treated as whole objects during the final stage of development, the genital phase.

The object-relationship and ego-psychological aspects of Freud's thought were not reflected in his clinical formulations. Although by postulating his structural theory (Freud, 1923a), he laid the groundwork for the understanding of character structure and its distortions, Freud did not use this comparatively new frame of reference to broaden his perspective on psychopathology.

I will not review the subsequent history of object relations theory and ego psychology, but will simply indicate a few areas especially important in helping us to understand the more subtle aspects of the structural defects seen in the majority of outpatients. Such an understanding might well suggest technical maneuvers useful in maintaining the analytic setting.

Infantile Trauma

Many of our patients have had extremely traumatic infantile backgrounds. Among patients from lower socioeconomic groups, seen usually in clinic settings, assault and neglect during infancy sometimes reach horrifying proportions. It is to be expected that the earliest developmental phases would be disruptive and that this would affect all subsequent emotional integration and structure formation.

Fixation at primitive levels, however, is not restricted to the psyches of low-income groups. It is found in all strata of society and is dominant in the patient population of all psychotherapists, psychoanalysts included.

A casual perusal of the infancies of some patients may not reveal anything particularly unusual. This may be due in part to the patient's faulty perceptions and incapacity to face the more unpleasant aspects of past relationships. The patient may need to use primitive defensive adaptations such as denial. The full impact of parental sadism is often recognized only after many years of treatment, though its effects are readily discernible.

Furthermore, although early childhood settings may give the appearance of having been gentle and benign, disturbing interactions may occur that neither child nor parents are aware of at the conscious level. In these patients' backgrounds the parents are usually intelligent and well educated, and appear to be sensitive, understanding, and concerned about their children's welfare. The traumatic, violent environments more often encountered in lower socioeconomic groups are superficially quite diffrent from the backgrounds of our more affluent patients. Yet the emotional disturbances they present are just as severe as those found in clinic patients, and it remains an enigma how this could have happened, given such relatively benign backgrounds. I recall a prominent child analyst throwing his hands up in despair after I had described such a situation. In an exhausted fashion he exclaimed—only somewhat facetiously—that perhaps what we had here was a "bad seed."

I believe, however, that if we could thoroughly study childhood backgrounds we would discover devastatingly traumatic elements in early object relations that are hidden by "false self" interactions. A patient of mine, described more fully in Chapter 3, was charming, aristocratic, and the epitome of grace and gentility. She spoke in a soft, well-modulated tone, and displayed sensitivity and insight regarding family and friends. She was always considerate of my feelings and was pleasant to talk to. Nevertheless, I had to adhere to a strict schedule with her. I could see her only in the morning, because in the afternoon, after lunch, she would drink continuously until driven home in the evening, dead drunk. I had learned of this behavior from the referral source, her family physician. The patient acted as if she drank very little, and then only with decorum and when socially appropriate. I would never have suspected how disturbed her behavior could become were I receiving information from her alone.

The patient's defensive adaptation demanded that she maintain an image of herself compatible with ancestors she considered illustrious, gracious, and noble. This adaptation was only partially successful. She was depressed and anxious enough to overcome her initial resistance to psychotherapy, and was grateful for our daily sessions. She obviously derived considerable support from our relationship, which for many months she used to reinforce her defensive self-deception. She eventually attained enough sense of security, however, to reveal her vulnerabilities. Slowly and gradually, over the course of three years, she became increasingly able to discuss how she had destroyed her life and the lives of her children.

I will not dwell on details here (see Chapter 3) except to mention that she revealed how little attention she paid to the maids hired to raise her children, how insensitive she was to their needs, and how inept she was in caring for them. This information was reconstructed bit by bit; the patient was far from aware of what she had or had not done. She had not been directly sadistic or attacking. Perhaps she had had good intentions, but she was so inadequate, needy, and vulnerable that her children were raised in a nightmarish setting to rival any of those described for disturbed ghetto children. Still, in her family, no one talked about unpleasant topics or experiences. Covering up was not only a way of life but a vital method of psychic survival. Furthermore, she seemed unable to register these early traumatic interactions intrapsychically and thus could not spontaneously reproduce them. Her husband joined her in walking around with psychic "rose colored glasses."

Because of structural defects, many patients have defective perceptions. To some extent, all perceptions are determined by various attributes of our characters. Patients massively damaged during infancy demonstrate extensive lacunae, both in their sensory appraisal of the external world and in recalling the past. This is the structural parallel of the childhood amnesia Freud described as the outcome of the repression of infantile sexuality.

My patient, in her role as mother, lacked the integrative capacities to understand the harmful aspects of her behavior toward her children. Children are known to have been assaulted as early as the first weeks or even hours of life, a time at which there is insufficient mentation for mnemic integration to occur.

Of course, traumas tend to be continuous; they may extend into developmental periods that can be remembered. By that time, however, the sensory system is sufficiently defective that it registers experiences in a mode quite different from that observed in persons whose infancies were more benign. What might be suffered as overwhelmingly painful and horrible by a person raised in secure circumstances may be experienced as standard operating procedure by severely disturbed patients.

The frequency with which these traumatic pathological distortions are encountered in clinical work requires that modifications be made in our thinking regarding development. As the treatment relationship allows us to understand more thoroughly the emergence of the patient's character from childhood trauma, the concepts of transitional phenomena and transitional space (Winnicott, 1953) acquire a central position in our formulations regarding structural defects and characterological maldevelopment. This book contains discussions of other phases, the symbiotic stage for instance, in order to determine where they belong on the developmental timetable and how they can be damaged by trauma.

Countertransference and Working Through

The treatment of primitively fixated patients stresses that interactions within the transference–countertransference axis become the most important factor in successful therapeutic outcome, as opposed to insights about events retained as unconscious memories. The more we learn about treatment, the more we must focus on countertransference responses. The patients we commonly see have the capacity to agitate therapists to a much greater degree than could traditional psychoneurotics, who are presumably struggling with intrapsychic conflict and use defenses to maintain repression of aberrant and unacceptable impulses. Basically, the psychoneurotic is struggling with oedipal conflict, to which defenses provide a regressive solution—a regression to earlier stages of psychosexual development. In the course of transference development, psychoneurotics assign various roles to the analyst in attempts either to support defenses or to gratify underlying id impulses. These roles are clear enough and should not threaten the analyst's integrity. Such patients are said to be dealing with impulses and with defenses against them; they do not threaten the analyst's psychic structure, because their own personalities are supposedly intact. Dealing simply with the projection or displacement of impulses, it is said, should create no countertransference impasses.

Of course, disruptive countertransference reactions can in fact develop with any patient, not necessarily because of idiosyncratic factors in the therapist. Psychoneurotics are often quite skillful in detecting and exploiting a therapist's vulnerabilities.

Interactions based on defective psychic structure are potentially more threatening to the therapist than those determined by intrapsychic conflict. The projection of damaged parts of the self into the analyst is often intended to disrupt and to injure. The patient attempts to create a setting that strains the very limits of survival. The main function of the analyst in such cases *is* simply to survive the patient's destructiveness. Such difficult situations can easily lead to untoward countertransference reactions.

Therapeutic resolution and working through also depend on the acquisition of insights. If the patient does not recover memories of infantile traumas, how can he gain insight that might lead to further psychic integration? It must be remembered, however, that it is *emotional* insight, a reliving of past experiences in the current setting with the analyst, that leads to understanding. Freud (1914d) stressed that the past must be remembered rather than repeated in action. Forgotten memories must be recovered, and this constitutes the lifting of infantile amnesia. Something similar, although short of total cognitive reconstruction, must occur in contemporary psychoanalysis and psychoanalytically oriented treatment. In case presentations, I seldom hear of the actual recovery of memories, even when the patient has been diagnosed as psychoneurotic. The transference–countertransference interaction, on the other hand, brings into focus traumatic and constricting relationships, an experience that has a potentially liberating effect.

Creative Integration

If, as therapists, we devote our attention to the primitive levels of the psyche, we occasionally get glimpses of the higher, integrative functions of the mind. The understanding of primitive mental states gives us insights into the highest human functions—artistic accomplishment, scientific discovery, aesthetic contemplation. Although much about the creative process remains mysterious, it is likely that all levels of the psyche participate simultaneously in the act of creation.

The creative personality is associated with various character traits and unique childhood experiences. These are variables that cannot be generalized for all creative persons. Furthermore, the constitutional elements of innate talent and genius cannot be ignored. Still, there seem to be certain combinations of early infantile relationships, developmental vicissitudes, and the organization of the perceptual system that favor the emergence of creative potential. As we make inferences about factors leading to character defects and psychopathology, we can use the same approach to discover what shapes a creative character—the forces that favor its development.

Conversely, in learning about higher psychic functioning, as we partially characterize creative activity, we will also broaden our perspectives on the primitive end of the mental spectrum. One would assume a wide spectrum between higher and lower levels for the creator, and a narrow one for patients suffering from severe and crippling psychopathology; but the width of the spectrum is not rigidly fixed; it can achieve breadth or become narrow, depending on the impact of environmental and intrapsychic forces. During treatment, a concretely oriented, unimaginative, and constricted patient may develop the ability to function creatively as he gets in touch with parts of the psyche that were previously in states of fragmented isolation. The reverse may also occur. Creative persons may become submerged in their psychopathology and seek treatment; their defenses will not only drain psychic energy previously used for creative accomplishment, but will interfere with what once had been a free and easy communication between different psychic levels. When such talented persons seek treatment, they usually complain about feeling inhibited and being unable to create.

It is striking that many severely disturbed and constricted patients present this same complaint: that they are unable to be creative. I have often encountered the poet or novelist who could not write, the musician who could not perform or compose, the would-be scientist who had never finished his dissertation. These are familiar character types to anyone who practices analysis. Though many of these patients have no real talent, some do, and they seek liberation of their potential through psychoanalytic treatment.

It is no mere coincidence that many of our patients who find the analytic experience rewarding also value creativity. I surmise that there are important similarities between the analytic and the creative process. Analysts, as a group, are fascinated by the mental operations of creativity, as evidenced by the popularity of papers and workshops on this topic at meetings. Their interest in the arts, music, and science is much greater than that of the average intellectual, and an unusually large number of analysts have some special artistic or musical talent. There must be parallels between analytic work and creative productivity, and this is experienced by both patient and therapist.

If the analytic interaction is governed by factors similar to those guiding the creative process, then perhaps treatment itself is a creative experience. Unlike ordinary creativity, however, it is a shared experience that enhances both participants—an act of mutual discovery. Though revealing hidden facets of the patient is its aim, often enough, especially with severely disturbed patients, the analyst digs up certain aspects of his own character, aspects not always pleasant to face. Patient and therapist expand the dimensions of their personalities, and this is an accretion, just as the creative product is an accretion to reality (Giovacchini, 1960, 1971). As will be discussed in Chapter 11, the dynamic interplay that occurs in recovering lost parts of the self and unearthing hidden feelings and anxieties is essentially the same as what happens in the scientist's mind when he produces something novel, something that adds a new dimension to reality. Expansion of the mind and expansion of reality are in many ways equivalent.

Thus, there may be an inherent creative element in the analytic interaction that makes analysis intensely interesting to persons who value creativity, analysts and patients alike. Beyond the element of discovery, however, there may be additional features in the analytic relationship that are significant in the creative endeavor as well. I am referring to the interplay of fantasy and reality, and reality and delusion. Every patient, whether psychoneurotic or suffering from a character disorder, has his own private view of reality, a reality modeled after that of the infantile world. How it matches with consensual reality determines whether we label him as delusional or as having good reality-testing.

We must become involved with our own primary process in order to better understand our patients. We must in some sense fuse with their mental operations and have our fantasies resonate with their realities. This is similar to what happens in creativity when the innovator's fantasies overshadow and often replace reality. *With patients, however, there is a reverse process operating; it is not fantasy that replaces reality, but reality, the patient's reality, that replaces fantasy.* The therapeutic task is to convert the patient's reality back to fantasy.

This is a complex subject that will be discussed in later chapters. Here I will briefly note that the technical maneuvers of treatment enable the patient to incorporate the external reality he has created back into his inner space, so that he can gain control of what had previously been viewed as unpredictable and threatening external circumstances. To remold reality in a fashion that is more compatible with the external world, and to acquire new adaptations and controls, is a creative achievement. The setting for such changes is the transitional space, the area of play, fantasy, and creativity postulated by Winnicott (1953). The interplay of fantasy and reality need not be a destructive interaction. Gradually, with therapeutic progress, it becomes a pleasurable activity and may acquire playful qualities. This is serious play to be sure, but what in the context of psychopathology was experienced as overwhelmingly threatening and painful has now become a rewarding activity with creative dimensions.

Part I

Psychic Development and Psychopathology

Chapter 2

Developmental Factors, Fusion States, and Narcissism: Is Narcissus a Myth?

Structural Considerations

A shift in emphasis from oedipally based intrapsychic conflicts to psychic structure has caused clinicians to place considerable importance on early developmental stages. In clinical formulations, Oedipus is more and more often replaced by Narcissus. Consequently, the narcissistic phase of development, as postulated by Freud (1914c), must be soberly reexamined.

The findings of such investigators as Brazelton (1963), Emde, Goensbauer, and Harmon (1976), Emde and Robinson (1984), Freeman (1971, 1979), and Klaus and Kennel (1982), to mention but a few, are relevant to psychoanalytic formulations regarding the production of psychopathology. Their recent observations have stressed further the influence of very early interactions on the formation of character, and it seems appropriate at this point to extend and modify some of our concepts regarding pregenital phases. Tustin (1981) has studied autistic children and placed them in a developmental conceptual framework that takes into account early cognitive abilities that had not been suspected before the systematic direct observation of infants. Neonatalogists now recognize the early exercise of cognitive capacities, greater sensitivities to specific interactions with the external world, and the existence of the bonding experience. All these have changed or at least modified our conceptions regarding both normal development and disturbances of emotional development that lead to structural defects and psychopathological adaptation or withdrawal.

Freud's ideas about narcissism have not been contradicted either by longitudinal studies or by recent findings in neonatology. Nor have they been validated, however. This is understandable, because the data so far collected allow no more than inferences about complex mental processes. Such data deal with actions and interactions and are of necessity limited to phenomenological sequences. These may be suggestive of narcissistic attachments, fusion states, and various regressive adaptations, but in no way can they even approach conclusiveness. Studies using observations of the analytic process, however, permit us to make formulations about early mental processes and also lead us to inferences about normal development that may differ from Freud's, in terms of sequence if not the qualities of the various stages. Inferences from the psychoanalytic interaction, if not more easily derived than those from phenomenological data (though I believe they are), have greater plausibility, because they are clinically useful and help us to understand our patients.

We can begin by questioning the primitive end of Freud's developmental spectrum, that is, his ideas about primary and secondary narcissism. Our experience with patients who fall into borderline or psychotic categories, that is, patients who have characterological defects, has taught us that their psychopathology involves disturbances of these early phases. Clinical necessity requires that we learn more about the quality of structural defects and how they affect adaptations to the external world and the development of object relationships.

Focusing on Freud's sequence from autoerotism to secondary narcissism raises several questions. I will not discuss auto-

erotism here, because this phase, as postulated by Freud, antedates psychological processes. If it exists at all, it would belong
to what I have called a prementational phase (Giovacchini, 1979b;
Giovacchini and Boyer, 1983)—the earliest biologically based
developmental phase, one preceding the construction not only
of mentation, but also of even minimally organized affects.
Instead, I will concentrate on psychological processes in general
and those involving narcissistic fusion states in particular.

Freud's model of emotional development, because it is a
developmental timetable, raises the question of its own inevitability as a preordained sequence. Must one particular phase
follow another? As the organism progresses toward a more
differentiated organization, does a similar or parallel organization occur in the psychic sphere? Certainly we make such an
assumption when we view psychic states along the axis of a
progressively structured hierarchy. Our concepts of regression
and progression, fundamental to our understanding of both
psychopathology and the therapeutic process, depend on viewing development as a forward-moving differentiation, both spa-
tially (higher and lower levels) and temporally (archaic past and
present secondary process).

Structural progression is well illustrated in the differentiation of the self and the outer world and the progressive structuralization of object relationships. Consequently, it is consistent
to postulate an initial amorphous psyche that eventually
becomes organized in a discrete manner, consisting of well-
delineated subsystems resulting in an integration of perception
and adaptive behavior. The steps that lead to higher, more
complex differentiations vary according to different authors.
Freud (1920) postulated an initial and undifferentiated id which
develops an embryonically organized core that receives modulated stimuli from the outer world and leads to higher psychic
organization. Hartmann (1939) wrote of an id–ego matrix as the
initial psychic state, whereas Glover (1930) described the coales-
cence of ego nuclei. Piaget (1937), Melanie Klein (1946), and
many other investigators and clinicians have introduced developmental sequences that vary from one another, but nevertheless describe a movement from the global to the structured. This
movement has important implications for the development of

object relations, the construction of the self-representation, and the formation of ego boundaries.

Despite what seems to be agreement as to developmental progression and its inevitability, we may still question whether certain way stations, so to speak, are essential to the process of structuralization. For example, do we need to assume that the child hatches from symbiotic fusion, as Mahler (1972) has postulated? Is there a movement from a global and amorphous preobject psychic organization to fusion with the mother, followed by a gradual separation that results in individuation and the capacity to relate to external objects? In short, are we to accept that the essential way stations during these early phases are amorphous states, fusion, and separation–individuation?

In a similar vein, we can ask whether secondary narcissism as a way station to the formation of object relationships is an absolutely essential transition phase. Even though some authors (Balint, 1968) have argued against the feasibility of postulating a phase of primary narcissism, the latter seems to be much more consistent with biological maturation than secondary narcissism. The process of psychic energy being focalized around that portion of the psychic apparatus which interfaces with the outer world just before there is an awareness of the outer world is analogous to the development of sensory systems as they process external stimuli. In so doing, these systems structuralize further so that, in a positive feedback sequence, they are able to relate with greater sensitivity and perceptiveness to the very same and other stimuli (Herrick, 1956).

In the psychic sphere, we have a parallel situation, inasmuch as the stage of primary narcissism precedes an ego that will recognize and relate to external objects. The ego has to be sufficiently energized (cathected) so that it can direct itself to the external world, to the not-me. As it does so, the ego's perceptive capacities expand, and it becomes better able to process outer stimuli and to recognize external objects in an ever-increasing totality. The ego thus progresses from a primary narcissistic position, in which there is no distinction between the inner and outer world, to the establishment of object relationships. The assumption of an in-between phase of secondary narcissism, however, that is, the construction of a self-object and symbiotic fusion state, has no parallel in biological maturation. This is not to say that secondary narcissism, because it is synonymous with self-object and fusion as a stage of development (Boyer & Giovacchini, 1967, p. 269), is invalidated by the data that come from either biology or neonatology. I am merely suggesting that there are alternative ways of viewing early emotional development that are more useful to our study of clinical phenomena and the treatment of patients.

Clinical Implications of Healthy and Pathological Symbiosis

Beatrice (1985) has placed healthy symbiosis fairly high up on the developmental ladder when he describes it as a process that leads to positive identifications. In the hierarchy of psychic mechanisms, identification is fairly sophisticated. As selective aspects of the personality of external objects are incorporated, the self-representation undergoes further cohesion and gains in depth, and dimension. To achieve this, the ego has had to develop rather sensitive discriminations, and it perceives the external world in a structured fashion. This capacity is well beyond what has been described as the ego state of the infant who is emerging from symbiotic fusion, and becoming aware of the external world as separate and distinct.

Is Freud's concept of secondary narcissism and the construction of the self-object similar to healthy symbiosis? Inasmuch as secondary narcissism is a way station on the path that leads to the formation of object relationships and the consolidation of ego boundaries, it would seem to be a nonpathological process. The question can be repeated as to whether it immediately follows primary narcissism or, to be conceptually consistent and clinically relevant, whether it might require further intermediary steps to complete or, at least, add to the developmental spectrum.

Before discussing this question further, I wish to examine pathological symbiosis as occurs in disorders of narcissistic equilibrium. The treatment of narcissistic disorders and borderline states—that is, characterological problems in general—resembles or becomes organized around the mother–child interaction to a much greater extent than the treatment of better-structured ego states. This gives us an opportunity to study early psychic processes associated with individuation and the formation of primitive object relationships. The relevance of fusion can be evaluated as we examine regressed ego states in the context of the transference.

Formulations about early fusion states have been made from the adult's viewpoint. During treatment the analyst relies heavily on his countertransference reactions to assess the patient's ego state and developmental level as it is reproduced in the transference. The patient, however, is not a neonate, and his mental processes are based on the capacities and acquisitions of later developmental phases. Is there a symbiotic fusion between therapist and patient based on ego states at similar levels? To a large measure there is such a fusion, which recapitulates the mother–infant relationship. Still, it is the patient's adult ego that has regressed, and his experience differs markedly from the neonate's. The analyst's reactions, however, are usually responses to the patient's neediness and helplessness as maternal and nurturing feelings are evoked in him.

As he attempts to respond intuitively to the patient, to get in tune with primitive needs and despair, the analyst may recognize that he is using fusion mechanisms. In turn, the patient fuses with the analyst. This analyst–patient fusion constitutes a symbiotic union, although the therapist's needs, that is, his therapeutic intent, are at a higher level than those of the patient.

Something similar occurs in the mother–infant bond and interaction, although there must undoubtedly be vast differences as well. Winnicott's (1956) view of healthy mothers as being in a state of "primary maternal preoccupation" is compatible with the thesis that the mother fuses with her child so that she can anticipate infantile needs and provide optimal nurturing and soothing. She is constantly around, supplying her ever-hovering attention. This is how she feels, and this is how we, as adults, view her. In this regard she is very much like the empathic analyst, although her dedication and devotion are total, whereas the analyst's involvement is both temporally and emotionally limited.

Even in the normal mother-infant relationship, it is not necessary to assume that the mother's and child's mental processes within the nurturing interaction are parallel to each other. The mother may perceive herself as being symbiotically fused with her infant, and her intuitive reactions support her orientation, but the child does not reciprocate at the same level.

I am equating secondary narcissism and symbiotic fusion inasmuch as both are conceptualized as a self-object that represents a pathway to object relationships. The term "symbiosis" can be questioned if we view the relationship as based on equal needs of the fused pair. The mother can obviously survive without the infant, whereas the reverse is not true. Still, there is a strong mutual dependency in a psychological sense that justifies the term "symbiosis." Regarding secondary narcissism, however, it is not an implicit assumption that the object the infant fuses with reciprocates in a similar manner and receives gratification of vital needs. Nevertheless, since it is the nurturing person, the mother, that is usually the object of the child's narcissistic attachment, she would also be involved in the fusion, and the interaction could be viewed as symbiotic.

There are, of course, many caretaker-infant interactions in which the caretaker is not symbiotically attached to the child. Undoubtedly, this is the basis of serious psychopathology. From a developmental viewpoint, the role of secondary narcissism can still be examined even when the child's nurturing source has not formed a symbiotic attachment. It is conceivable that the child could fuse with an external object without the object reciprocating and fusing with him. In this case, however, it is likely that we are dealing with a particular type of psychopathological merger that represents a deviation from, or a distortion of, normal development.

During the phase of secondary narcissism described by Freud (1914c), the child enters the world of external object relations by first attaching himself to the mother, at first viewing her as part of himself. The devoted mother described by Winnicott (1953, 1956) does not disturb the illusion of her child, who feels in complete control and the source of his own nurture. Winnicott describes these interactions in terms of the transitional object in the context of the mother's orientation of primary maternal preoccupation. Fusion mechanisms are not required in his developmental model.

I am emphasizing that perhaps we can discard Narcissus as an important figure in *the course of early emotional development*. This would imply that when we find evidence of narcissistic object relations in our patients' material, we are usually witnessing the manifestations of psychopathology. There are, however, narcissistic and symbiotic elements which we encounter clinically that do not have serious implications about emotional disorders.

I will refer to such situations later, but now I wish to further discuss narcissistic attachments that run, so to speak, in one direction. In treatment it is well known that during deep transference regression, patients merge, more or less intensely, with the analyst. The patient is recreating an early infantile relationship, but the analyst's response will help to determine whether this interaction retains its psychopathological significance. I am referring to how much, in turn, the therapist fuses with the patient. Is the therapist's response similar to what the patient experienced during infancy, or does the analyst react in a different, benign fashion? The latter does not imply any role playing; it simply refers to maintaining a benevolent analytic perspective.

There is a spectrum of merger responses emanating from the therapist as well. They may range from one of minimal fusion, in which case there would be a relative absence of symbiosis, to almost total merger, which could result in complex countertransference difficulties. Somewhere in the middle of this spectrum may be an optimal countertransference response, an optimal fusion, that can undo or, at least, help to undo the effects of early trauma. *The analyst's orientation toward the patient can create a symbiotic transference that is not a repetition of the infantile setting. Rather, it represents a rectification of childhood deprivation.* The therapist's counterfusion is different from both the infant's and the mother's psychic states at the time the child was just beginning to move into the outer world. The mother's fusion in psychopathological circumstances is often more of an engulfment based on her vulnerabilities and destructiveness rather than a smooth symbiotic union designed to foster an intuitive resonance that enables her to be in immediate touch with her child's needs.

The patient has never known the maternal sensitivity that is the essence of an optimal nurturing and soothing relationship. The analyst places himself in a psychic position that enables him to merge with the patient based on his need to analyze and to foster autonomy and individuation rather than on personal idiosyncratic needs. The analytic setting becomes a soothing environment, and through timely interpretations, the analyst provides symbolic nurture. This is an entirely new experience for the patient. This comfortable state of fusion, however, is often achieved only after considerable turmoil and the terrifying experience of having repeated in treatment the early traumatic maternal destructiveness.

This discussion implies that there is both healthy and pathological narcissism, a formulation Federn (1952) made a long time ago. To carry this formulation just a little further, it also implies that within the state of narcissistic fusion, there can be both healthy and pathological symbiosis. The position of these phenomena on the developmental scale is a factor in determining what is healthy and what is the effect of emotional maldevelopment. I have already indicated that healthy narcissistic and, therefore, symbiotic attachments occur only when object relationships begin to become fairly well established and ego boundaries consolidated. There is also considerable cohesiveness to the self-representation.

Early traumatic relationships, a consequence of the mother's pathological symbiotic needs, distort the infant's development so that when he reaches later stages, narcissistic isolation becomes a defensive and psychopathological adaptation to maintain a false self (Winnicott, 1960). I am also distinguishing between narcissism as a psychopathological defense from the healthy fusion of secondary narcissism as part of a post-individuation developmental phase. In psychopathology the patient, as Freud (1914) described, is withdrawing libido from the external object as a defense against fusion. Symbiotic fusion is experienced as terrifying. In analysis, such patients, during the transference regression, reexperience the maternal assaultive engulfment in the context of an early helpless and vulnerable ego state. I have placed this ego state at the primitive end of the developmental spectrum, one in which mentation is just beginning and before the external world is separated from the psyche.

The traumatic fixation point to which these patients regress is a much earlier developmental stage than the psychic organization that enables the psyche to fuse with external objects or that is able to perceive, at conscious or unconscious levels, external objects fusing with it. Still, as we repeatedly observe in the therapeutic interaction, when patients regress, they still retain many psychic mechanisms and adaptations that are characteristic of advanced developmental stages. Consequently, fusion and symbiosis in treatment can be experienced in the context of very primitive psychic organizations, something that cannot occur during the course of ordinary development. The amplification of these topics related to pathological processes can help in clearing up some inconsistencies and contradictions that have not been resolved in our understanding of how the psyche progressively structuralizes.

I will present a clinical vignette to highlight disturbances of development during what is usually considered to be an early symbiotic phase, but which can be better explained in terms of disruptions of transitional phenomena. I discuss in Chapter 4 how the patient has been used as a transitional object, and in Chapter 3 how disorders of early soothing mechanisms manifest themselves in treatment. This vignette illustrates many features that are focused on in these two chapters, but some are highlighted here as they are relevant to our investigation of fusion states and the developmental process.

Clinical Material

A woman in her early forties, who had been in treatment with me for many years, was unable to become involved in an intimate heterosexual relationship. She had been married three times and had innumerable affairs, but all these relationships turned out badly. Because she is personable and intelligent, she attracted charming and successful men. Similar to her, however, they had difficulties in sustaining intimate relations. Apparently they were highly narcissistic persons who used the patient to enhance their narcissism.

To summarize drastically, the first two years of this patient's analysis were exclusively concerned with revealing how inadequate and empty she felt. Though she continued to function at high levels in her daily life, she regressed to a state of helpless vulnerability in the consultation room, revealing a self-representation consumed with feelings of worthlessness and self-hatred. She emphasized her lack of ego boundaries and the lack of cohesion of her identity sense. She exemplified this ego state by picturing herself as an empty bottle that was buffeted around by both angry and capricious waves. She felt she did not exist as a person; she was there only to do the bidding of others.

Her self-denigrating attitude was also quite visible in the transference. The patient idealized me and blamed herself entirely for what she viewed as her lack of progress and for her pervasive sense of misery. She frequently lamented that she was failing me, because I could not count her as one of my therapeutic successes. I would be neither personally nor professionally enhanced for having treated her. It was evident that she saw herself as having a definite role in the treatment beyond the needs of a patient and beyond the wish of her therapist to be helpful and a catalyst to the developmental process. Clearly, she expected me to use her. How was quite vague, other than by gaining professional prestige. In any case, her needs were to be totally subjugated to mine.

She often referred to herself as a dirty rag doll, and frequently quoted the negative definition of a little girl, "a rag, a bone, and a hank of hair," which made me think of a much mishandled transitional object. I felt impelled to reply "sugar and spice and everything nice," but I did not make this quote until much later in her treatment, when she was able to construct polarities. During this stage of therapy she could only deal with her dehumanized manipulated self.

This period was followed by many sessions in which she experienced intense anxiety and despair and finally started vociferously attacking me. This began with her accusing me of using her—in the very way she felt she *should* have been used during the first two years of our relationship. Now she felt that I was manipulating and exploiting her, that I insisted on treating her like a rag doll. To my mind, this represented a mother transference, but it was also evident that by attacking me, she was reversing roles and identifying with her mother, treating me as she felt treated as a child. Between attacks, I felt as if I did not exist, so much so that to some extent, I welcomed her abuse, because at least under these circumstances, I was being acknowledged and not simply ignored and controlled as a nonhuman object.

I was reminded of Modell (1968), who believes that the characteristic transference of borderline patients is to treat the therapist as a transitional object. Feinsilver (1980, 1983) has written in a positive sense of transitional relatedness in treatment, and Searles (1976) has addressed himself specifically to transitional phenomena in the context of symbiosis. I definitely felt as if I were being controlled like a transitional object as the patient was reenacting the repetition compulsion in the transference regression, but she was taking the active role instead of being passsively vulnerable, a reversal first described by Freud (1920). At this stage of treatment I did not feel at all fused with her, nor did she with me. In fact, she had never felt intimate closeness with anyone in her life. She was now, however, retrospectively aware of intense rage for never having been acknowledged as a person with her own needs and separate from others.

There were, of course, as in any analysis, many facets to the transference. To focus on specific elements of the interaction in isolation from the patient's complex and varied feelings may give the impression of a clear-cut continuity that does not, in fact, exist. I will, nevertheless, emphasize certain elements that can lead to some conclusions about the symbiotic phase and its significance for psychopathological and normal development.

Gradually, the patient began once again to have positive feelings toward me, but without the intense idealization that had characterized her initial reactions in treatment. She felt she had made considerable progress, and she had developed faith in herself as a person. She was proud of how she was able to do things in a self-assertive but not intrusive fashion, and spoke of situations in which she was managing quite effectively, whereas previously she would have been overwhelmed by her vulnerability. She was especially proud of her ability not to be taken advantage of by men.

She also started reading some of my writings and adopted many of my viewpoints. She felt very much identified with my position and saw our closeness as mutually enhancing. Her associations indicated concern over whether I found my relationship with her to be valuable, which I did indeed, because of the pride I took in her progress and because of what I was learning from her. This sanguine state lasted six months, during which time she had at least a dozen dreams stressing that we were fused in a symbiotic attachment with each other.

Then the analysis became an increasingly unpleasant experience for her. Her concern about whether I was getting something out of her treatment mounted, and she finally concluded that I was exploiting her. At this point in treatment, I had become her paranoid object, and she was reenacting her psychopathology within the transference context.

The patient was gradually able, through interpretations, to understand how she was repeating certain maladaptive patterns and reexperiencing infantile relationships. The paranoid fervor completely subsided as we continued working in an atmosphere of mutual cooperation.

She repeatedly emphasized that she could not have survived, and perhaps neither could I, the paranoid period had she not built up her self-esteem when she felt herself to be symbiotically fused with me. She believed she had gained a sufficiently stable sense of identity, and that it had enabled her to maintain the integrity of her ego boundaries as she viewed herself in an unprotected state of helplessness to withstand my oppressive and exploitive onslaught. Furthermore, the treatment had provided her with a unique experience, the opportunity to fuse with a benign, helpful external object, something that had never occurred in her "real life," as she put it. Later, she no longer responded to me as if I were benign, but this represented a regression as she was getting in touch with the more primitive levels of her psyche and revealing aspects of defective development.

Discussion

The study of this patient permits us to draw inferences about normal emotional development by emphasizing specific developmental phases. Psychopathological distortions highlight the existence of the underlying ego state, and working through these distortions can give us a picture of what the psyche might have been like if it had not been pounded by infantile trauma. During regression in treatment, patients retain later developmental levels alongside the primitive ego state to which they have regressed. The analyst has the opportunity to observe distorted and maladapted patterns of high and low levels simultaneously. In some instances, attitudes and behavior that constitute the patient's adult adjustments are clearly reflections, that is, upward extensions of earlier, more primitive structural malformations. In other patients, there seems to be no connection whatsoever between later and earlier adaptations. The earlier ones appear to be ineffective and unreasonable, whereas the later ones are reasoned and reality-oriented. There seems to be discontinuity between various psychic levels that is manifested by puzzling behavior. The patient can be eminently sensible one moment and act bizarre, perhaps psychotic, the next. Such psychic discontinuity, which is discussed in detail in Chapter 4, was indicative in the case under discussion of difficulties in the patient's emotional passage through the transitional situation.

My patient had been traumatized early in life. Maternal caretaking had been defective, discontinuous, or nonexistent since birth. Instead of relating to her as an individuating child, the patient's mother treated her as if she were a transitional object. Rather than being involved on the basis of the child's needs, she needed the relationship only insofar as she felt in control and did not have to give anything of herself. It is unlikely that the mother felt fused with her child in the sense of having recognized her as separate and then merged with her. I am postulating that the patient, in turn, did not fuse with her. I do not mean to indicate, however, that she was totally incapable of forming narcissistic attachments and fusion: I would conjecture in fact that the complete absence of a psychic mechanism is a very rare phenomenon. I am indicating only that the patient demonstrated this deficit in the transference–countertransference interaction.

I repeat Freud's (1900) caveat that it may be untenable to extrapolate hypotheses about normal processes from the study of psychopathology, but he proved how useful this method can be, especially in his discussion of the psychology of the dream process. Granted, simply because some patients indicate that they did not fuse during their infancy, we cannot generalize from psychopathology. Still, if during treatment, the developmental process is once again set in motion and symbiotic merger occurs, it behooves us to try to determine just where this happens to fit on the developmental timetable.

In this instance, the patient had already begun to feel that she was an individual in her own right; she had developed some aggressiveness and self-esteem *prior* to incorporating my values, beliefs, and attitudes. Merging seems to have represented an advancement and enhancement of the individuating process. She then regressed to a pathological state of fusion in the transference, viewing me as the exploitive, controlling, destructive mother who used her as a transitional object. This was a feeling state that she had never experienced before the transference regression in treatment. In fact, it was created *by* the therapeutic relationship, and the patient stressed that *I* was fusing with *her*. She was not fusing with me; in fact, she was trying to escape my pursuit of her. She finally succeeded in maintaining separation by constructing a paranoid defense.

Symbiosis and fusion are complex processes that cannot be conceptualized on a simplistic basis, whether they are defensive constellations, aspects of normal development, or manifestations of defective emotional development because of the impact of psychic trauma. They seem to serve a variety of functions, both adaptive and maladaptive. To place such processes exclusively at the primitive end of the developmental spectrum, however, is conceptually inconsistent and is not borne out by clinical data.

The nature of trauma is a subject that requires considerable exploration. We have moved away from Freud's early formulations of sexual trauma as the chief psychological etiological factor in the production of psychopathology (Freud, 1905). Although today we are faced with more and more examples of childhood sexual abuse, we are learning that there are many factors in addition to disruptive sexual assault that are responsible for the damaging effects of these early encounters. We view early trauma from a broad perspective that includes the total infantile environment, with emphasis on the nurturing relationship. The development of the self-representation is determined by how well the child was nurtured and soothed. Self-esteem and the sense of security are, in turn, dependent on the cohesiveness of the self-representation, which is also reflected in the development and continuity of object relationships. The solidity and flexibility of ego boundaries are determined by how well the ego is integrated and the stability of the self-representation, as they evolve from a relatively nontraumatic environment. Trauma could be defined as a setting that interferes with the sense of security and the feeling of safety—the confidence that nurturing and soothing needs will be met. Homeostatic balance is lost or disrupted, and the long-term effects of such disturbances are seen in various forms of psychopathology.

The interaction between the caretaking adult and child can be considered from many perspectives. The axis that I have been examining concerns the fusion or lack of fusion between parent and infant. The mother I have been discussing treated her daughter as though she were her transitional object. She used her child to maintain control of inner disruption, to soothe herself so that she could maintain a tenuous connection with the external world. The infant, in response, does not develop a cohesive self-representation and a sense of aliveness, a true self with discrete boundaries.

Patients such as the one I have presented construct characteristic defensive adaptations as a response to having been controlled and used as the mother's pacifier. They suffuse the environment with their inner disruption, that is, create external chaos and thereby gain relief of inner tension (see Chapter 4). My patient recapitulated the mother–infant relationship in her dealings with me. Her mother had used her as a nonhuman object to support her narcissistic defenses. But this experience had also enabled the patient to live calmly in a chaotic world. Her personal life was highlighted by a continuous series of crises that she dealt with efficiently and calmly, always maintaining her distance and never permitting herself to develop feelings about or reactions toward her surroundings. This attitude was useful, because she was just about the only person who kept sane in that mad world, and this allowed her to be effective and to get the job done.

By this behavior, the patient was illustrating a reversal of roles, that is, she was relating to her environment as her mother had related to her. She was also continuing the infantile relationship inasmuch as she was treated as a transitional object in her current object relations. The latter problem was the chief manifestation of her psychopathology and had become so painful that it motivated her to seek treatment. She saw her numerous affairs as leading nowhere.

Her reversal of the early mother–infant relationship, although a defensive adaptation, nevertheless indicated that the patient was able to effect a fusion in adult life, something she was unable to do in early infancy. It was a pathological state of fusion, however. In treatment, when she was incorporating my values, the situation was different, because she believed she was gaining something valuable rather than manipulating me. As stated, this was a new experience that first occurred during treatment. This type of fusion was somewhat similar to what occurs during normal development, after some degree of individuation has occurred and ego boundaries are somewhat consolidated.

These conceptual reflections could be significant for our understanding of the symbiotic psychosis of children as described by Mahler (1952) and others. Child psychiatrists and social workers who work in residential treatment centers have reported data that do not support the thesis that such children are locked in a symbiotic fusion. Rather, the mother's propensity not to let the infant separate from her is prominent, but the reverse is not usually the case. In fact, I have been presented with examples which clearly indicate that these children have an incapacity to incorporate elements of the external world and make them parts of themselves, although they may demand the constant presence of the nurturing caretaking source. In fact, it is this inability to survive without the actual presence of the mother that signifies that the child cannot fuse with her. Apparently these children have not achieved the capacity for object constancy (Fraiberg, 1969); they cannot form and hold a mental representation without the reinforcement of the external object (Giovacchini, 1979b). To fuse requires the establishment of an internal object representation so that the self-representation can merge with it. These mothers, for their part, need to be with their children at times when they feel agitated. On the other hand, they have more defenses available to them, and can find substitute objects or even withdraw as the child becomes inadequate to serve as an effective transitional object because of the intensity of the mother's painful and disruptive feelings.

As mentioned, there are different types of infantile traumatic relations that lead to various forms of psychopathology. I have described character defects that basically prevent patients from forming intimate relations because they have been raised as transitional objects. There are other types of mother–infant fusion, usually more primitive mergers wherein the mother destructively fuses with her child, using the son or daughter as the receptacle for the hated parts of the self. This situation has been written about more frequently, especially by Melanie Klein (1946). The children go through life being panicked about fusing and about getting close to anyone, and, often, they use schizoid defenses to keep their emotional distance, whereas the patients I have described are not usually anxious. They are simply incapable of merging because of a developmental deficit. They have considerable rage, but it first surfaces in treatment as they relive with the therapist the early traumatic relationship.

These studies of psychopathology have implications for technique and the theory of emotional development. I cover treatment issues extensively in Chapter 8. It suffices here to point out that we are faced with transference reactions and elements of the repetition compulsion that have to be understood in terms of the unique features of infantile traumatic relationships. The latter are different from what we are accustomed to in our usual treatment of patients. If we do not recognize the patient's need to treat us as a transitional object or appreciate how angry he is at us for feeling we have reacted to him in a nonhuman fashion, then we are likely to have disruptive countertransference reactions that could easily lead to impasses that eventually disrupt the treatment.

Regarding emotional development, Winnicott's concept of the transitional situation gains much greater prominence. As the child structuralizes from the prementational phase to beginning mentation, he gradually becomes aware of the existence of a space that is separate from the self. This is accomplished by the construction of a transitional space—transitional in that the child perceives it as part of the inner world, whereas the adult sees it as a segment of the external world of reality. Objects within this space are transitional objects that the child uses to maintain control of inner tensions and to soothe himself. Gradually, as children feel increasingly secure that tensions will be calmed and needs met, they are able to relinquish control of some of the objects in the transitional space and begin to recognize them as something in their own right, rather than as just the servants of their needs. Winnicott (1969) wrote about the use of an object as part of the process of relinquishing control over it as it moved from the transitional space into the outer world. This passage through the transitional space signifies the beginning of the recognition of the outer world and the establishment of object relationships, at least part-object relationships. This process is discussed in greater detail in Chapter 4.

The process of emerging individuation does not require fusion mechanisms, but symbiotic attachments occur later as external objects become further differentiated. With increasing security that needs will be met, and with the growth of trust and confidence, children can allow themselves to become dependent and to relax their ego boundaries in a fusion state without feeling threatened or vulnerable. Disturbance of the earlier transitional phase will make the passage of objects from the transitional space into the external world traumatic and create disturbances in the later establishment of symbiotic object relationships.

The further examination of developmental factors and the revision of concepts about emotional growth are important endeavors for the clinician. For the most part, we are dealing with severely disturbed patients who fill their lives with misery.

Knowing about the adaptive significance of their despair and how they are repeating dehumanizing experiences in their current life may enable the therapist, through his understanding and survival, to help guide the developmental process in the right direction. Of course, we have to know what that direction is and where Narcissus enters the picture.

Chapter 3

Early Levels of Psychopathology

Diagnostic and Developmental Considerations

I have so far focused on developmental factors as they are relevant to the production of psychopathology. Fusion processes, transitional phenomena, and the transitional space have become important concepts in helping us to understand various types of characterological disturbances. Such disturbances can be more precisely defined and classified in terms of early developmental levels, amplifying considerably what we have learned about difficulties at later stages of psychic integration.

I have repeatedly stated (Giovacchini, 1975a, 1979b) that I find categorization of emotional problems of limited usefulness; the categories too easily become preconceptions that interfere with listening to our patients' material with an open mind. Eventually, however, we do make formulations, whether overtly or covertly, as to how our patients' minds work and where their psychopathology fits into some diagnostic scheme. Our currently modified views about the neonate's developmental sequence and the early mother–infant interaction have interesting implications for that process.

It should be noted that psychoanalysis has made special contributions to the task of diagnostic categorization. Before Freud, emotional disorders were defined phenomenologically, by clusters of symptoms and by other external factors, such as age and type of onset, the acute or chronic quality of the disturbance, its duration and spontaneous prognosis, and so on. Freud's in-depth viewpoint, based on a psychodynamic approach, provided a new perspective for understanding different types of emotional disorders. Rather than concentrating simply on the external manifestations of psychic disturbances, Freud distinguished among various neuroses on the basis of fixation and regression; that is, he determined where they belonged on the developmental spectrum. He did this by noting that certain defense mechanisms are frequently found grouped together and are characteristic of a certain phase of psychosexual development. For example, he saw that undoing, isolation, and reaction formation often occur together, and that they are typically found during the anal phase of psychosexual development, which dominates the ego orientation of the obsessional neurotic. Thus Freud introduced other variables to make nosologic distinctions. He arrived at his diagnoses by using several frames of reference simultaneously: the ego's fixation point on the psychosexual scale, intrapsychic conflicts, and the types of defenses that determine the patient's adaptations.

As I pointed out in the introduction, Freud (1914c) separated the transference neuroses from the narcissistic neuroses on the basis of whether or not a patient could form a transference. Whether Freud's ultimate conclusions about these two patient groups is correct or not is irrelevant in this context; but the particulars of his distinction saw to it that he concentrated mainly on what he called the transference neuroses, that is, the psychoneuroses—hysterics, phobics, and obsessive compulsives. He also studied the psychoses, particularly the paranoid state and the depressions, but most of his efforts were directed toward the psychoneuroses, because he believed psychoneurotics capable of cathecting the analyst and so being influenced by him.

By contrast, this book focuses almost exclusively on what I am calling the character disorders. I am distinguishing the character disorders from the psychoneuroses in a way that roughly corresponds to the distinction between physiological and anatomical abnormalities in medicine. The psychoneuroses are the outcome of conflicting intrapsychic forces where the structure of the psychic apparatus appears to be fairly intact. Character disorders involve defects in the architecture of the personality that are the outcome of faulty development. Severe traumatization of early developmental stages affects all subsequent phases in ways that specifically determine the extent and nature of psychopathology. Freud's diagnostic variables are also useful for the study of this group of patients; the main factor distinguishing the character disorders is that the basis of their psychopathology involves the ego–outer world axis rather than the id–ego axis. Again, the emphasis is on psychic structure, in that the problems these patients have in relating to the external world affect their capacity to function in general.

The nosological division I have posited is valid primarily for didactic purposes. Such distinctions are seldom clear-cut when we are dealing with patients. On the other hand, this division implies that we can use concepts derived from both id and ego psychology. We need not favor one frame of reference over the other. The type of disorder, whether psychoneurosis or character disorder, will determine which conceptual scheme is most appropriate.

Because the psychopathology of the character disorders is based on defects in structure, the different types of characterological problems can be separated in terms of developmental factors and structuralizing processes in the framework of early object relationships. I have therefore constructed a developmental sequence that focuses on the earliest phase of emotional elaboration. Again, the subdivisions of the character disorders I am about to describe are not distinct and clear-cut. There is considerable overlapping, even between groups that are fairly well separated on the developmental scale. Moreover, what I am about to postulate must be considered tentative and subject to revision as we continue to collect data from the treatment of patients as well as from other areas of observation.

The Sequence of Psychic Development

The Prementational Stage.   At the very beginning, the infant's mind can be viewed as functioning at a prepsychological level, a phase before the development of the capacity for mentation. I have called this the prementational stage, a very short period of neonatal life that precedes perception and encompasses an organization that is restricted simply to the recognition of states of comfort and discomfort. Perhaps comfort and discomfort are too sophisticated in terms of affect organization to be integrated by such rudimentary psyches. It might be more accurate to say that neonates experience, in some vague and indefinite fashion, fluctuating states of tension as they attain or lose homeostatic balance.

State of Early Mentation.   Following the prementational phase is a state of some psychological awareness. The infant begins to feel in a fashion that approximates the adult's feelings regarding internal sensations. In the state that Winnicott (1956) called primary maternal preoccupation, the mother can, within herself, evoke needs that resonate with those of her child. Again, these are tension states, and they refer to comfort and discomfort, but they are better organized at this point in terms of identifiable needs—hunger, for example, or irritation because of a wet diaper. These sensations approach states of pleasure and displeasure, but in a very rudimentary fashion.

I believe this phase, which may last up to two or three months, can be designated as a stage of amorphous ego organization. The previous prementational stage is probably very short-lived, and the continually reported findings from the observation of newborn infants keep pushing it back in time to hours and days. As with most mental phenomena, there is considerable overlapping, and one developmental stage does not replace another. Rather, they blend into each other, and elements of all phases coexist.

The amorphous ego cannot yet distinguish the inner and outer worlds, and the ego boundaries are imperfectly constructed. Consequently the infant does not have the capacity to acknowledge external objects. This is a preobject state with minimal mentation.

Again, this sequence is self-evident if we think in a biological context. "Structuralization" is a term indicating a movement from a more amorphous configuration to one of greater complexity. Embryology traces the development of the organism from a unicellar zygote to a complex being with an astronomical number of cells and a multitude of systems and subsystems. The ego can be conceptualized as structuralizing in a similar fashion.

Around the age of six months, infants develop stereoscopic vision. They move from a two-dimensional to a three-dimensional mode of perceiving. Fox, Sheas, and Dumas (1980) and Held (1981) describe experiments demonstrating the acquisition of stereopsis in infancy. Roth and Blatt (1975) study spatial dimensions in dreams in their endeavor to further their understanding about ego structure and psychopathology. Szajnberg (1983) discusses the implications of these findings for psychoanalytically derived theories of development. He compares externally observed prospective data with the retrospective, subjective psychological data of severely regressed patients, and then makes inferences about the first six months of life, using Spitz's genetic field theory of ego as a theoretical framework for biopsychological integration.

These studies have implications for those aspects of the developmental sequence that are related to the ego's construction of boundaries and its perception of the outer world in a comprehensive fashion. A two-dimensional perspective is associated with a primitive, rudimentary concept of an environment that is still attached to the periphery of the psyche.

The world is flat because externality is incomplete; the distinction between the ego and the surrounding ambience is still indistinct. External reality has not yet achieved the depth and perspective that reflect the complexities of the surrounding world. With the ego's further differentiation, reality, as it were, moves further and further away from the self and is perceived in an ever-increasing scope. This would constitute a three-dimensional, in-depth view, and it would include a more integrated view of the psyche as well. In other words, the perceptual modality has expanded in both directions, toward the inner world of the mind and toward the external world. Three-dimensional perceptions eventually lead to a sensitive appraisal of the outer world and an introspective approach to the operations of the mind. The latter is associated with psychological-mindedness, and it stands in contrast to the flat, concrete orientation associated with a two-dimensional view of the world. These distinctions are especially relevant clinically, because many patients suffering from character disorders have not progressed beyond two-dimensional modalities.

The Transitional Stage and Object Relatedness.   I will outline in some detail the psyche's entrance into the external world, because it is precisely during these stages of emotional development that psychic trauma has its greatest impact for the patients I discuss. In the previous chapter, I presented both theoretical and clinical arguments as to why I believe that secondary narcissism and fusion mechanisms belong to later object-related ego states. Here I will simply state that I believe the next developmental stage following an amorphous ego organization is best conceptualized in terms of Winnicott's (1953) theory of the transitional state. Briefly, by constructing a transitional in-between state, the ego structuralizes to the degree that it is finally able to recognize objects in the outer world. This is to acknowledge a world over which the ego has no control, in contrast to the illusory power it had over objects in the transitional space.

Within the context of object relations, the ego continues to structuralize, and its area of functioning is correspondingly expanded. It becomes capable of finer integration and perceptual discriminations. As it becomes increasingly involved with external objects, it begins to incorporate aspects of them and to integrate them as part of the developing self-representation. The psyche's repertoire of adaptations is enlarged through introjection and projection, psychic mechanisms that are constructed through the continual interaction of the inner world of the mind with external reality. Similarly, because of newly acquired integrative processes, the child can fuse with emotionally supporting caretakers, more often than not in a symbiotic merger (see Chapter 2). The child thereby stabilizes useful introjects and endopsychic registrations that maintain homeostatic balance and enable instinctual gratification.

This developmental model stresses the importance of interactions with external objects as the most significant factor in the structuralizing process. The role of instincts and constitutional factors is thus minimized, but not by any means abolished. The ego, its subsystems, and the perception and expression of drives (basic needs) are all components of a complex psychic structure that can undergo many vicissitudes in its development and suffer from distortions, lacunae, and other defects.

Character Disorders on the Developmental Scale

Character disorders stem from different fixation points on the developmental scale. In the clinic or in the consultation room, the diagnostic distinctions are not often illustrated in a pure form. Most cases are a mixture of these categories, and, to some extent, all developmental levels contribute to the structure of the psyche and to psychopathology. On the other hand, there is usually a focus on infantile trauma that had its greatest impact on a particular early phase.

The Schizoid Disorders. At the primitive end of the psychopathological hierarchy, I place what I call the schizoid disorders. These are patients fixated at the beginning of the developmental spectrum, the prementational stage, so that later stages of development are extremely constricted, and the patients' range of adaptations is severely limited. These disorders are perhaps best characterized by the patients' paucity of adjustive mechanisms and their withdrawal from the activities of living. Such people remove themselves from the external world and live in a state of schizoid isolation. Their inner world is equally impoverished and demonstrates a lack of fantasy and imagination. They tend to be concrete in their thinking and literal in their perceptions.

The schizoid disorders are difficult, but not necessarily impossible, to treat. Such patients find it difficult to sustain a cathexis of the analyst and to think in terms of psychological connections. Their concrete orientation makes therapy tedious and often seemingly nonproductive. On the other hand, the analyst's persistent presence is generally felt sufficiently that the patient may tentatively venture into the outer world and partially give up his schizoid withdrawal. I have reported in detail the treatment of such a patient, emphasizing that the analyst helps the patient to reach a level of psychological awareness by reacting to concrete modes of communication as if they had symbolic meaning (Giovacchini, 1979b, Giovacchini & Boyer, 1983).

The Borderline Disorder.   The next classification of patients has received the greatest amount of attention from clinicians—the borderline patient. I define the borderline disorder somewhat differently than Kernberg (1975) and Masterson (1976) do, in that I push the fixation point somewhat further back, but not by much. They believe the borderline patient to be arrested at the stage of beginning separation–individuation, and they stress the patient's poorly formed self-representation. I agree that these patients do, indeed, have problems in their identity configuration, but I would add that their egos are more amorphously organized than the psychic structure that characterizes beginning separation–individuation—Mahler's (1972) hatching phase. They can minimally relate to the external world in a "borderline" fashion, but they do not have the adaptive techniques to function well as separate persons. Rather than being on the threshold of integrating a relationship with the world of external objects, they are still fixated in a transitional space in which they exercise defensive magical and omnipotent control, techniques that are totally inadequate to deal with reality. Many borderline patients also have little fantasy activity, and the need for control is not necessarily part of an elaborate fantasy or delusional system. It can also take the form of a concrete, simple manipulation, much as a child might throw a rag doll around in order to feel strong and powerful.

When facing the surrounding world, borderline patients feel profoundly inadequate. I have often quoted a patient of mine who stated this situation most eloquently when he said that he had an arithmetic mentality but lived in a world of calculus complexity.

Most clinicians think of the borderline patient as a person who can easily become psychotic, but who reverts back to a nonpsychotic state rather quickly. In my experience, this is true for all patients suffering from structural defects, that is, for the character disorders in general. I reserve the term borderline for patients who are borderline in two respects: 1) they make borderline adjustments to the external world, in that their adaptations are inadequate to cope with the complex demands of reality, and 2) they may lose their psychic equilibrium and become psychotic. The psychoses of borderline patients usually emphasize their vulnerabilities, helplessness, and inadequacies, and may, as happens with the schizoid patients just discussed, be characterized by schizoid withdrawal. As a rule, these patients lack the florid and complex delusions that are part of the paranoid state.

The Character Neuroses. As the psyche moves through the transitional space into the outer world, the identity sense consolidates, and the ego acquires the capacity to relate to external objects. When psychopathology is the outcome of trauma that affects this developmental period in particular, there is a discrepancy between the organization of the external world and that of the psyche. This discrepancy is different from the inadequacy of the borderline. Unlike borderline patients, these patients have developed relatively complex adaptations, but they are not in synchrony with, and thus not particularly functional in, the world they inhabit. I call this group of patients the character neuroses.

Unlike schizoid patients and borderlines, these patients have at their disposal a variety of defensive adaptations, whose aim is to create harmony between the inner and outer worlds. In a sense, this would be true of any adaptation, but the character neurotic attempts to achieve this state of harmony by changing the environment or by relating to some special segment of it and withdrawing from the rest. This is not a unilateral process, however. The ego selects some portion of reality that is, to some extent, in resonance with its needs. In this way the ego forms a "false self," but not like Winnicott's (1960) false self, which refers exclusively to the ego that molds itself to the external world, a psychic structure that is the outcome of compliance. Rather, I am describing a defensive interaction in which the psyche selects a particular aspect of the external world which will stimulate the formation of a psychic configuration that can adapt to it, but the external world is also accommodating to the psyche's adaptive capacities.

The reality this patient chooses to live in is similar to the infantile setting, and the closer the latter is to the current reality we generally recognize, the closer the psyche approaches the formation of a true rather than a false self. Adaptations will be more functional and efficient because they will encompass wider segments of the surrounding world. In the character neurotic, there is generally sufficient difference between the infantile and current environment that the construction of a false self is necessary.

The false self is "false" in the sense that it is not smoothly integrated in the mind as a continuous extension of the lower levels of the psyche. The character neurotic exhibits a fair amount of fragmentation and thereby tends to use splitting and projective mechanisms. Kernberg would define these patients as borderline (1975), but, for the reasons I have just discussed, I prefer to reserve the diagnosis of borderline for an earlier fixation point.

Included among the character neuroses are those patients known as narcissistic personality disorders, which have been described by many other authors (Boyer, 1983; Giovacchini, 1979b; Kernberg, 1975; Kohut, 1971; Searles, 1975). They have constructed narcissistic defenses to overcompensate for what are experienced as deficiencies in the self-representation, which create a pervasive sense of inadequacy. Other patients reveal their feelings of inadequacy directly, presenting the familiar picture of the alienated patient who functions poorly and has very low self-esteem.

The Depressed Patient.   The final category of patients on the developmental continuum encompasses those who have moved into the world of external objects and who have replaced split-ting defenses with ambivalence. They are able to direct polar-ized feelings of love and hate toward the same part object, and the clinical manifestations of their psychopathology are those of depression. These are fairly well-structured personalities, al-though they may be harder to treat than more primitively fix-ated patients. I have discussed depressed patients elsewhere (Giovacchini, 1979b), and mention them here to complete the developmental scale.

The Psychoses.   The psychoses belong to a different diagnostic frame of reference and are not easily assigned specific and characteristic fixation points. I do not believe that they can be understood as entities independent of the character disorders. *They cannot be placed on a continuum with them because they are, in themselves, hybrids of schizoid states, borderlines, char-acter neuroses, and affective disorders* (see Chapter 6).

As is well known, many of the character disorders can be the precursor of a psychotic state, usually a transient one. The stabilized psychoses also have a structural configuration similar to the respective character disorders that precede their onset. In other words, the prepsychotic state is based on a specific char-acter disorder, even though there are additional features that may help to explain why in one instance the patient regresses to a short-lived psychotic episode and remains borderline, and in another instance, the patient becomes psychotic in the tradi-tional sense (see Chapter 6). Undoubtedly constitutional factors are also operating.

Tension States and Disruptive Agitation

In light of the foregoing sequence of disorders, I now propose to investigate a group of psychopathological entities that demon-strate the effects of very early traumatic interactions on the nurturing process. Such patients have been puzzling but increas-ingly recognizable in our clinical experiences. We find them difficult and enigmatic because they cannot be understood in terms of conventional intrapsychic conflicts. This is due, in part, to the fact that a large portion of their problems stem from the prementational phase and cannot be expressed psychologically. Rather, we are dealing with tension states and agitation without content. The maternal bond has not been effectively established, and the nurturing experience has been painful and disruptive.

To understand how psychopathology can develop at these early stages, we have to examine the various components of the caretaking interaction—the background and foreground. The background of the caretaking interaction refers to the holding environment—literally. It is characterized by how the baby is held, how the infant is soothed so that the infant can be fed in the most satisfying and beneficial fashion. A fussy baby cannot gain much nurture if fed in an unsoothed state. The mother must be able to soothe her child in order to feed him; in turn, the feeding experience causes the infant to feel further soothed. This is a positive experience that promotes psychic growth. The background and foreground of the nurturing process must be synchronous and coordinated with each other, and must feed back into each other in a positive way. A series of such equilibrating experiences leads to the infant's endopsychic registration of a nurturing modality that has a significant influence on the course of emotional development and the construction of object relations. As is readily evident, much can go wrong during the neonatal period, and the caretaking experience can be inadequate and traumatic in a variety of ways.

We can immediately think of potential deficiencies in the mothering relationship, what I have called errors of omission (Giovacchini, 1979b). Spitz (1945) has described tragic situations in which there was not even the slightest attempt to soothe the child while he was being fed. He describes the situation in an orphanage where the children were kept in cribs surrounded by high walls that did not reach the ceiling. They were fed punctually, but there was no interchange whatsoever between nurse and child. The children were not related to as human beings. Regarding the nurturing process, we can surmise that these children were not offered a holding environment, and they were not soothed. This means that the maternal bond was never established, and one would expect their emotional development to be severely impaired. As it actually happened, their physical development was also affected, and most of them died before they reached one year of age.

The children Spitz described would seem to be extreme examples, but I do not believe they are. They are extreme only in that their situation is obvious. The nurturing interaction was characterized by lack of both warmth and emotional attachment; consequently, the children were nurtured neither emotionally nor physically. There are many children, however, who are raised in conditions approximating those of the orphanage, but they are not so clearly recognized. Their situation is not so obvious. The traumatic interaction is not openly manifest, but it is nevertheless severe, and the effects on the infant's character are drastic. I am referring principally to traumas that have their chief impact on the soothing aspect of the caretaking interaction. The infant does not form what we might call a *soothing introject*. As a consequence, the child lacks the capacity for internal regulation of tension states. As adult patients, such people are often in a constant state of agitation.

Tension is a manifestation of various emotional disorders; it possesses specific qualities that can be helpful to our understanding of underlying psychopathology. Usually we tend to regard unpleasant emotional states as the manifestations of either depression or anxiety or both. These elemental affective states define certain types of intrapsychic conflicts. The situations I am about to discuss are considerably more complicated, because they emphasize complex structural defects related to the beginning stages of emotional development.

The lack of certain endopsychic regulators, such as soothing mechanisms is characterized by specific behavioral responses and compensatory adaptive reactions. These patients often respond in a manner that, from superficial observations, appears paradoxical. I wish to comment about and distinguish various types of tension states.

Chronic Disruptive Agitation

The first group of patients display a chronic and often constant state of disruptive agitation, although in some instances there is a rhythmic pattern. I recall a 23-year-old single man who complained of always being anxious. He was constantly in "emotional pain," he said, and nothing would give him relief. Nor did anything in particular precipitate his tension. It was just there all the time. I looked in vain for causal factors or ancient traumatic episodes that could explain the onset of his symptoms. The patient protested that they had had no onset; they had been there as long as he could remember. Throughout his life he had seen a series of therapists, none of whom had been able to help him, either with psychotherapy or with drugs. He had also received extensive diagnostic workups that failed to uncover any organic factors.

The only change his symptoms appeared to undergo was that they were worse every time he saw me. He would tell me, for example, that he had never felt so bad in his whole life, that this was the worst he could possibly feel. But the next session he would say he felt worse, and calling attention to what seemed to be a contradictory hyperbole had no effect whatsoever on him.

I continued to look for unconscious conflicts that would explain his all-pervasive anxiety. I covertly indicated my interest in dreams, but he seldom reported any, and when he did, they were almost exact replicas of reality. He would dream with amazing concreteness of detail about some event in his daily life that he had actually experienced. I felt frustrated, and then agitated, because I was confused and could not grasp some understanding of why he felt as miserable as he did.

The patient responded to my efforts with disdain. He told me that I was "barking up the wrong tree," but I did not, at first, understand what he meant. Then it slowly dawned on me that he was trying to say that there was no underlying content to his anxiety and agitation. I had been trying to fit him into a construct that assumed ego states at a much higher level of psychic integration than he was capable of attaining.

I had already begun to think specifically of problems regarding soothing mechanisms when it occurred to me that I was agitated at the end of every session. Contrary to what I might have expected, I did look forward to seeing him. He was a challenge, and I actually saw our sessions as encounters, anticipating them with both freshness and vigor. Still, about the time the patient was ready to leave, I was aware of being uncomfortable and agitated. This was especially so during sessions when he would lie on the couch silently for long periods, although his physical demeanor clearly indicated that he was very tense. Unlike other patients (some of whom I discuss later in this chapter), he did not feel calmer after the end of a session. I felt disrupted, but apparently he had not succeeded in getting me to absorb his agitation.

My capacity to maintain inner calm, to preserve a homeostatic balance, was temporarily disturbed by our sessions, but just as I felt puzzled by the source of his tension, I was in a parallel way perplexed by my untoward response. I was aware that I found him frustrating because I could not fit him into a comfortable conceptual scheme. I also felt dismayed by his vociferous complaints that he was always getting worse, implicitly blaming me for his worsening condition. Still, I did not believe these factors were sufficient to explain the intensity of my reaction.

I reached my conclusions about what was happening to me after a session in which I practically fell asleep. About 10 minutes after the session had started, I was aware of mounting discomfort: My eyes felt heavy, my neck was tense, and I was experiencing the onset of an occipital pressure headache. The headache became increasingly painful, spreading like a tight band around the temporal and frontal region. My reaction was to feel drowsy; I had to struggle intensely to stay awake. Finally I fell into a hypnogogic reverie that was primarily auditory rather than visual.

The patient happened to be quite verbal during this session, in contrast to the sessions when he was anxiously silent. As I fell into a somnolent reverie, his voice became indistinct, although it increased markedly in volume. Soon it lost both its communicative and human qualities as it reached a discordant and cacophonous pitch and intensity. I felt as if the sound were piercing my eardrums, and the consultation room became a cross between a noisy, smoky discotheque and the clanking boiler room of an ocean liner. I was experiencing the patient's voice as total chaos, a disorganizing experience that completely upset my sense of inner calm and emotional equilibrium. I realized that I had momentarily lost my ability to soothe myself. When I recovered from the hypnogogic state, I was able to view the patient in a somewhat calmer perspective.

I do not believe that I had absorbed the patient's tension. Rather, he had succeeded, perhaps not consciously, but with unconscious intentionality, in disrupting my inner soothing mechanisms. I had many visual images to depict my feeling state. For instance, I thought of foreign bodies getting caught in and stripping the gears of machines that had been running quietly and smoothly. The more I became aware of the nature of my disruption, the less agitated and more comfortable I felt with the patient. This occurred gradually over a period of nearly a year, during which, for the first time in his life, he began experiencing some relief. At first, he tried to sedate himself by drinking. He had tried alcohol in the past and had never attained relief, but now it seemed to help. If he drank two or three shots of vodka, he was able to "take the edge off" his tension. He still felt anxious, but his anxiety was not as intense as it had been. Finally, he was able to stop drinking altogether and was able to feel soothed by our sessions.

I will not pursue the course of this patient's treatment further, because it is not relevant to the investigation of prementational agitation and defects in internal soothing mechanisms. I will add only that as he was able to acquire some psychic equilibrium, he was able to work on various intrapsychic problems, problems that had been completely submerged by his chronic and intense tension. He also began to experience increasing quantities of anger, apparently in direct proportion to the amount of soothing he was able to achieve.

I wondered and still wonder about what exactly occurred between us that accounted for the amelioration of symptoms that had been constantly present for many years. Once I recognized that my internal soothing regulators had temporarily stopped functioning when the patient presented me with his agitation, I was able to regain equilibrium. Previously, before my disruption, when I had been calm, the patient did not benefit from it; and later, as mentioned, when I felt upset, the patient also did not improve, indicating that I was not absorbing his agitation. Following my disruption, however, when I was once again comfortable, he was able to feel better, as if he had internalized my capacity for self-soothing. Whether the sequence of my feeling disrupted and then being able to recover from a temporary disequilibrium was an important factor in the patient's acquisition of self-soothing mechanisms is difficult to determine, but I believe it did play a role. It was important for the patient to know that he could have an impact upon me, but it was even more significant that I was able to recover from his disruptive influence.

He had been able to frustrate and upset many persons, including therapists, but none had been able to regain inner peace when confronting him. He had been afraid that those persons he upset would not survive his distress, and that made him feel worse, if that were possible. These reconstructions were made with me as the treatment progressed; previously he had not been consciously aware of his concern about destroying others.

As already mentioned, he claimed he was never aware of feeling angry, either. Now he did feel angry, and at times he could direct it toward me, but for the most part he experienced it as a diffuse feeling without any particular target. Still, he was comforted by it. He compared it to a stabilizing anchor that helped him to organize otherwise chaotic and inchoate feelings.

I concluded that affects such as anger and erotic feelings possess a degree of structure; when superimposed on primitive prementational tension states, they help to reestablish homeostatic equilibrium. Apart from any other meaning or functions they might have, structured affects can act as soothing organizers. When the patient attacked me, I could see that he was in good control of inner feelings, and I did not feel at all threatened by it. The patient I have just described was remarkably undefended when I first saw him. He could not soothe himself, and he had very few, if any, adaptive techniques to calm himself. There are other types of patients, patients who are familiar to therapists, who have similar problems in maintaining inner regulation, that is, they also have defective soothing mechanisms, but who have been able in certain object-related contexts to obtain relief. They have defensive adaptations to compensate for a basic structural defect.

I am referring to visible and fundamental differences between patients such as the one I have just described and this group from which I will give an example. These patients can be calm for long periods and can be soothed, but in unique and sometimes bizarre situations.

In Chapter 1, I mention an aristocratic, genteel, but alcoholic dowager, whose children all suffered from severe emotional problems. She was particularly concerned about her teenage daughter, who drank sufficiently herself to be considered an alcoholic, had problems in school, and used drugs in a self-destructive fashion. This daughter also had episodes of behavior that some psychiatrists diagnosed as hypomanic. Although lithium did not help, methylphenidate had had some effect. As a child, she had been diagnosed as hyperkinetic, that is, as having a minimal brain damage syndrome.

The mother was, if anything, motorically retarded, although she had been known to have moments of extreme agitation when she was sober, which was a rare occurrence. She was not drunk when she saw me, because we had our sessions regularly at the same time five mornings a week. But after she left me, she would go out to lunch with friends and drink continuously until she stumbled into bed at night and passed out. She kept herself drugged and sedated with alcohol, so that she felt numb and anesthetized, if not exactly calm. She claimed she was comfortable, but it was easy to detect her underlying disturbance. Nevertheless, she rationalized her need to see me, which was quite obvious, by insisting that she needed help in handling the many problems her family presented. Indeed, there were many.

Her principal concern was with her daughter, who had become the bane of her existence. The girl had been suspended from school because of her drinking, and she was getting into trouble with the police as well, because of petty thefts and shoplifting. At times, she would become terribly agitated and run away from home, saying that she could not stand it there anymore.

Interestingly enough, from what was apparent, the home situation was fairly comfortable. The house was orderly and quiet, and there were many servants who took care of the family's needs. The daughter of this affluent household lacked nothing material, and no one made any demands of her. She could come and go as she pleased and had more money at her disposal than she could spend. Nonetheless, in these quiet and seemingly calm surroundings, her tension would mount until it reached a crescendo, and then she would run away, get drunk, or start taking dangerous quantities of drugs. In fact, if she did not resort to drugs or alcohol, she was chronically angry, as though she had a chip on her shoulder. She was petite and pretty, but she looked mannish and belligerent when she was in such a combative mood. Although she did not act out sexually, she was unquestionably having problems controlling inner tension.

It is tempting to explain this girl's behavior as the manifestations of intrapsychic conflicts or as the consequences of events that recapitulated early traumas. For example, she could have experienced the quiet house as an extension of her loneliness and isolation, and as the absence of warm, loving, supportive relationships. Her mother was usually in a quiet, drunken stupor, and the father was aloof and withdrawn, if not actually absent, when she was at home. Rather than experiencing the house as a source of stability and security, she may have felt as though she were in a mausoleum.

As with any patient, many factors stemming from different psychic levels will determine the extent and nature of psychopathology. My concentration here on prementational states of agitation and defective soothing mechanisms should not be taken to indicate the exclusion of other factors. Still, there is considerable data about this young woman which indicate that the impact of traumatic circumstances during the earliest developmental stages was extremely significant in producing her current difficulties.

I was able to learn something about her early childhood from my patient, who spent many of her sessions talking about her daughter. For instance, she told me in graphic detail and with considerable gesturing how she had fed the girl as an infant. She demonstrated how she would lift her baby, picking her up in an awkward, clumsy fashion without neck support, and then roughly swinging her in a wide arc around her shoulder. Apparently, she would hold the infant for a moment in the crook of her arm, and then go through some pinching movements. As she conducted this ritualized procedure for me, she kept humming in a cacophonous, very unpleasant manner. At least I found it grating and annoying. Ultimately, as indicated by her pantomime, she would shove her daughter onto her lap, no longer holding her with her arms, and push the bottle into her mouth. This was quite a remarkable performance, and I suspect that my patient had begun to drink a little earlier than usual that day, having had a few cocktails before our session.

With such infantile experiences, it is understandable that the daughter would have problems in controlling inner tension. Unlike the patient I discussed earlier, who seemed to have no techniques for calming himself, this young woman had some defensive adaptations to protect her against inner agitation. Most of what follows was derived from data obtained from various therapists to whom I referred her.

As is apparent from her behavior, the daughter was similar to her mother in her attempt to quiet herself by sedating herself with drugs and alcohol. This method might provide relief for a short period of time, but the hangovers and aftereffects she suffered following a bout of drinking or smoking marijuana were even more painful than the disruption that had driven her to such frenetic activities in the first place. She felt particularly resentful, because she believed that her friends and siblings, all of whom were alcoholic, did not have such untoward sequelae.

There were more effective ways that enabled her to achieve solace. She felt totally at ease in smoky, noisy disco-theques in which the music blasted loudly and painfully. Although many adolescents and a fair number of adults do feel at ease and sometimes pleasantly elevated or even exhilarated in such surroundings, this particular young woman's reaction seems paradoxical to me. My opinion is based on the fact that she finds peace and quiet painful, and is soothed by loud noise.

The paradoxical nature of her reactions is further illustrated by a fantasy that has been with her for years: She is driving her car into the parking lot of her high school on a very cold winter's day. The lot is covered with hard ice, on which she parks. The doors to the automobile are locked, and she sits inside, smoking cigarettes. The lot is for faculty only, however, and she is not supposed to be there. Two policemen have recognized her as a student and try to arrest her, but they cannot get to her, because they cannot open the locked doors. They become extremely upset and angry and are thumping on her windows, but to no avail. She simply continues to sit there, placidly blowing smoke rings at them as she watches them become increasingly frustrated.

This fantasy is especially meaningful in view of the relationship she constructed with two consecutive therapists. She would quietly sit smoking, not saying anything spontaneously. She would answer the questions addressed to her, but tersely. The two therapists, both of whom were fairly young, had each discussed with me how frustrated they were by the situation. Indeed, the first had become so agitated that he discontinued treatment, which is why the patient was now seeing the second. Both therapists felt a tremendous amount of guilt; each believed that he should not be tense and anxious if he was to function in an efficient, professional manner, and each was further upset because he felt sexually aroused by the patient. In fact, the first therapist kept suppressing fantasies of raping her.

As I thought about these therapists' reactions, I could not help but recall the two policemen in the patient's fantasy. Clearly the young woman had a need to agitate others, but she had a purpose: to obtain relief from her own inner agitation. Others absorbed her tension, and she was soothed. On the other hand, because her early nurturing experience had been characterized by deficient soothing, when she needed to recreate that environment, she chose surroundings that were intrusive, the way her mother had been with her. Why she would want to repeat a traumatic situation, however, is a question that requires exploration.

The first answer to come to mind is the repetition compulsion. The young woman was actively repeating a situation from infancy that had been characterized by passive helplessness. This is a well-known phenomenon in treatment, and it occurs frequently outside of therapy, too. But this explanation is inadequate, or, rather, it is insufficient. I believe that the patient chose an experience that most of us would find jarring specifically because it would soothe her. There are several factors operating simultaneously to account for her paradoxical reactions.

Apparently the patient had never been nurtured in a calm

and pleasant ambience; all she had ever known was the jarring, cacophonous environment in which she had been fed and related to. Without a relationship like that one, all she knew was a void, loneliness, and isolation. Such a relationship was painful, but it was a relationship nonetheless, and she could tolerate the pain as long as she felt acknowledged—even if the acknowledgment were negative, as occurred in her fantasy. In her current life, she did not have any relationship with her mother, who, apart from the time she saw me in the morning, kept herself in a constant drunken stupor. The daughter, therefore, had to seek commotion elsewhere.

All of the daughter's calming experiences occurred in frenetic, highly charged settings. She managed to create such settings just as she created the fantasy and the relationship with the two young psychiatrists. As I have discussed, she was able to externalize her inner chaos, a process that has many similarities to the mechanism of projection, but which also differs somewhat from it. The difference, in fact, places emphasis on the points I have been making about this young woman's paradoxical need for a jarring ambience, and her ability to get others to absorb her agitation.

During projection, the patient unconsciously places feelings and parts of the self into the analyst or into other external objects. Sometimes the analyst reacts to these projections as if he had really incorporated them; on other occasions, the patient believes that others are reacting to him on the basis of his projections, but this is simply fantasy. The externalization of inner chaos is different.

Externalization (Giovacchini, 1967) refers to the creation of the infantile environment either in the consultation room or in the external world. If there is considerable congruence between the childhood setting and the current one, then the ego can easily cope with reality. If not, there will be serious difficulties.

One might consider, for example, the master sergeant who adapts easily to battle conditions—who actually thrives in violent and dangerous circumstances. He knows exactly what strategy to follow in order to survive, whereas the ordinary civilian would panic and be functionally paralyzed, either because he would not know what to do or because he would be unable to put his knowledge into action. The background of our hypothetical sergeant may have been dominated by violence. Perhaps his father was a brutal man who physically attacked his wife and children. During childhood the sergeant may not have known a world of peace, and consequently, if he returned to civilian life, he would not have the adaptive mechanisms required to cope with the exigencies of a nonviolent environment.

Of course, this is an oversimplified illustration. There are many other psychic elements that are instrumental to the ego's capacity to maintain inner equilibrium and to adjust to the surrounding environment (see Chapter 4). Still, it indicates that the bases of adaptive mechanisms are acquired early in life. These mechanisms enable the psyche to function in the early environment, which, one hopes, reflects the world in general. Then one can build on the foundations of the ego's executive system to effect a smooth transition into the adult world. In many patients with character disorders, however, something has gone awry.

Projection, then, describes a mechanism in which discrete impulses and parts of the self are moved outward from the psyche onto an external object. Externalization describes the ego's attempt to create an outer world or to construct a reality that is fashioned after the infantile world. Of course, reality ordinarily has many facets, and most of us seek out familiar aspects with which we know how to deal. If the world offered few choices, and the chief modalities of surviving consisted of climbing trees to pick coconuts or throwing spears to hunt game, then a person who had been trained to conduct psychotherapy or psychoanalysis would be hard pressed to find a niche that would enable him to use his skills (see Chapter 4). Happily, our world offers a wide variety of choices; but some patients are limited by the traumatic environment of the past, and by its particularity—the component aspects of that environment may have been too vastly different from what most people have known.

I am suggesting by this discussion that *there is no absolute reality*. In treatment, patients present their private realities, and we have to understand them by seeing the world through their eyes. The young woman I have been discussing experienced nurturing in a unique and disruptive fashion, but she did learn to adapt to her trying circumstances.

I have been implying that the soothing aspects of reality are very important determinants of psychic equilibrium. This is especially true of patients who are fixated at primitive levels of development. The logic of this is clear when we turn our attention to the way in which infants perceive their surroundings at the very beginning of psychic life. Granted, our thoughts about the neonate's perceptions must remain speculative, and there is an irresistible urge to adultomorphosize. Nonetheless, we can make some assumptions based on our observations and interactions. In view of the infant's alterations of sleep and wakefulness, of apparently calm contentment and fussiness (taking the latter as a sign of discomfort), and other sequences that appear to denote cycles of gratification and neediness, it seems reasonable to postulate that the baby's earliest perceptions are fluctuations of tension. Thus, clinical variations of calm and tension, the latter perhaps leading to states of disruption, would be expected of an organism that is functioning principally on the basis of circadian rhythms, as happens during the first postnatal weeks.

Obviously the neonate has very little, if any, capacity for mentation, unless we accept that there is a psychic life even *in utero*. This does not seem likely, however, bearing in mind the data of biology and neuroanatomy, which stress the immaturity of the central nervous system during the first several months of postnatal life. The neonate's sensory system would thus appear limited to the perception of states of tension and nontension. This phase of development is compatible with the operation of cyclical circadian rhythms, and with nurturing as the infant's earliest contact with the external world. Nurturing, as previously defined, is characterized by a foreground that consists of the gratification of basic needs, such as occurs with feeding, and a background holding environment that provides soothing. Although the infant does not yet distinguish at these early phases an inner personal world and an outer reality, it is possible that in a very rudimentary sense, he feels surrounded by an ambience that provides soothing, and is subject to an inner pressure when biological needs are activated. The latter corresponds to the coenesthetic mode of perception that Spitz (1957, 1965) discussed.

Thus, the quality of the nurturing situation represents the infant's first awareness, which at this stage has nothing to do with separating the psyche from external reality. The nurturing and soothing elements of the mother–child interaction affect the diurnal cycle and determine whether biological rhythms continue in an unimpeded, well-integrated fashion. This depends on whether the mother–child interaction is in synchrony with diurnal variations, or whether it is disruptive and interrupts a smooth sequence. Throwing a monkey wrench into the psychic machinery, so to speak, creates a painful state of agitation that later produces clinical pictures such as the ones I have described. It also leads to specific defensive adaptations that I will describe in the next section of this chapter.

The infant's response to the nurturing situation, either calm satisfaction or painful tension, constitutes the neonate's first sensory experience, and it presages both the way the infant will view and construct the external world. That is why the daughter of my patient adapted herself to what, for others, would have been disruptive intrusions, such as noisy and smoky discotheques. The external world these patients seek out is in synchrony with their first sensory constellations—what I will call *primal awareness*. This state of synchrony is a supraordinate state and is the outcome of the meshing of a disruptive nonsoothing stimulus and an internal state of agitation. This produces a paradoxical type of harmony: The ego and the external world are in synchrony with each other, but that synchrony is based on disrupting relationships.

This is an interesting but difficult situation to understand because of the paradoxes involved. Agitation is calming. A state of tension produces some bizarre type of comfort. It may appear as if I am stretching the adaptive value of some psychic states too far. To reproduce later in life early states of primal awareness, when these were states of disruption, seems to have no purpose and is confusing.

We must realize that these patients are *intrinsically* confusing, and because most of us have had different types of primal awareness, it is extremely difficult to empathize with them. Our natural tendency is to assign to their responses complex purposes that could exist only with later stages of development, when paradoxes may be understood as reaction formations or masochistic defenses—mechanisms that, in any case, eventually attempt to reestablish homeostasis rather than continue disruption.

The daughter of my patient appeared calm in her fantasy. Apparently she was able to maintain a state of quiet equanimity in discotheques as well. Granted, in the latter situation, she could work herself up into a frenzy as she danced to the loud music; but even then, there was a smooth rhythm to her state, along with some organization to the music and the dance steps. If a young woman requires a disruptive environment to preserve an inner disruption, because that is a familiar state to which she has learned to adapt—and perhaps the only state she has known—then where does her demeanor of calmness come from? How does our hypothetical master sergeant maintain the determined coolness that enables him to function in a calm and efficient manner under chaotic conditions?

These patients are manifesting the effects of psychic processes that emanate from different parts of the same ego state. They can effect a synchrony, a balance, because they have found or created a current reality that is based on an early infantile reality. Disruption was the essence of their reality as neonates; it was their whole world, one that had not yet separated from the self. As the first world they knew, it is the only one they can live in with a modicum of harmony. It is this paradoxical harmony that causes them to appear at ease, and this is confusing. I have referred to the paradox of finding solace in disruption as *primal confusion* (Giovacchini, 1979a), but the confusion is mainly ours. It is a reaction to the patient's first constructions of reality, which are based on the way in which the early holding environment—in particular, the background of soothing—functioned to establish either internal harmony or disruption.

These patients are not altogether comfortable, however, as is generally made clear by their various defensive adaptations to control agitation and to deaden pain, such as my patient's continual sedation of herself with alcohol. They also seek treatment to obtain relief. Even if there is a psychic need to experience pain, pain is still pain, and it can eventually become unbearable. Moreover, if the environment is one of harmony and balance, then coping with it will require a degree of organization based on inner equilibrium and calm scrutiny. There may not be enough external disruption for these patients to experience themselves in a familiar setting. Perhaps this is why the daughter of my patient constantly carried with her the fantasy of the two policemen trying to break into her automobile. Such patients may have to resort to other adaptations to feel some degree of stability and security.

Using the Environment as an Adaptation

To some extent, we all create a world in which we can adjust and function so that our needs (basic and otherwise) are met. But there are differences between the creations of patients who have defective soothing mechanisms and those of people who have had fairly satisfactory and adequate nurturing experiences.

Ordinarily, the world that people construct is already there to be found, whereas the patients I am discussing, to a much more significant degree, have to seek out facets of reality that are unknown to most of us and, in many instances, are not considered in synchrony with the world at large. At best theirs are fringe worlds that do not harmonize and blend easily with the sociocultural milieu. In essence, I am referring to tempos and modalities of relating. I am not talking about complex constellations of customs and mores requiring specific responses so that the ego can relate to all of its masters, as Freud (1923) stated—the outer world, the id, and the superego. The primitively fixated patients I have described find themselves, rather, in what we might call a more elemental and primitive reality, one that has the same level of complexity as their minds.

As children grow into adulthood they have to learn many techniques and skills so that they can function as autonomous human beings in a commonly accepted reality that is in balance with their surroundings. Childhood and adolescence are periods of preparation. The child must learn to become part of a complex milieu that demands interaction from many different perspectives. He must adapt to various types of object relationships and develop specific ego executive functions in order to integrate the self with the outer world. As I have emphasized, the ego seeks out those aspects of its surroundings to which it can best relate. In this sense the ego creates its own reality, because it seeks and locates those areas of the environment that are specifically suited to the types of psychic structure acquired through development and maturation.

By contrast, primitively fixated patients are relating with an infantile ego to an infantile environment. Patients with defects in their capacity to be soothed find situations that are replicas of the intitial nurturing experience. As I have mentioned, they maintain their emotional balance in an atmosphere of emotional disruption. This would indicate that the ego's executive system has not progressed far beyond the primitive ego state on which such patients are fixated. They have a paucity of adaptive techniques, and so cannot cope with a world that requires the development of complex psychic structures in order to function and maintain autonomy and self-esteem. Their world is comparatively simple, but because it generates disruption, it is often insensitive and brutal.

As discussed, reversal of infantile roles is one of the primitive, unsophisticated mechanisms that characterize these patients' adaptations. On the other hand, they are also thrust into situations where they once again experience the original trauma, as indicated by some of the clinical material I have presented. I will now present additional clinical data in order to demonstrate further how these patients manipulate the world and, in turn, are manipulated themselves in their attempt to maintain a defensive adaptation to a specific segment of their surroundings and somehow achieve a degree of psychic equilibrium.

The nature of the psychic trauma of these patients also warrants further exploration. Beyond her disruptive provocation, what can we postulate about the character structure of the mother whom I have been describing? What elements in the parent–child relationship may be considered extensions of her initial defective soothing interaction?

In the next chapter, I discuss in considerable detail how a mother may use her child as a transitional object so that she can maintain some perspective toward the external world. Now, I wish to concentrate on the nature of the pathological holding environment that such a mother creates for her child, and how the child, in turn, learns to handle these early traumas.

It is difficult to ascertain the exact content of early traumas, because the patient reporting them may have subjected the memories to considerable distortion, and in most instances, the traumas occurred so early in life that they cannot possibly be remembered. The parents, because of their own defenses, are usually unable to reveal how they have assaulted their children, either physically or emotionally. Even if we cannot reconstruct what actually happened, however, we can still make inferences about the impact of the traumas as we learn about the structural defects of our patients.

Years before the discovery of neuroleptic drugs, I saw a middle-aged schizophrenic woman on the back ward of a state hospital. She was sitting in a rocking chair, with her legs spread apart, and as she rocked back and forth, she was masturbating by rubbing a small doll against her genitals. Rather than appearing sexually aroused, however, her expression was beatific and calm.

I mention this episode, because it seems relevant to understanding the background of two patients who claimed they had been sexually abused by their parents. Both had been treated like dolls during their childhood, and from their treatment it became obvious that they had been used as transitional objects. They had soothed their mothers by absorbing their agitation, rather than having been soothed by them. I learned indirectly about the actual childhood experiences of one of these patients, and I believe that the other's background may well have been similar. I will briefly mention what I learned and then discuss how these patients defensively adapted themselves to the external world.

One of these patients told me a dream; in it she is three-years-old, and she and her mother are engaging in mutual cunnilingus. The mother quickly reaches orgasm and then suddenly stops, leaving her daughter in a state of pent-up tension. Although she was only three-years-old in the dream, the patient felt aroused as an adult, and being left without relief was painful.

The other of these two patients frequently referred to relationships in which she felt "dropped," meaning that she would become involved with someone, often sexually, but not necessarily, only to be left when the other person seemed to have received what he or she needed from the relationship. The patient always reacted to these situations by feeling intensely agitated, and sometimes by crying loudly, screaming, and moaning. This initial reaction was usually followed by drunken sprees or promiscuous sexual escapades.

It does not necessarily follow, of course, that either of these two women was actually used by her mother sexually. Both may have had experiences in which they were able to soothe their mothers and, then, as the second patient put it, were "dropped," leaving them in a state of chronic tension. Later in life these patients may have eroticized the trauma and reenacted it in a sexual context. *Eroticization, in itself, functions as an organizer that binds agitation.*

It is certainly possible, however, that what they reported did in fact occur; as we know, cases of sexual abuse of children are coming more and more to our attention. Still, it is the effects of trauma on character structure and adaptations that concern the clinician, and not the exact reconstruction of the infantile traumatic setting. These patients had similar vulnerabilities and compensatory defenses.

Often adaptations are conspicuous because they have antisocial qualities. Patients may have a propensity to act out, trying to calm themselves by excessive drinking or by the ingestion of drugs. Though soothing, such behavior is frequently self-destructive and provokes the family or society to intervene, whether by punishing them, containing them, or finding help for them in a psychotherapeutic relationship.

Often, in a more subtle way, these agitated persons can contain themselves by evoking a mood or affect. We have all encountered patients who appear to be chronically angry, as though they had a perpetual chip on their shoulders, yet do not espouse a rebellious cause. They just seem to be generally angry, and this affect quickly establishes itself in the transference. I recall one such patient who, for three years, constantly found fault with everything I did. She began each session by reminding me how much she hated me and how stupid and inept she thought I was. In spite of her reviling me, I believe that my inadequacies really did not upset her. In any case, I did not find her attacks threatening.

Anger represented an affect that had an organizing potential and thereby had a soothing effect. During one memorable session, this patient told me how she had struggled the night before to organize her criticisms about the treatment, but all that would occur to her about me were good things. I had always suspected that she valued the treatment in spite of her deprecations. I could understand now that she valued the treatment *because* she could depreciate it and feel safe; she had learned that we would both survive.

As I have mentioned, sexual feelings can also be used to organize tension states so that psychic equilibrium can be re-established. Many promiscuous patients frantically pursue short-lived relationships in a desperate attempt to gain some relief from unbearable inner tensions. Some patients who act out sexually eroticize all their relationships by getting their partners to absorb their unsoothed inner state and then seeking with them to discharge the pent-up disruption through sexual activity. Unfortunately, this type of relationship is sometimes re-enacted between patient and therapist.

In a legitimate treatment experience, patients find contentment by identifying with the therapist's analytic attitude, a viewpoint that combines observation and understanding with a calm, nonjudgmental outlook. As I have said, this attitude, in some ways, is like the mother's intuitive understanding of her infant. When agitated, some patients can reestablish equilibrium instantly by calling their analyst; sometimes just hearing the therapist's voice, even on a telephone answering machine, will suffice.

The attachments made by some of these patients are interesting and can present paradoxical features. Ordinarily we think of a relationship, especially a heterosexual relationship, as mutually enhancing and the source of pleasure; that is, we think of it as adding a new and exciting dimension to life, because it permits the mutual sharing of experiences and the gratification of needs. Patients who have problems with self-soothing, however, use their relationships defensively, so they can adapt to the surrounding world. The unusual and paradoxical factor in these relationships is that instead of trying to reconcile themselves with life, they seek partners who will help them to escape life by preserving a state of deadness.

For such patients, life is equated with feeling, but feelings are painful. Therefore, to be soothed, that is, to achieve a state of lowered tension, is equivalent to death. This paradox stimulates disturbing countertransference reactions, which I will discuss in Chapter 9. Here I wish to stress the defensive potential of relationships based on deadness and to describe briefly how they may evolve.

Flarsheim (1975) presents an extremely interesting example of an anorectic young lady who illustrates this type of "deadness" relationship. As an infant, she was a fussy baby, and the parents hired a nurse who boasted that she could change a fussy baby into a nonfussy baby in a matter of weeks. Her method was simple and effective. She immediately responded whenever the child expressed a need, but she did not respond to that need. For example, if the infant cried because she was hungry, the nurse would change the baby's diaper; if the infant needed to have the diaper changed, the nurse would feed her. She also put some contraption on her hands, an "iron glove," to prevent her from sucking her thumb.

Later in life, as her treatment revealed, this patient reacted to inner needs with pain. Her needs were painful, and this meant that living and life were painful, because the sense of aliveness, to some extent, is based on an awareness of needs.

She constructed defensive adaptations to protect herself against the paradox that to feel alive is to feel pain. She oriented her life around the axis of being in control, which represented an attempt to deny that she had *any* needs. Her anorexia signified complete autonomy by virtue of the fact that she was totally independent of both her environment and her body. If she did not need nourishment, then basically she had no needs, and she did not have to rely on any external objects.

The relationships she formed were curious; they were characterized by intense involvement, and yet they were dull and colorless, consisting simply of two depressed individuals, suffering from anhedonia and needing to be with each other in the context of mutual deadness. There was absolutely no verve or zest to her relationships.

One of my patients, a middle-aged woman whose marriage was based on a fusion with deadness, had a fantasy in which she and her husband were sitting in armchairs facing each other in their living room. Instead of being live people, however, they were stuffed replicas of themselves that would survive forever, as if in a diorama. I believe that the relationship was a means to ensure survival for both patients, but this was accomplished in a context of deadness. As my patient demonstrated by viewing herself as a lifelike dummy, she appeared to be alive, but she lacked the attributes of life, such as feelings and needs.

As we become increasingly aware of the various and subtle manifestations of the impact of traumatized early developmental phases on the production of psychopathology, we are able to understand certain behavioral constellations patients present to us that in the past were extremely puzzling. When patients complained about feeling agitated or anxious, we tried to explain these symptoms in terms of libidinal forces being in opposition to the organization of higher ego or superego levels. The participation of a prementational phase was not considered.

Clinicians may find it frustrating to treat primitively fixated patients, because we are accustomed, as psychoanalysts, to dealing with psychological content in psychologically-minded persons. We have a need to force meaning on behavior and reactions that we cannot otherwise understand. Without such meaning, it seems as if we have nothing to analyze.

Granted, these are difficult situations, but in many instances it *is* possible to discern meaning in behaviors and reactions that are in fact derived from later developmental stages. Still, early soothing defects will have had their influence on the construction of these later phases, and this will be reflected in the transference reaction. It is important, therefore, that we continue to recognize the sequence from prementational disruption to later developmental distortions.

The adaptations these patients construct are also derived from more advanced psychic states. As just described, seeking a partner to alleviate painful feelings of aliveness by forming an object relationship based on deadness is typical of such patients, but it is, nevertheless, an adaptation that corresponds to a fairly sophisticated ego orientation. It requires relatively clear boundaries between the inner and outer worlds. As discussed in Chapter 2, the ego is able to construct object relationships, even if they are based on primitive fusion states.

I discuss the treatment of these patients and others suffering from primitive mental states in the next section of this book, which concentrates on technical factors. Here, I will simply mention in passing that, as is true of all treatment relationships with patients exhibiting character disorders, countertransference responses are responsible for principal impasses and complications. With these patients we have two types of reactions that can create problems and often lead to the dissolution of the treatment relationship.

I have already mentioned how the therapist may absorb the patient's inner disruption; this can escalate to the degree that it becomes unbearably painful. The other possibility is that the therapist can be put in the position of representing the object with whom the patient wishes to fuse in the context of deadness. This can be an especially complex interplay, because such a fusion sometimes occurs, and when it does, in my opinion, the therapist is always unaware that it is happening. If it were otherwise, his sense of aliveness would resist having deadness as a way of life imposed on him.

What frequently happens is that the patient unconsciously, or perhaps consciously, recognizes that the therapist has a depressive core. (We have to admit that there are many depressed but competent analysts.) The patient is then able to fuse with the depressed parts of the therapist's psyche, and this is reflected in the course of the treatment. It has the semblance of a therapeutic relationship, but it is a dead relationship, because nothing is happening beyond the preservation of the status quo. The foregoing is an extremely difficult situation, and more often than not, its optimal solution is transfer to another therapist.

In many instances, however, the therapeutic setting can eventually be converted into a holding environment in which the patient can be soothed. This causes life to be experienced as pleasurable rather than painful, an achievement that leads to the attainment of higher levels of psychic integration. This may be a slow, arduous, seemingly interminable process, but when successful, it opens vast dimensions of pleasure and satisfaction for patients whose view of life had been one of torment, and whose perspective of the world was two-dimensional, flat, and colorless.

Chapter 4

The Transitional Object and the Psychoanalytic Paradox

Moving forward from the prementational phase, the psyche begins to function in a rudimentary psychological fashion. It becomes capable of experiencing some inner feelings and embryonic affects, such as nuances of pain and pleasure; and it experiences global perceptions of the outer world that are not yet distinguishable from the inner world. Psychopathology that is the outcome of fixations at these stages of amorphous ego organization is characterized by specific clinical features.

As I have emphasized throughout this book, most analytic patients today present pregenital fixations and, because of characterological defects, have problems relating to the outer world. Study of the so-called borderline patient dominates many clinical expositions (Kernberg, 1975; Masterson, 1976). As we gain wider clinical experience, however, we are able to distinguish varieties of structural psychopathology that have unique and recognizable impact on the therapeutic setting.

This chapter focuses on patients with a type of character

defect that should be distinguished from the typical borderline state. These concrete and needy patients present themselves in a way that would seem to preclude analysis, but they are capable of using insights, and ultimately they reveal aspects of their personality that are sensitive, intuitive, and creative. This mixture of concrete, stubborn resistance and subtle understanding, which includes the capacity for insight, is especially puzzling to the analyst, who must somehow decide whether such patients are analyzable. The problem becomes even more difficult when the patient displays similar polarities between psychotic behavior and behavior that is eminently reasonable and sane.

These phenomenological antitheses have led clinicians to label such patients "borderline," especially when they appear to be normal with only isolated periods of "craziness." I am purposefully using the word "craziness" here, because it comes up so often in informal descriptions of such patients' psychopathology. It is not meant to be a pejorative term; it seems to be an apt characterization. The term "psychotic" implies a fixed, serious state. Although the patients I am now discussing are, indeed, seriously disturbed, they are sometimes difficult to *take* seriously, at least at the manifest level of their material. They are borderline in the sense that it is difficult to determine whether they are ever truly psychotic, although they may have all the manifest elements of a psychosis.

For example, one of my patients, a middle-aged businessman, casually reported that he had grown tired of his cat, so he drowned her in the toilet bowl and then threw her in the garbage. He related this without any affect, as if it were something quite natural. His lack of feeling for the animal was striking—the fact that it did not make any difference to him whether she were alive or dead. On the other hand, he dealt with many inanimate objects as if they were alive. I often find the tendency to anthropomorphize in this type of borderline patient.

I have never determined whether the incident with the cat actually occurred; such an act would have stood in marked contrast to the man's general humanistic, nonviolent attitude toward life. For technical reasons I did not think it wise to pursue the matter further. But even if the story had no foundation in reality, the material struck me as bizarre, rather than being typically psychotic and delusional.

These distinctions would have no particular significance, in and of themselves, if they did not give us insights about psychic structure. They do, however, and such insights can help us to anticipate a sequence of events in treatment, which, if properly handled, can lead to a favorable therapeutic outcome.

With patients of the sort I am discussing, the analyst may despair that they will ever present analyzable material and is led to abandon the psychoanalytic method. Many sessions are dominated by the patients' complaints about "never getting anywhere" or about finding themselves against a "brick wall." At the same time, these patients make the almost arrogant pronouncement that they have nothing to say, as if they were *determined* not to produce any analyzable material. They are aware of pressing needs, but are unable to articulate them. They are also aware of the inaccessibility to their unconscious and that they are not free associating; but they blame the analyst or the treatment for their inability to produce unconscious derivatives.

These responses are familiar enough and would ordinarily represent nothing more than rigid, concretely oriented patients who are very difficult, if not impossible, to analyze. As stated, however, these trying sessions are interspersed with others in which these same patients present rich and revealing material, often in a charming, entertaining, and creative fashion. I treated a young man who could be antagonistically concrete for weeks on end, and then suddenly he would bring me transparent dreams that could be understood both from their manifest content and in relation to recent therapeutic interactions. He could not or would not free associate to them after he reported them, but he did talk about many topics imaginatively and creatively, suggesting that he was making some connection with his unconscious mind. In contrast to the concrete sessions, in these sessions he did not merely complain and focus on surface events. On the other hand, he still did not free associate in a transference context.

Through dreams we learn about the patient's unconscious thoughts and reactions; but with the patients I am now discussing, the therapist's understanding seems to be of no help. Usually these patients ignore any analytic comments or interpretations. The analyst's frustration increases further, because he is unable to discern any ostensible transference elements in the patient's material. Indeed, the patient seldom, if ever, alludes to the therapist either in his remarks or in his dream material, except to complain about the treatment's lack of effectiveness.

In short, these patients are characterized by extremes of behavior—from reasonable, realistic, imaginative, and creative interactions to bizarre, psychotic-like episodes. They are capable of presenting material that can be easily understood in terms of its unconscious derivatives; yet they continue to act as if their unconscious were completely inaccessible to them. Furthermore, as Freud (1914c) wrote about the narcissistic neuroses, transference seems to be totally lacking. This combination of phenomena would not seem to make for a sanguine outlook.

Developmental Factors

We need to view the psychic structure of such patients from a different perspective. There are certain features common to their backgrounds, and these features have determined a particular type of structural defect. These borderline patients had traumatic backgrounds, but they were not as severely deprived as many psychotic patients and patients with severe character disorders. Their parents related to them and, to some extent, were able to respond to their needs. As infants, these patients did not suffer from the privation that Winnicott (1963a) has described. They knew what it meant to be gratified; but satisfaction of needs was a traumatic experience, in part, because the parents did not accept their children as individuals in their own right.

The most striking structural defect exhibited by such patients is a poorly structuralized self-representation. This is obvious in treatment as patients constantly demonstrate the blurred boundaries between the external world and the internal world of the mind. They emphasize their tenuous identity by not knowing who they are, what the purpose of their lives is, or where they fit in the general scheme. They have little sense of themselves as distinct and separate from others or from their surroundings. One adolescent patient saw himself as merged with both animate and inanimate objects. If he sank into an armchair, he would feel himself to be part of the chair. He did not experience panic, as often happens when patients merge and lose their ego boundaries. On the contrary, he felt comfortable and did not make distinctions between the animate and the inanimate. His tendency was to consider everything around him as animate. He would talk to the furniture. At night, he would say elaborate good-nights to the various chairs and tables in his room.

This patient—all patients in the group I am discussing—was treated by his parents as if he were an inanimate object. He was never related to as a human being with a mind of his own and distinct needs. He knew that his parents looked after his material needs; but after seeing that he was fed and clean, they more or less ignored him. When he showed any curiosity, enthusiasm, or interest, no one would respond to him. Winnicott (1952) would have said that the boy's dilemma was due to a lack of ego-relatedness; his id needs had been met, but his ego needs had not.

The lack of cohesiveness of the self-representation was the outcome of a specific type of defective mothering. During the earliest developmental stages, there is an endopsychic registration of the nurturing experience. The psyche's progression to the next stage, however, is difficult and traumatic for a patient whose mother has used him as a narcissistic extension of herself. This kind of background is not unusual for patients suffering from character defects; with the patients I have described, however, the narcissistic extension is unique.

Ordinarily, when a mother–infant relationship is based on the mother's narcissistic needs, the mother treats the child like a *self-object* (see Boyer & Giovacchini, 1967, p. 269). She projects the devalued parts of herself, her bad introjects, into the child. In other words, narcissistic attachments should be understood as based on elements of part-object relationships. Children who have experienced this kind of fusion with their mothers usually develop a hateful image of themselves. They revile themselves because of their badness and, in general, are self-destructive.

The self-representation of the patients being discussed here is somewhat different. Such patients may also revile themselves, but this is not a consistent response. They are often grandiose, but this is also true of other patients who have passed through a traumatic transitional phase; grandiosity represents an overcompensatory attempt to overcome a miserable sense of unworthiness. What is really striking about these patients is how often they feel that they do not exist. This is not a typical existential crisis. Like the adolescent patient mentioned earlier, they do not panic. They do not distinguish the animate from the inanimate nor the self from their surroundings. They do not feel real, and all of their feelings are also felt as unreal. They do not exist as live entities; they view themselves much as they would a piece of furniture that has no living status.

During infancy, the parents did not relate to the child's emerging sense of aliveness. After these infants were made comfortable by having been fed and changed, they were ignored. If they showed any interest in the environment or indicated a wish for play, they were simply not responded to. As they reached toward the external world, there was no reciprocity.

One patient complained that she did not know how to play any games except those that required intellect, such as bridge and chess. She felt awkward around children and was astounded when a friend, a young mother, played pat-a-cake and peek-a-boo with her 7-month-old son, who was hilariously delighted with these games. The patient was confused, as if she were witnessing a ritual performed by strangers from an alien planet.

As a rule, these patients do not have intimate object relations as adults. Their object relations are marginal. They may have friends, in some instances many friends, but there are no close ties or emotional attachments. If they are married, the relationship between husband and wife lacks feeling. The absence of feeling may be so pervasive that we get the impression they relate to persons as objects rather than as living beings.

In treatment there seems to be an absence of transference, from which patients infer that they do not project feelings or parts of themselves into the analyst. Furthermore, they have periods in which everything is considered in a concrete, mechanistic fashion, devoid of any unconscious connotations. An inanimate object does not have an unconscious. On the basis of these phenomena, it is reasonable to assume that they experience the external world, in general, as inanimate. *I conjecture that their mothers did not project elements of their inner psychic life into their children. I propose that they treated them, rather, as inanimate objects in general, and as transitional objects in particular.*

I recall several female patients who were named after the mother's favorite doll. For these mothers, it was important that the doll remain a doll—that she not grow up and become a woman. Another patient, a middle-aged man, was named after a pendant his mother had been given when she was less than a year old. The pendant looked like Pinocchio. The patient would burst into tears whenever he heard the story of Pinocchio, or saw a movie or cartoon about him. His psychic equilibrium became totally disrupted when he thought about the wooden puppet becoming a boy. He was overcome by a poignant longing that was unbearably painful. Ordinarily, he was without feeling, and during the first part of his treatment, there was, in fact, a wooden quality about him.

The transitional object, as described by Winnicott (1953), is an object that serves the psyche as a tentative entrance into the external world. The child's behavior toward it is ruthless, not because of organized hate or anything that is projected into it. It is part of an in-between space; it is an inanimate object on which the child's security depends; and it emboldens the unformed psyche to structuralize progressively and to form boundaries between the self and the nonself. In this in-between space where the transitional object resides, the infant exercises omnipotent control, and the transitional object is the target of that control.

Ordinarily, we are not much concerned with the transitional object itself—its treatment, its reactions, and its fate—because traditionally, the transitional object is inanimate, and inanimate objects have no feelings. But patients who have represented transitional objects for their mothers were not inanimate, they were simply treated as if they were. This has led to specific constellations of psychopathology.

The concept of the transitional object is confusing, because various formulations about it are not altogether consistent with one another (Grolnick, Barkin, & Muensterberger,1978). I discussed the following developmental sequence with Winnicott, who agreed that my views of the transitional object both reflect and restate his own views. I emphasize different facets of this developmental phenomenon, however, because my intention is to focus on its relevance to a particular structural defect and its resulting psychopathology.

As the child individuates, he constructs an intermediary space between the inner and outer worlds, and this construction eventually helps to consolidate ego boundaries. The transitional area between "me" and "not-me" houses the transitional object. It also represents an extension of ego boundaries, within which, according to Winnicott (1953), the child believes he can exercise omnipotent control. Thus, the transitional object is part of both the child and the external world, but it still resides in a space that is completely under the developing ego's control. The "good enough" mother supports the child's illusion of omnipotence (see Chapter 3).

Dr. Winnicott agreed with me that the transitional situation is characterized by an ego that contains an endopsychic registration of the nurturing situation; in fact, he added that the transitional situation could be considered characterized by the establishment of this nurturing matrix. The child who has had optimal mothering gains the conviction that the source of nurturing resides within the psyche rather than outside him in the external world. Actually, the external world is not yet recognized as such, because the child does not yet distinguish between the inner and outer worlds. This is an infantile state of omnipotence.

I believe the word "omnipotence" to be an unfortunate term. It connotes megalomanic, grandiose feelings, a heightened sense of importance and power. These reactions are much too sophisticated for a preverbal infant. What we usually mean by "infantile omnipotence" is the psychic state of a child who is tranquil and satisfied and experiences the maximum security that inner needs will be met. Because there is a sense in which the child has the feeling that he or she is the source of his or her own nurture, we use the term "omnipotent": The child would appear to believe that he or she is in complete control of his or her destiny and needs no one. These formulations are obviously adultomorphic and should not be taken literally. I am referring only to tendencies to experience states of satisfaction and emotional equilibrium. What the infant actually feels is difficult, if not impossible, to ascertain. Our language is mainly geared to an adult perspective, and perhaps we do not have the proper words to describe these early psychic states and developmental stages.

Winnicott (1971) conceptualized three spaces: (1) the inner space of the psyche, whose periphery is the ego's boundaries, (2) an extension of those boundaries to the border of the external world, and (3) the external world. It is the second of these spaces that I find useful for understanding a particular type of borderline psychopathology.

Winnicott called this second space the in-between space, the transitional space that is the area of play and creativity. The nurturing matrix characteristic of the transitional situation is projected into an object in this middle space, and by way of this projection it becomes the transitional object over which the infant exercises omnipotent control.

What I have described is not exactly projection. In order to project, the ego has to have more distinct and structured boundaries than those involved in the construction of the transitional object. Projection requires a certain amount of separation; the external object must be clearly recognized. The infant who is creating a transitional object still has blurred ego boundaries; there is not sufficient psychic structure to project psychic content from one distinct ego system into another. Rather, the child's psychic periphery seems to stretch outward, much like the pseudopodia of an amoeba engulfing and incorporating an external object. Even so, there is no incorporation from the infant's viewpoint; the infant experiences the external world as part of the self.

The viewpoint of an adult is different from that of a child. To the adult, the in-between transitional space belongs to the external world, whereas the child does not recognize an external world and regards this middle space as being part of his psychic world. According to Winnicott (1953), the "good-enough" mother does not challenge the infant's viewpoint. With optimal mothering, the child's needs are met in such a way that he does not recognize nurture as coming from the external world—the world that is outside the area of his control. The mother supports the illusion that the source of nurture resides within the child's psyche.

What happens when the mothering interaction is traumatic and the illusion is not supported? What are the psychopathological consequences if the mother does not support the formation of the in-between space and the construction of the transitional object? Some mothers may have such a need for omnipotent control themselves that they cannot let their children experience having some control over their immediate surroundings, their transitional object, and the nurturing experience.

A mother's character may have many psychopathological variants. The mothers of the patients I have been discussing were unable to allow their children to individuate or to emerge from a fusion state. They opposed their children's separation and individuation (Mahler, 1963, 1972). I wish to make clear, however, that this formulation is not the same as the hypotheses of Masterson (1976) and Rinsely (1982), who believe that borderline patients exhibit fixations at the stage of separation-individuation. Rather, I believe that the child experiences the impact of the traumatic environment from the very beginning of life, so that distortions of ego development and defects occur in both preobject and later phases.

In analysis, the mother of such a patient generally reveals that she is afraid to let her child grow up, because she believes unconsciously that if the child achieves separation and autonomy, he will murder her. Frequently this turns out to be a projection of similar feelings the mother had toward her own mother. Thus, such women feel they have to keep their infants at an immature level of psychic development. They impede separation and the construction of distinct boundaries, as would occur with the delineation of the inner space, the transitional in-between space, and the external world. Such a mother finds herself somewhere on the periphery of what would be the in-between space if the infant were to progressively structuralize. To permit that structuralization would mean feeling controlled by her child, and that could mean being destroyed by him. If she were to move into the external world, she would also feel herself to be in danger. As Winnicott (1969) wrote, when the object moves from the transitional space to the outer world, the infant loses control over it. He added that it is also destroyed in the mind of the child. Colleagues who discussed this conclusion with him would often ask why such a reaction *must* be assumed to occur. Would it not be easier to assume that the child merely decathected the object as it became external to the self? Winnicott remained adamant about his formulation and insisted that the child killed the object. He said, in fact, that the child *had* to kill the object first to be able to acknowledge and accept it later.

Winnicott's formulation has been difficult to accept, because he was ascribing this sequence to the course of ordinary development rather than to a course distorted by early psychic trauma. This would mean that *all* children have murderous impulses that must inevitably emerge; advances in psychic structuralization would depend on psychically murdering the nurturing source. Yet, for the patients under discussion here, Winnicott's assertion seems apt. The mothers I have been describing had strong unconscious feelings and fears that their children would somehow destroy them. Consequently, I wonder whether Winnicott was generalizing from this particular mother–infant psychopathological constellation.

From the analyses of these mothers and their children (as adults), I have noted some characteristic defensive patterns the mothers used, which produced various reactions in their children, reactions that define their borderline psychopathology. As mentioned, this kind of mother may be preventing her child from separating and individuating because she feels threatened by him or her. Putting the child in *her* transitional space reverses this perceived threat. She now has control rather than being subject to what she feels to be her child's murderous omnipotent manipulations. By keeping her infant in the sphere of her own omnipotent control, she feels protected. She thus renders her child helpless and safe.

There are other reasons for a mother's relating to her child as though he or she were a transitional object. She may be attempting to move into the external world by using her child as an intermediary step. That is, she may be trying to recapitulate the infantile emotional development that she was unable to achieve during her own childhood. This strategy does not enable the mother to progress beyond her fixation point, because, obviously, as an adult, a person cannot develop further emotionally by using techniques and relationships that would have been appropriate in infancy. On the other hand, a woman who uses her child in this way can achieve a sufficient degree of psychic equilibrium to function relatively well in the external world. But this is at the expense of her child.

The child remains fixated, cannot fully consolidate ego boundaries, and does not feel truly human. As already described, such a child does not distinguish the animate from the inanimate. The child never feels any security in his or her sense of aliveness. Internal feelings are imperfectly developed and dimly perceived. As patients, these people often comment that they really do not know what they feel, or if what they feel is real and belongs to them or is borrowed from others.

The in-between aspects of the transitional space that houses the transitional object are reflected in such patients' reactions and behavior. They feel that their whole life is a transition, and they do not know what their goals are or where they should be going. A patient told me of a repetitive dream he had had since childhood in which he was jumping between two objects but never reached the object he was jumping toward. He would find himself suspended in air and, on occasion, would become anxious about falling. Frequently such patients also bring dreams about bridges, but the shores are not discernible. The transitional qualities of their lives are even more striking in their relationships with people.

In treatment these patients begin to recognize how they have been used by their parents and often by persons in their current lives as well. Frequently their parents have cast them in the role of the go-between. For example, one mother had consistently used her daughter, my patient, to manipulate the father so that he would be compliant to the mother's needs. The patient felt her mother would have died without her help, although at the time, she was not entirely aware that she was doing her bidding. Nevertheless, she became very astute at relating to her father on the basis of manipulation, and as an adult, she constantly demonstrated her cleverness in bringing people together. She could behave in a highly sophisticated fashion and was quite adept socially. At other times, however, she was totally irrational, and would lock herself in closets or bathrooms or tear her clothes to shreds.

The mother of another patient, a man in his early twenties, had used her son to soothe herself, as well as to fend off her husband's sexual advances. Whenever she felt that her husband was sexually interested, she would go to bed early and bring her infant son into bed with her. (Husband and wife slept in separate twin beds.) She continued sleeping with her son in this way until he was 7 years old. As an adolescent, the boy was often seduced by older women and had innumerable affairs. In spite of his successful sexual experiences, however, and the fact that he was exceptionally attractive, he was consumed by painful feelings of inadequacy. He considered himself worthless and ugly, if not in body then in spirit, and incapable of doing anything worthwhile. He did not trust his own motives and questioned whether there were even one good feeling in his "miserable soul." The extremes of behavior illustrated by both the patients just discussed would indicate some fragmentation of the psyche.

The Borderline State and Psychic Discontinuity

The great difficulty that clinicians have in determining whether the borderline patient is presenting a delusion or whether his behavior is bizarre, but not necessarily psychotic, stems from what I have discussed as extremes of behavior. Sometimes they function exceptionally well and have good insights about themselves and their friends and family. All of this is inconsistent with the limitations and constrictions of a psychotic state. Nevertheless, as also discussed, such people can become concretely oriented and lose all their psychological-mindedness. Furthermore, the movement from a normal to a disrupted ego state occurs precipitously. There is no continuity from one to the other, no transitional period of gradual deterioration or progressive recovery.

A well-integrated psyche encompasses a broad spectrum that ranges from primary to secondary process, from early, primitive elements to later-acquired, rational realistic, sophisticated adaptations and perceptions. As feelings or sensory impressions move up the psychic hierarchy, however, they smoothly traverse the various levels: there are no abrupt boundaries; one level gradually blends into another. Freud (1923a) described this continuity when he stated that the ego dips into the id.

Patients who have been used as transitional objects for their mothers lack precisely this continuity. In a sense, they are fragmented, but this is a unique kind of fragmentation. Ordinarily, we conceptualize a fragmented ego as one in which various parts are split off from one another. The split-off parts are outside the main ego current (Freud, 1938). They are not connected to each other in a hierarchic sequence.

I am discussing a different psychic constellation. Rather than having split-off parts, these patients lack bridges between lower and higher psychic levels, between levels that should be part of a hierarchic sequence. There is no smooth dipping of ego into id. Rather, there are abrupt differences between the primitive and the sophisticated. Psychic structure contains lacunae, and as various elements traverse the mental apparatus, their cathectic regulation resembles quantum jumps.

Because these patients have remained fixated at an in-between transitional space, they have not developed a continuum that encompasses their inner mental life, the transitional space, and the external world. This lack of continuity helps to explain the sudden fluctuations between sophisticated, rational behavior and bizarre, primitive reactions. The latter occur in an explosive fashion. These patients do not seem to have the capacity to tame or to modulate their reactions.

I recall a patient who clearly illustrated psychic quantum jumps that were the outcome of lack of psychic continuity and connecting bridges between the various layers of the mental apparatus. This male patient ordinarily was reserved, polite, mild-mannered, and exhibited a low-keyed demeanor, but his behavior on the couch was surprising and striking. On occasions he would interrupt his associative flow quite suddenly by screaming, kicking, twisting, and writhing on the couch. He would shout loudly and piercingly and grimace as if he were in great pain. Then he would calmly resume associating, without commenting on his explosive outburst. Some sessions were punctuated with 20 or 30 such episodes.

When I realized that he was never going to say anything about this bizarre behavior, my curiosity increased to the point where I finally questioned him about what he was feeling during these episodes and what they could possibly mean. The patient explained that he felt extreme agitation deep down inside himself. This feeling propelled itself to the surface with great force, seeking to put into words; however, it was too strong and powerful to be contained by words. As it traversed up the psychic apparatus, it was not toned down or modulated; it was not tamed the way feelings usually are when they reach secondary-process levels of expression. At these times, language was no longer a method of communication. Rather, words had become a vehicle of discharge, in which feelings would accumulate and intensify into an explosion. I thought of two electrodes topped by spheres with a spark jumping between them. Spontaneously the patient compared his behavior to a Van de Graaff generator.

This patient, like others, had fantasies of an empty space inside him, a hollow void surrounded by organs. This void represented the missing intermediate area that tames raw feelings and controls and modulates behavior. I recall two women patients who also described having an empty space inside. Each would lie quietly on the couch, not moving at all, and then suddenly "motorically explode," jerking her limbs in a spasmodic fashion. From time to time each of these women also had the fantasy that she lived in this inner empty space. All these patients showed extremes of behavior in their daily lives, although the patient who grimaced and shouted as if he were in great pain generally led a fairly quiet life. His perception of his surroundings was bizarre, however, and his fantasies were unusually gruesome and perverse.

The Psychoanalytic Paradox and Technical Problems

The patients I have been discussing in this chapter produce disturbing but interesting treatment dilemmas. The character structure produced by viewing the self as a transitional object and by the absence of modulating bridges has a specific impact in the treatment setting. These patients may create what I have referred to as the *psychoanalytic paradox* (Giovacchini & Boyer, 1983; Giovacchini, 1975a, 1979b).

I define the psychoanalytic paradox as a situation in which the patient's character structure and psychopathology is in opposition to or incompatible with the analytic method. This incompatibility may involve anything from the formal elements of analysis, such as free associating and lying on the couch, to particular aspects of the relationship between analyst and patient.

Some intensely narcissistic patients, for example, refuse to use the couch, because not being looked at by the therapist signifies a loss of narcissistic supplies. I recall two attractive women patients, both of whom were very conscious of their need to be admired, and protested vehemently when I explained the analytic procedure and told them they would have to lie down. One patient ultimately did, but the most the other could manage was to lay her coat on the couch as a substitute for herself. After six months, it became clear that we were not able to establish an analytic relationship, but the treatment of the patient who reluctantly agreed to follow the "rules" progressed in a relatively satisfactory manner.

Surprisingly, patients who are unable to hold and form mental representations without the presence and the reinforcement of the external object in the perceptual field—Fraiberg's (1969) and Piaget's (1952) evocative memory—usually do not have problems getting on the couch. Even though they cannot actually see the therapist, they nevertheless feel his presence, which is sufficient reinforcement to form a mental representation that helps them to achieve psychic equilibrium and to maintain a holding environment. On the other hand, those patients who were treated as if they were transitional objects and who could sometimes be extremely concrete, refused to lie down.

The reasons for this involve more than the inability to hold a mental representation without external reinforcement. Intrapsychic conflicts are also involved, conflicts that are based on profound feelings of vulnerability. Lying on the couch is equated to loss of control. Such patients feel defenseless and exposed inasmuch as their status as a transitional object gains dominance. The analyst becomes the manipulating mother who will use the patient as personal whims dictate. Consequently these patients have to be alert and vigilant, defensive states that they do not find compatible with the supine position.

In treatment, these borderline patients create an analytic paradox that derives from the unique nature of the patient–analyst relationship. From a phenomenological perspective, the therapist is similar to the nonresponsive mother. His objective observational focus—what is referred to as analytic neutrality—is experienced by the patient as a recapitulation of what he suffered during infancy. The analyst is equated to the mother who never smiles, lacks radiance, and feels no pride or pleasure in her motherhood. Transference projections and the creation of the infantile ambience in the consultation room are virtually impossible to interpret, because the patient is convinced that the therapist really is reacting to him the way the mother did and has the same feeling toward him. The situation becomes complicated when the therapist relentlessly clings to what he considers to be analytic decorum as the patient's dissatisfaction increases. The analyst may react to the analysand's complaints as being psychically assaultive, and because of countertransference disruption, he may, in fact, withdraw from the patient. Understandably, the impasse intensifies and is further fixed.

Does this type of background and character pathology mean that analysis is contraindicated? In many instances these patients have vigorously sought analysis, but they believe they need an analyst who reveals his feelings, as opposed to the analyst who strives to be no more than a reflecting mirror, and they assert that analytic functioning can occur with more personal involvement. I believe that the creation of the psychoanalytic paradox by the patient who has had only minimal acknowledgment as an emerging human being forces us to reconsider our formulations about treatability and what the analytic method encompasses.

Most analysts agree that the essence of the analytic method is the interpretation of the transference. Is it possible to conduct analysis at a "higher decibel level" than analytic neutrality and still strive for the resolution of basic conflicts and traumas and the acquisition of further psychic structure? Or, to reverse the question, is it possible to gain analytic resolution in the case of primitively fixated patients *without* the therapist becoming involved? How are the effects of infantile trauma to be undone and the developmental process, which has been fixated at primitive levels, to be once again set in motion? In the aforementioned cases, the developmental process has progressed no further than the formation of the transitional space.

Psychoanalysts do not attempt to gratify infantile impulses. I doubt that anyone can actually do that anyhow. What was appropriate nurture and soothing in infancy will not suffice for adults, even if their egos are fixated at primitive developmental levels. Such egos have acquired elements of later developmental phases, resulting in a variety of adaptive techniques and regulatory mechanisms that make requirements for sustenance much more complex than those at the level of fixation. Mother's milk, literally, is not adequate. Even when the ego regresses to the fixation point, later adaptations are not lost. Most patients can still talk, walk, and remain continent.

Undoing the effects of infantile trauma, however, is not the same as the gratification of infantile needs. Rather than the substance of nurture, clinicians today are dealing with modes of relating that are pertinent to emotional development and the acquisition of psychic structure. The analyst can furnish the patient with a type of relationship that is different from the traumatic mother–infant interaction that contributed to psychic maldevelopment and the creation of ego defects. The therapeutic process can help the patient to acquire a sense of being. The therapist's attitude and the intensity of his responses can see to it that these seriously disturbed patients feel acknowledged for the first time. Such responses demonstrate that the analyst reacts to his patients beyond their basic needs and takes pleasure in their developing sense of aliveness.

This is a corrective experience. It is not, however, to be confused with Alexander's (1961) concept of the corrective emotional experience. What I am discussing does not involve role-playing in a transference context. Rather, the therapist's responses are a natural, spontaneous therapeutic reaction to the patient's specific form of psychopathology. I do not view the treatment of such patients as modified analysis; I believe the therapist is behaving in an appropriate analytic fashion, given the patient's emotional distress and decompensatory defenses. I can best substantiate these opinions by giving a clinical example.

I have described this patient, a withdrawn adolescent college student, in greater detail elsewhere (Giovacchini, 1979b). He was referred to me by a university student health psychiatrist because of an acute crisis. The patient had totally withdrawn in his dormitory room, not sleeping, bathing, or eating; there was a complete physical and emotional deterioration. Finally, the young man's classmates literally carried him to the student health clinic, whereupon he was hospitalized with a diagnosis of acute schizophrenia. The diagnosis was changed to identity-diffusion syndrome (Erikson, 1959; see also Chapter 6, p. 140) when he suddenly became alert during a visit from his parents. After his dismissal from the hospital, he was sent to me on an outpatient basis. When I first saw him, he looked withdrawn. He offered absolutely nothing on his own, and was reserved and cryptic in his replies to my questions. I soon felt that his monosyllabic answers indicated he experienced my questions as intrusive and irritating, so I told him that I did not want to keep bothering him because of my curiosity. I said, it might be better if he lay down, so he could be alone with his thoughts if he wanted to be. I would be nearby, however, and he could tell me his thoughts if he so decided. He was visibly relieved and did lie down, saying nothing for the remainder of the session. He continued that way for several sessions and then tentatively started asking questions about pedestrian matters.

With certain patients, I find questions irritating and ordinarily do not answer them. I tend to deal with each statement the patient makes as though it were a declarative sentence, regardless of its actual grammatical form. With this adolescent, however, my attitude was entirely different. I could not *not* have answered his questions. It would have been both analytically unthinkable and out of character for me to remain silent or to resort to the frequently used ploy of throwing the question back by asking why he had asked it. I have certainly done this on other occasions. I have remained silent, and I have asked patients why they were asking their questions and felt perfectly at ease. With this patient, however, this sort of strategy would have been impossible, and it felt wrong.

The patient spent many sessions asking me how to conduct himself in the external world. He would ask what kind of clothes were appropriate for certain occasions, and how to get to certain locations in the city. Once he even asked me how to make a telephone call to ask a girl for a date. We were calm and comfortable with such exchanges.

One day he appeared distraught and agitated. He was extremely upset over an insignificant change that had been made in the schedule of the train that he ordinarily took to my office. I immediately felt as agitated as he did, and we began having an intense, anxious discussion about it. If outsiders had been able to see us talking, as through a one-way mirror, without hearing the content of what we were saying, they would have concluded that we were concerned about an impending global catastrophe—as though a nuclear bomb were to be dropped within the next 10 minutes. In point of fact, however, the change in schedule caused no difficulties whatsoever in his transportation to and from my office. If anything, it made the trip more convenient for him.

This patient's analysis lasted for many years and had many stormy moments. His transference reactions were quite complex and involved many layers of his personality. During the middle phases of treatment, he made considerable use of splitting mechanisms, and his transference was dominated by projective identifications. I briefly mention these elements, because I wish to emphasize only that our initial intense involvement was not all that occurred between us. I do believe, however, that the analysis of the transference would not have been possible had we not established a relationship through such interchanges.

This patient had a poorly established self-concept, and his main adaptation was defensive withdrawal. He was a schizoid personality plagued with feelings of nonexistence. At any rate, he did not see himself as having a separate existence apart from a tie to his parents. As the analysis later confirmed, he did not feel he existed on his own; he always had to retain a connection to his mother.

He described his mother as apparently concerned with his welfare, but cold and intellectual. Much like the other patients I have been describing, he did not recall his mother ever smiling spontaneously at him, or talking or playing with him. When she did talk to him, she gave him orders or planned his future.

My spontaneous "high decibel" reactions represented responses that were quite different from anything he had ever encountered in the past. Although he was not consciously aware of it at the time, he was beginning to feel that someone was interested in his potential for experiencing life and defining his boundaries. He was recognizing that he had needs of his own and that there was someone in the external world who shared and encouraged that recognition.

My mode of relating, to my mind, was not an extraanalytic maneuver, or, as Eissler (1953) called such maneuvers, a parameter. Rather, I regard it as a unique aspect of the holding environment required for patients with particular infantile backgrounds. It was part of the analytic decorum, which, to some extent, has to be tailored to the patient's individual needs. The analyst generally creates a benign, calm atmosphere designed to foster understanding and to promote introspection. As the patient gradually recognizes himself to be an object of interest and concern, an experience that was seriously lacking during the vulnerable years of emotional development, he also accommodates to the analytic ambience.

I do not believe that analysis is possible for the borderline patients I have described unless the analyst takes measures to avoid the unwitting recapitulation of the early mother–infant relationship—even if the resemblance is only superficial. Whatever modalities are employed, they must acknowledge the patient's existence and express the analyst's concern for his further emotional development and autonomy. With less disturbed patients, these therapeutic attitudes are implicit, and the low-keyed objective analyst does not interfere with them. The patients I have been describing need special affirmation, and the holding environment has to be constructed so as to demonstrate explicitly what other patients would take for granted. In this way the analyst's involvement can make up for what was lacking in the past. Again, however, the therapist's responses are spontaneous; they in no way involve role-playing.

An interest in the patient's development of autonomy is not the same as an expectation of cure. Often, in fact, the patient experiences the latter as an intrusive assault and an attack on his autonomy. With some schizophrenic patients, the therapist's slightest anticipation of change can be catastrophic. Rather than an edict to get better because this would be gratifying to the analyst, involvement with the patient should indicate acceptance of his attempts to enter and to explore the external world, a world that has always been experienced as rejecting and exploitive.

The Missing Transference and the Inability to Free Associate

Some borderline patients are considered to be unanalyzable. Although I have distinguished the group of patients discussed in this chapter from what I call typically borderline, they do exhibit some borderline characteristics, namely, a rigid character structure and the inability to become emotionally involved with persons and ideals.

These patients often tell their analysts that they have nothing to say. If they bring a dream, and their dreams are often bizarre, but rich in material, they have nothing to say about it. If asked for associations, they usually reply that they have none, without giving themselves the time to relax and to be receptive to what emerges.

They have similar attitudes about their therapists, in that they have a concrete, constricted view of them. They may even blame the therapist because they, as patients, cannot "open up" to them. At the same time, the therapist is made to feel as if he did not exist.

This would seem to present a therapeutic dilemma, given that such patients cannot free associate and apparently cannot form a transference. They appear to be totally alienated from the unconscious mind. Thus, the deeper parts of their psyches are inaccessible, at least in the consultation room. Even when they are behaving in a primitive fashion, they display no capacity for insight. They are apparently unaware of intrapsychic factors and unconscious motivation. Psychic determinism is incomprehensible to them.

This inability to recognize the importance of the unconscious mind in determining behavior, feelings, and attitudes is the outcome of their structural defects—the stated lack of continuity between primitive and advanced psychic levels. These patients can reveal unconscious material, but it has no relevance for them in the contemporary setting, because it is unconnected with current ego states.

The lack of transference would seem to preclude analysis. It is sometimes possible to establish a psychoanalytic frame, however. The missing transference itself becomes a form of transference, because it also represents the essence of an infantile object relationship as well as the manifestation of structural psychopathology. Furthermore, in spite of these patients' complaints and threats to stop therapy, they covertly value the therapeutic relationship, and are quite upset if the analyst cancels an appointment or suggests termination.

They have formed an attachment to the therapist, but cannot acknowledge it. As with all their feelings, they are unable to integrate their positive responses into the main ego current (Freud, 1938). This is not just a matter of structural deficits; the situation also has psychodynamic implications. Conflicts about basic trust and the fear of loss of control are involved.

Often these patients are obliged to devalue what they value. They feel vulnerable to the therapist, especially if he has become powerful enough to help them, an example of the negative therapeutic reaction (Freud, 1923a). Such patients are afraid to trust anyone and sensitive about relinquishing control of inner forces or external objects. Their function as a transitional object for their mothers is a significant determinant of their defensive stance.

Even so, inner conflicts are important. A middle-aged professional man unconsciously wanted desperately to be dependent but was afraid of being destroyed if he allowed himself to form a dependent relationship. Consequently, he formed strong defenses against dependent feelings. An important antecedent of this conflict was his relationship with his father, who was unusually sensitive to his son's needs and had remarkable intuition about his inner feelings and distress. He could react to the patient in an appropriate, sensitive, and warm fashion, but only for a short time. As soon as the patient began to respond and become involved, his father would lose interest and "drop" him. As an adult, the son was wary of all relationships, and I could feel how he distanced himself from any intimate or primitive feelings except to recite bizarre dreams. He tried to divest me of any significance or influence.

I was not disheartened, however, because in spite of his denials, I felt that I was being useful to him and that he liked me. After about a year of treatment, he acknowledged that he had improved and was feeling somewhat fond of me and of the therapeutic relationship. In fact, he became increasingly positive to the degree that he felt safe and secure in his reliance on me. He had developed the capacity to free associate and was demonstrating the existence of a traditional transference.

Creating a setting that permitted him to sustain idealization enabled him to connect lower psychic levels with higher, structured ego states. This was not always a comfortable experience, however, and there were occasions when it was so painful that his previous inability to free associate—that is, his tendency to keep a distance from primitive unconscious levels—became even more understandable. For example, he began one session by stating that he felt especially relaxed. He was feeling warm and grateful toward me and toward the treatment. But gradually he became frightened, a disruptive feeling that slowly intensified to terror. His voice became tremulous, and he began to whine like a wounded animal. As he sobbed, I could occasionally hear him form words, such as "Please help me." He was choked with overwhelming, painful affect that was bordering on panic. There was no content attached to these feelings.

He had suffered a massive regression, but at the end of the session, was able to integrate. He had to sit in the waiting room for half an hour before he had regained sufficient composure to return to work. This sequence is not too unusual in borderline patients, but it was a unique experience for this patient. Ordinarily, he was well controlled, although, like other patients I have been discussing, he had regressed episodes of erratic and bizarre behavior. These episodes seemed to have an existence independent of the rest of his personality. On the couch, he did not show evidence of fragmentation. He began his session at a high psychic level and then gradually moved to primitive ego states, eventually reaching basic levels of vulnerability and helplessness.

This regressed episode and several more that followed indicated that he now was able to connect primitive infantile elements with secondary-process-dominated orientations. In a manner of speaking, he was able to fill the lacunae between upper and lower levels. This was an extremely frightening experience, however, and it threatened his psychic survival.

Later in the analysis, we were able to attach content to the terrifying affect he had experienced. Paradoxically, along with his panic, he felt a sense of "aliveness," but it was devastatingly frightening. His associations quickly led him to a view of himself as having been inanimate; he believed he was now undergoing a metamorphosis.

At this stage of treatment, he revealed traumatic infantile constellations and clearly reenacted them in the transference, which now developed a paranoid tinge. Briefly, he viewed me as wanting to block his progress, as not wanting him to grow up and move away from me. He accused me of not supporting his endeavors for individuation and autonomy because of my inflexible view of how analysis should be conducted, an orientation that was not suited to his needs. These attacks on me could be traced to displaced feelings that were initially directed toward his father, whom he could not trust.

His fear of becoming alive represented a reaction toward his mother, who wanted to keep him in the transitional space. If he could remain wooden and "frozen," he did not have to fear her engulfing murderous rage.

It became clear why he had to keep me at a distance and remain alienated from primitive feelings and levels of the psychic apparatus. If he were able to make contact with these early levels, he would have formed a bridge, thus moving out of the transitional space on the path to separation–individuation. This possibility produced a situation of intense conflict because of the traumatic relationships in the infantile environment.

Concreteness, lack of transference development, and the inability to free associate were the outcome of structural defects and protective defenses against early traumatic object relationships. Yet, if we include infantile adaptations in the transference as well as the projection of feelings and parts of the self, all these aspects of his personality could in themselves be considered transference manifestations. Although our natural tendency is to judge such qualities as analytically undesirable, and even as insurmountable resistances, I believe it was necessary for me to be with the patient as he used the defenses that were necessary manifestations of his psychopathology.

"Being with" such patients means surviving their rage and not attacking or rejecting them, which is what happened in the infantile environment. This may lead to periods in analysis when the analyst is idealized, a marked contrast to these patients' usual reactions. But this is not the usual idealization characterized by power and grandiosity. Rather, it is more of a warm glow in which the patient feels comfortably held. It is an attribute of a secure analytic ambience. It also seems to be a necessary precondition for the emergence of underlying traumatic conflicts and the acquisition of psychic structure.

Summary and Conclusions

I have focused on a group of patients whose biological needs for nurture and comfort were adequately met, but whose mothers never related to them beyond simple caretaking. These mothers never smiled at their children, and they derived no pleasure from playing with them or from their emerging sense of aliveness. From the analyses of both these patients and their mothers, it appears that the mothers used their children as transitional objects. As a result, the children's emotional development became fixated in the in-between transitional space.

This kind of fixation leads to specific types of character structure and ego defects. Early developmental levels have not formed a smooth continuum with higher later-acquired adaptive ego states. Extensive lacunae in the middle layers of the psychic apparatus manifest themselves as defective modulating elements. Such patients show extremes of behavior, marked polarities of sane, sensitive rationality and episodes of psychotic-like irrationality. There are no transitional gray areas between black and white. They exhibit a peculiar kind of fragmentation, or splitting, in which connecting bridges between higher and lower levels are missing.

There are many such patients who seek analysis, and they present special problems in therapy. These can be explained in terms of the psychoanalytic paradox. The mother's attitude toward her infant has some similarity to the low-keyed objective analytic attitude sometimes referred to as analytic neutrality. These patients require different modes of relating which will indicate that the therapist, unlike the mother, is very much concerned with the patient's developing autonomy and with his entering and exploring the world.

These are variations of analysis, not modifications of or deviations from analysis. They are elements of the analytic process necessary for the construction of a holding environment appropriate for specific types of psychopathology.

Chapter 5

Object Constancy and Mental Representations

This chapter explores in some detail how attributes of the external world become part of the psyche. This is an object relations focus, which highlights interactions with external objects and the acquisition of developmentally higher levels of psychic integrations. The clinical interactions that I discuss involve both primitive and relatively advanced stages of ego integration. These patients illustrate character disturbances that reflect the structural defects of higher developmental levels.

The acquisition of psychic structure is a reciprocal process. Beneficial experiences with the surrounding world lead to endopsychic registrations and to the structuralization of functional units that later coalesce into adaptive ego executive mechanisms. As the ego's capacities expand, the psyche can seek out and profit from further potentially beneficial segments of reality, beyond what it had been previously able to incorporate. The boundaries between the internal and external world are fairly well constructed, at this point.

Our current focus on character structure relies heavily on the investigation of cognitive factors, which again emphasizes the role of object relationships, both in psychic development—the progression from early amorphous prementational states (Giovacchini, 1979b) to cohesive ego organizations capable of tripartite modalities of relating—and in the ego's ability to carry on various psychic functions relative to the inner and outer world—functions that are characteristic of particular developmental levels.

The current conceptual and technical atmosphere encourages clinicians to phrase their formulations in terms of object relations theory and ego psychology. These are not, however, two separate frames of reference. Object relations is a facet of ego psychology, a subcategory, so to speak. Similarly, id factors do not constitute a separate frame of reference; they are also part of the psyche, and must be taken into account in our formulations of the development of the mind and psychopathology. Psychodynamic formulations have not been rendered useless as we move into structural and cognitive areas. These additional viewpoints should not lead to the replacement or condemnation of certain clinical concepts as erroneous or anachronistic, but can enrich our perspectives about the variability and range of the human mind (see Wallerstein, 1981, 1983).

From the other direction, there has been considerable discussion and controversy over the clinical worth of the structural focus and some question as to whether these conceptual models even belong in the psychoanalytic frame of reference. Many of these articles take Kohut's works (Kohut, 1971) as a point of departure and illuminate various facets of his ideas, often supporting them and occasionally modifying or criticizing them. I have criticized most of Kohut's basic new formulations and definitions (Giovacchini, 1977, 1979b) and propose here to refer instead to areas that other authors have elaborated which will help us to understand the structural and cognitive factors relevant to two patient groups: those patients suffering from primitive mental states and those patients who have achieved relatively high degrees of ego organization and developmental advancement, but who are capable of deep regression, in which many sophisticated structures and functions are for the moment lost. Indeed, such a regression represents the essence of their psychopathology.

I believe that arguments about what properly belongs in the domain of psychoanalysis are counterproductive. In order to treat patients psychoanalytically we have to understand both how their minds function and something about the structure of the psychic apparatus. However unique a treatment modality, it can hardly exclude the exploration of psychic structure and early pregenital developmental stages from our assessment of psychopathology. Furthermore, we gather information about these areas from the standard psychoanalytic treatment of patients.

Some clinicians have objected that we have had to modify our treatment procedure sufficiently that it can no longer be considered psychoanalytic; but then what are the essential elements that would permit us to classify our treatment technique as psychoanalysis? Certainly any treatment that is nonjudgmental, respects the patient's autonomy, is based on the principle of psychic determinism, and primarily uses transference interpretations for the promotion of insight and further psychic integration is basically psychoanalytic. The analyst may find it indispensable not only to deal with conflicting drives, but to relate to various facets of the mental apparatus of the patient as they merge with his mind in transference projections.

Conflict is not necessarily restricted to the drives. The term can be applied to psychic states. Dorpat (1976), for example, distinguishes between structural conflict and object relations conflict. Dorpat, however, is attempting to create a dichotomy that emphasizes intrapsychic conflict without involving the drives. This is to subdivide structural problems into two types, one that involves intrapsychic *structural* conflicts rather than clashes between opposing drives, and the other concerning faulty relationships with external objects. I find it difficult to maintain such a dichotomy because, as I am certain Dorpat would agree, the intrapsychic always affects the quality of object relationships. It is simply a question of emphasis. Freud (1924a, 1924b) had something similar in mind in terms of drives, when he contrasted the neuroses and the psychoses. He asserted that the former were the outcome of intrapsychic conflict, a

conflict between the ego and the id, and the latter the outcome
of rifts between the ego and the outer world—from our contemporary vista, the outer world of external objects.

To approach this problem differently, Levine (1979) reminds us of the importance and structure-promoting qualities of
sustaining object relationships. According to Eisnitz (1981), the
barometer by which to gauge psychic structure is the self-
representation, because it offers us a framework by which we
may view clinical phenomena. It is a final pathway evolving
from the id, ego, and superego and "provides the 'set' that
organizes and gives a special quality to ego functions and object
relations under pressure of unconscious wishes." Wallerstein
(1981) recognizes the importance of all aspects of the psychic
apparatus, the self as well as the drives. He believes we should
not unnecessarily subordinate or diminish the traditional focus
on the vicissitudes of sexual and aggressive drives.

Many clinicians would agree with Eisnitz about the importance of the self-representation, particularly when dealing with
borderline patients (Kernberg, 1975) and other patients suffering from character disorders (Giovacchini, 1975b). Sandler and
Rosenblatt (1962) were among the first to conceive of the
psyche in terms of self- and object representations and the
representational world. It was Hartmann (1950), however, who
first mentioned the concept of "self," which he introduced into
the psychoanalytic literature. He distinguished the self from the
ego, understanding the former to be connected with a subjective sense of being and the latter to be an abstract concept of a
particular functional unit of the mind.

I agree with those clinicians who prefer to use the term
"self-representation" to designate an ego subsystem that incorporates various aspects of a person's identity. The self-representation can be contrasted with other intraego formations that are
depictions of external objects, but are preserved internally as
object representations. This is in accord with Jacobson's (1964)
orientation. The term "self" has a much looser connotation and
can be thought of as a general reflection of the psyche in its
totality. Federn's (1952) attitudes about self-feeling are similar
to this viewpoint about the self, and they highlight the contrast
between the self, a supraordinate structure, and the self-representation.

Self-Representation and Object Constancy

Fraiberg (1969) approaches the establishment of object constancy as a clinician who realizes how important the understanding of early development is to our assessment of character structure. Noy (1979) also discusses cognition from a clinical viewpoint, but his theoretical base is broader than Fraiberg's. He distinguishes primary- and secondary-process cognitive elements, and investigates whether the perceptual apparatus is focused primarily on the inner or the outer world.

Fraiberg is well known for her description of two different types of memory, recall and evocative memory. In recall memory, the sensory apparatus recognizes an object when it appears in the perceptual field, but it does not retain a reproducible memory trace of that object. There is undoubtedly some mental representation, but it is not sufficiently structured to be evoked without the presence of the external object; it is not sufficiently cathected to be consciously experienced. This does occur with evocative memory, however, and this is the same capacity Piaget discovered in his experiments. It enables the psyche to "remember" an external object even when it is not actually present.

These distinctions are significant, because they have implications about emotional development and the achievement of psychic structure. Spitz (1957) believes that object constancy occurs considerably earlier than do other psychoanalysts, such as Fraiberg (1969) and Anna Freud (1951), who place its beginning at 18 months. Spitz postulates that it begins at eight months, when stranger anxiety is first manifest. He links the ability to maintain a mental representation of the mother to a "special stress situation," meaning that the child cathects the mother's internal representation when the stranger appears. Because what appears in the external world is different from what is internally cathected, the child cannot integrate the external object. It remains a foreign object and produces anxiety. By contrast, Anna Freud writes about libidinal object constancy as a stable inner object representation, even when there is no need, or when the object is experienced as unsatisfactory.

Piaget (1952) concentrated on cognitive rather than libidinal factors—from our viewpoint an ego–psychological rather than id focus. He worked with three interrelated concepts: object permanency, object constancy, and evocative memory. Permanency refers to the inherent stability and organization of the mental representation of the object—its independent status in time and space. The object may lose its cathexis, but not its structure. He viewed object constancy as the stabilized (permanent) intrapsychic representation of an object, regardless of its actual presence or absence. He saw it as a structural achievement that occurs with the capacity for evocative memory. He agrees with many analysts, in that he places these developmental events around the age of 18 months.

Piaget's experiments were conducted using inanimate objects, but he believed that the structuralizing processes responsible for animate and inanimate object constancy are the same. In fact, according to Piaget, animate object constancy occurs slightly before inanimate object constancy. His experiments established a hierarchy that is important to both the study of normal development and psychopathology.

The ego progressively structuralizes and acquires a multifaceted internal object representation that is retained despite large libidinal fluctuations. As these cognitive functions are established, there is a corresponding formation of the identity sense. Along with the refinement of the object concept, as Piaget called it, there is a parallel structuring of the self-representation. The qualities of both self- and object representations are the outcome of either the ego's integrity or its psychopathological defects.

With progressive structuralization, object representations become more cohesive, integrated, and sophisticated, as boundaries between self- and object representations become increasingly distinct. The self-representation, similar to object representations, achieves permanency and then constancy; and as it becomes further consolidated, it is experienced as an enhancement of the identity sense.

In essence, then, there is a parallel development between object constancy and the constancy of the self-representation. The failure to reach such levels of integration has many psychopathological consequences. The inability to attain *self-represen-*

tational constancy, or the loss of it through regression, is the basis of much of the psychopathology we currently see in our patients.

Frequently, our patients suffer from intense anxiety, because they cannot maintain a cohesive identity sense in the presence of changes in their familiar environment. They have little or no flexibility. They require an absolutely constant environment to support the shaky integration of the self-representation, and to be able to preserve the boundaries of object representations. If they can no longer continue in their usual minimal construction of boundaries of self- and object representations, there is the danger of destructive fusion when circumstances upset their usual equilibrium.

Another frequently encountered clinical phenomenon concerns the loss of self-esteem. Borderline patients who suffer from structural defects uniformly demonstrate a profound sense of worthlessness, and a lack of purpose and definition of values. These are all associated with an amorphous self-representation, one that has not achieved object permanency, let alone object constancy. In treatment, this negative self-appraisal may prove to be especially impervious to analytic resolution, because neither the patient nor the analyst is able to relate it to any focal internal conflicts, external precipitants, or etiological infantile traumas. There is nothing in the patient's background that is specific enough to account for the looseness of integration and the rigidity of the self-representation.

The patient has learned how to adapt to the infantile world, and within such a context, he is able to maintain adequate amounts of self-esteem, and to keep self- and object representations somewhat differentiated. When he moves outside the confines of this ambience, as is inevitable, his usual equilibrium is drastically upset, and adaptations designed to maintain self-esteem become ineffective. The analytic setting itself represents an ambience that is different from the infantile environment, and it is intrinsically threatening to some patients suffering from particular types of psychopathology. Within such a context, infantile defenses cannot continue functioning.

This discussion implies that the integration of self- and object representations and their internal consistency or constancy can be conceptualized from the vantage point of different levels of psychic structuralization. For example, the self-representation can be well organized and cohesive but at a primitive level. This type of self-representation has achieved some degree of permanency. Kernberg (1975) believes this is typical of the borderline personality organization.

Organization of the self-representation within a primitive context is now familiar to most analysts as we have come to understand our borderline patients better and our clinical experience broadens. Object constancy, however, has been considered an attribute of a relatively advanced developmental stage and has not been thought to belong to earlier phases. This makes sense, given the assumption that emotional development proceeds from states of lesser structure to states of greater structure. The study of cognition has, to a large measure, supported this viewpoint.

Our clinical experience, however, dictates that we reconsider our assumptions. Our patients are providing us with data that require us to think out how what might be an ordinary developmental sequence becomes distorted by psychopathology, and contributes to the final pathologically constructed ego organization. The borderline patient is a case in point. If we accept that he has a relatively stable integrated self-representation, although primitively organized, we must infer that *a primitive state need not be equated with a lack of structural organization.* A primitive organization may nevertheless be an organization that has some permanency and stability.

What can be said for the self-representation also applies to object representations and object constancy. Some primitive ego states, the outcome of psychopathology, can relate to the external world on the basis of object constancy. The ego is able to maintain a mental representation of an external object without its actual presence. Still, the psyche, by and large, has achieved only a minimum of differentiation, and the boundaries between the inner and outer world are poorly established. This particular situation is characteristic of specific types of psychopathology and modes of relating. It is also characteristic of patients whose behavior seems contradictory because they can be sensible and irrational at the same time.

For example, certain patients relate to the analyst and people in general only on the basis of their needs. They can be exasperatingly childish and needy. This would be expected of patients who are experiencing an analytic regression, but this orientation is not limited to the treatment setting. The analyst learns that this inability to recognize external objects as persons, along with a total lack of mutuality and reciprocity, are characteristic of all their relationships. Nevertheless, they do not lose mental representations when the external object is absent. They can also function quite effectively at times.

In analysis, these patients are often intense and clinging. As a rule, they are humorless, and their viewpoint about themselves, their friends, and the world is constricted. They may be vociferously demanding and can have a tremendous impact on the analyst because of the immediacy of their needs. In fact, because of being treated only as an object and as a nonperson, the therapist may react defensively with analytic neutrality.

Some clinicians, Modell (1968) in particular, consider this type of relating, which in treatment leads to specific disruptive countertransference responses, to be typical of narcissistic patients. Undoubtedly this is true, but patients who phenomenologically display no signs of a narcissistic orientation also may relate in this way. Their object relations, as discussed in the previous section, are preoedipal and narcissistic, but their ego structure is characterized by a lack of rather than what seems to be a surplus of ego-libido. The apparent surplus usually represents an overcompensatory defense to bolster a self-representation plagued with a profound sense of inadequacy and worthlessness. These patients are totally preoccupied with themselves, but they also reveal, and sometimes parade, their feelings of worthlessness. There is a diversity to their underlying character structure, which ranges from borderline states to depressive and even obsessive–compulsive organizations.

Clinical Material

Developmentally, it is possible to trace a continuum from an amorphous, preobject ego state with unformed intraego structures to one that contains well-differentiated self- and object representations and operates on the basis of object constancy and mature whole-object relationships. With psychopathology, there are varying degrees of regression and fixation that were first (Breuer & Freud, 1895) described in terms of drives. This section discusses how the mechanisms of regression and fixation affect the structure of self- and object representations. I will begin by describing patients who exhibit very primitive fixations.

These patients have fairly amorphous self-representations and have not yet achieved object constancy. As is generally true, absolute distinctions are difficult to make when dealing with emotional states. The type of patient I am about to describe demonstrates a relative absence of object constancy. In some very primitively fixated patients, this can approach total absence.

Loss of Mental Representation

A married woman in her late thirties demanded daily appointments. She told me during her first session that she could not tolerate my being away. She realized that I would occasionally take a vacation or otherwise leave the city, but she found this extremely upsetting. Even though she knew she had to accept that I would leave from time to time, she demanded that I let her know well in advance. I told her about my next trip almost six months ahead of time, but this turned out to be of no particular help, inasmuch as she spent most of that time reviling me for wanting to leave her. She accused me of deserting and abandoning her.

I learned that the patient felt she needed me to be constantly present, seven days a week, 24 hours a day. Reluctantly accepting that this was impossible, she at least had to know where I would be at all times. She revealed that if she did not know my location, her mental image of me would fade away. She could not hold a mental representation of a person unless she had some communication with him or her. Indeed, she had the itinerary of all her friends, and she was in daily contact with about a dozen of them by telephone.

Her life had a frenetic quality to it. Everything she did was done with intense excitement, or, more accurately, with considerable agitation. She suffused the consultation room with an all-pervasive tension that both of us experienced as painful. Although the patient could be clever and sometimes witty, her excitement was usually grim and humorless.

She complained that she knew very little about pleasure, but she was not particularly depressed. She was describing a state of anhedonia. Her general attitude seemed pathetic, but it was difficult to classify it definitively.

For all ostensible purposes, she was incapable of feeling. For example, she literally did not know if she were hungry, thirsty, sexually aroused, or had to defecate or urinate. All she felt was an amorphous inner tension, and she relied mainly on its predominant anatomical location to determine which organ system was primarily involved.

She perceived herself in the same amorphous fashion as she experienced feelings. She had no sense of who she was, where she fit in the world, or the purpose of her life. She had been unable to continue college in another city, because she apparently had suffered from a severe emotional decompensation that had necessitated hospitalization.

She had a poorly defined identity sense that could be accounted for by early life experiences, especially by the fact that she had been the neglected younger sister of identical twins. The diffuseness of her self-representation reached such intense proportions that she sometimes wondered whether she were even alive. She was in constant terror that she would "dissolve into nothing."

Returning to the discussion of amorphous feelings, she reported always feeling anxious, but was unable to define what she meant better than that. She had not been able to connect her anxiety, if indeed that is what it was, to any situation that might either precipitate or terminate it. Nor did her associations (she did not report many dreams) supply clues about the unconscious conflicts that would account for her diffuse feeling or for its intensity. I could not understand its source.

One session she surprised me when she said that she herself was the source of her anxiety. She told me she could turn the feeling on and off "like a faucet." Then she proceeded to demonstrate what she meant. She had been relatively calm and composed at the beginning of the session, but as soon as she said "Now I will feel anxious," it was as if she had commanded her autonomic nervous system to respond, and she showed all the visible signs of anxiety. Her pupils dilated, she developed "goose bumps," and I could see small trickles of perspiration on her brow. She then stated that she would no longer feel anxious, and just as suddenly, all of the autonomic signs of anxiety vanished.

Although her affective tone was poorly discriminated, she was, nevertheless, able to generate feelings. She had a modicum of conscious control, as she so dramatically illustrated. Still, she was far from being in complete control, in view of the fact that she was driven to produce anxiety. When she did not, she experienced what she called "apathetic terror," which she associated with her fear of dissolution. Clearly, she was describing an existential crisis.

Federn (1952) used the same words this patient did—"apathetic terror"—to describe an ego that is losing its cohesiveness and integration. Byschowski (1952) described similar subjective states in schizophrenic patients who were not only withdrawing from the external world, as Freud (1911) discussed, but whose identity sense was crumbling. That is indeed the way my patient viewed herself. She was terrified that if she did not create anxiety, she would cease to exist. She compared it to pinching oneself to make sure that one is awake. To feel nothing meant she was dead. To feel something, albeit painful, reassured her that she was alive. Without anxiety, she perceived herself as a vacuum, as an empty, terrifying void. She was producing an affect that was phenomenologically similar to anxiety as protection against a more fundamental anxiety, the fear of annihilation.

To summarize briefly, this woman is one of a class of patients who have practically no capacity for object constancy. This is evidenced by an inability to form and to hold a mental representation of an external object without the presence of that object. This does not mean, as it did with Piaget's (1952) children, that the object must be within the subject's visual field. With adult patients, the knowledge of where a person is, if not too far away and immediately available (at least by telephone), suffices to maintain an internal object representation.

Correspondingly, the self-representation is tenuously constructed, and these patients suffer from severe identity problems.

Fear of Fusion and Loss of Self-Esteem

Analysts are becoming increasingly familiar with patients who vigorously resist beginning treatment or who later create an impasse that threatens to disrupt therapy (see Giovacchini & Boyer, 1975). These patients have a greater, although still minimal, degree of object constancy than the patient just described. There is a quantitative continuum between these two groups, and the tenuous self- and object representations account for the difficulties in constructing and maintaining an analytic setting.

One such patient, a successful, very bright young man in his early thirties, was extremely conflicted about starting analysis. On the surface, this was odd, because he had tried for many months to get me to see him. Because my schedule had been full, I had tried to refer him to various colleagues, but he had adamantly refused to see them; he was afraid they would think he was "too sick" and would not want to analyze him. It was particularly surprising, therefore, when he tried to manipulate me into not analyzing him.

For two sessions he gave me a long detailed history, obsessionally filling in every detail of past development. For my purpose here, I will briefly mention that he had a successful but passively uninvolved father, and a beautiful, apparently narcissistic mother who doted on him. The patient was an only child who attracted considerable attention because of his innate talents and intellectual precocity.

At the beginning of the third session I briefly instructed him about free association and the use of the couch. I knew this was an interruption of his intention to give me further information concerning his past, but I saw no purpose in letting him go on as he had. Usually, I do no more than ask patients to lie on the couch, letting them decide whether they wish to talk and what they wish to talk about; but this patient, although he had initially seemed eager for analysis, I believe would have gone on indefinitely sitting up and continuing with his narrative, avoiding the couch.

He politely listened to my instructions, but seemed bewildered. In fact, he approached the couch, but moved the pillow to the other end and proceeded to lie down, a position in which he would be facing me. I corrected him immediately, and he turned himself around. He started speaking in a less organized fashion, often hesitating and indicating some anxiety. Five minutes before the end of the session, he sat up and said, "I've had enough." He did not leave, however; he continued talking until the end of the session.

The patient cancelled the next four sessions, each time having what appeared to be "legitimate" reasons. For example, he cancelled his next appointment because he had the flu with a fever of 103°. He recovered rather quickly, but not until he had missed the second session. After that he was unexpectedly sent out of town by his firm, which caused him to miss the last two sessions of the week.

When he finally returned, he walked toward the chair, but I motioned him to the couch. Again, he walked toward it reluctantly, but this time he did not lie down. Sitting up, he told me that his problems were current and immediate and he did not want to get lost in the morass of his past. In view of the fact that he had gone into such extensive details about his early childhood and development, this seemed bizarre.

I had some vivid feelings at this point, which I discuss later when dealing with technical factors and countertransference. For the moment, I will confess that I had to resist the impulse to tell the patient angrily that he should stop wasting my time. Either he should let me analyze him or go elsewhere. I restrained myself by remembering the simple principle of psychic determinism. The patient had to be reacting to some profound anxiety that prevented him from relaxing and regressing in an analytic context. So I explained that it was up to him whether he talked about the past or the present—in this regard, he had complete autonomy—but that for technical reasons as well as for my personal comfort, I required that he use the couch. I said that if I believed treatment could progress in any other fashion, I would be glad to conduct therapy in a way that would make him feel more comfortable; however, I and the psychoanalytic method had limitations, and I knew no other way in which I could proceed. I also told him I believed that by letting him sit up we might be evading some fundamental problems. He did not seem happy about what I said, but he acquiesced. I somehow felt we had avoided a power struggle.

I learned later that the patient's initial reluctance to begin analysis was the outcome of his ambivalence. He desperately wanted analysis, but he was frightened. He understood that the aim of analysis is to foster autonomy, but he was afraid of losing control. To lie on the couch and not be able to look at me signified that he was helpless and vulnerable. He would feel humiliated and lose his last vestige of self-esteem. Looking at me meant that he was in control, because he was maintaining his vigilance.

Apart from obvious masochistic, homosexual transference elements, he was dominated by the fear of fusion, of recapitulating the traumatic infantile fusion with his mother. The fear of pathological merger made it difficult to begin analysis, and during treatment, he experienced transference regression in a frightened, painful fashion.

Still, he had considerable resiliency and integration, and had developed enough trust in the analytic setting to be able to move in and out of regressed states that recapitulated his early relationship with his mother. It was interesting to note how he came out of the regression, that is, how he used certain adaptations to protect himself from fusion.

Fusion, as discussed in Chapter 2, was a terrifying experience for this patient, and this was the psychopathological consequence of a traumatic maternal relationship. His mother apparently needed to use her son for support, and clung to him. She related to the external world primarily on the basis of a false self, as she maintained an air of aristocratic self-sufficiency and gentility. Underneath this veneer she was depressed and plagued by intense feelings of inadequacy. In spite of her superficial savoir-faire, she was terrified by people and painfully shy. As the patient recalled, she took extreme pride in his intellectual precocity and used him, in a diversionary way, as a conversation piece, so that she would feel at ease in small gatherings. He experienced this as a merger that stifled his individuality.

When regaining his composure after a period when he felt

that I was "swallowing" him to make him part of myself, as his mother had, the patient would become rigid and concrete in his observations and attitudes. This is the way he usually conducted himself in his daily life. The patient recognized that his fear stemmed from his infantile past, but he still experienced it intensely and painfully. In the regressed state, he perceived me in a vague, blurred, indefinite way, and had extreme difficulty in maintaining a coherent image of both me and himself. As he emerged from such a state, and he returned to his usual rigid, concrete observations and attitudes, we both became very distinct in his mind and sharply separated.

At these moments, he lost his ability to free associate, and became outwardly directed. He no longer had any capacity for introspection. He would ask me innumerable questions, the types of questions that are usually directed toward physicians, such as, "Are we making progress?" and similar queries that I had no inclination to answer. During these periods, he had assigned us specific roles. He was the patient and I was the doctor. Although he also viewed himself in terms of his work and various social roles, his concepts about himself, me, and the world in general were stilted and mechanical.

His memory was unusually good when he exhibited these concrete qualities. He could retain a mental representation of me with unusual clarity, and could recall in detail my mannerisms, the inflections of my voice, and exactly what I had said. This was in sharp contrast to his orientation during regressed states, when self- and object representation lost their distinct qualities and became fused.

Clearly, his concrete state manifested itself as a resistance, and was a defensive adaptation to protect him from the dissolution of his self-representation, which he feared would occur in a state of fusion. Thus he had achieved object constancy, but it was not entirely a developmental achievement. Object constancy was part of a defensively constructed ego state that did not permit him any access to the deeper layers of his personality. This was reflected in his behavior and general functioning: He was inflexible, unfeeling, and inhibited in working creatively, a severe handicap in view of his professional position. He was free of anxiety, however, and maintained a modicum of self-esteem.

In contrast to the previously discussed patient, who had problems in forming and maintaining mental representations, and in essence had achieved only a minimum, almost nonexistent, object constancy, this patient had traversed a considerable distance on the developmental scale. The fact that he could construct an ego state based on object constancy, even though it was defensively motivated, is indicative of basic integrative capacities.

Much more can be written about the disruptive nature of fusion or lack of harmonious fusion. There are various psychopathological constellations of the mother–infant merger, including an inability to merge. These range from mothers who totally abandon their infants to mothers who sadistically attack their children, either actually or symbolically. I believe that patients suffering from severe structural psychopathology have not been able to fuse comfortably with the internalized representations of their mothers, and their mothers, in turn, were unable to relate intuitively to their children because of structural defects of their own that interfered with their maternal capacities.

Lack of fusion or defective fusion is the outcome of psychopathology. My patient, like other patients who are characterologically similar, organized himself around the axis of what we might call a pathological object constancy to defend against the threat of being fused to a mother who would stamp out his individuality in order to enhance herself. *From one viewpoint, he was using elements of a later developmental phase to protect himself from an earlier one. He was paradoxically regressing in a forward direction.*

Still, the stage that included defensive object constancy was primitive in many respects, as evidenced by its concreteness, rigidity, and insular isolation from other developmental phases. The patient's narrow, constricted view of the world and his limited responses indicate an infantile, vulnerable orientation, rather than the maturity associated with nondefensive object constancy.

Such a defensive ego state is characterized by strict definitions of values. These patients deal mainly in polarities. Everything is good or bad, true or false, and based on the strict dichotomies of love and hate. There is no in-between room for illusion.

Constricted View of External Objects

The final group of patients to be discussed have achieved object constancy; but their view of external objects, although stable, is inflexible and constricted. In some respects, their outlook is similar to that of the patients described in the previous section, but there are significant differences in psychic structure. For this group, the construction of object constancy is not a defensive adaptation—a protection against fusion. Instead, this particular type of object constancy is the outcome of defective development, and the resultant ego organization causes specific orientations toward the outer world and specific behavioral patterns, that is, unique ways of relating to external objects. In treatment, such patients' modes of relating create characteristic transference reactions and countertransference difficulties.

The distinction that I am making between defensive adaptations and behavior that is the outcome of trauma and maldevelopment is not absolute. All behavior can be viewed simultaneously from various perspectives. For analysts who adhere to the principle of psychic determinism, patients' reactions and orientations are understood to have purpose and meaning. We think in terms of stratification of the psyche and oppositional forces between different layers of the mind. Although many clinicians prefer a theoretical framework based on structural factors, they view the ego's responses as defensive adaptations. With the patients I am now discussing, the defensive potential of their constricted behavior is a matter of degree. Furthermore, as Freud (1926) pointed out, constrictions as inhibitions can acquire a secondary defensive function.

Although the type of psychopathology this group presents is not particularly severe or bizarre in its manifestations, the treatment of such patients is often experienced as tedious. For example, I found myself reacting to a 35-year-old married man with annoyance, although there were no obvious reasons for my having such a feeling.

The patient was a highly successful professional man, quite articulate, with an excellent command of the language and considerable wit. His descriptions of inner feelings and outer events were picturesque and entertaining. Thus my feelings puzzled me.

Perhaps I had anticipated what would happen. He went on, session after session, in the same clever style, but turned from describing his environment and the inner world of his psyche to nagging and complaining about treatment. He had a rigid, obsessive character configuration, and similar to the patient I discussed in the previous section, he became demanding in a concrete fashion. Unlike that patient, however, his concreteness was not as pervasive. He could easily become psychologically minded and make use of free association, fantasies, and dreams for introspective purposes. Even his nagging and complaining were transient. Although he periodically became concrete, rigid, and demanding, this orientation alternated with other attitudes that are more propitious for analysis. Most of the time he presented material that was helpful in maintaining an intrapsychic focus. Yet, paradoxically, his preoccupation with himself, rather than being favorable for analysis, struck me as being a deterrent to treatment, and it disturbed me.

Unlike with other superficially similar clinical situations, the patient did not seem to be withdrawing from me, shutting me out, or even diminishing my worth by projecting feelings of inadequacy into me. There were some such projections, but they did not dominate the transference, and even if they had, there was no reason for them to have interfered with the course of the analysis or upset me. In fact, none of the defensive adaptations I have mentioned should have been reason for concern. They are common enough defensive stances for patients suffering from structural problems and intrapsychic conflicts.

What I found disturbing about my patient's mode of relating is that I had the impression he was not aware of me as a person. He made me feel as if I were unidimensional and lacked depth. I was only a vehicle for his needs, and the external world revolved around him, having no other focus. My description might suggest the orientation of a narcissistic patient, who deals with external objects as if they were self-objects. The analyses of such patients often cause an analyst to feel that he does not exist in his own right, apart from the patient. Under such circumstances, the therapist may even feel the type of anxiety that is characteristic of an existential crisis (Giovacchini, 1972, 1979b). This was not the situation with my patient. He did recognize me as separate and apart from himself, but in a limited way.

At the beginning and end of sessions, he was always courteous and respectful, which stood in contrast to his occasional outbursts of recrimination and sarcasm during the sessions. When feeling especially mellow, however, he might spend all his time discussing topics he knew I found exciting and sharing intellectual interests with me. He *seemed* to be relating to me as a person; nevertheless, I did not feel as if he were. I still reacted as if I were being excluded, although clearly this was not so.

I then realized that I was responding to the emotional tone, rather than to the content, of what he was saying. Although his material was interesting, the way he presented it was tedious and dull. He never smiled, and although, as I said, he could be witty, he was totally devoid of humor. He often looked depressed, confused, and perplexed, but never animated, enthusiastic, or happy. The fact that he directed everything back to himself combined with his humorless mode of presentation made me uncomfortable. I was able to relax only when I understood our relationship in terms of his infantile past.

His mother, because of a chronic depression, had been in treatment with a prominent analyst as long as the patient could remember. When he was six months old, she had been hospitalized for several months. In spite of her severe emotional difficulties, he was told she was a good and devoted mother. He remembered being well taken care of as a child, but he could not recall ever chatting or playing games with his mother. Apparently she was constantly depressed and never smiled.

She related to his needs with a sense of immediacy, but she could not go beyond the need-gratification level. I was able to partially reconstruct and to speculate about the early maternal interaction from the way the patient related to me and from my countertransference responses. I also had the opportunity to gather information about the mother from her analyst, who emphasized that she had not been able to recognize her son as a person, but simply as a baby who had to be fed and changed. He confirmed that she had never sung or cooed to him. In fact, because this analyst had been interested in his patient's mothering behavior, he had asked her about the various developmental milestones of her son's life. When questioned, she did not recognize that her child had had a smiling response or felt stranger anxiety. Certainly, she had not tried to evoke a smile from him, or, as far as her analyst could tell, she had not smiled in his presence. She did not seem to have derived any pleasure from her son. He was a chore that she conscientiously took care of, but not a person whose presence would fill her with pride and a sense of accomplishment.

I felt exactly the same way. I felt no pride or sense of accomplishment about the treatment relationship. We did not smile at each other, and I took it to mean that he was not pleased to see me. To him, that lack of interchange meant nothing, because, as with his mother, smiling was a foreign habit.

I have emphasized that the patient did not ignore me in the way that some narcissistic patients will totally exclude external objects and concentrate only on themselves. The mother's analyst was again helpful. He did not classify his patient's relationship with her son as having been primarily narcissistic or engulfingly symbiotic. He believed that, because of her depression, she could only relate to external objects in a constricted fashion, which, in regard to her son, meant that she could relate only to the immediacy of his needs. She could not deal with him as a person in his own right, emerging and developing as an autonomous human being. She had no intuition or empathy; she could not establish emotional resonance with him. She simply looked after him in terms of his physical needs. This permitted him to reach a developmental level that includes object constancy, but it gave him a constricted view of external objects based on his needs. He neither received nor gave emotional sustenance.

He had, of course, received some emotional sustenance;

otherwise, he would not have been able to achieve even a constricted form of object constancy. He had also reached levels of psychic development that enabled him to realize a fairly successful career and moderately adequate social relationships. He was much further advanced emotionally than the children Spitz (1945) described, whose physical needs were taken care of but who were kept isolated in cubicles. This patient could relate fairly well to the external world, but he was considered selfish, eccentric, and rigid.

Many patients suffering from characterological problems have similar backgrounds, and evoke disruptive countertransference reactions during treatment. Such patients make demands of us that we cannot or do not want to meet. Our antipathy to them may become so intense that we would rather not treat them. The analyst has to understand the patient's structural defects and constrictions in order to overcome his reluctance to continue analysis.

The Tenuous Treatment Relationship

Although the following section focuses on technical issues, some remarks about treatability are appropriate here. There are no specific recommendations or techniques that will make the patients I have been discussing analyzable. If the therapist is highly motivated to treat patients who cannot maintain mental representations without external reinforcement, he might have to alter his work style drastically.

The first group of patients discussed in this chapter have serious ego defects and behave in an irrational, unpredictable fashion. Their infantile world was irrational and unpredictable by virtue of the fact that their early object relationships were inconsistent. Frequently the mother was totally absent. Their unreasonable demands often represent an attempt to establish a sense of continuity, to create a world in which they will not feel abandoned or vulnerable. Because they are recapitulating the traumatic, unreasonable elements of the traumatic infantile environment, they repeat childhood frustrations that disrupt the analytic setting.

The second group of patients I discussed have a much less disruptive impact on the therapeutic action than the patients just described. Nevertheless, they may be very difficult to treat, because they often cannot accept certain formal elements of the analytic process, such as lying on the couch and free associating. The treatment impasse usually occurs at the beginning of treatment, and if the analyst is unwilling to modify the analytic approach—for example, by letting the patient sit up—the patient may abruptly terminate.

The young man I described in this chapter did use the couch at my insistence, although he protested vehemently. In two similar instances, however, the patients terminated. A middle-aged woman did not return for her next appointment after her first hour on the couch, and another patient, after three months of treatment, moved away to join her mother in another city, claiming that she had received enough benefit from analysis that she could now continue on her own. These patients had intense resistance to analysis.

The inner conflicts of such patients are reinforced by the "rules" of analysis. Throughout their lives, they have erected defensive adaptations to deny their basic feelings of vulnerability and helplessness. Inasmuch as their self-representations are perceived as tenuous, and object constancy is not firmly established, they fear analytic regression. They are terrified of fusing with the analyst and have to be constantly vigilant in order to maintain control. Consequently, to lie on the couch and to free associate are especially threatening.

The analyst has to decide whether to modify the therapeutic stance, perhaps by permitting the introduction of parameters, as Eissler (1953) described. If the therapist maintains the analytic setting, he runs the risk of losing the patient early in treatment. I have tried both approaches.

The analyst's personal orientation is especially important in choosing an effective method of treatment for this group of patients. When I have tried to treat these patients on their own terms, so to speak, I have not been particularly successful. On several occasions, the patients were pleased and felt they had benefited from treatment, but other than some rearrangement of life circumstances—in one instance a divorce—I did not feel that much had been accomplished, at least not in terms of their acquiring further psychic structure and resolution of intrapsychic conflict.

Undoubtedly, idiosyncratic elements of my character contribute heavily to my evaluation of these treatment situations. Countertransference is an important determinant for how we wish to treat patients. I found myself reluctant to relinquish my analytic identity, which is part of my professional ego-ideal, by offering these patients something other than analysis. Because their self-representations are tenuously constructed, and because they have achieved only a precarious type of object constancy, I feel more secure if I hold firmly to my analytic orientation and continue to view external objects (patients) from that perspective. This attitude may very well have influenced what I evaluate to be a lack of therapeutic accomplishment when I have tried to practice nonanalytic therapy.

Still, the number of patients who have fled from analysis is comparatively small. More were able to begin treatment by tolerating analysis, and as they came to understand their vulnerability as the outcome of their fear of fusion, they adjusted well to the analytic setting. In fact, some of the patients who left returned later, and I was glad that I had not jeopardized my potential for conducting analysis by attempting another form of treatment.

To summarize briefly, the treatment of the second group of patients, those who fear fusion and relinquishing control, may become complicated due to certain formal elements of the analytic setting and to untoward countertransference reactions. Analysts may feel their professional ego-ideal threatened when patients refuse to accept basic analytic procedures, such as the fundamental rule and the use of the couch. In contrast to the first group of patients, who are unable to hold mental representations without external reinforcement, and who threaten to disrupt the analytic setting by destroying its temporal boundaries, these patients are much more circumspect. They reject very specific factors to defend themselves against a basic vulnerability that is the outcome of tenuous object constancy and a blurring of boundaries between self- and object representations.

The third group of patients present treatment difficulties

because elements of analytic technique bear some similarity to the nuances and modes of relating of early object relationships, a situation I have called the psychoanalytic paradox. The patient's reactions to these similarities lead to specific countertransference problems.

In Chapter 4, I emphasized that these patients relate to objects in a constricted manner, a reflection of the way their mothers related to them. They have attained a constricted form of object constancy. As discussed, this means that the mother related to the infant in terms of the immediacy of his needs, but not as a potentially autonomous evolving human being. She related to her child in a unidimensional fashion, only in one frame of reference.

Patients may perceive the analytic relationship as identical to the early interaction with their mothers. They may view it as unidimensional and confined to a single frame of reference. Indeed, the analyst wants to restrict the psychoanalytic focus to the intrapsychic world and not enter the patient's external world. For many such patients, the intrapsychic focus is expressed by urgent needs, and living in the outside world is equated to being accepted as a person in their own right. They want the analyst to relate to them in both frames of reference.

Under the pressure of the repetition compulsion, they also try to create a situation in treatment that repeats the early mother–infant relationship in the transference. Usually the reverse of that relationship is recapitulated, in that the patient treats the analyst the same way the mother treated the patient. The problem is intensified, because the analyst, or rather the analytic method, aggravates potential problems, and the repetition compulsion is reinforced by the analytic approach. The transference may be impossible to analyze.

Specifically restricting the interaction with the patient to interpretations and the maintenance of a neutral stance is reminiscent of the constricted relationship with the mother who could allow herself no emotional involvement with her child. The analyst is equated with the unavailable mother. The patient suffers the same infantile deprivation in the current treatment setting. This ordinarily happens in the transference relationship, but usually the analyst's neutrality creates a backdrop that causes infantile transference elements to stand out. With these patients, however, infantile reactions blend with the analyst's operational mode. Consequently, their transference implications are obscured, and the patient believes he is confronting a reality similar to the one he knew in infancy.

Patients need to repeat infantile deprivations, but they also want to be gratified, to make up what they lacked in their early object relationships. This is a compensatory attempt characteristic of patients who have achieved a degree of psychic structure that supports object constancy and allows them to seek segments of the external world that lead to gratification from the analyst. In adult life they are able to make demands they could not make in infancy, because at that time they did not have sufficient ego structure to assert themselves; they also felt too vulnerable and helpless. Similarly, patients suffering from primitive mental states do not have the resources to reach out toward external objects.

The resolution of transference depends on the patients recognizing that their feelings are, for the most part, based on infantile projections, and their ability simultaneously to view the analyst as analyst. If these two frames of reference cannot be kept separate, then the therapist is confronted with the difficult clinical complication of a psychotic transference. If the analyst responds to the patient's manipulations by assuming, in part, the role of an infantile object, the treatment impasse becomes compounded. The analyst often becomes angry and confused and feels threatened in his analytic identity. The patient has put the therapist in the untenable position of failing him. This may create havoc, especially if the analyst does not recognize that it is inevitable. As a consequence of the repetition compulsion, these patients view therapists as not relating to them, as withdrawing, and as being constricted and unempathic. Because of his professional ego-ideal, the analyst finds it difficult to accept such a nonanalytic evaluation and may resist it.

The patient's nagging complaints become painful. Whatever the therapist gives the patient by way of interpretation is off the mark. The analyst is not "in tune," not "locked in," with the patient's feelings. Insights do not help, and this is taken to mean that the analyst does not understand the patient or want to. If the therapist does not maintain his analytic focus, that is, view these complaints as analytic material, he may feel discouraged, frustrated, and guilty. He is faced with the problem of determining how much of what a patient says is, in fact, a correct appraisal, and he becomes increasingly confused. He may even attempt to compensate for what he begins to feel as his uselessness by becoming more interpretatively active, but the patient continues to feel misunderstood.

Recently I saw a hospitalized adolescent schizophrenic patient who demonstrated some of these issues more clearly than patients who have not regressed to such a primitive level. This young man felt that no one cared for him, and he described himself as "emotionally isolated," even though the hospital personnel did everything they could to relate to him, and catered to his physical needs as quickly as possible. They even tried to anticipate his needs, but were remarkably unsuccessful. Consequently, the patient would frequently experience mounting agitation, often culminating in a physical attack on some staff member. He would then be put in restraints. After such episodes, the patient would become paranoid, feeling that people disliked him and attacked him because they felt he was unlovable. However, this paranoid orientation was not fixed and would dissipate as he resumed participating in ward activities.

When I saw him in consultation, he was relatively calm at the beginning of the interview. Because he was not particularly spontaneous, I asked him some questions concerning the reason for his hospitalization and how he was getting along on the ward. He gradually began to volunteer information, so instead of continuing with my questions, I just listened and occasionally made a comment about what he had said. For a while we seemed to be chatting amiably and fully at ease. Then the mood changed. He found fault with every comment I made. Somehow I had missed the point. I had misunderstood him, or I had misplaced his emphasis. He communicated these reactions in a covert fashion, but his disagreement with the direct statements I made was explicit. He also became increasingly agitated. He leaned forward on the edge of the chair and looked as if he were about to spring. He appeared conflicted, as if he was struggling to control himself.

I viewed him as a hurt, confused child feeling ashamed and humiliated, as if he had been overcome by his feelings and had a tantrum. He appeared as if he had been badly hurt, and without knowing how, I felt responsible. I remained silent for a few minutes and let him talk without interruptions. He became a little calmer, and then I said that, apparently, I had not been in tune with his feelings and had not really understood what he was trying to tell me. He smiled, visibly relaxed, and described in considerable detail some of his paranoid preoccupations. He was, however, discussing situations from the remote past, far removed from the current setting.

My comment about not having been in tune with his feelings, not having been in emotional resonance with him, established a bond between us. He was then able to focus his rage on specific external situations and objects in order to maintain our relationship on an empathic level. His paranoid ideation was both temporally and geographically distant.

In the analysis of nonpsychotic patients such as those in the third group I have been discussing, the recognition that the analyst has to be experienced as nonempathic helps establish a bond, a relationship based on the premise of being understood and recognized as a person, a situation favorable for analysis. To achieve such an optimal relationship may require some suspension of analytic neutrality and objective interpretation— objective in that it lacks subjective elements and is experienced as impersonal.

Circumstances frequently mitigate against the establishment of a bond between patient and therapist emanating from the analyst as well as the analysand. Because of the repetition compulsion, as I have discussed, the patient needs to have the analyst relate to him in a constricted, unfeeling fashion. He behaves in a way that causes the analyst to despair, and in reaction, perhaps even with revenge in mind, the therapist does not want to relate to the patient's emotional needs. Martin (1975) described what he termed "obnoxious patients," who are intrusive and make demands that are designed to pull the therapist out of the psychoanalytic frame of reference. The patients I am discussing are more subtly disturbing.

A 40-year-old married woman repeatedly emphasized how

much she needed me to tell her things about the external world, because she was too inept and helpless to make critical judgments that would enable her to cope with the exigencies of her daily life. This meant that I was to evaluate everyday events and relationships so that she would know how to respond judiciously. If I did not grant her what she required, she warned, she would alienate her husband and children and generally create chaos. She acknowledged that she was asking me to breathe for her. She dependently clung to other persons as well, who eventually distanced themselves from her because of her intense neediness. Her self-centeredness finally antagonized her family and friends, and I began to feel the same resentment. This patient did not recognize anyone except in terms of her needs, an example of the constricted object constancy that I have been discussing.

She quietly attacked me for not giving her what she needed. These were not vociferous attacks. On the contrary, she would revile herself for her weakness, but she was nevertheless adept at quiet reproach. She indicated that I was being remiss in my role as therapist, because I never talked to her, and she asked me numerous questions, which I usually did not answer. In many instances, I did not know the answer, but I was also aware of an inner resistance that made me reluctant to respond.

Still, I was far from being entirely silent. I answered some of her questions and often made interpretations. Whatever I said, however, did not seem to count. She did not recognize my interpretations as interpretations or as answers. She viewed them as criticisms and either started arguing with me or attempted to justify herself, although I had been extremely careful to be nonjudgmental. I could feel her reaching out to me, and, then, when I responded, she ignored the fact that I was trying to reciprocate. If she acknowledged my attempt to impart some understanding, she would follow what I said with another question demanding further clarification. If I fell into her trap, she would continue questioning every one of my responses. She reminded me of a child who endlessly asks, "Why?" She was insatiable.

Her reactions made me feel that I was simply a tool of her needs, without any human qualities. I felt frustrated; I had to view my countertransference in terms of the immediacy of her needs and her constricted maternal relationship, in which she had felt constantly frustrated, a frustration she now provoked in her external world.

The following material clearly illustrates how irritating she could be. While having her hair done, she was chatting with her hairdresser, telling her about some of her problems with her children, especially with a son who was having difficulties during his freshman year at college. The hairdresser responded to her request for advice by making some sensible suggestion. The patient objected and revealed another aspect of the problem. Again, the hairdresser offered her a solution, and again the patient argued that it would not work. At the end of the appointment, the patient was astounded when the hairdresser angrily told her she did not want to see her in her shop again.

Summary

The development of object constancy is parallel to the formation of the self-representation. It is a characteristic achievement of an infantile phase of object relations in which the child is able to maintain a mental representation without the reinforcement of the external object's presence in the sensory field. Object constancy is associated with evocative memory.

The vicissitudes of object constancy become clear in a psychopathological context as maternal character abnormalities and defective maternal care lead to faulty integration of self- and object representations in the child. I have traced a continuum of patients suffering from varying degrees of disturbance in maintaining object constancy. This continuum implies that object constancy is not simply the end product of a progressively structuralizing developmental process. The traumatic infantile environment causes a type of object constancy which is, to some extent, adaptive in preserving a psychopathological equilibrium. I have described three types of psychopathology that lead to specific treatment problems and disruptive countertransference reactions.

The first group of patients suffer from almost a complete

lack of object constancy. They have only recall memory and are literally unable to hold a mental representation without the actual presence of the external object somewhere in the familiar environment. The second group has a tenuous object constancy and a precariously held together self-representation. These patients need to have control over their feelings and the external world to protect themselves from fusion, which is experienced as total annihilation. This type of character defect is commonly encountered in a variety of clinical syndromes that have commanded the attention of clinicians. I believe, for example, that many cases of anorexia nervosa can be explained on a similar basis (see Chapter 6). The third group has a constricted form of object constancy that causes the patient to relate to external objects only in terms of the immediacy of needs. The external object is not recognized as a person with feelings and a potential for growth.

The structural defects of all three groups presented cause problems in treatment. These technical difficulties are created by what I call the psychoanalytic paradox (see Chapters 4 and 6), a situation in which psychopathology becomes imbricated into the analytic setting and leads to treatment impasses and upsetting countertransference responses. The first group of patients disrupts the general setting; the second group objects to specific elements of the treatment procedure; and the third group reacts adversely to the analytic stance of neutrality, the technique of interpretation, and a strict adherence to an intrapsychic focus.

I have discussed the impact of these types of structural psychopathology on the analyst's equanimity. This can lead to trying, even impossible, situations in treatment, but an understanding of infantile trauma and the resultant maldevelopment of self- and object representations often makes it possible to overcome inner disruption and to continue analyzing.

Chapter 6

Schizophrenia:
The Persistent Psychosis

The psychotic state continues to fascinate and puzzle clinicians. In spite of our greater knowledge about neurophysiology and neurochemistry and our ever-increasing sophistication about developmental sequences and structural psychopathology, schizophrenic patients still present us with an aura of mystery, especially when we attempt to confront their delusional systems. Their private worlds create an enigma that affects our therapeutic efficacy, and the impact of their delusions can disrupt our psychic equilibrium, the stability of our self-representations, and our sense of values. The lack of congruence between the psychotic's reality and our view of the world produces a jarring lack of resonance that is experienced as painful and paralyzes our capacity for understanding (see Giovacchini, 1979b; Giovacchini & Boyer, 1983).

Schizophrenics present us with a very difficult and confusing but very interesting dilemma, that must be intrinsic to their psychopathology. Since antiquity, madness has been held in awe. Psychosis has fascinated both experts and laymen; it has been revered and reviled. Some apparent schizophrenics have been elevated to sainthood; others, the greater majority, have been ostracized, feared, and tortured. Mankind has been aware of the psychotic state since the dawn of civilization, more so than of any other mental aberration, and yet, until recently, has done very little to understand it from a rational viewpoint (Ellenberger, 1970).

Perhaps there is something inherent in the schizophrenic condition that evokes a strong emotional response in the observer, impeding our efforts to remain within a rational, objective frame of reference. It may be that their psychopathology is characterized by certain disruptive elements that are intended to defy our capacity for understanding. In order to preserve their world, schizophrenics may have to make inroads into ours. For us to enter the schizophrenic's world in an attempt to achieve some degree of empathy, it is necessary that we keep at least one foot firmly anchored in our own reality. The schizophrenic patient who becomes engaged in treatment may not be able to accept any world other than the one that is constructed by a personal delusional system. The latter could clash with the therapist's orientation toward reality.

Thus, it is possible that the psychic structure and ego defects of schizophrenic patients are not particularly complex and difficult to understand, but that we feel threatened, sometimes even terrified, of their overwhelming delusions or the bizarreness of their thought processes. If we could overcome our emotional response, perhaps we could develop some capacity to make contact with them and to understand how their minds function.

I wish to concentrate here on the mental processes of psychotics, rather than to make formal diagnostic distinctions, which have received and continue to receive considerable attention in the psychiatric literature. When I refer to psychotic patients, I am discussing schizophrenics and excluding the affective disorders. This book is concerned with the emotional problems associated with primitive mental states, and although depression and mania may be extraordinarily difficult to treat, these disorders belong to higher levels of the developmental scale.

The conditions focused on thus far in this book involve a mind that is in the process of formation, that is, a mind still in a state of transition and evolution. The deviations from normal development may be enormous, but because of the unformed qualities of the psyche, there is some resiliency, and this may lead to the acquisition of further psychic structure and the achievement of higher developmental levels.

Schizophrenics, on the other hand, are known for their rigidity and their resistance to progressive change. From a developmental perspective, their points of fixation are difficult to place on the continuum of ego stages. They seem to have a fixed organization that traverses many levels of psychic structure. The resiliency attributed to other patients suffering from primitive mental states does not seem to be a characteristic of schizophrenics.

Nevertheless, it is difficult to make generalizations for psychotic patients. Whereas most such patients hang on tenaciously to their delusional systems and continue to use primitive defenses, we occasionally encounter a patient who changes dramatically and gives up his psychotic system. We have called such patients borderline, but I believe there are patients whose character structure is typically psychotic and whose adaptations depend on the construction of a delusional world. In treatment, therapist and patient may rather quickly establish a bond that emboldens the patient to take steps into the therapist's world. This may be the outcome of an exceptionally good fit between the two, but what exactly does that mean? Understanding that interaction will help us to understand the innumerably more frequent relationships in which a bond is imperfectly formed or is not established at all.

One might question why anyone would want to treat schizophrenic patients with a psychotherapy based on psychoanalytic principles. Psychopharmacological advances have made it possible to control psychotic behavior to the extent that schizophrenics often can make some kind of adjustment to the external world. Analysts, however, find the goal of adjustment to reality, by itself, to be unsatisfactory. Instead, we direct our attention to deep etiological sequences and try to undo the effects of early and persistent traumas. Perhaps we find schizophrenic patients to be especially fascinating because, in spite of being helpless, vulnerable, and constricted, they also have the creative potential to construct an external world that makes extensive use of primary-process operations.

A reality based on primary-process thinking is inherently fascinating. It is, of course, an incomplete and unacceptable reality, but it commands our interest. We sometimes have the feeling that if the patient worked further on his picture of the world, gradually introducing secondary-process elements, the final product would represent an ingenious and creative view of the surrounding reality. The psychotic patient seems not to have completed the developmental task of reality-testing.

The reality-testing function is arrested, but this involves more than fixation. The patient has imbricated elements of the traumatic infantile world and worked them over with primitive defenses that are not guided by reality-oriented principles. The resultant external world is distorted by the patient's projections of the past to the exclusion of most elements that are not part of his psyche. As a rule, external objects are not recognized as separate and autonomous, but are recognized only inasmuch as they play a role in supporting the patient's psychotic adaptations. They belong to the patient's psychotic reality and are not acknowledged as part of the external reality most of us recognize. This enables schizophrenics to control both internal and external objects, because no objects are actually recognized as external; the world and all of its inhabitants exist only to thwart them or to serve their needs—functions that, for them, are not incompatible.

I believe this is another example of the pathological distortion of the transitional phenomenon. The patient cannot detach his psyche from the external world. The environment remains attached as an appendage to the schizophrenic's ego. The inner and outer worlds are united, and there is no consensual reality beyond them.

As I have emphasized in Chapters 2 and 4, during the course of normal development, a transitional space is established between the inner and the outer worlds, and this space enables the construction of the external world with its real limitations. The schizophrenic patient never moves to the final position of relating to a secondary-process-oriented reality. His delusion lies within the transitional space, but, for the psychotic, this is not an in-between space. Nothing exists but the delusion. That is one of the reasons the psychotic cannot acknowledge or recognize anyone as belonging to the external world, and this makes such patients difficult to treat.

I am specifically distinguishing here the role of the transitional space from that of the transitional object in the production of psychopathology. The various character disorders that I have discussed were treated as and felt themselves to be transitional objects; but the schizophrenic has specific defects in structuralizing beyond the transitional space, a space that contains the delusional system.

This does not mean that all schizophrenics are completely oblivious of the commonly accepted reality. Indeed, they are not. Many of them are very shrewd in their dealings with their environment and can function extremely well. They are especially adept, however, at seeking segments of the external world that they can manipulate and keep within the framework of their delusions. When they are successful in their manipulations, their behavior seems rational and reality-oriented, but it is still based on psychotic premises. This mixture of surface sanity and underlying insanity can be extremely confusing to the clinician.

Interestingly, I have found that the better I understand a schizophrenic patient, the less certain I am that the patient is schizophrenic. This is somewhat like the dictum that if a patient is treatable, you can rule out the diagnosis of schizophrenia. This nihilistic viewpoint made untreatability a criterion of diagnosis, as it were, the definition of schizophrenia—untreatability at least from a psychotherapeutic or a psychoanalytic perspective. This attitude, which has some support from Freud (1914b), ties our hands from the very outset of our endeavors, because it dogmatically holds that our efforts will be fruitless. And if they are not, then we are not investigating what we think we are.

It is true enough that a patient who walks into the consultation room as a schizophrenic may not be one when he leaves. But the dictum will not allow that this outcome may depend on the atmosphere the therapist creates. Sometimes the analyst gains a quick intuitive grasp of the patient's inner torment and unconsciously responds in an empathic, nonthreatening (which usually means nonchallenging) fashion. Because the patient's personal reality is not disturbed, the therapist can be acknowledged and allowed to remain in his own sphere, at least for the moment. Thus, the patient has added another dimension, an extension, to his reality, and by having done so, is less psychotic than he was.

When investigation and treatment are conducted in the same setting, the therapeutic relationship has notable effects on both patient and therapist. Still, as clinicians, we have the opportunity to assess the many variables that are involved in the patient's shifting psychic equilibrium as well as the resonating fluctuations within ourselves.

Structural Considerations

Although formulations about schizophrenic psychopathology reflect the seemingly infinite variety of clinical pictures these patients present, there are several factors that practically every clinician accepts. Even the most unpredictable behavioral sequences are based on fairly specific psychic processes such as projection, denial, and dissociation. From a structural viewpoint, the schizophrenic patient has poorly defined boundaries between the inner and outer worlds, leading to defects in reality-testing, accompanied by thought disorders. Consequently, object relations are disturbed, and this disturbance parallels a faulty construction of the self-representation.

All this is well known and has been frequently stated about the schizophrenic. The same mechanisms have also been postulated for borderlines and other patients with ego defects. On the other hand, although a frankly psychotic patient can be easily distinguished from the compensated mental state often associated with borderline psychopathology, the differing underlying psychic processes and fixations are poorly understood. Perhaps absolute distinctions between schizophrenics and non-schizophrenics can never be made, and this may, in part, account for the fluctuating clinical picture seen in so many psychotic patients. Granted, there are immutable and fixed psychoses, such as were commonly found in the back wards of state hospitals, but with the introduction of the neuroleptic drugs, even these patients frequently become manageable, and to some extent can adapt to the external world.

Some psychoanalysts (Bion, 1957; Klein, 1946; Winnicott, 1952) speculate that a psychotic core exists in all emotionally disturbed patients. In fact, some psychoanalysts believe that such a core is universal, the product of ordinary psychic development, which may or may not have psychopathological consequences. These are debatable hypotheses, but the concept of a psychotic core underlying various forms of severe psychopathology may be useful and shed further light on both schizophrenic and characterological disorders. More specifically, the psychotic core can be viewed as a primitive structural constellation that is the outcome of specific psychic traumas the child has endured within a particular maternal–infant matrix. Emotional development then proceeds in a faulty fashion, resulting in structural defects, a lack of consolidation of ego boundaries, a psychopathologically constructed self-representation, developmental fixation, and overcompensatory defenses and adaptations, possibly involving delusional distortions of the external world. The extent to which the latter dominate would determine whether we are dealing with a psychotic or a nonpsychotic state. The factors that determine one outcome or another, however, are largely unknown and, at best, can be reconstructed only retrospectively.

Schizophrenics, as I have already emphasized, do not seem to belong to this world. This lack of contact with the environment is sometimes expressed both by an unawareness of what is going on around them and by an inability to define themselves. I have frequently heard schizophrenics, and borderlines as well, complain that they are neither "fish nor fowl."

As is now well accepted, these phenomena can be explained on the basis of blurred ego boundaries and an amorphous self-representation. Also, ego subsystems lack integration; they do not function in harmony and coordination with one another. Psychotics are fragmented and make extensive use of splitting mechanisms in constructing defensive adaptations. Although this is also true of borderlines and other forms of character disorders, schizophrenics are not constrained by the limitations imposed by our current reality, and they are thus more adept at letting various parts of their psychic systems operate independently of one another.

To illustrate these structural defects, I will place them in a clinical context by calling attention to a type of adolescent emotional decompensation first described by Erik Erikson (1959) as the identity-diffusion syndrome. Erikson did not consider this state to constitute a psychosis, because it was only a transient condition. These patients decompensated when they left home to go to college, that is, when the familiar frame of reference of the family environment was abruptly changed and they could not adapt to the new and strange surroundings of the dormitory and the university. However comfortable or uncomfortable the home setting might have been, the patient's ego had learned how to adapt to it, and it possessed neither the flexibility nor the adaptive executive techniques to relate to and to cope with the new milieu. In consequence, patients suffering from the identity-diffusion syndrome collapse psychically. They feel helpless and vulnerable as their integrative capacities fail them. They lose whatever cohesion there had been to the self-representation, and this loss accounts for the specific qualities of the clinical picture.

Briefly stated, these young people withdraw from their companions, stop attending classes, and just sit in their rooms, staring into empty space, doing nothing. Their personal habits and hygiene deteriorate: They stop washing, brushing their teeth, and do not change their clothes. Usually they are brought into student health services because their classmates can no longer stand the stench. Phenomenologically, they resemble either catatonics or simple schizophrenics.

In addition to withdrawal, there may be periods of intense panic, and these also claim the attention and help of their colleagues. During these states of affective upheaval, such patients are confused and frequently disoriented as to time, place, and person. They literally do not know who they are. Because the clinical picture seems to be typical of an acute schizophrenic breakdown, that is how these young people are usually diagnosed.

Erikson believed that the resiliency of the ego distinguished the identity-diffusion syndrome from schizophrenia. Once these adolescents were returned to their homes, they quickly reintegrated and returned to their usual mode of adjustment; in some instances, this meant a fairly high level of functioning.

Whether these patients are examples of true schizophrenia is not relevant to the point I am making. They demonstrate in bold relief those structural defects which, to my mind, characterize psychotic states.

To put this another way, the identity-diffusion syndrome can be viewed as a paradigm that can be expanded to include complex psychotic orientations. The self-representation or the identity system is always involved in severe psychopathology, and it is especially disturbed or defective in adolescent psychosis. Perhaps such defects can be considered core disturbances around which a variety of clinical pictures develop. *The role of the self-representation in producing psychoses is analogous to that of anxiety in the production of the psychoneuroses.*

Freud (1926) viewed anxiety as a nidus that sets certain defense mechanisms into motion. He understood the latter to be manifested by behavioral constellations that defined clinical syndromes and the various psychoneuroses. This understanding was the basis for Freud's hypotheses about nosology and neurosogenesis. He postulated that there was a struggle within the psyche, because the mental apparatus had to maintain equilibrium and protect itself from the potentially disruptive effects of anxiety. This was a defensive struggle, and it was the expenditure of energy to contain aberrant, dangerous impulses responsible for the production of signal anxiety that ultimately caused impairments of functioning and the constrictions of different psychoneuroses.

As already mentioned, the psychodynamic frame of reference is not as much in the foreground in the study of psychoses as it is in the investigation of the psychoneuroses. In our use of the structural hypothesis to establish a foundation for our conceptual scaffold, we have so far determined that defects in the self-representation are prominent. These have profound effects on various ego systems, such as the executive and the integrative, which, in turn, lead to the construction of a specific psychotic syndrome. The resultant overall disruption involves

reality-testing, and the intensity of the latter's disturbance determines whether we are dealing with a psychosis. Whatever other
features we choose to focus on, the ego's incapacity to relate to
or to perceive a commonly accepted reality is the *sine qua non*
of psychosis.

When I say disturbances of reality-testing, I am not referring to a homogeneous area. The type of disturbance depends
on what aspects of the outer world are alien to the patient. To
restate one of the premises of this book, reality itself is not a
homogeneous entity. Because *there is no absolute reality, in a
sense, there is no absolute psychosis.*

A salient difference between neurosogenesis and the production of psychoses involves the process of defense. Whereas
signal anxiety leads directly to the formation of defenses, defects in the self-representation do not lead directly to defenses in
any comparable fashion. Rather, such defects exist in context
with a generally defective ego, and they add to the difficult task
of coherently perceiving and relating to the external world.

In Chapter 4, I focused on psychic discontinuity, a lack of
connecting bridges between lower and higher levels of the
psyche, bridges that would have created a smooth, cohesive
continuum within the structural hierarchy. Schizophrenics also
demonstrate psychic discontinuity, but, to construct a metaphor, the disturbances it causes are not of a vertical nature, but
occur in many directions. The discontinuity discussed earlier
involves the unmodulated movement of impulses and feelings
that originate in the primitive layers of the mind, as they burst
forth into higher ego levels. Psychotic patients, on the other
hand, seem to be generally fragmented and not limited to a lack
of coordination between different levels. Multiple splits may
occur within the same level, and these will have specific behavioral manifestations and effects on thought processes.

For example, I have seen severely regressed psychotics
move around with jerky, robot-like, uncoordinated movements.
I recall witnessing this type of spasmodic jerking behavior years
ago in wards that housed chronic schizophrenics. Then we considered it to be a type of hebephrenic posturing, usually without
any symbolic significance or meaning; but in some instances, it
was apparent that the patient was, in a crude and somatic form,

expressing some primitive desire. A middle-aged noncommunicative man, diagnosed as a simple schizophrenic, would quietly walk around the ward, and then, without warning, would suddenly squat, and as the muscles of his face and trunk convulsed in a myoclonic spasm, would scream at the top of his lungs in a high-pitched keening wail. This was a bizarre sight, which reminded some of us of a person in an attitude of constipated defecation. I have also observed nonpsychotic patients move in such a clumsy fashion that I was concerned about the safety of breakable furniture, such as table lamps, in my consultation and waiting rooms.

From a psychological viewpoint, thought processes and perceptions have the same uncoordinated qualities in severely disturbed patients as the physical clumsiness found in less primitively fixated or regressed patients. *When reality becomes fragmented beyond a certain point, it acquires bizarre qualities that, to a person accustomed to synthesizing perceptions, appear delusional.*

Early Traumas and Defective Development

The backgrounds of many schizophrenics are often conspicuously traumatic. They have generally been raised in such a strange and weird fashion that they seem to come from an alien planet. Yet patients who can articulately describe their background are frequently unaware of the fact that their early world is in any way different from the one in which most of us live. Massive psychic trauma has become a way of life.

Infantile trauma impedes the ordinary course of emotional development; that is, it leads to fixation points to which the patient may regress later in life when facing stresses that are associatively connected to these early disruptive experiences. Freud (1905, 1916) often formulated psychopathology in such terms, and, as discussed, he outlined a developmental progression designated as a sequence of psychosexual stages. When dealing with patients suffering from primitive mental states, however, the definitive stages Freud postulated are difficult to observe, and we seldom, if ever, witness a neat regression to an easily discernible fixation point. Rather, primitive ego states are amorphous and chaotic, and they are reflected in the way patients view themselves.

In fact, traumatic interactions have disrupted the formation of an orderly sequence of progressive developmental stages. There are different ways in which this may occur, according to the nature of the trauma. Traumas can be divided into two principal categories, those of commission and those of omission.

A trauma of commission consists of an assaultive environment in which a child has been brutally mishandled. Such children have never known gratification—this is the state of privation Winnicott (1963b) described; all they have experienced is tension, disruption, and later, during their development, pain. A trauma of omission is the absence of positive and organizing experiences that lead to ego synthesis and cohesion, experiences that would compensate for and undo the damaging effects of the ordinary impingements that are unavoidable.

Klein (1946) and Winnicott (1952) believed that children, in the course of ordinary emotional development, reach a paranoid–schizoid stage of organization. Although I do not find this a plausible formulation about normal structuralizing processes, I do agree that having external persecutors can be an organizing experience for psychopathological states dominated by destructive internal objects. The paranoid patient needs persecutors, around which he can anchor his ego and achieve stability and synthesis. The persecutors are created by the projection of these disruptive internal objects. Winnicott adds that positive experiences will counteract the damaging effects of such objects.

There is an interesting sequel to early assaultive traumas. The schizophrenic's world was filled with traumatic attacks on his integrity; but rather than being devastated by them, schizophrenics survive and use their traumatic experiences to advantage. In a primitive fashion they make such experiences adaptive. The resultant ego is, in a sense, hypertrophied (Giovacchini, 1975a; Gitelson, 1958); although it can exist in environments that would devastate most of us, it is a constricted ego. It is also uniquely malformed.

The absence of positive synthesizing experiences makes its own contribution to the psyche's structural malformations. We would expect that both assault and what is essentially deprivation will lead to developmental arrest. There would be a halt in the forward motion of the structuralizing impetus that must be inherent in the mind. The schizophrenic patient's development illustrates an interesting but malignant negative feedback sequence that has unique consequences for the formation of the psychotic character.

When there is inadequate or minimal gratification, the neonate does not develop a coherent representation of the external world. The inability to internalize and to integrate the surrounding environment is reinforced by the impact of assaultive trauma, which causes the psyche to perceive the external world not only as a jarring asynchronous bundle of incomprehensible stimuli, but, later, as a painful entity that cannot be controlled if the mind is turned toward it. It is similar to looking at a bright light that is so strong it will burn out the retina if the eyes keep staring at it. One has to turn away completely to survive. This metaphor is particularly apt in describing the impact of assaultive trauma, because the intensity of the stimuli is so great that the sensory systems are overloaded and damaged. With the neonate, the capacity for receptivity is severely damaged, and all later stages of development, as we recognize them, are malformed. The construction and stratification of progressively structured ego states depends on interactions with the external world that can be internalized. By definition, trauma breaks through the stimulus barrier; it cannot be modulated and disrupts the homeostatic balance and psychic integration (Freud, 1920). Its intensity contributes to its damaging effect.

Schizophrenics suffer from the most damaging combination of the two types of trauma: They are not protected from unbearable intensities of threatening stimuli, but they are also the victims of understimulation. They are abandoned as well as attacked, and, understandably, this contributes to the formation of structural aberrations. As neonates, they are both defending themselves by the use of primitive defenses, and unable to cathect the external world because there is nothing to cathect.

External objects in the environment do not make their presence felt sufficiently so that the child can develop psychic structure from the relationship.

One must assume that some positive experiences took place in the background of psychotics, because otherwise they would not have survived. Still, the overwhelming impact on the psyche has been caused by intrusive interactions that were often physically as well as emotionally assaultive, and by deprivation and abandonment. Consequently, the psyche does not smoothly progress to higher ego levels; rather, the psychotic constructs an ego based on primitive defensive adaptations, such as schizoid withdrawal, dissociative mechanisms, and faulty introjective–projective processes. Such an ego encompasses all the psychosexual stages, but it has combined them as a result of primary-process operations, such as condensation and displacement, familiar elements of the dream work. The minimal positive influences of the environment have permitted the psychotic to grow physically rather than die, and to form some adaptations that maintain a modicum of homeostatic equilibrium.

There is a close parallel between physical maturation and emotional development, each having effects on the other. As discussed in Chapter 2, we can assume that there is a preordained sequence of stages of emotional development that can be correlated with a similar maturational sequence. If the child is provided with a marginal environment that permits physical development, there is an accompanying emotional development. In schizophrenia, however, the process is so distorted that elements of all stages of emotional development are mixed up with one another. To put this in terms of a spatial metaphor, it is as if the psyche had expanded horizontally instead of vertically.

Such a psyche is precarious. Schizophrenics have to be selective about whom they will relate to in the external world, and, as repeatedly stressed, they are extremely vulnerable. This is reflected in how they adapt to external objects and to the vicissitudes of their environment. They seem to be operating at levels so primitive that they antedate the formation of coherent object relations; thus, correspondingly, schizophrenics do not perceive themselves as autonomous human beings; sometimes they do not even feel human.

Not feeling human creates a perspective in which the non-human aspects of the external world become dominant. As I have discussed in Chapter 4, some patients relate to surrounding inanimate objects as if they were alive, an extension into adulthood of the anthropomorphization of childhood. Their external objects are modeled after their self-representations, which, as emphasized, have remained arrested at the transitional-object stage of development. Consequently, these patients treat people as they themselves were treated, and in humanizing the nonhuman aspects of their environment, they continue operating in the familiar transitional space.

Schizophrenic patients, because of the lack of stratification of a structural hierarchy, also do not have sufficient psychic integration, structure, and perceptivity to have human relationships. Their disturbance is even more profound than the very disturbed patients who have been classified as severe character disorders. Rather than directly relating to external objects as might be permitted by their arrested and distorted ego states, schizophrenics withdraw from our familiar reality and then construct another one that is uniquely their own. I have already focused on the creation of the psychotic's reality. I wish to stress that what appear to be object relations within the schizophrenic's world are not genuine interactions between two persons based on an exchange of feelings, even if there are many primitive and infantile elements to the apparent exchange. Though schizophrenics appear to be relating to objects, they are really reacting to different parts of the self.

Everything in their world reflects some aspect of the psyche, as occurs in dreams. In dreams the ego loses its integration and organization, something the psychotic patient has developed only to a minimal degree. The feelings they display reflect their concern for the maintenance of this marginal integration, and for guarding their compensatory defensive adaptations from onslaughts from our world, which they refuse to acknowledge. For example, a patient described a poignant episode from her childhood, which she remembered as having been excruciatingly painful—so painful that life became unbearable, and she was obliged to "deaden" her feelings. In fact, she became autistically withdrawn and was sent to a residential treatment center for four years. What had happened was that a tree in her backyard had died. She could recall hugging that tree and crying inconsolably. It was as if a major part of her life had been lost with the death of the tree, and at the time, she reacted as if she herself had ceased to exist. She lost all sense of personal awareness, and the years at the residential treatment center were a total blank.

This patient, and other psychotic patients, are not really relating to objects any more than the dreamer is relating to the various persons in the dream. The frequently made comparisons between schizophrenic views of the world and the dream are apt. The schizophrenic has been referred to as a dreamer who is awake. To relate to the world on its own terms and not as though it were part of one's dream requires reasonably well-defined ego boundaries and a recognition and capacity for assessment of the external world. To summarize briefly, the undeveloped distorted psyche of the psychotic is not capable of making contact with the outside world. The psychoses are different from other types of character disorders. Nonpsychotic patients have made some sort of contact with external objects, even though the kind of contact made is the outcome of structural defects. Both schizophrenics and other patients suffering from primitive mental states interact with the nonhuman aspects of their environment, but with the psychotic patient, this is primarily an intrapsychic phenomenon.

The Nurturing Interaction and Psychopathology

Fromm-Reichman (1959) has written about the schizophrenogenic mother. In view of the various clinical pictures that are considered schizophrenic, I do not believe we can outline a specific personality type that can be made responsible for the production of psychosis. There are too many variables involved, including genetic and constitutional factors. Still, we can focus on certain elements of the mother–infant interaction that can contribute to our understanding of the developmental vicissitudes that underlie psychopathology.

As I have said, the nurturing process can be divided into two components, a foreground of feeding, that is, actual nurturing, and a background of soothing. This corresponds to Winnicott's (1963a) distinction between the object mother, who relates to instinctual needs, and the environment mother, whose function is to soothe, to provide a holding environment, and to relate to ego needs. There may be disturbances in either one or both of these components, causing the child to develop specific vulnerabilities and character defects.

I am separating elements of the mothering process for heuristic purposes. In actuality, psychopathology is not particularly selective and involves all facets of the mother–child interaction. Nevertheless, some specific aspect of the relations may be predominantly implicated, highlighting an imbalance between nurturing and soothing elements.

A person cannot survive with a total absence of mothering, whether this means a complete lack of nurturing or soothing. Spitz (1945) has demonstrated that the child cannot survive the absence of the environment mother even if nurturing has been adequate. The neonate does not have inner soothing mechanisms. The outer world has to supply regulators and modulators. Freud (1920) discussed how the mother modulates external stimuli for her child by acting as a stimulus barrier. She also soothes the infant, reestablishing inner calm that might have been disrupted by internal sensations.

The mothers of schizophrenics often demonstrate a total lack of comprehension of soothing interactions. They sometimes believe they are engaged in caring and calming their children, when, in fact, they are having just the opposite effect. Bateson (1951a, 1951b) spoke of the "double-bind" message, a type of communciation that he believed was characteristic of the mothers of schizophrenics.

The double-bind message is characterized by contradiction. The mother expresses her wishes or opinions to her child, but means the exact opposite. If she gives instructions on how to behave, she is really encouraging the antithesis. Johnson and Szurek (1952, 1964) wrote of a similar phenomenon when they discussed superego lacunae in parents who forbade certain behavioral aberrations, but who, in actuality, were pushing their child to act out their own forbidden impulses. A good example of both the double-bind message and superego lacunae is the mother who constantly warns her daughter not to be promiscuous and get pregnant, yet simultaneously drives the daughter to irresponsible sexuality and inevitable pregnancy.

Unlike Bateson, who believed that schizophrenia is the outcome of such mixed messages, Johnson and Szurek were not limiting these interactions to the production of psychosis. They found these parent–child relationships in the backgrounds of nonpsychotic children. Obviously, there are other variables besides the double-bind message that are required for creating a psychosis, and it is doubtful whether mixed messages are a necessary condition for the production of schizophrenia. Nevertheless, we can see how damaging being subjected to such confusion can be for an ego that is precariously held together and extremely vulnerable.

To emphasize the effect of receiving contradictory messages, I will review briefly what I have formulated about the psychopathological elements of the schizophrenic's character structure. Because the impact of the environment has such destructive and devastating consequences, the ego of the psychotic patient has to be viewed in terms of primitive fixations. By contrast, Bullard (1984), in studying the egos of psychotic adolescents, concluded that both regression and maldevelopment play an essential role in the etiology of schizophrenia. Because I conceptualize schizophrenics as not having the stratification of a progressive hierarchy of ego states, I would say that even if the ego state of a schizophrenic is defective and the manifestation of maldevelopment, regression could not have occurred, at least not in the ordinary sense of a backward movement from higher to lower psychic levels. It is also this lack of stratification that causes the double-bind message to have such traumatic effects. It makes damaging contributions to the psychotic ego along with being partially responsible for its creation. The former effect could be considered part of a regressive process, and the latter refers to maldevelopment.

If one is to question the role of regression in the construction of psychotic symptoms, how does one account for the commonly observed phenomenon of the compensated psychotic who functions well in the external world and, then, because of some crisis, disintegrates into a schizophrenic psychosis? In terms of functioning, this is certainly a regression, but is it a movement from upper to lower levels? As I have stressed, there is no such thing as pure regression. Higher levels of adaptation are not entirely lost when a patient regresses, and the patient does not return completely to the corresponding maldevelopmental infantile stage. Sophisticated adaptations coexist alongside primitive defensive operations. Whether the patient functions in an efficient nonpsychotic fashion or is schizophrenically disorganized or maintains a delusional organization depends on whether one or the other is dominant. It would seem more useful for the clarification of schizophrenic psychopathology to conceive of a spatial metaphor. I picture a mixed ego state operating with both advanced and primitive psychic processes, rather than a longitudinally arranged ladder-like layering of ego states, containing varying degrees of primary- and secondary-process elements. The concept of topographical regression (Freud, 1915a) would not be applicable to such a structural configuration.

The double-bind message is thus directed at an ego that has many primitive features. The parent's message, as it is consciously expressed, is directed to the better organized, reality-oriented aspects of the psyche. The true meaning, however, is conveyed to the psychotic parts of the ego, because the parent is speaking to the child from a similar and unconscious level. The parent is operating at a reality-oriented and *regressed* level simultaneously. The child responds to this regressed part and further cathects primitive elements. This is a maldeveloped ego, because the impetus for growth and development—positive integrative adaptations—is not supported by the parent–child relationship. Rather, the parent's relating at an unspoken, unconscious level reinforces ego distortion and leads to a pervasive fixation. *The double-bind message is more than just a message; it is the essence of a relationship that has to be observed in its total context.*

As therapists, we frequently experience the trauma the helpless child suffered when we deal with the parents of schizophrenic patients. In spite of their protestations that they want the best for their children and will do whatever is necessary to promote their recovery, we find them sabotaging our efforts in many ways, some that we could never have predicted. Fortunately, we have defenses, strengths, and adaptations that their children did not have, so these parents have lesser impact on us, although there are moments when our frustration reaches unbearable proportions.

I had a consultation with the mother of a schizophrenic adolescent in order to decide how to plan a therapeutic program for her son. He was in the hospital at the time and had been heavily drugged. Several family members were mental health professionals, and they were of the opinion that the young man had been reduced to "zombie" status by the heavy doses of phenothiazines he had been given. They described him as "a living vegetable," and wanted me to clarify the situation to the mother so that the patient could become engaged in a psychotherapeutic or psychoanalytic relationship. When I saw the mother, she was cordial and affable and seemed very impressed by my recommendations. I suggested a therapist whom I believed to be especially sensitive and skilled in treating very disturbed adolescents, and the mother agreed that she would call him at once and arrange an appointment as soon as her son was discharged from the hospital.

She never called. Instead, she found a psychiatrist who is well known for his indiscriminate use of drugs and electric shock therapy. He continued the son on heavy doses of drugs and gave him outpatient shock treatments. Somehow the patient himself managed to reduce his drug intake, and finally one evening found enough energy to hang himself in his apartment. The mother blamed his death on the fact that he had not continued with the dosage of drugs that had been prescribed.

The tragedy expanded with another son who had also been diagnosed as schizophrenic. He had been institutionalized in another city, but seemed well enough at the time to come home. His psychiatrist stressed the importance of the son's moving back into his old room, and advised strongly that little pressure be put on him. The parents were also told that the son should become engaged in psychotherapy. They agreed, and told their son that they would find an analyst for him. Instead, they made an appointment with an organically oriented psychiatrist who prescribes heavy doses of drugs and does not believe in the existence of the unconscious. Furthermore, they forced him to live alone in the same apartment in which his brother had committed suicide. After this young man's first appointment with the new psychiatrist, he returned to the apartment and killed himself by taking an overdose.

Quite obviously, the mother, and perhaps the father, harbored dangerous death wishes toward the children. Although on the surface, both seemed appropriately concerned for their sons' welfare and appeared to be sincere in their resolve to follow the advice they had been given, their subsequent actions were mercilessly destructive. These are examples of double-bind behavior at its tragic worst.

In these two instances it led to death. But, in a sense, the schizophrenic has already experienced psychic death, inasmuch as the world that would be equated with life has been unbearably painful. *Underlying the contradictory messages of the double bind are destructive wishes that would crush any semblance of living spontaneity and zest for life.* The portals to the external world are opened wide and beckon the infant, but at the same time there are forces in their vicinity that threaten to destroy him if he dares pass through them. A schizophrenic patient had a recurrent dream of foreboding gates engraved with "Abandon all hope ye who enter here," but he said that these were not the gates of hell; they were the gates of the world, of life. Life was viewed as a series of endless tortures, a perpetual trauma.

Psychopathological Adaptations

Because psychotic patients live so much in their own private world, and external reality is generally not acknowledged, they are especially vulnerable to the exigencies of their environment and must construct special adaptations. I said earlier that the psychotic's inner world blends with the transitional space, and this construction represents the outer world in its entirety. From another viewpoint, we can conceptualize the psychotic's ego boundaries as blurred, and the inner world, the outer world, and the transitional space as fused together; this situation would lead to a psychic state of chaotic confusion. Schizophrenics are locked into a fusion state that parallels the traumatic mother–child fusion, or in a state that represents a defense against such a fusion. As adults, they continue to feel assaulted and manipulated by their introjects, and their helplessness and vulnerability are augmented by a poorly established nurturing modality.

Schizophrenics, as is characteristic for many patients suffering from primitive mental states, use splitting and projective defenses. They may project inner assaultive forces into the outer world, and so manifest the familiar paranoid constellation. To protect themselves from their all-pervasive, terrifying feelings of abject helplessness, they become compensatorily megalomanic. They often attempt to relate to what we understand as the external world as if they were in complete control. This is the reverse of their infantile situation, in which they were controlled and assaulted; their psychopathology is the outcome of an overcompensatory effort to master through omnipotence and grandiosity their feelings of terrifying vulnerability. This represents a pathological exaggeration and distortion of the control normally exercised over the transitional object.

As always occurs in the construction of overcompensatory defensive adaptations, the frightening traumatic situation that is being defended against still emerges in a threatening disruptive fashion. As the assaultive introjects are projected, they are endowed with omnipotence. This is partly due to the fact that patients view their introjects very much as they did the corresponding infantile objects, when everything in the external world appeared to be gigantic and malevolent. In addition, defensive megalomania, initially attributed to the self, is also projected into the surrounding world and becomes attached to their projected introjects. The latter is facilitated by semipermeable ego boundaries.

The comparative lack of distinction between inside and outside sees to it that what began as defensive omnipotence becomes self-destructive. The patient has created for himself the same traumatic milieu that surrounded him during infancy. If the psychotic, as an adult, attaches himself to a person, cause, or object, he eventually feels controlled by the relationship, rather than the reverse.

Often schizophrenics attempt to create a state of self-sufficiency, which is actually a delusional exaggeration of the infant's illusion that he is the source of his own nurture. This attempt is the outcome of a defective or nonexistent nurturing modality along with a traumatic environment incapable of soothing the infant. Schizophrenics often reveal a delusion that some insidious poison is damaging their inner organs, eating them up, or causing them to rot. To protect themselves from being devoured by a poisonous nurturing modality, schizophrenics split off this part of the self and omnipotently deny any dependence on the external world. This gives them unlimited power. The space surrounding them is similar to the transitional space of childhood, in which they have omnipotent control.

As just discussed, however, there is often a power reversal, and schizophrenics end up feeling controlled rather than being in control. Because this reversal is based on what occurred in the traumatic infantile environment, the situation is an example of the repetition compulsion.

If the repetition compulsion becomes overwhelming, it disrupts the schizophrenic's equilibrium, which is based on the delusion of omnipotent fulfillment, and the corresponding psychic state becomes unbearably painful. This sequence stimulates even more drastic defensive adaptations.

Perhaps the most extreme defense, extreme in the sense of moving away from reality, is catatonic withdrawal. The patient totally removes himself from the environment, and seems to be completely oblivious of its existence and significance. Such a withdrawal alleviates pain by removing its source; and by denying needs, there is no pressure or inner yearning that requires a response from a world on which one may be dependent. Catatonia is an intensely regressed condition and, in some instances, may be terminal. During the last decade, however, I have treated several patients who had catatonic episodes that lasted a matter of hours or days, and they did not seriously interfere with the course of therapy.

What the catatonic patient implicitly expresses is overtly acted out by the patient who suffers from anorexia nervosa. Ordinarily, we do not think of such patients as being schizophrenic, although there are more than superficial similarities in their extensive use of denial, which can have fatal consequences.

As with schizophrenics, the anorectic's illness frequently begins during adolescence, and the patient does not acknowledge any dependent feelings. By not needing to eat, these patients feel completely independent of both the outside world and the inner world of the psyche. The sequence of binge eating, vomiting, and anorexia is characteristic of the anorectic patient's vital need for control, perhaps the only need they can allow themselves to be aware of, inasmuch as they are able to translate it into action.

All the adaptations I have been discussing are directed toward the external world. Even though schizophrenics do not emotionally participate in that world, they nevertheless develop psychic mechanisms that enable them to establish some type of harmony in what are mainly pseudorelations or pseudotransactions. These are defensive interactions that seem to be responses to structural deficits rather than to intrapsychic conflict. Pao (1979) advances a theory that holds the schizophrenic process to be based on conflict; but with psychotic patients the distinction between conflict and deficit is not so distinct. In certain stages of schizophrenic disorganization, psychotic patients view everything as part of the psyche; thus, as distinctions between the inner and outer worlds recede, all defensive and adaptive processes would be responses to inner conflicts. These conflicts would not necessarily involve discrete instinctual impulses; rather, they would be derivations of clashes between and maladjustments of various parts of the psyche. The conflict or deficit can, nevertheless, be converted into an adaptation that makes it possible for the patient to achieve inner equilibrium, and to adjust to our reality in a passable fashion.

For example, a middle-aged patient had managed to hold himself together by creating a delusional world that was dominated by omnipotence, magic, and power. Delusion is a quality of adaptation that defines the psychotic condition. This patient defended himself against his frightening and threatening sense of vulnerability by constructing a world in which he was in total control. His megalomanic orientation included an ability to travel outside his body to various "astral" planes where he would join a godlike person who was absolutely omnipotent. He also heard voices that would instruct him how to solve problems and handle difficult situations. He identified the voices as actual persons, and said that one of them was residing within himself.

The patient believed that in general he was getting along well. His wife and parents disagreed. He had given them and others some indication of his delusions, and they had become alarmed. In fact, he had lost his job, and he was becoming embarrassing to his family as he began to reveal more and more about his delusional system on social occasions. They finally institutionalized him, and after several months he appeared to be much improved. He had been put on very heavy doses of Mellaril.

I had seen him before his hospitalization, and afterward I noted a striking change in both his demeanor and appearance. Whereas previously he had been talkative and, at times, animated, he was now taciturn, morose, and withdrawn. He looked haggard, and there was a jerky quality to his movements. He looked more like a zombie than a human being. Yet when he did talk, he was eminently rational and attuned to reality. When asked about his delusions, he explained that the various phenomena he had previously dwelled on were fantasies, omnipotent wishes, and the personification of various parts of himself. In the past, I had ventured some tentative interpretations about the helpful voices; I had suggested that they stemmed from within himself and were the achievement of a particularly sensitive auditory system. He now seemed to be in complete agreement with such explanations. He did not discuss his former beliefs with family or friends; if asked, he would simply state that he had recovered, and no longer had such "nonsense" in his head.

He managed his life with some degree of efficiency and was even able to set up a small business in which he could use some of his technical skills, but he was functioning at a considerably lower level than he had previously. Everything he reported to me was dull, drab, and colorless, and he seemed to plod along in a depressed, withdrawn manner. His family was not concerned about his somber mood, as long as it was sober and did not embarrass them. By contrast, I felt that this so-called "reality-oriented" person was not a person at all. To me, he appeared to have had something vital torn out of him, and all I was seeing was an empty shell. At first, I thought this was a complication of the heavy doses of Mellaril he was taking, but nothing changed after the drug was discontinued.

Perhaps I missed his delusions. At least when he had been delusional he had not created such a gloomy, oppressive mood. In fact, he had been occasionally vivacious and often spoke with enthusiasm. True, he was often miserable even with his delusions, and I had seen him when he was feeling desolate and isolated, but now there was no relief in sight. All he presented was a picture of utter dejection. In any case, I asked him about the voice that he had said resided inside him and whether he missed it. As usual, he answered me mechanically, and said that he did not hear the voice, and indeed never had. He had just been referring to a part of himself. He seemed to be playing back to me, as one might from an acoustically poor tape recorder, something I might have said to him. His response was so mechanical that I doubted his sincerity.

I focused on his assertion that he had *never* heard a voice from inside himself. This was an astonishing statement, because I remembered countless sessions when he had extolled the wisdom and perspicacity of the inner voice that belonged to an actual person who used his body as his home. Almost reflexively, I challenged him by saying that I *knew* he had heard that voice as well as other voices, and I doubted that they were absolutely silent even now. Rather than being offended by my confrontation, as I might have expected, he stretched out in a relaxed posture, and I could see the flicker of a smile at the corner of his lips. He then confessed that he did, indeed, hear the voices, and he still had all of the same beliefs. He simply could not talk about them outside my office, because they would "lock him up" if he did. He was very much relieved, however, now that he could continue talking about them with me. My consultation room became the only place in the world in which he could reveal what he considered to be his true self.

His appearance and mood drastically changed. He was henceforth able to relate to the world in an outgoing manner, but he felt he derived the strength to carry on from our sessions, in which he could reinforce his sense of control through his megalomanic ruminations. In the outside world, he behaved appropriately; but this was an act, a false self that protected him from the assaults of external objects, who could never possibly understand him or appreciate his needs. He had learned to adapt the delusional system that maintained inner integration so that it did not clash with the demands of reality. He also continued to pay attention to the voices outside the consultation room, but he did it unobtrusively. If someone were astute enough to notice his self-preoccupation, he would account for his lapse of attention rationally, stressing that he was either planning the next day or thinking about some chore he had to complete.

The treatment had become supportive of his delusion, and paradoxically, his delusion was providing him with enough structure and integration so that he could continue functioning in the external world in a way that was acceptable and nondisruptive to his environment. As stated, this was the extreme of a false-self adaptation, but he had achieved some stability. I had become part of his adaptation, but he had to struggle against me to maintain it. He obtained support for his delusion because the treatment setting was designed to promote autonomy, and this meant, among other things, that I would respect the world he had created. My task was to see reality through his eyes. On the other hand, my task was also to understand his creations in terms of their adaptive significance and their infantile antecedents. Rather than being merely accepting, I was supposed to be pursuing why he needed to look at the world the way he did.

The patient gradually became aware that I was developing some uneasiness about not fulfilling what I believed should be my analytic role. He was using me as a gymnasium where he could keep in shape, but he was strengthening his adaptations rather than his muscles. On the other hand, I had begun to feel that I was reinforcing a delusion, and my ambivalence made me less useful to the patient in terms of how he wanted to use me. When I tried to make inroads into his delusions by trying to analyze them, the patient became terrified and withdrew.

It became clear that if I challenged his delusions by trying to analyze them, he would decompensate to the extent that he would have to be hospitalized. In any case, the patient would not permit me to analyze him, because he would withdraw and literally not hear my interpretations. After about 18 months, we decided that he no longer needed regular appointments. He returns three or four times a year to talk about his delusions. I surmise that the infrequency of our contacts protects them against the threat of being examined, and thus placed in another context, which would rob them of their adaptive potential.

The Structure and Impact of Delusions

As repeatedly stressed throughout this chapter, the delusional world of schizophrenics, the one they live in, replaces the world most of us live in. The stability of a delusional system varies, ranging from a fixed solid structure to rapidly fluctuating beliefs. The latter emphasizes that the schizophrenic patient's bizarre beliefs are the content of the delusional system. Accordingly, a delusion has often been defined as a false belief. Sometimes we observe a rigidly established delusional system of long duration suddenly disappear or become drastically altered.

To illustrate what I mean by a highly structured, stable delusion, I refer to a schizophrenic man in his thirties, an artist, who believed that he was living in prehistoric times, and that his environment was primordial and inhabited by dinosaurs. He spent most of his time painting scenes of the landscape he felt himself to be observing from atop a knoll. His pictures were remarkably realistic, although not quite photographic. He insisted that they represented actual landscapes that he was copying from nature.

I asked him to loan me a painting for two weeks so that I could bring it home and show it to my family and friends. He was glad to let me have it, and was further pleased when I asked him to paint the same scene again. I was, of course, interested to see what kind of copy he would be able to make when he had no picture of that landscape in front of him as a model. To my astonishment, he reproduced the same landscape with dinosaurs with such faithful accuracy that, had it not been for the difference in size, it would have been impossible to distinguish one painting from the other. The new one was about three-fourths the size of the first, but other than being smaller, it was identical: Every blade of grass was slanted in the same direction, the proportions and posture of the animals were the same, as were all the other innumerable details that constitute a painting. He must have been able to create these scenes with eidetic sharpness. He viewed the world in terms of his projections, and constructed an environment that endured and which he could vividly perceive.

I assume that he hallucinated the scenes he painted, although, unlike the typical hallucination, which is focalized, he generalized his projections to encompass his ambience, rather than focusing on an object or part of an object, such as its voice. He created an environment that symbolically represented the archaic infantile environment. He focused on the background of his past, an adaptive reworking of the traumatic holding environment, rather than concentrating on the assaultive persons of his infancy. The dinosaurs did, in fact, represent fossilized external objects, dumbly grazing in an innocuous, stupid fashion. He was able to render dangerous introjects harmless by projecting them into the external world he had created, and by turning them into mindless dinosaurs. Nevertheless, he was off at some distance on top of a knoll, lying there hidden, and watching them.

I have seen other patients whose delusions were as stable as that of the artist patient, although it was difficult in those cases to know how visually sharp their hallucinations were. Sometimes a delusion will have endured for years, and then, suddenly, it will become transformed into something quite different from that to which the patient had tenaciously clung. Often a signficant external event will trigger this change. For example, I was on call as a resident when the atom bomb was dropped on Hiroshima. The emergency room was full of patients who had brought the bomb into their delusional systems. I had known several of these patients previously, either because they had been hospitalized or because they were being seen in the outpatient clinic.

In one instance, the changed delusional system included changes in somatic symptoms. For years, one middle-aged man had believed he had little men in his throat who delighted in blocking his respiratory pathways, causing him extreme physical distress and anxiety. He had been diagnosed as having asthma, but treatment had been only moderately effective.

From the day the atom bomb was dropped, he never again talked about those tiring internal persecutors. Instead, he was plagued by squadrons of tiny self-propelling atom bombs that burrowed underneath his skin and selectively exploded. He felt immense burning, pain, and itching at the site of the "explosions," and he had developed a chronic, ugly rash that was refractory to treatment. All this occurred in just a few hours, and his new delusion became chronic.

Another patient, a woman in her fifties, had a very complex religious delusional system. She was one of the apostles and met daily with Christ, although he kept himself invisible. She had gained omnipotence from him, but it frightened her because of its potential to get out of control and lead to catastrophic calamities. Therefore, she had to be extremely careful not to unleash her divine powers in a destructive fashion. When the atom bomb was dropped, she completely and, it would seem, instantaneously altered the setting of her delusion, although the theme persisted. The bomb was her creation, and she had control of it. The FBI had managed to steal one out of her arsenal, and had given it to certain Army generals, who were actually Communist secret agents. They were the ones responsible for destroying Hiroshima, but she would see to it that they were punished. She wrote innumerable letters to the President of the United States and to various senators and congressmen. She continued in this paranoid fashion for many years, and as far as I know, she clung to this delusion until her death about 15 years ago.

There was no particular change in the *structure* of the delusions of these two patients; rather, they revised the scenery, so to speak—the manifest content—and thereby modernized them. As the patients acquainted me with their new editions, I was reminded of the custom of presenting a classical play or opera, one that depicts a myth or takes place in an ancient Greek or Roman setting, by doing it in modern dress. The manifest content of these patients' initial delusions was bizarre and had little correspondence to persons, situations, or events in the external world. Even the little men of the first patient's delusion were a special breed. But the atom bomb had suddenly become a dominant element in our world, and even though both patients remained quite psychotic, they were bringing their delusional systems more into line with what was actually happening around them. This does not mean that they were less psychotic; it simply indicates that the differences at the manifest level between their delusions and reality were not as great. They were not more sane; the world had become more insane.

I realize that by making clinical assessments of society I am straying into areas that require different disciplines involving other types of variables to be understood. Diagnostic judgments are the conclusions we reach about persons, and they are not suitable for classifying culture. Still, as I have repeatedly stressed, the quality of symptoms and the content of the clinical picture are very much determined by the sociocultural milieu. Defensive systems require a setting that will support them, and this occurs through the process I discussed earlier, called externalization (Giovacchini, 1967). In a similar fashion, schizophrenic patients will seek out segments of the external world that support or reinforce their delusions. They seek and find the psychotic sectors of reality, or those elements of the environment that lend themselves easily to delusional elaboration. The destruction of humanity by bombs is a case in point.

A person adapts more or less successfully to the milieu. Usually we think of psychoneurotic patients as being able to cope with their environment in a fairly adequate fashion, whereas patients suffering from structural defects are characterized by their difficulties in adjusting to the external world. Schizophrenics, through their delusions, have created their own world, but they are not always successful in achieving some degree of psychic balance. The delusional system often does not work well enough to hold the patient together by preventing the ego from fragmenting. Even a relationship with the various elements of a self-created world may be fraught with conflict and threatening. I am describing the familiar state of psychotic decompensation.

Decompensations are frequently precipitated by an event in reality that somehow threatens the stability and the adaptations of the delusional system. On other occasions, internal pressures intensify to a degree that cannot be contained by the various primitive defense mechanisms that operate in the formation of delusions. Even in the latter instance, however, the environment participates, because it interferes with the functioning of adaptive defenses, such as projection, or it stimulates internal needs and heightens anxiety, causing other defenses to function beyond their integrative capacities. For example, a dissociation that protects the psyche by separating bad from good internal objects can become so intense that the ego fragments to the extent that it loses whatever structure it had been trying to preserve.

In the emergency room, we often encounter patients in a state of panic because they believe they are falling apart. They may describe this feeling quite literally, complaining that they have lost parts of their body, both external appendages and internal organs.

These are intense, acutely agitated states that may degenerate further into uncontrolled violence, necessitating restraint of the patient or heavy sedation. From a psychic viewpoint, the latter represents an acute regression: A state of previous, although possibly delusional, organization has deteriorated into total chaos. Apparently the patient was not able to maintain his integrative delusion because it was too disruptive to the general external world. This was the situation with the patient I described earlier, who used the treatment to help him keep, as well as to hide, his delusion. Or certain inner forces have been intensified to the extent that the delusion cannot process or contain them. These, then, would be uncontrollable inner forces.

Biologically oriented psychiatrists would attribute the buildup of inner tension to defects in physiological controls, and peculiarities in neurochemistry. These are endogenous causes and supposedly independent of characterological defects and a failure of psychic adaptations. From such concepts about etiology springs the rationale for the psychopharmacological treatment of the psychoses. This organic orientation seems to be especially apt for the manic-depressive disorders.

When dealing with severe disorders of ego development and primitive psychic organization, the interplay between biological and psychological factors is especially prominent. I have repeatedly emphasized the importance of an initial prementational stage of emotional development, a stage that is primarily biological and antedates the construction of psychological mechanisms. The fixations and regressions of psychotic patients include a high percentage of prementational elements. Consequently, in many schizophrenics and manic-depressives, it is difficult to distinguish between psychological and biological causality. This is an intrinsic aspect of primitive psychopathology, and it is especially true of manic-depressive states, where it is frequently impossible to find precipitating factors for the acute onset of either a depression or a manic phase.

There are certain physiological processes that are characterized by automaticity and referred to as circadian rhythms. These consist of energic sequences that have a cyclical character, reaching peaks and minimum ranges periodically. Such fluctuations are the familiar diurnal variations, and are far removed from psychic factors and conscious control. Many psychotic patients seem to have regressed to modes of functioning that are dominated by automatized cyclical patterns, and when the peaks go beyond a certain intensity, the whole psychic apparatus appears as if it had collapsed.

Are there psychic forces, the outcome of conflict or traumas in the external world, that intensify inner tension to the degree that a defective, vulnerable psyche cannot maintain its cohesion? Undoubtedly, in many instances, such stimuli are operative, although they may be difficult, if not impossible, to detect. Can the psyche collapse, however, without such stimuli? Can a breakdown simply occur because of an endogenous accumulation of tension due to faulty neurophysiological mechanisms? The biological psychiatrist would stress that it does.

To argue these alternatives, I believe, leads only to needless controversy. Nowhere can we see as clearly as we do in our observations of psychotic patients the close interplay between disruptive environmental influences and constitutional vulnerability, the latter exemplified by a reversion to what can be considered primitive modes of physiological functioning. *In schizophrenia and manic-depressive states there is significant physiological as well as psychological regression.* The ego, because of inherent weakness, either constitutional or the consequence of a traumatic infantile world, most likely both, when facing stress reminiscent of early assaults, regresses to circadian sequences without the modulating controls of more sophisticated biological and emotional adaptations. Because it cannot turn to the external world for support (it is foreign and alien), its threshold for enduring inner tension is extremely low. Consequently, a breakdown that may seem to have been caused by endogenous factors alone may actually be the product of subtle regression-stimulating interactions that undermine the capacity of the delusional system to achieve psychic equilibrium.

As is true of any adaptation, a delusional system requires support and reinforcement; it cannot exist in a vacuum. As I have just discussed, the delusion may be undermined or even violently rejected so that it cannot sustain itself unless the patient completely withdraws from the current reality. There are specific types of delusions that require reinforcement from the external world in order to maintain their organization. Others, those seen in severely psychotic persons, require an almost complete exclusion of the external world. Still other delusions cannot sustain themselves at all because of conflicting elements of their manifest content. They are unstable and crumble in the context of general psychic disintegration.

This latter type of delusion directly incorporates elements of the traumatic infantile environment, whereas a more stable delusion would contain defenses against the disruptive and assaultive elements of the patient's early interactions, which would be either internalized or projected into the external world. One schizophrenic patient, for example, believed he had a genie who was always nearby and ready to carry out his wishes, but this apparently utopian arrangement caused great anguish and misery. More often than not the genie would get out of control, pick the patient up, and run amok with him in his arms. The patient would react with such terror that he frequently reached a state of panic and would have to be hospitalized. As discussed in the previous section, the function of a delusion is to achieve control and to compensate for helplessness and vulnerability. If the assaultive introjects continue to be active, as occurs in the repetition compulsion, the adaptive potential of the delusional system is severely impaired, leading to psychic collapse. In the example I have just described, this collapse occurred within the context of the delusion.

In other instances, psychic breakdown can occur when the

delusion ceases to operate and loses its impact as a protective fortress. The patient described earlier, who for a while denied his delusion both to me and to the external world in general, did, in fact, give up his omnipotent world for a short period of time. His acceptance of consensual reality was heralded, however, by a devastating nightmare. In his dream he is standing on a gloomy knoll, dressed as a medieval knight in armor. A much larger Zeus-like figure, also dressed in armor, slowly approaches him and then quickly plunges a short sword into his chest and cuts out his heart. The patient awakened in terror. When he was once again delusional, he had absolutely no recollection of this dream. Quite clearly, the delusion held him together, producing an armor that was resistant to penetration.

Another patient, as a consequence of treatment with phenothiazines, no longer had auditory hallucinations, and the hospital discharged him as recovered. Although the patient's reality-testing was good, he felt miserable. He came to see me because he wanted his voices back.

These observations emphasize that the structure of the delusion is precarious. True, some delusions appear to be rigid, tenacious, and impervious to influence, but there may be certain factors essential to the maintenance of their stability and cohesion, factors supporting their defensive potential. Delusions are protective devices that counteract the disruptive traumas and introjects of the infantile past, but the latter sometimes try to weave themselves into the fabric of the delusion and destroy it.

As is true of any adaptation, a delusion cannot exist without some support and reinforcement. Although it disavows the external world, that world must nevertheless be acknowledged. For one thing, whatever the content of the delusion, its manifest content is patterned after images and other sensory input from the external world. The delusional world is based on the environment most of us acknowledge, even though its elements are arranged in bizarre and idiosyncratic combinations that defy reality-oriented configurations. For another, to deny or to replace something experienced as dangerous requires that, to some extent, the object be acknowledged.

In the introductory section of this chapter, I indicated that the characteristic feature of a psychotic character structure is the dominance of the transitional space without the development of the space beyond it, the external world. This statement, however, is not absolute. I was stressing the significance of the transitional space with regard to a defective acknowledgment of the external world. Even the most regressed psychotic patient must have some minimal awareness of the surrounding ambience. Furthermore, to maintain a delusion requires a space outside it into which patients can project all the destructive introjects and parts of the self that are threatening psychic equilibrium. The act of projection requires an area into which the objectionable aspects of the psyche can be dumped. Schizophrenic patients, because they lack unity and cohesion, are compartmentalized, and various segments of the psyche have to be well delineated from one another. The bad parts have to be segregated from the good parts if the fragmentation or split is to survive and thus preserve psychic equilibrium. The delusion has to persist in an uncontaminated fashion if it is to function as a homeostatic regulator. Thus the external world can be accepted to the extent that it serves as a receptacle for projection. Klein (1946) has written extensively about these processes. The point I am stressing is that a minimal acknowledgment of the external world is essential for the maintenance of the delusion.

Schizophrenics often turn to their therapists to support their delusions, much as the patient I discussed, who hid his delusions from his family and friends. They want us to be on their side and share their hatred for their persecutors. Although frequently we also become persecutors, if the treatment has succeeded in forming a good holding environment, such patients can both view us on the basis of their delusions and still use us to support them. They want the therapist to join them in their delusional space, but they can simultaneously place another image of him in the hostile external world. At times, this can lead to an effective treatment relationship (see Chapter 8).

For example, an adolescent schizophrenic male was referred to me for treatment because, in spite of both his parents' and his internist's entreaties, he refused to accept the fact that he was extremely underweight. His internist, of course, wanted him to increase his caloric intake, but the doctor assured me that in spite of his weight the patient was amazingly healthy, and that although his intake was considerably less than it should be, he had a well-balanced, sensible diet.

When I first saw this young man, I thought him to be abnormally thin, but not emaciated or debilitated, as I have seen among more typical anorectics. He stressed that his father continually fought with him about his weight and tried as hard as he could to "fatten" him. Quite inadvertently I asked him how long he had been thin. He became furious and nearly walked out of my office. He angrily replied that he was not at all "skinny," and in fact he took very good care of his body, and ate selectively (he was a vegetarian). He shouted that I was like everyone else, that is, not really interested in his welfare. I just wanted to exploit him. I immediately realized that I had imposed my reality onto him, and that he had experienced my question as assaultive. He experienced it as an attempt to disrupt the world he had created, where extreme thinness was an ideal; indeed, it is an ideal that is shared by many who live in the world most of us find familiar. Somehow I was able to placate the patient, and he accepted another appointment, although he continued to be disgruntled. I suppose that the extent of my remorse for my "transgression" helped to reestablish the relationship, even though he remained suspicious and distrustful of me for many months.

I was on my guard, because I had concluded that he was quite vulnerable and sensitive and would react adversely to anything I might say that could be construed as a threat to his autonomy—the autonomy inherent in his delusional system. I noted that there were many instances when I could have commented or made a suggestion, but refrained from doing so, because it would have been experienced as intrusive. Occasionally, I slipped, but I was always able to salvage the situation. For example, on one occasion, he showed me a letter he had written to an uncle, a fairly well-constructed letter, but he had obviously misspelled a rather simple word. Knowing how obsessionally precise and sadistically critical this uncle could be, I gently pointed out the misspelling. I am sorry I ever did. Again he exploded, screaming that I was wrong and that he did not care what the dictionary spelling was. Again I was like "the others" who were against him and involved only with themselves. I apologized for having upset him, and we both dropped any further discussion about the letter. I believe the only reason he did not terminate treatment then was that we had established a good relationship prior to this incident.

The patient had recently dropped out of school because he felt his teachers did not understand him. Actually, he had never completed a project or held a job. He graduated from elementary school and high school, but his parents had told him everyone did. His grades were low, and he was always at the bottom of the class, although when tested, he scored with results of superior intelligence. He never accepted responsibility for his poor performance, and in his characteristic paranoid fashion, he blamed others for his failures. In fact, he did not recognize them as failures. He gave me innumerable examples of situations in which he was infuriatingly arrogant and self-righteous, especially in view of his lack of either talent or industry and his total unproductivity.

I had for the most part been successful in controlling my urge to "correct" his reality distortions, because I had come to realize that such comments would be placing me in the part of the external world that was "misunderstanding," or persecuting, him. I would have become imbricated into his paranoid delusion along with all the other paranoid objects he had been able to construct. Instead, I had been able to remain relatively nonpartisan, but still offered him support for his various endeavors.

The patient had no imposed routine, because he neither worked nor went to school. He had devised a schedule for himself, however, getting up at a certain hour, doing calisthenics, then going to the library to look up the literature for whatever project in which he was engaged. He was usually working on some electronic equipment, so he would spend the afternoon drawing complicated circuits. He also kept an elaborate diary about all his daily activities.

I saw him four times a week, and at the beginning of the week, he would bring me his diary of the previous week and whatever drawings he had made. It was absolutely necessary that I observe every detail of these drawings, although I understood very little, and that I read every word of his daily log. I learned that this constituted an acknowledgment of his existence, without which he felt he did not exist. My recognition of how he was functioning gave him the support he needed so that he could continue functioning.

This was an interesting situation, because on the one hand, I felt he was trying to provoke me into a transgression so that I would become a paranoid object; yet, on the other hand, his very existence seemed to depend on our relationship. I finally concluded that these were not two antagonistic currents so long as I did not participate in the process of becoming a paranoid object. On the contrary, it seemed that my being part of his paranoid system helped to cement the supportive holding-environment elements of the treatment. Nevertheless, whatever persecutory quality he attributed to me had to be minimal.

In this way he could maintain a balance. He could not replace current reality altogether with his intermediate world of persecutors. He was still very much dependent on external objects for his survival, because, clearly, he had no capacity to take care of himself. He was provided with food, shelter, therapy, and ample sums of money. The latter, however, was given to him grudgingly, and he was able to place his parents' "parsimony" in his paranoid system. In other words, he was glad to take whatever he could get, but was successful in not allowing himself to feel gratified. This was important, because if he were able to be appreciative of what they supplied, he would feel obligated to them and at their mercy. Thus, it was essential that he deny any dependency, because he equated it with vulnerability. In therapy, he had similar feelings as they represented the transference. I had become a basic supportive force that helped to maintain the cohesion of the self-representation. His repeated—and on occasion successful—attempts to provoke me into imposing my reality on him represented a need to defend himself against acknowledging how dependent he was upon me, and yet when I did not conform to his expectations that I would scorn or reject him, it strengthened the bond between the two of us. Though our relationship was strong and positive, I had managed to fail him sufficiently enough so that he could keep part of me in his paranoid world. For him, this was a comfortable balance, and I was able to accept it.

In the next section of the book, I will discuss situations in which the impact of the patient's delusion leads to disruptive countertransference responses such that the treatment cannot survive. As discussed, the therapist must have some access to his own world and not be completely submerged in the patient's delusional system. If the analyst can even partially gain the patient's confidence and trust early in treatment, the patient, in turn, can accept the part of the therapist's reality that he requires in order to keep functioning as a therapist.

Concluding Perspectives

Any treatise on schizophrenia will, of necessity, be incomplete. The variations of character structure and the pervasiveness of the delusional system defy our capacities to make comfortable generalizations. In many instances, we have to recognize our limitations and to accept our inability to treat psychotics within a psychotherapeutic or psychoanalytic context. Our success or failure will largely depend on our capacity to survive patients' delusional distortions of our role, motivations, intentions, and feelings, and on our being able to tolerate the demands and beliefs of their privately constructed worlds. These, of course, involve countertransference responses, which will also be discussed in detail in the next section.

No other group of patients has the personal impact that schizophrenics have on their therapists. If the analyst becomes engaged in the treatment process, it is likely that his dedication is intense. Somewhat like the patient, the therapist often finds that the schizophrenic manages to intrude himself into his private world. This experience can be both exhilarating and exasperating. Because the psychotic's character pathology predominantly involves defective boundaries, the treatment relationship is in danger of becoming disrupted as the unacceptable world of reality and the delusional system blend in chaotic confusion. Even when the treatment is progressing more or less successfully, however, there is always some merging of different realities, and this makes the therapy of psychotic patients unique.

The treatment of all patients suffering from severe psychopathology causes us to question our values, and this means examining our current reality from perspectives that we had not previously considered. This occurs with particular intensity during the psychotherapeutic treatment of schizophrenics. Paradoxically, the strangeness of their worlds, their alien and bizarre qualities, force us to justify—and in many instances to reject— the standards of our surrounding milieu. The schizophrenic's construction of a unique reality-space that contains the delusional system has profound effects on our stability as we begin to question the world we live in.

We learn that there are no absolutes to the function of reality-testing. External reality can be viewed from many perspectives. When we juxtapose our viewpoint with the psychotic's reality, we invariably become confused, and this is the outcome of another paradox. The strange, incomprehensible elements of the schizophrenic world are both alien and familiar to us. They make no sense, and at the same time they make profound sense. This is far from being apparent, especially when we can find fundamental truths in many delusions. This contradiction, at some level, however, continues to plague many therapists, and makes working with schizophrenics both exciting and exhausting.

Schizophrenics defend themselves from the traumatic infantile world with their delusions. Their assaultive environment is equated with reality in general, which they disavow. *Their traumas occurred in our world, which is the alien enemy.* We find ourselves belonging to this hostile territory, which also contains within its borders the capacity for understanding and empathy that is so essential to the treatment process. We are put in the position of possessing all the destructive elements of the traumatic past alongside the capacity to offer the patient something good from an area outside his private domain, an experience that he may never have had. This is confusing, because in order to be helpful, we have to accept the blame for all the ills and misfortunes these patients have suffered as they attack and withdraw from us.

The truths that are inherent in the delusional system are reflections of the injustices and inequities of our society, but they are concretized in an idiosyncratic fashion. We often tend to push the negative elements of our milieu into the background, because we do not want to let them interfere with our benign attitudes toward patients. The schizophrenic, in a manner of speaking, will not permit us to deny the destructive elements of our milieu. He will insist on our experiencing them as he has, but we cannot use them against the patient.

We have to acknowledge the inherent evils of our society, accept responsibility for some of them, and transcend them.

Patients' expectations of their therapists can also be destructive. From our viewpoint, they may be unreasonable. They may refuse to leave our offices, or want to be with us constantly. This assigned role of savior is even more difficult than the role of persecutor. We are forcefully made aware of our limitations as we are showered with omnipotence. The role of persecutor can be easily allied with a patient's other persecutory elements, but the role of savior may become part of the delusional system. This puts our boundaries and spatial organization in jeopardy as our world is invaded with oxymorons that are characteristic of the schizophrenic viewpoint. Still, if we can maintain our cohesion by regaining our therapeutic perspective, we can be enormously helpful to our schizophrenic patients.

Part II

Technique in the Treatment of Character Disorders

Chapter 7

The Handling and Mishandling of Resistance

Those clinicians who argue against the use of classical analysis for the treatment of character disorders have a point. Despite the fact that for many years, I have espoused what appears to be an opposite viewpoint, if the technique of classical analysis is rigidly defined, then it is easy to find elements that would create difficulties in the treatment of primitively fixated patients.

As I mentioned in the Introduction, the overcoming of resistance has remained since Freud the chief task of the treatment process and has become the hallmark of the classic psychoanalytic approach. Most analysts consider this struggle an immutable feature of the patient–analyst relationship, and the battle is understood to be won by the weapon of transference interpretations. Contemporary analysts, especially those who are accustomed to working with patients who are much more primitively fixated than with patients having oedipal neuroses, do not find the battle metaphor useful. But, if we are to view treatment as a cooperative venture rather than a continuous tug-of-war, we would need to modify considerably our attitudes concerning resistance, a phenomenon that has an unfortunate pejorative connotation (Greenson, 1969).

As I have already indicated, very early in his career, Freud (Breuer & Freud, 1895) literally commanded the patient not to resist; he understood resistance as a reaction against treatment, and he used every means at his disposal (Freud, 1911–1915) to do away with it as quickly as possible. At that time, he believed that the task of analysis was to make the unconscious conscious, and resistance thwarted his purpose by preventing free association.

Whether resistance is consciously contrived or unconsciously controlled is not entirely clear. In the *Studies on Hysteria* (Breuer & Freud, 1895), Freud tells us that he discovered resistance as he was trying to perfect the technique of free association. He was then using the pressure technique. He had the patient lie down, and instructed him that he was going to touch his forehead, and when he did, the patient would have some thoughts centering around the period when he first developed his symptoms. More often than not, however, when Freud touched the patient's forehead, the patient would say that nothing occurred to him, even though Freud had stressed that the patient should hold nothing back out of shame or because the thoughts seemed trivial, inconsequential, or embarrassing.

As we know, Freud was persistent and relentless. He told the patient that *something* had to occur to him, and sometimes accused him of holding back. He exhorted the patient not to suppress anything, and continued with the procedure of applying pressure to the patient's forehead. Finally, after several attempts, the patient would produce some associations, but he would also admit that these same thoughts had emerged even the first time Freud had touched his forehead.

This was an astonishing sequence: The patient was challenging the physician's authority, an unusual occurrence in those mid-Victorian times; he was also working against a treatment plan that was designed for his own welfare and the relief of distressing symptoms. Freud concluded that he was witnessing a powerful force that was resisting his curative attempts—a conscious phenomenon, because the patient was aware of what he was doing, but also unconscious, because the patient did not understand the purpose of his suppression. (Freud had not yet distinguished between suppression and repression.)

Later, in his technical papers (Freud, 1911–1915), Freud emphasized the unconscious nature of resistance, and linked it to the phenomenon of transference. The patient unconsciously transfers infantile impulses and attitudes to the analyst, and seeing him in terms of these infantile imagos becomes a therapeutic obstacle. Patients resist acknowledging the transference origin of their feelings, and insist that they are having realistically based reactions. Freud (1912a, 1914a) pointed out how both the hostile and erotic transference could become therapeutically disruptive.

Basically, Freud believed that there are defensive forces within the psyche that prevent unconscious impulses from becoming conscious. In fact, the unconscious is defined as a part of the mind that is barred access to consciousness. If resistance is an unconscious process that leads to repression of instinctual derivatives so that their meaning cannot be explored, then it is an inherent feature of the psychic apparatus as it is constructed along a topographical axis. Resistance is the natural consequence of the division between, and separation of, conscious and unconscious.

The topographical hypothesis was first postulated in the context of an id psychology that viewed the mind as the site of conflicting instinctual forces (Freud, 1900, 1915a, 1915c). The concept of resistance is well suited to this model, because one can easily visualize the phenomenon as a clash between two opposing elements. If psychopathology is based on intrapsychic conflict, which occurs because the preconscious mind finds certain unconscious elements unacceptable to conscious awareness, the patient's resistive behavior is the inevitable outcome.

After having postulated the structural hypothesis, Freud (1923) modified and extended his ideas about psychic processes. He still thought in terms of conflicting drives, but he included structural factors in his formulations. The ego contains both conscious and unconscious elements, and it represents the upper extension of a structural hierarchy, whose primitive base is the id. Because elements of lower levels cannot be integrated into higher levels, resistance is understood to operate from both id and ego levels.

In his early formulations, Freud had thought of resistance as emanating from the ego, much like secondary repression (Freud, 1915b), but in *Analysis Terminable and Interminable,* Freud (1937) wrote about the adhesiveness of libido, which describes a resistance of the id. This, too, can be compared to repression, but to what Freud described as primal repression. The latter occurs when the id exerts an attractive force on psychic elements that may have reached ego levels, but are associatively similar to id content. Something similar seems to happen with patients whose psychopathology can best be described in terms of structural defects, and who manifest resistance in the treatment setting.

If the psychic content of lower levels of the personality cannot be integrated into higher structural levels and so rendered capable of being communicated to an external object—the analyst—then our idea that repression or resistance involves a barrier or an obstacle is an oversimplification. Rather, the patient is exhibiting an inherent incapacity that is the outcome of structural defects. Primitive psychic structures have not been integrated into later-acquired, more sophisticated, adaptive ego states. Unlike a barrier, the absence of integration cannot be somehow breached. The patient cannot behave otherwise, and his inability to reveal himself and to get in touch with inner primitive forces and feelings is determined by the constrictions of his character structure.

With such patients, resistance is overcome as the consequence of successful treatment, which leads to the acquisition of further psychic structure. The analyst cannot make demands for the patient's cooperation, because this so-called lack of cooperation is an inherent part of the patient's psychopathology and represents a deficit. In fact, the patient may be seeking treatment to free himself from the very constrictions that do not permit him to be open with the therapist.

The difference between resistance and defenses is obscure, especially in patients suffering from character disorders. Analysts can ordinarily tolerate defenses, and are content to understand and to interpret them, whereas their attitude toward resistance, as discussed, is somewhat peremptory. Still, it should not surprise us that patients bring into the analytic setting the adaptations they use to cope with the external world. Especially at the beginning of treatment, they will relate to the therapist as they have to other significant external objects. If they have needed to be oppositional in the past, they will continue in the therapeutic present. Rather than trying to overcome this opposition, it should be analyzed as a defensive adaptation.

Resistance and the Need to Control

As I have discussed, there are certain formal elements to the analytic interaction that are superficially similar to traumatic elements of the infantile past. The analyst has often been imbued with authority and power that is realistically unwarranted, but is nevertheless encouraged by the analytic setting itself. This may not be as true today as it was in the past when analysis was considered mysterious and esoteric, but there are a substantial number of opponents of psychoanalysis whose antipathy is based on feeling threatened by the prestigious position they have attributed to the analyst.

Some patients need to exercise total control, and they view the analytic situation as impinging on their capacity to do so. Such patients often refuse to lie on the couch, because they believe they would no longer be in control and are exposing their vulnerability. Technically, this constitutes a resistance, because the patient is resisting the treatment procedure; but he is behaving as he is because he is terrified of being overwhelmed by inner destructive forces.

For example, a single man in his middle thirties had been hospitalized many times since his adolescence. He was apparently quite bright; he had been the valedictorian of his high school class, and had graduated *summa cum laude* from a prestigious university. He performed very well in a highly technical capacity, but would periodically become detached, and then withdraw completely from his family, friends, and fellow employees. He appeared to be in a fugue state, which would change over a period of days to one of agitation and terror. By that time he would be so disturbed that he had to be hospitalized.

He had seen several therapists on an outpatient basis, but he was always too agitated, literally, to sit still through an entire session. He would ramble on in a hyperactive fashion, either ignoring questions or answering them in a mocking noninformative manner. Not one of the analysts he saw believed he was acting in a psychotic fashion; they viewed him, rather, as being provocatively silly, a wiseacre behaving like a spoiled brat. One therapist described him as an adult version of a minimal-brain-dysfunction child, with some hypomanic features. All the therapists agreed that the strength of his resistance rendered him untreatable. Their conclusion was particularly interesting, given that resistance in this case did not mean resistance to free association, as was described by Freud. On the contrary, this patient always seemed to be free associating in a wild and bizarre fashion. His therapists, in essence, objected to the fact that he *was* so wild and bizarre. He did not present himself in a better-organized, secondary fashion; he did not sit still and let them take an organized history. They believed that the patient had the capacity to control his feelings, and that his choosing not to do so constituted resistance—he was refusing to follow a prescribed sequence that involved diagnostic assessment through history-taking.

When I first saw the patient, I also formed an immediate impression that he could behave in a calm, organized manner if he wanted to. I had no particular inclination to stop him, however, from rambling in a hypomanic fashion, and made no attempt to take a formal history. Remaining seated in a chair, he began to revile himself as an odious, "festering, polluted" person full of "pus and garbage." Then he had a fit of silly laughter, and talked about how successful and creative he could be. He told me how much admired he had been at work, and about the numerous innovations he had made. He also described his many artistic and musical talents. Nevertheless, he could easily return to attacking himself. At the end of the session, which he announced before I did, he stopped abruptly, said that we had accomplished nothing, and quickly left. I had made very few comments, just simply asked an occasional question to clarify something he had said.

The next session he began by stating that he had nothing to say to me, because he was certain that I could not help him. He did not want to reveal himself, because there was nothing I could offer him. In fact, he was a machine that no one could operate except himself. He continued in this way, telling me that I was useless, but he alternated in blaming me or himself. He then threatened to quit treatment.

I nonetheless felt fairly comfortable, and gently asked him to lie on the couch. He responded by screaming No, but did move to the couch and sat down. In a placating fashion, he said he would sit up but turn his head the other way so that we did not have to look at each other; however, he maintained a posture in which he could easily keep me within his range of vision. I replied that I would go along with this arrangement for a while, because I understood that he had a strong need to remain in control of the situation. I had no wish to compromise his autonomy, but sometime in the future, for the sake of the analysis, he would have to lie down. I added that this was not a personal wish of mine, but a requirement of the process, although I admitted I felt more comfortable when patients were lying down. He visibly relaxed and became calm. He sat on the couch for several sessions and finally lay down, and treatment progressed in a conventional manner.

Refusing to lie down is similar to suppressing associations, inasmuch as it represents an opposition to certain rules that have characterized psychoanalytic treatment. The relaxation of what had been the immutable requirements of analysis accompanies an extended viewpoint of indications for treatment. Still, the more classically oriented analyst, although he might approve of a modified approach, would be quick to point out that it is not analysis. At best, it is psychoanalytically oriented psychotherapy.

This introduces another variable regarding the definition of psychoanalysis. The more a therapist accedes to resistance, the less resemblance to psychoanalysis the treatment process retains. I believe, however, that this is a superficial approach; it ignores the deeper factors of therapeutic regression, the transference interaction, and the interpretative modality. If we include the holding environment (Winnicott, 1960) as an intrinsic factor of the analytic relationship, then the problem becomes further complicated. Accepting the patient's "resistance" may be crucial to the establishment of the holding environment.

I firmly believed, although I had not deliberately thought it out, that I had to let my patient sit rather than lie on my couch. Yet I can think of other patients who balked at lying down, to whom I would have given no further appointments had they absolutely refused. What determined my different reactions?

As an example of the latter, some years ago I saw a successful professional man in his middle forties, whose wife had urged him for a long time to seek analysis. She had been successfully analyzed herself, and was, because of her own changes, unwilling to continue the marriage on the same neurotic basis (Giovacchini, 1958a, 1965). She had been urging him to get into treatment even before her own analysis, but since being analyzed, she had been firm and unrelenting in her insistence. He finally realized that she would divorce him if he did not acquiesce, and he felt intensely anxious, almost panic-stricken, about losing her. As his anxiety mounted, he called me, and presented himself as a man desperately in need of treatment. Because he owned his business, he could accommodate himself absolutely to my schedule.

He was in a state of near-panic during his first session; he was afraid that I would not accept him for treatment, and this would mean the break-up of his marriage. It was clear that he had very little concept of treatment as something for himself; it was simply a means of appeasing his wife. When I indicated that I was interested in treating him, he became considerably less anxious.

Feeling reassured, he became less compliant. He gave me many reasons why he could not come during certain times of the week. He also informed me of several business trips that would keep him away for weeks at a time. He was obviously frightened of becoming involved in therapy and was resisting the beginning of treatment. During the second session, I asked him to lie on the couch, and he reluctantly did. We had a special problem arranging for a third session, because of his schedule, and I had the definite impression that my putting him on the couch had contributed strongly to our difficulty. Nevertheless, we were finally able to agree on a time.

Before that next session, I had set up a schedule of regular appointments that he would have to be responsible for; at least, he would have to pay for them whether he kept them or not. As soon as he arrived, he told me that he wanted some explanations, and asked that he be allowed to sit up. My response to his request was the diametric opposite of the one I gave the hypomanic patient. I tried not to show the strength of my reaction, but I firmly refused. If he had been adamant, I was prepared to terminate treatment then and there.

So the patient lay down, and I discussed, in essence, the analytic setting. He admitted that he did not really want to be analyzed, but wanted to be treated by me because he wanted to hold his marriage together. I accepted that this was sufficient reason for analysis, and the treatment relationship continued for many years, with a fairly successful outcome.

Looking back at that third session, I have wondered why I reacted so differently to these two patients. From a technical viewpoint, both were resisting. Each balked against following a procedure that most of us believe is an intrinsic feature of the analytic interaction. As is true of any reaction, however, there are many different underlying factors. These patients' resistance stemmed from different psychic levels. *There are different forms of resistance, and they cannot be dealt with uniformly.*

The first patient had, on occasion, been diagnosed as schizophrenic, but because he was, for the most part, able to function, the diagnosis was often toned down to schizoid, and hypomanic was frequently added. He was conceptualized as having a schizoaffective character structure. Whatever the diagnosis, he dramatically displayed the effects of splitting and projective mechanisms, and his sessions, as mentioned, were heavily punctuated with outbursts of both grandiosity and bitter self-incrimination and devaluation.

His life was a constant struggle between good and evil inner forces, and he had to somehow control the latter so that he would not be destroyed, or, more aptly put, so that he would not destroy himself. Basically, he had to be in control of his feelings, which also meant that he had to control the surrounding world, because the boundaries between inner and outer were blurred. At work, he was always on top of the situation; no one told him what to do. On the contrary, other employees were there to do his bidding. His home was said to be a marvel of electronic wizardry, in perfect harmony and run simply by pushing buttons.

Very early in treatment he presented me with a revealing dream, one that stressed the polarities of good and evil. Two Titans are standing in front of him, one dressed in white armor, the other in black. At first it seems as if they are going to engage in combat, but suddenly the black Titan moves toward the patient as if to seize him. The patient panics and runs for rescue toward the white Titan, who extends his arms to receive him. He is then carried in the Titan's arms to a cozy, warm cave. In spite of being protected and removed from the source of danger, his anxiety does not altogether abate. He feels helpless in his rescuer's arms, and is even aware of a sense of shame. He precipitously jumps out of his benefactor's arms, grabs his sword, and finds himself in the midst of a group of Roman warriors who are slaughtering peasants. The peasants beg him to save them, and he believes he could if he had the "power." Perhaps it is in his sword, but he is not certain. He awoke feeling frightened.

This dream can be studied from many angles. Incorporated in the manifest dream content are elements of the movie *Star Wars*. The Titans are figures in both Greek and Roman mythology; and Roman warriors reveal the transference element of the dream inasmuch as my name is obviously Italian. I have reported the dream, however, to stress this patient's fear of losing control and of being in the passive position—even when he is being rescued—and also to point out his need to be actively controlling, which is depicted in his running away from his protector and getting in the middle of the mêlée.

He demonstrated these anxieties and needs in his behavior during our sessions, and in his resistance to lying down on the couch. For a long time, he was hypomanic, and during the first few sessions he found it difficult to sit still. He would stamp his feet and writhe in the chair. He did not actually get up and pace around, but he wanted to. He verbally attacked me because he believed I forced him to stay in one place, and to some extent this was true. Although I never overtly demanded that he not get up and move around, I certainly expected him not to, and I probably conveyed that by my demeanor.

Asking him to lie on the couch, I believe, was equivalent to his being carried in the white Titan's arms. The patient had this dream at a point in the treatment when he was still sitting up on the couch. He felt helpless and vulnerable and in someone else's control; and even though he was protected by the Titan, he had to relinquish his destiny to someone else. This ultimately meant his destruction.

Thus, resistance was the outcome of fundamental conflicts related to his psychic survival. It was a manifestation of the core of his psychopathology and of his structural defects. His self-representation had not achieved a cohesive, stable integration. It was also being constantly threatened by hostile, destructive introjects, against which he had been able to construct overcompensatory defensive adaptations. These adaptations involved control, mastery, and grandiosity, and his innate talents and creativity helped to support them. To insist that he lie down was to directly threaten his *modus operandi*, his chief defensive modality.

The situation was different with the businessman. Though his reluctance to begin analysis was also based on intrapsychic factors, they belong to higher levels of the psychic apparatus than those operating in the first patient. The businessman's behavior seemed to be organized on a secondary-process basis, whereas the first patient's orientation was apparently following a primary-process axis. These distinctions would indicate that the second patient had the capacity to curtail his actions; he was not driven to resist in order to survive or to maintain the cohesion of his self-representation. He had much more flexibility.

Resistance as a reaction to the fundamental terror of the dissolution of the self-representation represents an expression of the deepest elements of the schizoid patient's psychopathology. The businessman's resistance was a manifestation of a surface defense, but a defense that could continue to exist even if it were prohibited one avenue of expression. It had many others at its disposal.

Had I not been willing to let the first patient sit on the couch for as long as he needed to, I strongly believe that he would not have been able to continue with me. I conjecture that, in a sense, I would have fed into his delusion by actively assuming the same role as his inner destructive evil forces. I would have become the black Titan that he had dreamed about. My not interfering with his need to control and to maintain ascendancy over bad internal objects helped to create a safe atmosphere. True, he will have to work out his problem at some point in his treatment, in a transference context, and deal with me as if I were the black Titan. If he can gain a feeling of security in the treatment setting, however, he will begin to understand that the setting's purpose is to foster maximum autonomy, and will acquire the confidence to face his hatred and rage. The delusional qualities of the need to control can be "tamed" to a striving for independence and self-sufficiency as his primary-process orientation achieves accretions of secondary-process elements. Accepting the patient's resistance, then, will have helped to create the holding environment that made analysis possible.

On the other hand, to have acquiesced to the other patient's request to sit up, and to have let him continue his cavalier treatment of the schedule, in my opinion, would have made the prospect of analysis impossible. This man had the propensity to gain his ends by manipulation. Indeed, his talent for manipulation had contributed to the patient's success in business; but the behavior was part of a defensive pattern that protected him from loss of self-esteem. Its basis was a competitive struggle with his father, who had died recently, and the patient's subsequent guilt. His attitude was a reaction formation, and in the analysis was a displacement both for his feeling of inferiority to his father and for his guilt about having wanted to destroy him. He also maintained distance from emotional involvement, because he was afraid of intimacy, but he was able to manipulate relationships so that, on the surface, they appeared to be close. In the same way, he wanted to appear to have an analytic relationship without having to become emotionally engaged.

In retrospect, I see more clearly that if I had responded to his request to sit up and "talk," I would have been colluding with him, and accepting a pseudorelationship for an analysis. Unlike the situation with my other patient, my refusal to accept his resistance did not threaten the foundations of his personality. He had many resources, many areas in which he could use the psychic mechanisms of reaction formation and displacement, and innumerable opportunities for forming pseudorelationships. Furthermore, the idea of conforming to his wishes felt out of character for me, whereas I was not particularly uncomfortable when I acceded to the wishes of the schizoid patient.

Resistance and the Loss of Narcissistic Supplies

Throughout the years, I have encountered with increasing frequency patients who signal at the very outset that they are going to be critical of the analytic method. They implicitly or explicitly criticize analytic neutrality and the relative inactivity of the analyst. They demand feedback and express a need to be "locked" into the relationship. They want an active give-and-take exchange. They also expect commentary, questions, and some kind of guiding organization.

If the couch is suggested, they are apt to refuse because they require eye contact. They complain about the anticipated sense of isolation. They need a "meaningful relationship," and do not want to be abandoned and left talking to themselves. They have to know what the analyst is both thinking and feeling, so that he and the patient can relate to each other as "whole" and "real" persons.

Although the purpose of analysis is to foster the patient's autonomy, the analyst has to feel his own sense of autonomy; he must be free to choose how he will relate in the treatment setting. In productive circumstances the patient's and therapist's autonomy do not clash. When patients make the demands I have just outlined, I experience them as intrusive, but again, the patient's resistance to treatment has to be assessed in terms of the level of psychopathology it represents. Ordinarily, these narcissistic patients can maintain their adaptations outside the treatment relationship and relinquish some of them in order to be analyzed. If they cannot, analysis might not be possible.

I recall two patients whose situations were somewhat similar, but whom I handled differently. In one instance, I was able to conduct analysis; in the other I was not. Both patients were middle-aged, married women who had been popular and attractive in their youth, and had received considerable admiration. One had been an actress earlier in life, and had gained a certain amount of celebrity status. The other had been a model, who had done many cosmetic ads. Each sought treatment because of anxiety and depression related to the fear of growing old and losing her beauty. In both cases, the children had grown up and left home, and the husband seemed somewhat indifferent; in fact, the former actress's husband was probably having an affair.

Each was quite agitated when I first saw her. The former model found herself "bored to death," and she was furious with her husband, although she could not give any specific reasons for feeling that way. He was simply dull, and did not relate to her in the vibrant fashion she required. As she looked back over her marriage, she evaluated it as a failure, although her husband seemed content with the way things were. He could not understand why she was unhappy and wanted treatment. In fact, he was opposed to psychoanalysis. She saw his attitude as further evidence of his insensitivity. She insisted that they were not in synchrony with each other, and that he had no concept of how to relate to her needs. Analysis was somehow to make up for these deficits in her daily life.

Though she tried to be charming and, to some extent, seductive, there was a peremptory quality to her demeanor. I definitely felt that the sooner we could formally enter analysis, the less demanding I would find her, so early in the second session I asked her to lie on the couch. She greeted my request with a storm of protests. She accused me of being as insensitive as her husband, and of not understanding her need for eye contact. She was infuriated by my suggesting a situation where, once again, she would just be talking to herself. She had discussed classical analysis with friends who were currently or had been in treatment, and that was not what she wanted. I replied that this struck me as odd, because she knew me as an analyst. I added that I could respect her sensitivities, but did not believe I could be of any use to her unless I tried to analyze her, and the process required that she lie on the couch. Of course, it was her choice, but analysis was what I had to offer. She chose to be analyzed, and she resentfully lay down.

For months, she was very angry, and saw me as a harsh taskmaster, but she continued coming, was always on time, and never missed an appointment. Briefly, throughout the years, she increasingly revealed how lonely and isolated she felt; she always had to perform and be attractive in order to receive any attention. She learned to "exist" on the acclaim she received. Without it she viewed herself as an empty void. Narcissistic supplies held together a fragile sense of self.

Her behavior markedly changed over this time; she was no longer histrionic and melodramatic, and did not avidly seek attention and admiration. She became drab and depressed, and expressed considerable tension and feelings of intense inadequacy. In other words, she had given up her narcissistic defenses, but gradually she began building up self-esteem and received gratification from my interpretations. She found employment, which made use of her fine sense of design, divorced her husband, and remarried.

I need not discuss further details of her treatment except to emphasize that this highly narcissistic woman presented defensive adaptations that seemed to be at odds with the analytic procedure. She was able to survive the requirements that I consider intrinsic to analysis because, in my opinion, she was able to continue to cope on a narcissistic basis in the external world. If I had accepted her demands, her resistance, as I felt it, I do not believe we would have ever achieved an analytic relationship.

The situation with the former actress supports my belief. When I suggested that she lie down on the couch, she adamantly refused. I had concluded that she was extremely fragile, and I had no desire to issue ultimatums, so I decided I would, at least for a while, let her sit up.

The patient also wanted to control the frequency of her appointments. Her life was extremely busy, and she really had very little time left in her heavily burdened schedule, so she would have to fit me in as best she could. At first, I thought she was devaluing treatment in order to enhance herself, as some narcissistic patients are prone to do. When I indicated that she was being somewhat cavalier in her approach to therapy, however, she vehemently denied that this was the case and wept uncontrollably. She said that people always misinterpreted her actions and did not understand how overwhelmed she felt. I sensed once again her underlying fragility, and viewed her high-handed manner as a desperate attempt to maintain her shaky self-esteem.

As was true for the schizoid patient presented earlier, she had to be in complete control. Regarding analysis, this meant that she would determine when or whether to come. She had to decide how much importance she would give to our relationship, because if she let me become emotionally significant, she would be eclipsed by me. Still, she was aware of her intense need for contact.

I had reconciled myself to accepting her conditions for treatment, believing that if I did not, she would terminate our relationship. Perhaps that would have happened, but as it was, she remained in treatment for only six months. During that time, I learned she was terrified of the transference regression, which would have led to her fusing with me, and feeling vulnerable and dependent.

These fears were the outcome of the repetition of a symbiotic relationship with a destructive and devouring mother who exploited her daughter's beauty and talents for her own aggrandizement. During this patient's treatment, as well as in her daily life, she defended herself against the anxiety of being submerged and destroyed, by seeming to attribute little importance to interpersonal relationships. What she was doing with me was typical of her mode of relating.

My accession to her demands, or from another vantage point, my giving in to her resistance, represented the acceptance of a defensive stance that she had adopted toward the world in general. I was, in effect, reinforcing a psychopathologically determined adaptation, thereby vitiating the opportunity to analyze it. Consequently, the treatment stagnated, leading to unsuccessful termination.

I had thought that this patient's narcissistic defenses were deeply rooted, and that I could not prematurely disrupt them.

As I said, I was impressed by her fragility. But now, in retrospect, I wonder whether I underestimated her capacity for maintaining integration. She has been skillful in manipulating her environment and achieving her ends. For example, her husband had strayed by having an affair. The patient retaliated by having several affairs, and the husband meekly returned and gave up his lover.

Treatment had not acquired any specific meaning for this patient. It was simply another facet of her life, which became part of her narcissistic adjustment. Her resistance to treatment, as I initially wanted to conduct it, was an additional manifestation of a general manipulative tendency, which made others defer to her, and protected her from a destructive merger with emotionally significant external objects. She managed to maintain separateness by not allowing anyone to become, at least from a surface level, emotionally significant.

I still believe that if I had insisted on certain conditions for treatment, such as a regular appointment schedule and lying on the couch, that she would not have come back. On the other hand, my allowing her to exercise her defenses in the treatment situation as she demanded also led nowhere.

The first narcissistic patient did not terminate when I insisted that she follow analytic protocol. Now I am inclined to deal with such patients in a standard analytic fashion. The patient may decide not to pursue analysis, but at least the therapist will have defined the treatment setting. The patient knows what to expect, and if he so decides, can return to a constant analytic environment.

Resistance and the Psychoanalytic Paradox

Resistance has been classically considered disruptive to treatment. Traditionally it was understood to emanate from the patient. But the analyst's reaction to the patient's material is highly significant in determining how effective resistance will be in thwarting the course and purpose of therapy. Thus, countertransference reactions can be incorporated into resistive forces and contribute to therapeutic impasses.

As I have discussed, there are formal elements in the psychoanalytic method and setting that may reinforce the patient's resistance or be experienced as a repetition of the traumatic past. The technical problems caused by the psychoanalytic paradox are related to the problems created by adverse countertransference reactions, although different facets of the analytic relationship are emphasized. For example, narcissistic patients, and those who have a profound fear of fusion, as I have said, often refuse to lie on the couch; and this may threaten the therapist's analytic identity. Allowing the patient to sit up, apart from technical considerations, may be disruptive to the analyst, because it is contrary to his work style. This is a rather obvious threat to an analyst's *modus operandi*. There are more subtle interactions.

Narcissistic patients in particular complain of the analyst's lack of participation and silence. Either overtly or covertly, they may demand responses to their material, sometimes to a dream. The analyst, for his part, feels his professional autonomy threatened; he wants to decide himself when and whether he will respond. The treatment may degenerate into a power struggle as the therapist continues to "resist" the patient's demands. This, of course, is itself a form of participation by the analyst, and it prevents the establishment of an observational frame of reference and an intrapsychic focus.

The patients discussed in Chapter 5, who have a constricted view of external objects, create extreme examples of the psychoanalytic paradox. Their reactions to analytic neutrality and objectivity are especially complex, and often threaten the integrity of the analytic relationship. The patient, overtly or covertly, stubbornly refuses to join the analyst on an observational platform. The fact that he is repeating the infantile past is vigorously denied as he uses the analyst as the target of all frustration and pain.

As discussed in Chapter 4, these patients do not distinguish between the analyst and the unempathic, aloof, constricted mother. The maintenance of the classic stance of analytic neutrality, rather than helping them to recognize and to resolve transference elements, operates in a diametrically opposite fashion. Analytic neutrality is characterized by low decibels, toned-down responses, and reactions that are supposedly required for the maintenance of objectivity. The analytic attitude of neutrality is designed to preserve an intrapsychic focus, and the analyst, by being in control of his feelings, creates an uncontaminated field of observation. For some patients, however, this situation is reminiscent of the traumatic infantile environment, and the analyst's objective attitude is confused with not caring and the absence of feeling.

Patients who have a constricted view of external objects illustrate especially well the point I have been attempting to make in this chapter. Whatever the patient does to interfere with the maintenance of analytic neutrality may be considered simply another way of defining resistance. If an analyst is not allowed to remain neutral, then his capacity to analyze is impaired, and this becomes therapeutically counterproductive. But all of the reactions exhibited by the patients under discussion, particularly those behaviors that interfere with the analytic process, are part of their psychopathology and cannot be treated as though they were outside the patients' main current.

Many analysts relate to patients as if their resistance were an independent phenomenon that they developed against being successfully treated. In addition to the refusal to free associate that Freud (Breuer & Freud 1895) wrote about, the examples of resistance most frequently cited by analysts are being late and cancelling appointments. Analysis is a new experience to which the patient apparently develops new reactions that oppose attempts at cure. Obviously, this view presumes a medical model that does not stress psychic determinism. The situation, however, is not so clear-cut. Even if we determine that all of the patient's reactions stem from intrapsychic sources, how much can they be controlled by the ego simply because they reside mainly at higher psychic levels?

I mentioned in the introduction to this chapter that Freud first thought of resistance as being conscious, and then later pointed out its unconscious component. How often is a patient actually aware that being late is connected with a resistance to treatment? We have to interpret repeatedly patients' reluctance to become involved with therapy, and often have to link that reluctance with more fundamental attitudes, such as the fear of intruding. The resistance to treatment turns out to be a surface manifestation of deeper and more basic anxieties and conflicts. It has to be dealt with analytically; yet, as I am also emphasizing, the analyst has to preserve the analytic setting before interpretations can hope to be effective. There are various reactions to resistance that are possible within a psychoanalytic context, depending on specific constellations of psychopathology.

If the analyst abandons a neutral stance, then many clinicians would assert that he has abandoned analysis, but what exactly constitutes analytic neutrality? We usually define it in terms of what an analyst should not do, namely, respond to the patient's material at the level of content. This can mean not volunteering information, not answering questions, or not responding to the patient's requests for advice and guidance. The less classical analyst might permit some response, but only after the material has been analyzed. Thus, the technique to preserve neutrality consists either of analytic silence, or of questioning the patient as to why he has brought up whatever he has. If the patient becomes uncooperative or otherwise disruptive, he is usually told he is resisting.

Loewald (1960) has a somewhat different concept of the analytic relationship and of analytic neutrality. He states that the analyst, because of his capacity to understand and to perceive better than the patient what is going on intrapsychically, is, structurally speaking, at a higher level than the patient. Within the treatment relationship, there is a differential that is structure-promoting. Loewald recognizes the similarity of analyst and analysand and mother and child, the former dyad promoting psychic growth, and the latter, both psychic and physical growth. The structure-promoting aspects of the analytic relationship do not necessitate any additional techniques besides transference interpretations, but these are easier to integrate and more acceptable if a comfortable holding environment has been established.

Neutrality, in other words, need not dictate specific reactions to the patient's material. It is an attitude, one designed to create an objective, nonjudgmental setting that emphasizes the principle of psychic determinism. How this is achieved cannot be generally prescribed. The appropriate responses for a therapist to make are determined by each patient's psychopathology, and what may be supportive of the analytic framework for one person may be disastrous for another. The only general principles that can be postulated are a calm, nonjudgmental outlook, a respect for the patient's autonomy, and a noninvolvement with managing the patient's life. An interpretative, understanding attitude frequently furnishes the integrative support a patient needs, and it structures a holding environment that can survive the vicissitudes of transference projections. Nevertheless, certain types of patients, such as those with a constricted view of external objects, require a different style of involvement that will stand in contrast to the lack of feeling they experienced in childhood.

For example, some patients (described in Chapter 4) have withdrawn from a disappointing, nongiving world, a world they have helped to construct in adult life by patterning it after the infantile world. In treatment, if they have been able to establish some confidence in the therapist, they may turn to him for help. Then they are intensely needy.

These patients attempt to use the therapist to make up for infantile deprivations by making many vague and sometimes incomprehensible demands, and by ignoring him as a person. What are the technical considerations in this situation? Should the analyst respond to the patient's entreaties, or should he remain uninvolved with content? The patient's overt or covert insistence that infantile needs be met might sabotage the treatment, because the therapist is forced into another, nonanalytic role, and this constitutes resistance. On the other hand, if the analyst does not respond, the treatment might end then and there, which, of course, is the ultimate resistance.

I have often found myself in situations where the patient made some demand to which I have instantly responded without any conscious deliberation. I recall one young woman who, very early in treatment, handed me a wooden statuette; it had an amorphous face, no arms, and was thin and emaciated. It bore some resemblance to a Giacometti sculpture, but I knew nothing about it, not even who had carved it. This patient had very low self-esteem, and her self-representation had many grotesque features. She felt that she could neither be nurtured nor held and soothed. The statuette had no facial features, no mouth, and, lacking arms, obviously could not reach out to anyone. It was clearly a female, however, as one could easily tell from its exaggerated feminine contours, and it had some prehistoric qualities. Even in that fleeting moment when the patient handed it to me, I had the distinct feeling that the statuette represented herself, or, rather, how the patient viewed herself. I felt no hesitation whatsoever in accepting it, and it remained in a niche in my consultation room for several years. As stated, I did not question or consider whether it was analytically proper to accept it. I simply knew that had I not, I would have lost a patient. Much later in treatment, my intuition was confirmed many times (see Chapter 9).

This patient needed to leave part of herself in my office. She had great difficulty in forming and holding a mental representation without the reinforcement of the actual presence of the external object. She reversed that situation with me; she kept herself around me so that I would not forget her, which would have meant losing her. By projecting herself into the statuette, she was also keeping me in her perceptual field. This was a fundamental need; it maintained whatever little ego cohesion she had. When I have an awareness of a patient's basic neediness for emotional supplies, I usually find it fairly easy to feel some involvement that goes beyond the need to understand him. My responses become intensified, and I develop some degree of excitement. This is not role-playing; it is something that happens spontaneously. This is especially so when a patient is attempting to move from a position of schizoid isolation into the external world. This usually happens tentatively; the patient is groping cautiously in order to begin to understand and to cope with a confusing and overwhelming reality. These efforts may still incorporate a resistance to analysis, a resistance to exploring inner terror and chaos, but can analysis proceed if the patient is not first helped to gain some access to current reality?

I have already described my treatment of an adolescent college student who said practically nothing for several months, then timidly started asking questions about such pedestrian matters as how to behave or dress for various occasions, or how to make a telephone call to ask a girl for a date. Under most circumstances, these questions would have struck practically everyone as dull for a young man, and in an ordinary analytic relationship, our tendency would be to view them either as a resistance to free asssociation or as the expression of infantile dependent needs, and not respond to them. Perhaps, because the patient had said so little, and there was only a modicum of exchange between us, I found what he asked interesting and responded with enthusiasm.

I felt a need to give him the information he requested, and as I mentioned, I also shared his distress even when there was no reason for either one of us to become upset. Again, I propose the argument that I do not believe treatment would have been possible if I had dealt with his questions and reactions either as material or as resistance. Colleagues have sometimes agreed that it was indeed necessary to respond to this young man, but hasten to add that this was not analysis. The argument has been further elaborated that this patient is an example of a patient for whom analysis is contraindicated, although the reasoning is somewhat circular. Because we accept that the patient will not stay in treatment if we try to deal with him analytically, then he is not analyzable. However, this requires that we also accept as the *sine qua non* of analysis the confrontation of resistance and the consistent direction of the patient to focus on inner motivations. This would mean that any other approach is nonanalytic.

The latter are techniques that we consider compatible with the maintenance of a calm, nonjudgmental attitude, and with an adherence to the principle of psychic determinism. Still, the confrontation of resistance frequently has critical overtones; the implication is that the behavior constituting the resistance is devoid of unconscious components and that the patient can willingly give it up. Isn't there a subtle contradiction present when analysts exhort patients not to resist? Is the analyst not taking sides against the defensive components of the psyche and therefore committing a breach of analytic neutrality? Strict adherence to an intrapsychic focus emphasizes neutrality, but does neutrality sometimes imply indifference? If it does, then a technique that rigidly conforms to such a perspective may defeat its purpose, and perhaps undermine the treatment relationship.

As discussed in Chapter 6, the schizophrenic patient has to keep part of the therapist in the external world while incorporating another part in the omnipotently controlled transitional space. Something similar, I believe, happens with all patients, inasmuch as the analyst has to straddle two worlds, the inner world of the mind and external reality. This means that there is more to the analytic process than the exploration of id impulses. Classical analysts realize that analyzing defenses is equally important; in fact, it is indispensable before the therapy can reach down into the id.

I have already mentioned the many similarities between the analytic relationship and the mother–infant interaction, some of which I believe are relevant to techniques for the preservation of the analytic setting. I have also discussed Winnicott's postulation of two mothers: the object mother, who gratifies id needs, and the environment mother, who responds to what Winnicott called ego needs (Winnicott, 1963a). The latter provides ego-relatedness. Winnicott implicitly stresses that both these aspects of the maternal relationship are essential for psychic maturation.

When I responded to the adolescent patient's questions and shared his excitement, disruptive or otherwise, I believe I was behaving like the environment mother. This eventually created enough of a holding environment that we were able to explore the deeper levels of the patient's mind.

When treating patients suffering from severe psychopathology, interactions cannot be judged simply by their surface qualities. We cannot rely on phenomenology, because what may have an incontrovertible meaning to us may be perceived in an entirely different fashion by the patient. In the last chapter, I gave an example of another adolescent patient who viewed himself as having a normal body, when he was obviously thin to the extent of being emaciated. The fact that I responded to his questions and shared his distress did not necessarily lead to his experiencing me as managing his life, giving him guidance, or joining him in facing dilemmas. At the time, he was simply reacting without any cognitive awareness. Later in treatment he viewed my responses in terms of fluctuating levels of energy. He saw our relationship as exciting and characterized by an intensity and tempo he had never before experienced.

The analytic relationship is complex. Many of its aspects are contingent. The underlying theory and the goals of analysis are clear enough and, to some extent, immutable. The vehicles of therapy—interpretation within the context of the transference, and the unfolding of the repetition compulsion—also possess some constancy. Working through, the poorest understood of our technical concepts (see Chapter 8), is essential for the resolution of intrapsychic conflict and the acquisition of psychic structure. These concepts and processes have remained the foundations of analysis ever since Freud first described this form of therapy.

By contrast, the frequency and length of sessions and the use of the couch have throughout the years undergone some modifications. Also, what and when the analyst will interpret cannot be rigidly predetermined and may not be entirely dictated by psychopathology. What may be appropriate for one analyst may not be for another, because the transference–countertransference axis will be different in each relationship. Sometimes the interpretation of resistance will have a disastrous effect in a treatment relationship that may otherwise have continued unimpeded.

I regard the foregoing aspects of analysis as *secondary attributes* that are not applicable to all patients, whereas an intrapsychic focus, the repetition compulsion, and a transference resolution through interpretation are primary. The therapist has a certain degree of flexibility that is determined by the patient's characterological structure and unique infantile experiences. Every patient has a need for a particular tempo. With the emaciated adolescent patient, I had to increase my tempo to relate to his lowered one.

Summary and Conclusions

The phenomenon of resistance in patients suffering from character disorders is considerably more complex than what Freud described in patients he believed to be examples of hysterical neuroses. Patients such as I have described often find the treatment process menacing because (1) it threatens to undermine defensive adaptations that compensate for ego defects, or (2) it becomes associated with the infantile traumatic environment and reinforces it.

Freud's recommendations regarding the handling of resistance are simple and direct: Discover the resistance and forbid it. This method is far from effective, however, for patients suffering from structural defects.

Our main problem as psychoanalytic clinicians is to determine when to adapt ourselves to the manifestations of psychopathology that emerge as resistance in the treatment setting, and when not to alter the psychoanalytic setting to make such accommodations. I have given several examples in order to illustrate how the therapist may have to respond differently to superficially similar situations. In general, if the resistance is the expression of core psychopathology, that is, if it represents the manifestation of a defense against a fundamental ego defect, then to insist on certain formal attributes of the psychoanalytic procedure will be counterproductive. If, on the other hand, resistance is the outcome of superficial defenses that can be relinquished in treatment because the patient can continue to gain gratification by exercising them in the external world, then the analyst can insist on maintaining his analytic *modus operandi*. Perhaps he will lose the patient, but it is doubtful that he would have been able to analyze him even if he had made the concessions.

Schizoid patients who withdraw and need to maintain control may balk at using the couch. They view lying down as being in someone else's power, and so being exposed in their fundamental vulnerability and helplessness. Often, they have not reached a sufficient level of psychic integration to deal with the external world and the treatment setting symbolically. They cannot understand the difference between symbolic submission and the concrete act of lying down. Similarly, scheduled sessions, payment of fees, and other facets of the analytic interaction are interpreted as literal expressions of the therapist's destructiveness—the kind of destructiveness that dominated the infantile environment.

Narcissistic patients may need to be constantly replenished, and so equate analytic objectivity with relative rejection and deprivation. This, too, is the outcome of a concrete orientation, devoid of the capacity for symbolic elaboration. Similarly, vulnerable patients are afraid of being intruded on, assaulted, or engulfed in a destructive fusion. All these patients, because of their concreteness, cannot separate the current world of treatment from the infantile environment, and this inability may be manifested as objections to one or another aspect of analysis, such as lying on the couch or refusing to free associate. Another group of patients are similar, but rather than any special feature, they generally find the tempo of analysis incompatible with their needs. Often these are schizoid patients whose chief defense is withdrawal. This group is not confined to schizoid character types, however. It may include many types of character disorders.

Resistance in patients suffering from character disorders cannot be viewed, then, as though the patient were simply creating a tug-of-war and pulling away from analytic involvement. There are many subtle interactions involving the patient's character structure, ego defects, and the analytic procedure that must be explored before we resort to the pejorative use of the term "resistance." Countertransference remains an important vector in determining whether analysis between a particular analyst and patient is possible. Resistance, therefore, has to be studied in terms of both the patient's and the analyst's character orientations and reactions.

Chapter 8

Working Through:
A Technical Dilemma

The two most enigmatic words in psychoanalysis are "working through." In the previous chapter, I suggested that the meaning of "analytic neutrality" is generally assumed to be self-evident, but that we actually have various definitions of the concept. By contrast, every analyst can give a fairly standard definition of "working through" without really understanding the essence of the process. We all agree that it is the fundamental basis of care, but most of us are uneasy about the mechanisms—if any— involved. The problem is compounded by our experience with both obsessional and needy patients, who complain that, in spite of all the precious insights we have given them, they continue to feel miserable. Why don't they feel better? We have to tell them what to do so they can get some relief from their depressions, inhibitions, or phobias.

To protest that they have to *integrate* our interpretations and *work through* their problems would appear to have the elements of rote recitation, and the words seem trite and useless.

Still, most clinicians resort to such replies when they feel help-less, because they cannot be any more specific. We feel exasper-ated, and often, as a consequence, we tend to blame patients for not responding, for not getting any better. The fact that they know more about how their minds work then they did previous to treatment seems to make little difference with regard to their symptoms. Freud's emphasis that the purpose of psychoanalytic treatment is to make the unconscious conscious does not seem to be enough of an explanation to get at the essence of the analytic process.

Psychoanalysis began as an id-psychology. First by hypno-sis, then by free association and the interpretation of dreams, Freud explored the unconscious and discovered the mecha-nisms that characterized unconscious processes. As I have stressed, he began to understand the psyche as a conglomeration of conflicting intrapsychic forces. Thus, psychoanalysis became conceptualized as a battleground whereon the analyst sides with unconscious impulses against the repressive, inhibiting forces of the ego. Freud did not wish to encourage the acting out of id elements; he simply wanted patients to bring them into con-scious awareness.

Freud next paid attention to the obstacles the mind creates to thwart the therapeutic task of revealing the unconscious. In this context, he discovered resistance (see Chapter 7) and trans-ference, which he considered to be a resistance. In fact, when-ever patients halted their flow of associations, Freud (1912a) suspected that they were blocking some thoughts about their analysts. Similarly, Freud believed that the hostile, or negative, transference (Freud, 1912a) and the erotic transference (Freud, 1914a) could also act as deterrants to free association, which, in turn, would impede the capacity to work through inner conflicts and maladaptations.

Freud concluded that the deleterious effects of these trans-ference reactions were the result of the patient's having success-fully undermined the analyst's professional orientation. Patients diminished the therapist's influence and authority by casting him in another role and losing sight of him as a specialist and an expert. In the case of the erotic transference, for example, Freud believed that the patient accomplished this by trying to debase the therapist to the status of a lover. In the next chapter, on countertransference, I emphasize that one of the main obstacles to the achievement of therapeutic resolution is indeed when patients successfully disrupt the therapist's professional self-representation.

Thus, transference, besides being a vehicle of cure, can also work against the process of working through, and the fact that it works both ways is confusing. Nevertheless, clinicians are familiar with phenomena in treatment that confirm Freud's ideas about both the integrative and disruptive aspects of transference. Such phenomena are difficult to explain conceptually if we rely on a hydrodynamic conflict model alone. We require structural concepts to understand the more subtle elements of transference interactions as well as the various factors involved in therapeutic resolution. When dealing with patients suffering from primitive mental states, working through involves the acquisition of psychic structure and increased integrative capacities as well as the resolution of intrapsychic conflict.

Freud (1914d) reevaluated the analytic process when he introduced the concept of working through. Initially, he (Breuer & Freud, 1895) viewed treatment as being directed to the uncovering of trauma and the circumstances surrounding it, followed by abreaction. Catharsis and abreaction were the essential elements of the curative process.

In the *Studies on Hysteria* (1895), both Breuer and Freud understood the cause of neuroses to be traumas that had not been affectively experienced. If the ego is unprepared or in a state of dissociation, it cannot appropriately respond to a threatening situation; it encapsulates the trauma and does not produce the proper amount of anxiety that would be appropriate under those circumstances. The affect becomes "strangulated," and this leads to the production of symptoms. Initially, the therapeutic course was to bring about the production and discharge of anxiety that should have been felt in childhood when the trauma occurred.

This approach was gradually modified inasmuch as the analyst does not actively pursue traumatic events. In fact, the hypotheses dealing with the etiology of neuroses have also been modified; we now tend to think of a total traumatic environment rather than a dramatic traumatic event or the impact of a series of such events. Freud's psychodynamic orientation led to a focalized viewpoint of psychopathology. Trauma was walled off like an abscess, but the surrounding psychic structures were considered normal. Within the higher strata of the mental apparatus, controlling and inhibiting processes operated, and these manifested themselves in therapy as resistive. Freud (1914d) came to believe that the main therapeutic task consisted of interpreting resistance so that the patient could overcome it and remember past traumas.

At this time, Freud paid little attention to character structure, although he did not entirely ignore it (Freud, 1916). Resistance could be separated from the deeper layers that contained the core conflict. Later (Freud, 1923a), he viewed all aspects of the psyche as interconnected, and no single response or function could be considered in isolation or separated from the effects of psychopathology.

The beginning phases of the working-through process are very much involved with remembering. The understanding of psychopathology depends on lifting the childhood amnesia that surrounds traumatic constellations. This is an ultimate goal in treatment, and it often occurs by the analysis of screen memories. To some extent, abreaction has been pushed into the background. Recovery of lost memories has replaced the massive discharge of anxiety, although the two can occur simultaneously.

According to Freud, screen memories counterbalance childhood amnesia. What is essential from childhood is retained in these memories, and their analyses become a vital factor in therapeutic resolutions, or working through. The analysis of screen memories is analogous to the interpretation of dreams. Screen memories are like the manifest content of dreams, and the memories that are lost in the infantile amnesia are their latent content. Thus, the screen memory *covers* a more significant and traumatic memory. (*Deckerinnerung* is the German word for screen memory, which literally translated means "cover memory.") The purpose of treatment is to uncover.

Memories supposedly refer to actual events, but we often wonder how much is fact and how much is fantasy. In treatment we tend not to be concerned with determining what actually happened, but find the patient's fantasies extremely helpful in understanding how the mind functions or malfunctions. Freud referred to fantasies as internal acts that can be analyzed, in contrast to external acts that serve as barriers to analysis and working through. Fantasies are psychic products that are connected in some way to forgotten memories, which, by remaining buried, perpetuate the development of neurotic symptoms.

Freud's statements (1914d) have implications that go beyond a view of the analytic process as a struggle between remembering and active forgetting. He enigmatically states that during working through, something may be remembered that could never have been forgotten, because it was never conscious. The effects on the patient are the same, though, whether it has been forgotten or not. Freud does not elaborate further on these curious statements.

They can be understood, however, if we think in terms of psychic structure and developmental stages. The impact of the traumatic environment may have had its damaging effects before the psyche was sufficiently structuralized to form endopsychic registrations (memories, introjects, or mental representations) of the disruptive ambience. The level of ego organization is prementational and unable to structure percepts. To some extent, any patient who has suffered infantile trauma must have had experiences that he has not been able to integrate, because the psychological systems that would enable this integration have not yet developed. The effects of trauma are felt from the very beginning, although a trauma may be phase-specific and have its chief impact on a particular developmental phase or psychosexual stage. Even so, in the treatment of patients suffering from primitive mental states, we invariably recover or, better stated, we construct memories that were never part of the patient's experience in the sense that they were once subjectively perceived. Once resistance is overcome, however, the patient accepts them even though he cannot recall them.

Regarding other memories that *are* capable of being recalled, some patients convert them into actions, which are frequently directed toward the analyst. Freud states that the compulsion to repeat is the patient's way of remembering.

This implies that the repetition compulsion (a more direct translation of *Wiederholenzwang* than "compulsion to repeat") is in opposition to working through fundamental conflicts, although later Freud admits that it conjures up a "piece of real life" and can be useful for therapeutic purposes. Nevertheless, his general orientation is that, as much as possible, everything should be kept in the psychic sphere. Because the repetition compulsion expresses itself in actions toward the analyst, it has become imbricated into the transference. I surmise that this is another reason Freud considered transference a form of resistance, although he frequently stressed that it is the vehicle that is responsible for a successful therapeutic outcome.

Resistance, Working Through, and Acting Out

Apparently because of his concept of treatment as a battleground, a struggle between opposing forces, Freud saw a close connection between those elements that work against therapeutic purposes and those that work toward successful completion. Resistance and working through, when placed in the frame of reference of the transference, are closely linked together. As discussed in Chapter 7, resistance represents a point of view. From another perspective, it can be considered an essential ingredient of the working-through process. Notwithstanding the patient's anxiety about getting in touch with the primitive parts of his mind, and his fear and reluctance to relinquish psychopathological defensive adaptations, working through can be thought of as operating from the very beginning of treatment.

I am referring to a therapy in which the patient and analyst are aware of a desire to work with each other. Some initial interviews are totally chaotic, and may not progress to a regular schedule in an outpatient setting. In these instances, the regressive process may have become so completely out of control that the patient's immediate problem must be managed either through hospitalization and/or medication. In such cases, the question of working through is not in the foreground; rather, the treatment is aimed at maintaining structure, and at producing a structure-promoting environment.

Although working through leads to higher states of ego integration, and is also a structure-promoting experience, Freud did not emphasize this aspect of the process. As I have repeatedly mentioned, he was not thinking so much in terms of structure as he was about conflicting mental forces. Still, both structural organization and the resolution of conflict begin very early in the treatment relationship, and they are at first dependent mainly on the therapeutic alliance (Zetzel, 1956) or on the holding environment.

Usually patients have very little insight when they first enter a therapeutic relationship. They have generally sought treatment because they feel distressed, inasmuch as their usual adaptations are not functioning well enough for them to maintain psychic equilibrium, and they are aware only of their pain and misery—especially those patients who are fixated at primitive mental levels. The process of self-revelation, which begins with a recounting of the patient's circumstances, either in a structured history or in a casual spontaneous manner, changes the patient's focus from being immersed in and surrounded by distress to being a collaborative observer.

The act of reviewing past and present circumstances in the presence of a sympathetic, nonanxious listener is itself a structuralizing experience that opens the pathway to conflict resolution. The analytic setting encourages organization, even though it is also the vehicle that simultaneously allows regression and disorganization. For the moment, I will concentrate on synthesizing elements, because they are relevant to our understanding of working through. Though patients are encouraged to be spontaneous and not to structure their thoughts, the verbalization of feelings and the recall of memories and experiences do occur in a sufficiently coherent manner for the analyst to use his potential for understanding. Gradually, as patients keep free associating, the material develops certain repetitive patterns that the analyst can identify, though the patient will most likely be unaware of them.

In fact, many analyses consist of a seemingly endless repetition of the same theme. I have seen many patients, for example, who use every session to complain about their spouses, and this can go on for years without change either in the material or in the patient's attitude. What gradually evolves is a connection between these persistent current orientations and similar patterns in the past. Sometimes the behavioral pattern replicates a pattern of relationship that existed in the patient's family of origin—for example, the parent's marital relationship; in other instances, the patient is repeating a relationship that he or she had with some significant person in the infantile world. I will give examples of both instances, and then elaborate further on how a life adjustment based on the repetition compulsion manifests itself in the transference and how it is related to working through and acting out. It often seems uncanny how faithfully the present recapitulates the past. Regarding the adult replication of a past relationship, I will cite the example of women who are married to alcoholics. These patients complain vociferously about how they are mistreated, even beaten, by cruel and indifferent husbands, who may be irresponsible, poor providers, sadistic, and unfaithful. Yet the few I have seen in treatment did not leave their husbands. It is a common observation that such marriages generally endure. If the husband stops drinking and reforms, often the wife herself begins to drink, and sometimes she becomes an alcoholic (see Giovacchini, 1958a, 1969).

Frequently in such cases the parents of the wife have behaved in a way that is practically identical to the behavioral pattern of the patient and her husband. The patient's father has usually been a brutal alcoholic, and the mother has remained a long-suffering victim.

This general pattern is found in many patients, though not necessarily such obvious sadomasochistic constellations involving blatant brutality and sordidness. In an analytic practice, we frequently encounter affluent patients whose husbands are professional men or wealthy and respected businessmen, but with whom the marital relationship is every bit as miserable as the ones I have just described. Frequently, these women may be closet alcoholics or drug abusers, the latter involving moderate or large amounts of cocaine.

In analysis, the wife generally fills every session with a litany of her husband's indifference, inconsiderateness, and her rage at him for all the injustices he has heaped on her; but as a rule, she will not leave him. She rationalizes her staying with what she depicts as an impossible situation by believing that a bad relationship is better than no relationship. She concludes that this is a male-oriented world in which middle-aged or older men can skip through life with impunity, particularly if they are wealthy, because their wealth and charm make them attractive to many women, whereas middle-aged wives have lost their beauty and charm, and are dependent on their husbands for the financial advantages they enjoy, the material things staying married provides, as well as the opportunity to receive psychoanalytic treatment.

The treatment finally reaches a plateau, where the patient talks of nothing else but her need for enhancement, sometimes sexual, while the husband actively or passively pushes her into the background. This pattern invariably turns out to be a repetition of past family relationships. One of my patients was repeating, to an astonishing degree, the relationship her mother had with her father. The patient's father and her husband both came from humble, poverty-stricken backgrounds. Each had had a burning ambition for recognition and wealth, and was ruthless in his pursuit of success. Both achieved their purposes, but they were so relentless and singleminded that they totally neglected their families, and the raising of the children was left totally to their wives.

Even the composition of the families was identical. The patient and her mother each had four children, two older sons and two younger daughters in the same age sequence. The elder sons in both families had been diagnosed as schizophrenic, and both had been institutionalized on and off for long periods of time. The other children all had serious problems. Some were drug abusers and alcoholics, and those who were married were very unhappy with their spouses.

My patient had resolved that she would never lead the self-sacrificing humiliating life her mother had. She was never going to put up with a husband who ignored her and had innumerable extramarital affairs. Yet, now she found herself in exactly the same circumstances. The life she was leading was clearly a repetition of her parents' relationship and their family constellation. She had identified with her mother to the extent that the role she assumed determined her whole orientation toward the world. She was desperate and unhappy, but had never thought of leaving her husband; in fact, she offered the rationalizations just mentioned for not doing so. It was clear, however, that under no circumstances could she break loose and leave her husband. He frequently told her that there was nothing in the marriage for him, and that he would like her to leave; but he made no effort to get a divorce either. It was obvious that they were tied to each other by constricting and neurotic bonds.

In the last decade, I have seen more and more patients similar to this one. These marriages sometimes end in divorce after 20 to 30 years, usually because the husband leaves, and he generally gets married again, often to a much younger woman. As I mentioned earlier, however, many such marriages do endure, and when a spouse (in my experience, usually the wife) is studied from a psychoanalytic perspective, the all-pervasive marital relationship can be understood as a manifestation of the repetition compulsion. My patient was repeating the traumatic constellation of her parents' marriage, and in her relationship with her husband was identifying with her mother's masochistic position.

I do not believe that it is unique to my practice that most of the patients I have seen with unhappy marriages are wives. Their husbands apparently seek their self-esteem in their professional or business successes, in the recognition they receive from their colleagues, and in extramarital relationships. Undoubtedly, at some level, these men need their wives, but the latter are so needy and vulnerable that the husbands do not have to acknowledge their own dependence or feel threatened in their sense of security. They are content to maintain the status quo, and the most they seem to want is to be left alone. Another patient, similar to the one just described, spoke for many years about nothing except how her husband mistreated her. To some extent, she was also reliving some aspects of her parents' marriage, but she was not as totally identified with her mother as the other patient. She was reliving an infantile relationship in the present with her husband, a relationship in which to be defeated and frustrated was inevitable. The frustration she suffered, however, had almost completely incapacitated her.

I first saw her when she was in her early forties. Oddly enough, she was feeling off-balance emotionally as her material circumstances substantially improved. For years, she and her family had lived almost at a povery level. Her artist husband could not at that time make a living from his work, and the wife had to take a job in order to make ends meet. She reviled and denigrated him for not meeting his responsibility to support the family. Apparently to console himself, the husband drank to excess, causing his wife to heap more abuse on him. He seems to have accepted her violent contempt and deprecations calmly and passively.

Several months before I saw her, the husband won a prize for his work, and he became immensely popular with his colleagues and particular segments of the public. His works sold, and he became important and wealthy. Along with his status, there was a dramatic personality change. He became aggressive, demanding, and autocratic. When his wife attempted to overshadow him with her domineering demands and insulting attacks, he retaliated by physically assaulting her and replying with long strings of obscenities. This was an astounding turnabout that completely overwhelmed the wife, and her personality also underwent a change: Her usual aggressiveness was now replaced by timidity, fearfulness, and vulnerability. She became increasingly vulnerable to the degree that she found it exhausting to carry out the simplest and most pedestrian tasks.

The first three years of her analysis were concerned with how important her husband was for the maintenance of her self-esteem. She needed his attention and solicitude, and he would not give them to her. Instead, he took lengthy trips away from home, and gave ample evidence that he was having affairs with other women. She was devastated by each of his transgressions, and would scream and moan during many sessions about how unfairly she was being treated.

I understood that her chaotic behavior was not confined to my consultation room. At home, she acted as if she were a terrified, wounded animal, easily startled by noises, and frightened of her shadow. She might lie in bed for days, because she felt her body was wracked with arthritic pains and she could not

move around. Physically, she was sound, and some of her asser-
tions and bodily concerns, at times, appeared psychotic. In
general, however, she was realistically oriented, and showed no
evidence of a thought disorder. Her inner disruption had overwhelmed her and rendered her unable to function.

She saw herself as emotionally paralyzed, and when she
was most regressed, it was difficult to make any sense out of
what she said. This was partially due to the fact that she cried so
loudly and screamed so much that she was incoherent. From the
first time I saw her, I was impressed by her capacity to regress,
and how needy and demanding she could be. Nevertheless, I
had a sense that in spite of her distress, she was a moderately
competent person who could, if need be, take care of herself.
Though she pleaded with me to take care of her and to hospitalize her, I did not feel any compunction to treat her on any basis
other than as an outpatient. In other words, I did not believe I
was witnessing psychic disintegration; rather, I believed that she
was demonstrating a state of deep regression, but one that was
repeating some very important interactions of her infantile past.
My opinion was based on her occasional displays of resiliency.
During a session or at the end of a session, she might pull herself
together and discuss a reality issue, such as our schedule, in a
calm and logical fashion.

As with the other patient I discussed, her parents' marriage
was remarkably similar to her own; however, her regressive
behavior could also be traced back to her relationship with her
father, who, similar to her husband, had been a failure and an
alcoholic, and then became wealthy. Unlike her husband, however, the father had inherited his money, not earned it through
the use of his talents. He was handsome and charming, but irresponsible. He was also seductive toward his daughter, prom-
ising her everything she wanted, but never keeping his word,
and spending very little time with her. She begged him to pay
attention to her, and although he always assured her that he
would, he never did. She recalled his not showing up for her
birthday parties and innumerable other disappointments. She
often responded by having temper tantrums.

In college and after graduation, she had a series of affairs
with narcissistic men who seem to have had more than a trace of

sociopathy. Similar to her father, they were grandiose in what they promised her, building up her hopes and expectations only to dash them to the ground. She never learned from any of these crushingly disappointing experiences.

Clearly, in treatment, she was repeating through her husband the frustrating experience she had with her father. She was reenacting for me an infantile attitude, and was reliving the frustration she felt then. She was also creating a similar situation with me, which could be understood as an important manifestation of the transference. She accused me of not loving her, of being unable to save her, and of not wanting to take care of her. At the same time, she would reassure me that I was the only person in the world who really understood her. Both patients were revealing significant aspects of the development of their psychopathology. They displayed their equilibrium and their adaptive modes in their complaining and behavior. Before treatment, their daily life was chaotic and confusing and lacked organization. After starting therapy, both women became more consistent in their behavior, even though they were disruptive. As the transference developed, the repetition of the infantile environment became strikingly clear. In one instance, the dominant theme was identification with the mother and all the attendant circumstances. The second patient was presenting her infantile self with little modification or disguise.

Although both patients were disruptive and, at times, capable of evoking disturbing countertransference reactions, they were eventually easy to understand. I could distinguish between the content and affect they produced, and the structure of their material. This point in the therapy could be considered the beginning phase of the working-through process, one that has to be experienced both to set the process in motion and to provide the analyst with a basis of understanding, which is vital for analytic resolution. Both the patients' material and the analyst's responses are essential ingredients of the curative elements of analysis.

Thus, working through is not a phenomenon that is confined only to the patient. It is the outcome of an interaction between patient and analyst. The patient produces material, and the therapist processes it. It is understood from the vantage point of a higher psychic level, and as the patient integrates the analyst's interpretations, there are various shifts of psychic organization that affect the course of further material. Working through requires the analyst's participation. The acquisition of insight leads to patients expressing themselves more clearly, and the connection between the past and current transference attitudes and reactions becomes easier to understand. The repetition compulsion crystallizes, so to speak, preparing patients for its resolution as the analyst gains an increasing grasp of its significance.

Through transference projections, the analyst is equated with important persons of the patient's past. He has a definite role assigned to him within the framework of the repetition compulsion. He has to accept that role and yet, at the same time, not participate to the extent that the patient demands. This can become a delicate situation that may enhance or hinder the working-through process.

Valenstein (1983) discusses several categories of psychic functioning dealing with sensory and motor responses. According to him, working through involves the action system. This means that insights, as they lead to higher levels of psychic integration, also lead to alterations in the action system, which may change some behavioral patterns. Within treatment, however, patients' behavioral patterns may change in a way that is disruptive to the working-through process.

Reality-adapted behavioral change is equated with working through, whereas acting out is usually thought of as resistance. I have often described acting out in terms of countertransference, that is, as behavior that the analyst cannot stand. Distinctions are difficult to make, however, between behavior that is associated with the working-through process and behavior associated with acting out, and they are not necessarily absolute. These processes all involve the action system, as described by Valenstein (1983), but their significance for the analytic interaction cannot be evaluated simply on the basis of furthering or blocking progress. There are elements that work both ways, and, as mentioned, to a large measure, their effects are determined by the analyst's responses.

The analytic setting causes the patient's material to structuralize itself so that definite patterns emerge. These patterns organize themselves under pressure of the repetition compulsion, and the analytic setting acts as a catalyst for the promotion of this sequence. The analyst often reacts, as a result of evoked countertransference, by developing feelings toward the patient that are consistent with the role that has been assigned to him. If the therapist's feelings overwhelm analytic objectivity, then the treatment relationship faces an impasse. Under these circumstances, patients are usually accused of acting out, and as Freud (1914d) stated, actions have to be converted into memories. To do so might require that patients suppress certain types of behavior, which would necessitate that analyses be conducted in a state of abstinence. Still, as Freud admitted, if some actions can be valuable because they bring a "piece of real life" into treatment, then when do analysts have to impose prohibitions? What determines which actions will be beneficial or harmful?

Perhaps these questions were easier to answer when Freud wrote his papers on technique and working through, because he was formulating guidelines on the basis of the psychodynamic discharge hypothesis. The prohibitions Freud insisted on consisted of not gratifying certain id impulses. In some instances he told patients to abstain in a literal sense, demanding that patients curb their sexual activities; in one instance he forbade masturbation. He also told his patients not to make important decisions, such as changing jobs or getting married. Apparently he believed that inhibitions were released by analyzing them, so that patients had to be careful not to act out underlying impulses and make choices they would later regret. The id had to be held in check, and to some extent, the activities of living had to be suspended during analysis. It must be remembered, however, that in those days analyses lasted a matter of months rather than years, as is the current situation.

Giving in to certain instinctual impulses by seeking to gratify them could be considered acting out, but what kinds of behavior are not forms of acting out? These would be complex action units that include many facets of the psyche with integrative and executive ego systems operating in a judicial, superego-controlled, reality-adapted fashion. Of course, id impulses are also operating in such behaviors, but relatively speaking, they are not as directly expressed as they are in acting out. Neverthe-less, in spite of secondary-process taming, primary-process ele-ments may erupt as the repetition compulsion gains momentum and brings the past into the present transference context. Thus, the distinction between acting out and the development of the transference under sway of the repetition compulsion is far from clearcut in the treatment interaction.

Survival of the Analytic Setting

I have emphasized that working through has to be examined in terms of an interaction between therapist and patient rather than a task that is performed solely by the patient. The analyst has to convert what in some circles is considered resistance and self-destructive acting out into a reenactment and then a resolu-tion of the repetition compulsion. For the most part, this is not a question of forbidding certain behaviors; rather, the analyst tries to use what the patient brings to enhance the working-through process. Of course, there are certain outlandish actions that would be destructive to any treatment relationship, and these have to be controlled from the beginning. I will discuss these situations in the next chapter. Aside from extremes of destruc-tive behavior, however, most of the material and some actions produced by patients can be helpful both to further understand-ing and to the achievement of higher levels of ego integration.

Even if some anticipated actions are prohibited, they have to be expressed to some degree, and the analyst has to respond to them; but to allow potentially destructive actions might lead to the disruption of the analytic setting. For example, when patients want to cut down on the frequency of their appoint-ments, the rationalizations usually offered are lack of money or time and commitments that make scheduling difficult or impos-sible. These can be significant reality factors and have to be weighed, but the consequences for treatment, even eliminating only one appointment a week, also have to be evaluated.

In the previous chapter, I stressed that certain elements of analysis, such as lying on the couch and the frequency of ap-pointments, are secondary factors. Once a schedule is agreed on, however, changes assume a significance that often goes beyond the change itself. The patient may be responding to the pressure of the repetition compulsion or using certain defensive adaptations that were constructed initially as protection against infantile traumas. In analysis, these defenses erect barriers against affective involvement with the therapist, and maintain distance so that primitive transference anxieties are avoided. True, the patient is displaying a vital adaptive segment of the psyche, but by manipulating the schedule, avoids bringing it into treatment and experiencing its full impact.

A colleague consulted me about a patient who wanted to cut down from a four-times-a-week schedule to three times a week. At first, this did not seem to make much difference, especially because this patient was, in fact, having financial difficulties that seemed to be out of his control. My colleague's dilemma was that he felt very strongly that changing the schedule was the wrong thing to do, but he also had some apprehension that the patient might terminate treatment if he insisted on continuing the four sessions a week.

The patient's infantile background had been chaotic and unpredictable, and he had frequently reacted to his inner disruption by having temper tantrums that would compete with the affective explosions surrounding him. He would outscream and outshout his parents and siblings, commanding attention and silencing them, often instantaneously. Then he would contemptuously isolate himself and sulk while his family apparently felt some remorse. In a modified way the patient had repeated this sequence in my colleague's office.

As the patient free associated, he was able to cathect disturbing introjects. This process manifested itself by the man's working himself into a frenzy, pacing around the office, and screaming at his analyst to "shut up and listen," and hurling obscenities and insults at him. Such outbursts had frequently led to his leaving the session before the time was up. At times, the analyst felt both confused and guilty. When the patient suggested that they meet only three times a week, the therapist was first inclined to agree because he wanted some relief, but he was also upset about changing their routine. He believed that such a change would destroy the analytic setting.

In general, a clinician would not be concerned about cutting back just one session a week, especially if the patient had financial problems; but neither my colleague nor I considered the proposed change to be a wise move in this case. Although we did not understand what was going on as well as we would have liked, we felt strongly—and my colleague especially so—that changing the frequency of appointments would disturb the tempo of the analysis and that it might not survive. The problem was that the analysis also might not survive if the analyst remained adamant.

Nevertheless, my colleague told the patient that he believed it was vital for the analysis that they continue on a four-times-a-week basis. Although one appointment more or one less, by itself, did not seem to be a major issue, he said, in view of the patient's background and need to devalue what could be potentially valuable, it was best that his feelings remain in the treatment rather than be avoided by his missing a weekly session. To the analyst's surprise—and mine later—the patient simply smiled and said "Fine," and continued the interview by pleasantly associating for the next few minutes. Then he burst out, screaming, shouting, and insulting for the remainder of his time.

We were surprised by his sanguine response, because our mood had become grim as we felt pushed to the edge of brinkmanship. The patient had survived his childhood by brinkmanship, having to be crazier and angrier than his surroundings or psychically perish. In treatment, on the other hand, he was pleased that his analyst did not allow him to withdraw, even if that withdrawal were more symbolic than real. Still, it was real enough, and in view of the patient's background, it would have constituted a form of therapeutically self-defeating and defeating acting out.

The therapist had been prepared to terminate treatment if the patient would not accept his imposed conditions, believing that he would at least be preserving the analytic setting for the patient to return to. Fortunately, this was not necessary. Instead, the patient indicated that he was pleased by the analyst's firmness and constancy, and sufficiently secure in such a setting that he could express the intensity of his feelings, knowing that they would neither destroy him nor his therapist. The survival of the analytic setting enhanced the working-through process.

Up to that point, the patient had been relating to his analyst on the basis of the repetition compulsion, a present-day complex of behavior that fairly accurately recapitulated the sequence of events and traumas that characterized the infantile environment. To a minor extent, the analyst was participating, in that his countertransference consisted of confusion and guilt. We can all empathize with confusion, because the patient's erratic behavior was intrinsically confusing; but it was his unconscious intent to confuse and to make others feel guilty as he had done with his family. Inasmuch as the patient succeeded in getting his analyst to have these feelings, therefore, he was infusing the consultation room with an almost pure form of the repetition compulsion. By reducing the number of his interviews, he was solidifying it further, and by that time, we could say that it was being expressed beyond the scope of therapeutic usefulness.

I believe this clinical example is especially instructive because it helps to delineate the boundaries between acting out and working through, and it highlights the analyst's participation in converting one into the other. If the patient relates to the therapist and to other persons in his world on the basis of the same anxieties and vulnerabilities he felt toward the archaic objects of the infantile world and uses the same adaptive defenses developed in the past, his behavior can be defined as acting out. The therapist's interventions, usually directed toward maintaining the analytic setting, introduce variables that did not previously exist, and demonstrate to the patient, either implicitly or explicitly, that his ancient fears are no longer warranted in the present context, and that his constricting adaptive defenses are outmoded methods of coping.

In previous publications (Giovacchini, 1984; Giovacchini & Boyer, 1975), I divided the analytic setting into two components, the analyst as a transference figure and the analytic ambience. Patients project instinctual impulses, feelings, and parts of the self into their analysts, and this constitutes transference. They also attempt to transform the analytic setting into a replica of the traumatic infantile environment, a process I have called externalization. This is another way of viewing the development of the repetition compulsion within the treatment frame, and analysts have to react in a fashion that furthers the working-through process. They make themselves available for transference projections, but they do not allow the patient to disrupt the analytic setting by infusing it with the infantile environment. This does not mean that they participate by accepting the roles that patients project into them. I simply mean that they do not try to stop or block them. If they were to behave according to the role that has been assigned to them, they would be colluding in the conversion of the analytic setting into a chaotic infantile setting.

My colleague, by insisting on the frequency and regularity of the analytic schedule, did not participate in the patient's attempts to relate to him as if he were a member of the patient's past surroundings. We have concluded that this prevented the treatment from being sabotaged. The patient was not able to destroy the analytic setting by replacing it with the infantile ambience.

The distinctions I have drawn between the infantile ambience and transference projections would indicate that the therapist did not allow the patient to externalize. On the other hand, he was able to continue relating to the analyst as an imago from the infantile past. Perhaps my colleague's maintenance of the analytic setting contributed to the fostering of transference projections.

All patients in some manner or another, attempt to externalize. One of my patients, a middle-aged, highly successful businessman, tried to bring the past environment into the consultation room in a subtle, hidden fashion. I mean hidden in the sense that the attempt did not involve the manipulation of what I have called the secondary attributes of the analytic process, such as trying to change the frequency of appointments. My patient was born in a ghetto in which violence and strife predominated. Because he was physically strong, shrewd, and intelligent, he became the leader of the ruling gang, and he was feared and respected in the community. At the same time, he did well in school and was able, through scholarships, to get a college and postgraduate education.

I have discussed this patient in some detail elsewhere (Giovacchini, 1979). Here, I simply wish to stress that he was enormously successful in business and had amassed a sizable fortune. The same technique—aggressivity, combativeness, and shrewdness—that permitted him to survive comfortably in the ghetto served him well in the jungle of the business world. He sought psychoanalytic treatment because he had recently had a fairly severe heart attack, and his doctor told him he would have to distance himself from the stress of the daily battles he was fighting if he wanted to live. The patient felt distressed at the prospect of giving up his *modus vivendi*. He was experiencing periodic waves of anxiety and, for the first time in his life, felt profoundly depressed.

During the initial stages of treatment, he presented himself as the personable, well-bred, highly educated person he was. He was considerate, polite, and courteous. Gradually, however, his demeanor and mode of relating changed; his language became coarse, and his mood was generally angry and belligerent. The atmosphere in my office was tense and electric, and I felt the man had a perpetual chip on his shoulder. I found myself beset with strong urges to reply in kind when he attacked me and psychoanalysis. He wanted me to help him make decisions, and become a sufficient influence in his everyday life. I then recognized that he was attempting to manipulate me, but because he was crude and insulting in his approach, I felt that he was trying to make the consultation room into a ghetto.

His life had become a series of crises, and he covertly blamed me for them. At least that is the way I felt. For example, a business associate had refused to live up to an important commitment, a default that represented a sizable financial burden for the patient. He felt that he had been taken advantage of, and he wanted to use me as a sounding board; but, as usually happened in such situations, he was not satisfied with my response. In a slightly paranoid manner, he believed that I was always siding against him, and, to some extent, this was true, because I felt somewhat irritated when he presented me with such material.

The patient was trying to use me as a lawyer, a financial consultant, and an accountant, presenting me with dilemmas in these areas and implicitly expecting me to bail him out. He filled his sessions with these everyday tumultuous situations, and avoided taking any responsibility for what was happening in his world. He seemed to have lost all appreciation of the concept of psychic determinism. He wanted me as an ally rather than as an analyst, and he was angry because I was not cooperating with him the way he thought I should.

I eventually realized that it made no difference whether I cooperated with him or fought back so I would not be manipulated; either way drew me further into the combative world he was trying to create in my consultation room. If I cooperated, I would be siding with him in a battle against his enemies. I could become an officer member in his gang. If I resisted his efforts, I would be fighting him directly. In either case, I would be getting involved in an aspect of his past life and participating in the repetition compulsion. He was making it very difficult for me to remain in an analytic frame of reference.

I gradually began to feel the distinction between what he was projecting and what he was externalizing. By projection, he had assigned me the role of disappointing caretaker. As he had with his father, he was trying to create an imago of me as a person who would care for and protect him, so that he could feel let down when I was unable to do so. To maintain his projection, however, he needed an environment that would support it, one in which he could attempt to construct an idealized imago and then, because of my ineptness, feel let down. This externalization could occur only if I responded to the content of his material. As mentioned, it did not matter how, either positively or negatively, for as long as I let his expectations dictate my responses, I was letting the ghetto of his past assume a tangible presence and, thus, destroy the analytic ambience.

Projection is facilitated by analytic neutrality, that is, neutrality as I have discussed in Chapter 7; whereas externalization requires some involvement by the analyst. The infantile environment invades and replaces the analytic ambience and destroys the holding environment. The patient may succeed in producing some security for himself, especially if the therapist sides with him; but this is a false or pseudo-holding environment, because it is supported by defensive infantile adaptations. There is only an illusion of security, which the analyst cannot keep fostering if he is to remain an analyst.

With my patient, once I realized what was happening, I simply stopped responding to the content of his material, and did not try to defend or justify myself. He became very angry, and accused me of not caring. At the same time, his tension mounted to the extent that he demanded hospitalization. I refused to hospitalize him, and emphasized that we had to deal with his feelings in the context of the current failure of past adaptations. I was very active interpretatively, but I did not waiver in my resolve to maintain our daily appointments. Although the patient protested, he derived considerable security from my not putting him in the hospital and felt reassured and supported by my implicit belief that he could regress considerably, and yet be able to retain sufficient control that he could continue functioning without being institutionalized. He was able later in analysis to tell me about these feelings and responses.

Not permitting the patient to sabotage the analysis by externalization is different from the corrective emotional experience (Alexander, 1961) although there may be some superficial resemblance. In the corrective emotional experience, the analyst responds and behaves in a manner contrary to the patient's transference expectations. This is done in an active, deliberate fashion and assumes the proportions of role-playing. The response to externalization also involves not conforming to infantile wishes, but this is accomplished by the analyst's refusal to abandon the analytic orientation and to disrupt the treatment setting. This prevents the patient from derailing the working-through process as the repetition compulsion reenacts the traumatic past; it can be understood rather than acted on.

The preservation of the analytic setting as an essential feature of working through means that the analyst has to survive the patient's attempts to convert the analytic setting into the infantile world. The therapist has to maintain an analytic integration that represents a particular high level of psychic functioning. To relinquish professional identity represents a regression, because whatever role the therapist adopts is the outcome of infantile projections. Granted, in order to be sensitive to their patients' needs, analysts permit themselves a certain degree of regression, but this is a controlled regression that operates simultaneously with the analytic *modus operandi*. In spite of the regression the therapist does not abandon his professional identity.

Survival of the Patient

In some instances, regressions may be harmful to the patient. The patient's regression may be so intense and deep that it gets out of control, and the holding environment aspects of the analytic setting may not be sufficient to maintain the minimal integration that is required for the promulgation of the working-through process. The patient may be overwhelmed by the impact of infantile trauma and vulnerability, and for many years psychoanalysts have cautioned against accepting patients for treatment whose egos are believed too fragile to withstand analytic regression. Again, we have to evaluate the extent of the therapist's contribution in determining whether a regression will be manageable or unmanageable.

A young, single man in his middle twenties sought treatment to enhance his professional training as well as to overcome a propensity to feel anxious in social situations and when performing before his teachers. He believed that analysis would give him psychic strength and enable him to no longer feel vulnerable. He had great hopes as to how much he would gain from the treatment situation and particularly from his association with me.

Clearly, he had idealized me and felt that working with me would lead to mastery and control. His fantasies and dreams indicated that what we were to accomplish bordered on grandiosity and megalomania. On the surface, he demonstrated complete trust and confidence in the therapeutic setting as he became increasingly convinced of our invulnerability.

I viewed his developing orientation as a defensive adaptation and had decided to make some gentle inroads into it by an occasional interpretation. Before I could, however, his underlying vulnerability emerged. At first he began experiencing mild episodes of dizziness as he got up from the couch at the end of the session. Moving from the analytic world into the external world upset both his psychic and physical equilibrium (Giovacchini 1958b). His difficulty in making this transition intensified to the point where he had to hold onto the edge of the couch to keep from falling. Finally, he would grope his way to the waiting room, where he would sit for 10 to 15 minutes until he felt sufficiently composed to leave. He referred to this interlude as decompression, my waiting room being the decompression chamber.

In the consultation room, his regression gradually intensified. He began experiencing waves of anxiety that often reached panic-like proportions. At times, he tried to reassure both himself and me by emphasizing that his faith in analysis had permitted him to put himself so completely in my hands, to give up his defensive compensations, and to reveal his feelings of childish helplessness. As his anxiety continued mounting, however, he began having doubts about the protective powers of the therapeutic relationship. He would lie on the couch trembling, repeating in a low, tremulous voice, "I am so afraid, I can't stand it."

I had expected that this patient, who had such a marked tendency to idealize, might get in touch with his underlying feelings of vulnerability, but I was not prepared to see him overwhelmed by them. The working-through process had been set in motion as he gradually relinquished his narcissistic defenses, but instead of the regression moving in the direction of integration, because of its intensity, it became a disruptive phenomenon leading to a breakdown of psychic cohesiveness. The analysis was floundering, because it seemed as if the patient could not survive the regression.

I found it hard to understand that his bringing infantile feelings into analysis should have such a devastating effect, and that he did not retain integrative islands of secondary-process functioning to protect against the onslaught of infantile feelings of helplessness. Regression is an inherent aspect of the therapeutic process, and working through includes regressed ego states within its framework. Both integrative higher-level secondary-process operating ego systems and primitive, early developmental phases are part of the working-through process. My patient did not seem able to strike a balance between second-ary- and primary-process functioning, and he felt inundated and overwhelmed by the latter. Was there something unique about his psychopathology that made him unanalyzable?

In the past I have repeatedly emphasized that although many patients are not suitable for analysis, judgments about treatment should not be made on the basis of psychopathology alone (Giovacchini, 1979b, 1984). The "fit" between patient and therapist is a crucial factor as well as the specific countertrans-ference feelings that are evoked. I gave much thought to this patient concerning whether his idealization of the analytic rela-tionship, and his idealization of me in particular, had any special relevance to the period of vulnerability that followed. I also recalled how pleasurable it had been to have the patient's com-plete confidence and trust, and how disturbing it was to see him in such a distraught state.

I finally realized that because he had so anticipated the inevitable successful outcome of treatment, an enthusiasm that he had projected into me, I had overlooked how really emotion-ally disturbed this patient was. I had absorbed his projections and his idealized self, without examining them as projections, and without evaluating their significance as defensive adapta-tions. I had become part of his false-self organization, represent-ing a person and an ambience for the patient that complied with his needs to be protected against his underlying vulnerability. The setting was so designed that instead of analyzing helpless-ness and vulnerability and the infantile traumas associated with such feelings, I was helping the patient deny their existence. We had created pseudo-strength.

This false-self type of security, however, cannot endure, because it has no solid supportive foundation. It leads nowhere, and completely sidesteps the working-through process, which itself contributes to the holding environment and enhances self-esteem and security. False-self security exists in a vacuum and is very fragile. If a person is starving to death and fantasizes or hallucinates eating a sumptuous meal, he may be helped tem-porarily, but the images do not furnish sustenance. Similarly, my patient discovered that idealization alone does not provide security. Yet, he was not disappointed in me, as might have been expected when the object of idealization fails to supply the anticipated omnipotence. He was not sufficiently object-directed to even blame me for his painful regressed state of help-lessness.

I thought if I could assign some purpose to the patient's disruptive and chaotic reactions, within a transference context, that it might help him to achieve some psychic organization, which could then be directed to examine his reactions instead of just simply reacting. I pointed out the obvious—that he needed to reveal the infantile parts of himself to me, and later I added that because I had failed to appreciate the extent of their power, he had been obliged to show them to me in a dramatic and intense fashion. This sufficed to make his regression manageable, and he was now able to talk about his feelings rather than to lose control of them.

There were, of course, many subtle factors in our relation-ship, and I am emphasizing only one aspect, because it helped the patient to regain his self-observing function (Sterba, 1934). It also helped him to reestablish the working-through process, which can now be schematically defined as a combination of a regressed ego state and a higher-level, self-observing function; these constitute a setting in which the repetition compulsion reenacts the infantile traumatic scenario.

As the analysis continued, the patient presented considera-ble material indicating how much he had idealized his father, only to find at the age of five that he had "feet of clay." This occurred when he was able to measure him alongside the fathers of his playmates in kindergarten. Also his mother, for reasons of her own, began to depreciate her husband for his crude manners and intellectual ineptness, in spite of the fact that he had been highly successful financially, and was a good and generous pro-vider. Our early relationship in analysis could now be fit into a pattern that had repeated itself many times throughout the years.

The process of working through had not been set in motion at the beginning of treatment, because my countertransference reaction had been an impediment to my understanding how emotionally disturbed the patient was. I was basking with him in the glow of idealization, and lost sight of the adaptive significance of his transference projections. They were no longer the manifestations of various facets of the repetition compulsion. Rather, they were overblown, megalomanically oriented survival techniques. As long as I participated in the construction of such techniques by not viewing them analytically, but accepting them as positive, supportive forces much as I would a good therapeutic alliance (Zetzel, 1956), I was creating a therapeutic impasse. I was also making it difficult for the patient to experience his past as past in the current setting, and to experience even some of his immediate disruptive reactions in the context of the repetition compulsion.

Regressive disruptive reactions that threaten the patient's capacity to survive as a patient can be viewed in terms of their adaptive significance, such as this patient's need to reveal dramatically how vulnerable he felt. It is doubtful, however, that the latter had such a communicative purpose from the very beginning. On the surface, his reactions appeared to be purely disruptive and disintegrative processes. As he was able to survive them and with the help of interpretations, however, the patient was able to elevate those reactions to a level of higher integration, give them meaning, and fit them into the context of the repetition compulsion.

Survival of the Therapist

Some patients, fixated at primitive mental states and suffering from severe psychopathology, bring so much rage into the treatment that the relationship seems to be enveloped in total chaos. Patients may attack and revile their analysts to such an intense degree that they render them ineffective. They are intent on destroying their therapists, and, in fantasy, they believe they have. Therefore, whatever the analyst does or says is meaningless, and this furthers the conviction that the therapist has been destroyed, at least in a functional sense. The patient has made the treatment worthless.

On the other hand, if the analyst does not react to the situation as though it were intolerable, the patient often continues to keep appointments, and in subtle ways indicates respect for the treatment. Patients may be courteous and polite at the beginning and end of the session, even though they heap all sorts of abuse during the interview. Basically, they want their therapist to survive their destructiveness. This is another example of a situation in which clinical material can reach such levels of intensity that what might have been an unfolding of the repetition compulsion and an instigation of the working-through process becomes a disintegrative, nonprotective, regressive experience. This time, however, it is the intensity of the therapist's feelings that has been disruptive. If the analyst can survive the patient's attacks, then something valuable may be accomplished within the therapeutic framework.

Clinicians are familiar with this group of patients, and the interaction is usually understood in terms of the patient's need to project hated parts of himself into the analyst. Frequently they refer to getting rid of their garbage, using the analyst as a garbage-disposal unit. I recall a patient who spent many months on the couch just reciting a series of nonsense words. Sometimes he arranged them in quatrains with a musical cadence, but they had absolutely no discernible verbal meaning. This was garbage material that he left behind in my consultation room. Though unpleasant, analysts recognize that the patient's projections develop important transference meanings and are required for analytic progress.

This type of clinical interaction can be explored from a somewhat different, although related, structural perspective, which will make clear some of the spatial qualities of the working-through process. I believe that Winnicott's (1969) ideas about the use of an object provide us with a valuable conceptual framework. As I reviewed in the previous section, Winnicott divided psychic space into three areas, the space of the inner world of the mind, the transitional space, and the space of the external world. He postulated that once an object moves into the external world, the infant's psyche has lost omnipotent control of that object. It survives apart from the psyche, and has an existence of its own. Because it has moved outside the transitional space, however, for the child, it ceases to exist.

I mentioned that Winnicott's idea was that the infant wanted to kill the object for leaving the sphere of omnipotent control. The child had to kill the external object in order to be able to find it again. It had to survive destructive rage. Winnicott believed that this sequence was an important aspect of normal development by which the infant achieves individuation and distinguishes between the internal and external world.

As I have stated, it is difficult to accept that in order for the psyche to differentiate, the child must feel that he has destroyed significant emotionally important persons in the infantile environment. It is not difficult, however, to discover murderous feelings motivated by the loss of an object in patients suffering from relatively severe forms of psychopathology. The group of patients I have been discussing are an excellent example of emotional problems that test the therapist's capacity to survive to the utmost, and such patients, of course, are impelled to act the way they do because of psychopathology.

Thus, in many instances, the chief element responsible for therapeutic progress is the analyst's ability to survive in the face of the patient's need to try to destroy him. Patients' outbursts have often been interpreted as a test to determine whether the therapist is strong enough to withstand their onslaughts; they need to build a foundation of trust to weather the turmoil that has to surface later. This idea is compatible with Winnicott's assertion that the external object has to be destroyed and yet survive so that it can be found. Does the object have to be destroyed, however, as evidenced by that object's, or the analyst's, reaction, or simply in the mind of the child, or patient? Certainly, the patients I am discussing have stored immense amounts of hatred within themselves, and they have to reenact early experiences of abandonment. They create situations in treatment that reproduce moments of helplessness and vulnerability, but at the same time, they also introduce protective defensive adaptations that were acquired during later stages of development. These involve control and megalomanic manipulation as well as a reversal of roles in which the external object is vulnerable. In treatment, they are demonstrating their need to maintain control. Loss of control is usually associated with murderous feelings; by trying to destroy the analyst, they are giving such feelings a target, and in a perverse way, they are regaining control.

Working through for these and other patients suffering from characterological defects, rather than the resolution of intrapsychic conflicts, mainly involves the acquisition of psychic structure and integration. As they destroy their analysts by allowing them to be part of the external world rather than perceiving them in the transitional space, they are forming stronger and better-differentiated ego boundaries. If not marred by disruptive countertransference reactions, the patient's attempts to destroy the therapist can be an essential aspect of the working-through process. The analyst's survival paves the road by which patients themselves enter the external world.

There are other reasons for patients' wanting to destroy their therapists. Sometimes they are directly portraying reactions to some important element of the repetition compulsion. Patients' anger, for example, may be aimed at disappointing parents who have failed them by being unable to either soothe or nurture. The analytic role is often equated with soothing and nurture, and if patients view their analysts as failures in these respects, then they have destroyed them, at least professionally.

This situation often leads to serious countertransference problems (see Chapter 9), because the analyst feels inept in carrying out the analytic task. This reaction is more disturbing than a response to patients needing to find their way into the external world of objects. One might say that in the latter instance, the analyst is destroyed in an impersonal fashion. What I am now discussing is an interaction in which the analyst represents an actual person of the infantile past, and the patient, rather than wanting to destroy in an abstract sense, is directing murderous feelings toward that person. Although this type of destruction is also an essential factor of the repetition compulsion and the working-through process, the therapist's reactive participation may derail the potential for resolution and integration.

Transitional Qualities of the Working-Through Process

Throughout this book, I have been using the concepts of the transitional space and the transitional object to explain various forms of psychopathology associated with severe structural problems. I believe that we can also view treatment interactions

in terms of spatial qualities, and locate special aspects of the
working-through process in the transitional space. The patient's
psychopathologically constructed or neurotically distorted reality becomes subjected to various manipulations that are characteristic of the in-between space.

I have emphasized a movement from the internal world
through the transitional space to the formation and recognition
of an external world of reality. Patients suffering from characterological problems have encountered difficulties in achieving a
balanced view of the external world and in constructing structured and integrated ego boundaries. This movement from the
internal to the external world has occurred in a defective fashion. In treatment, as part of the working-through process, the
course of development is reversed, and the repetition compulsion can be reenacted in the transitional setting. This is best
illustrated with clinical examples that involve delusions, because
delusions involve radical alterations of the external world. Experience with psychotic patients often highlights processes that
occur in the psychoanalytic treatment of less-disturbed patients.

Feinsilver (1980) writes about transitional play as an essential element of the treatment of some patients. The example he
gives is that of a schizophrenic woman who had delusions of an
influencing machine similar to the one Tausk (1919) described in
his classic paper. She believed that Feinsilver manipulated parts
of this machine in order to torture her. When she accused him of
maltreating her, the therapist humorously responded that he
was being paid to cause her anguish, that this is what he was
supposed to do. The patient must have understood that Dr. Feinsilver was stating that he was making himself available for her
projections. He was also conveying that he dealt with them in a
playful manner, taking them out of the realm of grim reality.
The patient responded by being amused and intrigued with his
response, and this helped her considerably in understanding, at
times, that she needed her projections, and she was able to
experience them in a nonanxious setting.

Delusions vary as to their tendency and disruptiveness, as
discussed in Chapter 6. Another quantifiable quality of delusions is their degree of grimness. The latter is associated with
how fixed they are and determines how amenable they will be

to therapeutic interactions. Some delusions are so fixed in the patients' minds that they practically replace our reality *in toto*. The artist patient described in Chapter 6, who painted prehistoric landscapes, is an example of a system of thought that seems to be intractable. Other delusions are more loosely organized and allow elements of the current reality to enter them. These I have called *transitional delusions*, and often they are experienced as amusing rather than grim.

A highly intelligent patient, who was in his twenties when I first saw him, heard voices when he was playing a musical instrument. These voices were clear and distinct and easily understood, and they were benign; they made constructive comments about how he was playing and instructed him as to how he could improve his performance. The patient was grateful for their help and he welcomed their criticisms. At other moments, however, the tone of the voices would change. They became angry and accusing and more typically paranoid, calling him a homosexual and derogating him for being passive and effeminate. Thus, from giving helpful criticisms, the voices degenerated into persecutors. By then he was in the midst of a common paranoid delusion.

The more benign state was also a delusion, inasmuch as he had auditory hallucinations and firmly believed that their source was in the external world. At the same time, the voices were directed toward a reality-attuned, creative endeavor that had purpose and a goal. The combination of reality-oriented activity and hallucination constitutes what I have referred to as a transitional delusion. The patient was always delighted when he heard these voices, and his mood was impish and playful. When the voices became persecutory, however, his demeanor changed to one of paranoid suspiciousness and anger. On occasion he had to be hospitalized.

Another patient believed that various philosophers and poets from antiquity would periodically visit him. These visits usually occurred after he had been reading the writings of these personages, and he would simply be continuing the discourse the book had started. He felt flattered by their attention, and believed he learned enough from them to write fairly good poetry. In other instances, he developed delusions characterized by megalomania and direct communications with God. Here, too, a transitional delusion would degenerate into a typical delusion as the patient's psychopathology dominated.

In treatment, the process of working through will change the course of the transitional delusion on the pathway to a psychotic organization. Aberrant impulses and parts of the self that have contributed to delusional replacements of reality are brought back into the transitional space, where they are subjected to psychic operations characteristic of that mental area. Feinsilver's (1980) banter with his patient helped to convert a grim delusion into a subject for playful scrutiny.

The paranoid patient who had benign auditory hallucinations furnishes another similar example. He had become extremely paranoid about me, and during a particular session, he emphasized how afraid he was of me. He was convinced that I was being paid a vast sum of money by the Mafia to pick his brains and destroy his mind. He meant "pick his brains" literally, as though I would open his skull and drive an ice pick into his cerebrum. He was very angry, and frightened to the point of panic. Quite spontaneously, I asked why the Mafia should have to pay me anything to pick his brains when that service was included in his fee. At first he was astonished, then he chuckled, and finally laughed. He replied that I really enjoyed my work, and I countered by stating that working with him was very instructive and that I was learning considerably. He was vastly pleased, and his previous fear, anger, and suspiciousness had disappeared. Instead, he started reviewing the context of both malignant and transitional delusions with an impish glee, evidenced by such questions as "Did I really do that?" or "Did I really have such bizarre thoughts and beliefs?" He was amused by the intricacy of his ideas and fascinated with their primitive qualities and their vast gaps in logic.

This was a crucial session, because we could return to some of the questions he raised and our conclusions during later phases of treatment. He continued having delusions that emphasized the paranoid transference, but they were no longer so intense that they disrupted him or our relationship, nor as intractable. My response had indicated willingness to be the recipient of transference-projections, which allowed him to join me in what I consider to be the transitional space, and to examine our interaction. I conceptualize our location as the transitional space, because the atmosphere became light and playful and involved illusions and fantasies rather than delusions.

Winnicott (1953, 1967, 1971) believed that the transitional space, besides being an area in which the infant exercises omnipotent control, develops into the space that contains play, illusion, and the "cultural experience." From the viewpoint of omnipotence, at first children have the illusion that they are the source of their own nurture; later they enjoy the illusion, and this is when the capacity for organized play develops. From these transitional activities, ego boundaries become integrated, and the child begins to recognize and relate to the external world. In working through, something comparable happens. The distorted external world is moved back into the transitional space; it is reacted to and evaluated in terms of illusions and play rather than delusions. The transference–countertransference aspects of the repetition compulsion are examined in this area, and the consequences of the understanding gained from such a scrutiny have significant effects on how the external world is perceived and reacted to.

There are some similarities to this back-and-forth movement in Freud's (1911) ideas about the production of a paranoid psychosis. Freud postulated that the patient first experienced an "end of the world" phenomenon, in which libido is withdrawn from the external world back into the psyche. If this is sufficiently intense, he said, the world is decathected to the extent that it no longer exists for the patient. This happens in catatonia. Regarding the paranoid process, Freud believed that the delusion represents the libido's return to the external world. It is an attempt to repair the "rent" with reality that was caused by the initial withdrawal of libido.

Freud did not formulate in terms of a transitional space, but his concepts definitely involved back-and-forth movements from the inner and outer worlds. The transitional space can be viewed as the vital factor that determines whether the movement from one space to another will lead to the production of psychopathology or to the achievement of psychic structure and integration as a consequence of successful working through.

Basically, this means that the reality created by psychopathological distortions becomes part of a fantasy system, and, again, as Freud repeatedly pointed out, fantasies have a tremendous impact on the achievement or the disruption of psychic equilibrium.

The interaction of play and illusion in the transitional space does not imply frivolity, though humor and wit may be involved. It is a serious exchange between patient and therapist aimed at bringing grim distorted reality into the realm of the intrapsychic. This is the essence of the working-through process, and it is relevant for nonpsychotic as well as psychotic patients.

Nondelusional patients also distort reality, inasmuch as they externalize the infantile ambience (see Chapter 7). The repetition compulsion is reenacted in the external world in many subtle ways. In this sense, it is similar to a delusion, because it replaces a common reality with a private reality. During an analytic relationship, the patient, to some extent, shifts his infantile focus from the external world into the analytic ambience. Once the patient can view his constructions in a transference-countertransference frame of reference, both analyst and patient are working in the transitional space.

Working through transforms concrete actions and attitudes into metaphors. My patient was an extreme example in his belief that I would actually macerate his brain. When we were discussing our relationship as if it were a fantasy, he could think of "picking brains" as a learning experience. This happens with other patients in less discernible ways. What the patient believes literally becomes a conjecture and an abstraction.

Summary and Conclusions

Working through, the essence of psychoanalytic integration, is the poorest understood concept in psychoanalysis. In this chapter, I have discussed the relationship of this process to acting out and to the repetition compulsion, and as a phenomenon that occurs in the transference–countertransference context.

Working through is not something that the patient does alone. The analyst's responses can either set it in motion or impede its development. In some instances, both the patient's and analyst's psychic survival are at stake.

Finally, I have discussed the spatial qualities of working through and have located the process in the transitional space. This is the area of play, fantasy, and illusion, a space that is the seat of creativity, and, as Winnicott stated, "the location of the cultural experience." The psychoanalytic experience is a creative endeavor in which concrete and grim orientations and actions are converted into metaphors that, in turn, expand the operations of perceptual and executive ego systems. How some of these changes occur is still very much a mystery, but the treatment of patients fixated at primitive mental states is a fruitful area that will help us fill many of the gaps in our understanding.

Chapter 9

Countertransference: Disruptive or Productive

In the *Concordance to the Psychological Works of Sigmund Freud* (Guttman, Jones & Parrish, 1980), the word "countertransference" appears only four times. Freud never wrote a specific paper on the subject; he simply used the term in passing, or when he was making a subsidiary comment while considering another subject. In 1910, he admonished analysts about having countertransference reactions, because they would interfere with analytic neutrality and be harmful to analysis. He advised further training analysis if such reactions occurred.

Today we have many papers dealing with the subject of countertransference. It is talked about freely and recognized as an essential ingredient of the analytic process, having either a destructive or a constructive potential. Analytic neutrality, as I

We wish to thank William Alanson White for permission to reprint portions of this chapter published in an article by Peter L. Giovacchini (1981) titled, "Countertransference and Therapeutic Turmoil," in the journal of *Contemporary Psychoanalysis*, 17: 565–595.

have discussed in Chapters 7 and 8, no longer assumes that objectivity and the therapist's personal reactions are incompatible (Poland, 1984; Shapiro, 1984). It is being increasingly recognized that analysis is an emotional experience for both analyst and patient; the analyst's feelings cannot be ignored any more than the patient's feelings. Especially when dealing with patients suffering from severe characterological problems, the analyst's countertransference responses can be one of his main sources of access to and insight about the primitive parts of the patient's psyche. This process often involves the analyst's access to the deeper levels of his own psyche.

Throughout this book, I have repeatedly emphasized the spatial qualities of psychopathology and have stressed the patient's need to put the analyst in the transitional space. Analysts cannot help reacting, to some extent, to their patient's projections, and they also have responses to being controlled and manipulated in the transitional space. The type of reactions, however, are of course determined by the specific strengths and weaknesses of the therapist's personality and by the structure and integration of his ego boundaries. How open analysts are with themselves is a crucial factor that determines whether countertransference will be destructive or constructive.

Freud's (1910) admonition that analysts "should not have" countertransference responses is not particularly helpful, because analysts will have them in any case. They are unavoidable. Feeling guilty because one believes that he has transgressed the standards of the professional ego-ideal, or the idealized self-representation, as Schafer (1984) prefers, can be a motivating factor for repression. Thus, in many instances, analysts are not aware of countertransference feelings, but this does not mean they do not have them or, more important, that they do not affect the treatment relationship.

Unrecognized countertransference can severely threaten the analytic interaction. The therapist may lose his analytic orientation, and, as Freud (1910) stated, this can lead to deleterious effects. The analyst's discomfort can generate an atmosphere in which the self-observing function of both the therapist and the patient is disrupted. Patients often feel a need to construct defenses against an analyst's reactive hostility. Frequently they withdraw and become silent, or they talk about current situations in a concrete and nonpsychological fashion. In many such cases, the therapist believes the patient is resisting; he is unable to understand that the patient is reacting to and defending against hostile countertransference attitudes. Although in these instances, resistance is an iatrogenic creation, more often than not the therapist becomes intrusive, and subtly blames the patient because the analysis is not proceeding as it should. He may make interpretations that are really criticisms designed to give him some relief rather than to furnish the patient with some insight about his mental processes. In extreme cases, the analysis is terminated either because the patient can no longer stand it or because the therapist decides that the patient is too sick and should never have been accepted for treatment in the first place.

These reactions are familiar examples of the destructive potential of unconscious orientations and impulses if they do not become subject to ego-integrative forces. One cannot conclude, however, that countertransference elements are always useful for analysis if they become subjected to conscious awareness. More than mere recognition is required. Therapists must understand their countertransference reactions in terms of their early development and infantile past. They also have to learn how the patient's psychopathology threatens some of their characterological adaptations. Finally, the interaction has to be placed in an analytic context; that is, both patient and therapist have to recognize in what specific ways the flow of the analysis has been interrupted.

To formulate in terms of an interruption in the flow of the analysis does imply that, from one viewpoint, countertransference responses are undesirable. It would be better if analysis could proceed along its course without any disruptions. On the other hand, can clinicians conceive of any analysis that has smoothly proceeded from beginning to end without any obstacles? Perhaps there are some analyses that have shown only continuous progress, but if so, they are extremely rare.

If obstacles in general are more the rule than the exception, and if in some instances they are not only unavoidable but indispensible for the resolution of certain types of psychopathology (Giovacchini & Boyer, 1975), then perhaps the impasses caused by countertransference reactions may also be unavoidable and indispensible. No less a clinician than Winnicott (1952) believed this to be the case, and Searles (1975) is a strong advocate of that position. I certainly respect their opinions, but I sometimes wonder if we must inevitably react to particular varieties of psychopathology.

If an analyst has had intense feelings toward a patient that he has been able to understand in terms of his past and the patient's repetition compulsion, he may be able to turn the transference–countertransference axis to therapeutic advantage. What began as turmoil can lead to analytic resolution. When another patient presents the analyst with a similar transference constellation, however, is it not possible that the analyst has learned something from his previous patient? Would he not have reached a higher level of therapeutic integration, so that he can deal with his present patient without feeling any significant emotional upheaval? This is similar to Schur's (1958) formulation about the hierarchy of anxiety. A person may experience the anxiety signal as a representation of a painful and dangerous situation, but some situations ultimately become so familiar that all one need do is be aware of the circumstances. A curve in the road for example, induces almost automatic reflexive responses in the driver, without his having to experience any disruptive affects. Similarly, an analyst becomes familiar with certain clinical situations because he has learned about them from his countertransference experiences with earlier patients. To learn from patients seems to be a reasonable objective.

To approach this from the other direction, there are some countertransference experiences that cannot remain quiescent even with further therapeutic experience and sophistication. I believe it is possible that in some instances the therapist must react in order to enable the patient to reach higher levels of structural integration. Certain analytic interactions may demand more than just interpretative understanding. The analyst and patient may have to share an emotionally meaningful experience so that the obstacles to the patient's emotional development will be, at least, partially removed. I believe this is especially true for patients who are fixated at primitive mental states.

What Is Countertransference?

Before enumerating instances of specific countertransference responses, I must first make clear what I mean by the word "countertransference." I believe that countertransference is ubiquitous; it is found in every analytic interaction in the same way that transference is. Just as with transference (Freud 1912a), countertransference mechanisms also operate in nonanalytic relationships. Everything that an analyst or a patient thinks, feels, or does can be viewed as a hierarchal spectrum. One end is dominated by unconscious primary-process elements and the other end by reality-oriented secondary-process factors. When a patient directs his feelings toward the analyst, the primary-process elements of the spectrum represent transference, and in much the same way, the part of the analyst's responses that stem primarily from the more primitive levels of his psyche can be viewed as countertransference. These assessments are quantitative.

Although every reaction in the analytic setting has either a transference or countertransference element, that element may not be significant or useful. In the external world, these elements are usually minimal, and patients may present us with material that is so reality-oriented that we cannot discern its unconscious transference component. Or perhaps we can discern it, but not interpret it. Nevertheless, it is there, as the principle of psychic determinism has taught us. With countertransference, we may have to be even more alert to the primitive infantile elements within ourselves, so that they do not interfere with our analytic objectivity—as Freud (1910a) has warned us. Equally important, not being aware of our countertransference may cause us to miss an opportunity that could become a turning point for the analysis.

There have been various classifications of countertransference responses. Racker (1968), for example, distinguishes two types of countertransference, one based on concordant identifications and the other on complementary identifications. In the former, the therapist is empathic and identified with some portion of the patient's id or ego; in the latter, the analyst is the receptacle of an unwanted projection. Some authors (see Epstein & Feiner, 1979) would restrict countertransference to direct reactions to the patient's transference, whereas other clinicians would use the term for any irrational response of the analyst, not just those stimulated by transference projections. I divide countertransference into two categories: homogeneous and idiosyncratic.

Homogeneous Countertransference. By homogeneous, I am referring to reactions that one might expect from most psychoanalysts. If a patient becomes murderously threatening, most of us would feel afraid. This is a realistic response, but it still has unconscious roots. More subtly, patients may produce certain types of material that most analysts would find disturbing. For example, a patient may project devalued parts of the self into us, or he may withdraw and shut us out. A large number of analysts feel a desire to pursue the withdrawn patient. Not that they are overwhelmed or would, in fact, react, but a feeling of some discomfort, if only transient, is common under these circumstances. Such human sensitivities are manageable as the therapist maintains his analytic perspective.

Idiosyncratic Countertransference. Idiosyncratic responses need not be disruptive, either, but they often are. The unique qualities of the analyst's background and his particular character make-up are responsible for especially disturbing reactions to clinical material that another analyst could take in stride. Not wanting to treat a patient because she is in many respects like one's mother is an especially clear and simple example of this type of idiosyncratic response. Sometimes this type of countertransference reaction is the outcome of the analyst's unresolved psychopathology.

On the other hand, an idiosyncratic orientation can be particularly favorable for the analytic treatment of some patients— for example, if the analyst's tolerance is greater than it is for the majority of analysts.

Some years ago, I was cochairman of a workshop. The members represented seven or eight psychoanalytic societies and institutes. One of our group was presenting a patient to us, and in the course of describing the patient's material, he said,

". . . and then the patient defecated," whereupon he continued his narrative without pausing or commenting. I did a double-take and then stopped him. I was momentarily confused because the analyst had reported the event so matter-of-factly, and I asked this group of experienced psychoanalysts whether patients defecating on their couches was a pedestrian occurrence. I was relieved to hear that none had ever had that happen in their offices. The presenting analyst protested that his patient was behaving as any good analytic patient would. This was a rigid, tight, obsessive patient who initially had difficulties in sufficiently relaxing so that he could free associate. As a result of analysis, the patient was able to relax both emotionally and somatically. Not only was his mind more flexible, but his sphincters also relaxed. Defecating, according to the therapist, was a sign of improvement and a mode of communication. All of us were convinced that he was right, but we still did not feel that we would be able to maintain an analytic decorum under the circumstances (see Lindon, 1967).

Clinical Examples

What follows are, for the most part, examples of the homogeneous type of countertransference. When dealing with human responses, however, absolute distinctions are neither possible nor desirable. Obviously, there will always be a personal element to even the most common types of responses.

Countertransference and Motivation

Many patients have been considered unanalyzable for lack of motivation. Analysts have sometimes required that prospective patients personally call them to make the first appointment, that they pay their own fees, and otherwise demonstrate that they are sincerely interested in being analyzed. In a sense, the patient has to pass a test in order to be granted the privilege of being treated. Still, there are clinical situations in which there seems to be no way of establishing a bond with the patient sufficient for treatment.

The therapist's attitude, that is, his countertransference, is an important determinant of whether some patients have or will develop enough motivation to set the analytic process in motion. Lack of motivation has been thought of as resistance, but, as discussed in Chapter 7, all of a patient's reactions must be viewed as manifestations of his character structure, and in some instances, as manifestations of psychopathology, which must be examined in a transference–countertransference context. It is easy to react personally to a seemingly nonmotivated patient, and an analyst may feel impelled to make demands that will be counterproductive to establishing a therapeutic relationship. On the other hand, a *laissez faire* approach might prove to be equally detrimental to the prospect of treatment.

Countertransference responses to the patient who indicates in one way or another that he does not want treatment are usually the outcome of the analyst's wounded narcissism. If the patient has been referred specifically for analysis (and not for diagnostic evaluation to determine what type of treatment is indicated), the analyst will have developed an analytic orientation toward him, as well as certain expectations of him, even before the initial interview. The patient's lack of enthusiasm or even outright hostility toward analysis creates confusion, and often upsets the analyst's calm and equilibrium, leading to exchanges that will upset whatever possibility there might have been to form a therapeutic alliance (Zetzel, 1956). Thus, to reemphasize, the analyst's contribution is a crucial factor in creating a manageable or nonmanageable treatment setting.

As an example of what superficially appeared to be a hopeless situation, I will discuss a young and articulate executive who called me for an appointment to discuss the possibility of analysis. He was emphatic about wanting analysis and no other form of psychotherapy. I soon learned why. A judge had, in a manner of speaking, sentenced him to analysis. He was ordered to see a psychoanalyst and to report back to his probation officer every several months to determine whether he was still in treatment and making progress. Otherwise, he would go to jail.

The patient, a practicing homosexual, had approached another man in a train station. His intended lover turned out to be a detective, a member of the vice squad who had been planted

there specifically to trap homosexuals. (Obviously, this occurred some years ago when homosexuality was considered a
moral and legal offense.) The judge, perceiving that the defen-
dant was a well-bred, educated, ambitious person, did not want
to disgrace him by giving him a jail sentence. Having had some
personal experience with analysis, this judge mandated that the
young man get treatment. When I discussed this patient at a
"special problems" seminar, my colleagues all agreed that this
was an impossible situation for analysis and that the patient was
being manipulative—trying to exploit analysis to keep from
being sent to jail. He had no real interest in being analyzed.
They felt quite angry with him, something I did not notice at the
time, because I also felt resentful, and as if I were being used.

When I saw the patient again, I began to wonder if our
collective anger was justified. Should analysts demand that all
their patients be dedicated to analysis? Wasn't there always
some ulterior motive? Patients do not, as a rule, want to give up
their symptoms or defensive adaptations. They want relief from
their misery and tension, but they are not seeking basic character changes. If they were unambivalently committed to gaining
mutative insights, we should not encounter resistances. Were my
patient's reasons for seeking treatment fundamentally different
from any other patient's? Isn't there always some pressure or
circumstance in the outside world that prevents the patient's
usual adaptations from functioning as well as they should to
maintain psychic equilibrium? In any case, examining my reactions made me feel that my anger was a countertransference
response derived from a narcissistic threat to my professional
self-representation based on my expectation that the patient
would have better motivations for treatment than merely to
keep from going to jail.

I decided that I would try to analyze him and see where the
material led. To my surprise, there was nothing particularly
unusual about his analysis. He did not create any special obstacles, and he seemed genuinely interested in the treatment. I had
practically forgotten the circumstances that led him to see me.
After three years, I learned that he never asked for anything
directly. As a child, for example, if he wanted a bicycle, he
would ask his father for a wagon. His father would violently

reject his first request, perhaps even beat him, and then would buy him something different—very likely a bicycle instead of a wagon. Although it seemed unlikely that a person could deliberately set in motion the sequence of events that had led to his being in analysis, especially his coming to the attention of a psychoanalytically oriented judge, we both wondered about the power of psychic determinism.

The lesson I learned was that I should not have made a value judgment about the patient's motivations. It would have been a grievous error to accept them at face value, because it would have deprived him of analysis, an experience he really wanted. Because of childhood experiences and traumas, however, he could not ask for it directly. It had to be forced on him.

I have already mentioned the middle-aged businessman who wanted to be analyzed because his wife had threatened to divorce him if he didn't. She had given him the same ultimatum once before, several years earlier, but the psychiatrist he saw at that time refused to accept him as a patient, because he felt that the man was not sufficiently motivated. The wife was not as adamant then as she was now, so the matter was dropped. As I have already described, when I first saw him, the patient was anxious that I might not accept him; he was certain that his wife would divorce him this time if he did not get into analysis. Recalling my experience with the patient first reported, I decided to start treatment.

As stated, once he felt secure that I would not reject him, he created all sorts of obstacles to setting up a schedule; he wanted to converse with me and refused to lie on the couch, because he needed to maintain eye contact. He displayed all of the manifestations of resistance. I felt a mounting resentment over being manipulated and used for nonanalytic purposes. My countertransference response was based on feeling forced into a role that I did not want to assume—that of preserving his marriage. I was aware that my feelings were interfering with my capacity to remain objective and to understand the patient's resistance as a manifestation of intrapsychic conflict. Nevertheless, I did not believe I could continue with this patient unless he stopped acting out his apparent lack of motivation by sabotaging my efforts to create an analytic setting. In a sense, he had to behave in a fashion that would assuage my disruptive countertransference responses. Consequently, I insisted, as conditions of treatment, that we set up a regular four-times-a-week schedule, and that he lie on the couch. I also briefly explained the principle of free association. The patient did not like what I said, but I felt better that I had clarified the situation. He has been in analysis for two years, and the treatment continues.

In this latter example, unlike the situation with the first patient, the lack of motivation was not a manifestation of a specific adaptive pattern. It was, rather, the outcome of the patient's unwillingness to give up certain types of infantile behavior, but his wife had forced his hand. The patient's resistance to analysis threatened my capacity to analyze him, and I could not continue seeing him without a confrontation.

These are situations in which the analyst's countertransference reactions are stimulated by threats to the narcissistic integration of his professional self-representation. Similar to these reactions are those that are evoked when patients make inroads into the analyst's ego-ideal. The seemingly nonmotivated patient reveals himself in a specific way that directly threatens the analyst, whereas patients who attack the analyst's ego-ideal do so in a subtle way. Their attempts to undermine the analyst's values are embedded in their verbal productions, and their purpose is often well hidden.

Countertransference and the Analyst's Ego-Ideal

The following situation illustrates the difficulty of maintaining an analytic perspective when a patient threatens one's values. A 26-year-old male patient's life had been a series of failures. He had never successfully completed any endeavor. He could not hold a job, so he had been unemployed for many years. In fact, he had never really been employed. Although of superior intelligence, he had dropped out of college in his second year. Since then, he had enrolled in numerous courses and programs, but he always left before he was able to see them to their conclusion. Usually the instructor would become enraged with him and angrily tell him that he was wasting everyone's time, because he had neither the talent nor the skills required for that particular project. His latest humiliation had occurred when his teacher, a well-known writer, told him that he might as well forget becoming a creative writer, because his productions were crude, shallow, and sophomoric; he had absolutely no talent.

He came to me directly after this narcissistic injury. In general, I would have expected to feel some sadness about the patient's unhappy experiences, and to some extent, I did. Still, I was surprised that my reaction was fairly superficial.

The young man quickly settled into therapy. He spoke freely, kept all of his appointments, was never late, and paid his bills on time. He indicated faith in analysis and seemed to show me genuine respect. In spite of all this, I found myself feeling irritated with him, and I did not look forward to his sessions. I could not understand my reactions, because he was not doing anything that was unusual or unpleasant.

I asked his permission to tape record an interview, which he was eager to grant. I then played the tape to both colleagues and students, and I was interested to observe that almost every listener felt similarly irritated with him. Some stated that he was not free associating, but they could not specify how they had reached this conclusion or why this should induce negative feelings. Others referred to the patient's pontifical tone, but they were also puzzled as to why this should bother them, because they were otherwise at ease with patients who presented themselves in such a fashion. In some way we all felt threatened by him, but could not understand why.

As I continued listening to the tape and recalled particular sessions, I gradually reached the conclusion that I was feeling hampered in my functioning as an analyst. This patient was somehow upsetting my professional stance and threatening my analytic identity. His material was infuriatingly rational, and it did not seem to offer any openings that would enable me to look with him into his unconscious. I can best illustrate this quality by describing the content of his discussions.

This patient was involved in many fringe movements, such as fad diets, oriental herbs, and particularly astrology. The fact that I have referred to such activities as "fringe movements" implies that I am reacting with value judgments, an attitude that must, to some extent, be nonanalytic. The patient presented his position eloquently, and tried to convert me to his viewpoint. I sometimes felt that he was taking the extreme position of wanting me to give up psychoanalysis in favor of astrology.

Again, this is not an uncommon clinical situation, especially with patients who suffer from relatively primitive fixations. To attach oneself with grandiosity to a cause often holds together patients who are suffering from terrifying feelings of helplessness and vulnerability. These are psychopathological adaptations, but they are nevertheless adaptations, so why should they cause adverse countertransference reactions not only in me, but in colleagues and students who heard the tape-recorded interview? Had it not been for that common response, I would have classified my own reaction as an idiosyncratic type of countertransference, and would have tried to explain it solely on the basis of some peculiarity of mine.

I finally concluded that the basis of my difficulty was the patient's combination of rational logic and megalomanic devotion to systems that have no scientific foundation. I found myself disrupted and unable to maintain a calm, nonjudgmental attitude toward him. If it had not been for that combination, I do not believe I would have had any problems.

Most of us, that is, those analysts who are willing to treat serious emotionally disturbed patients, are comfortable with obvious craziness. We view delusion as a necessary adaptation, and do not threaten it or feel threatened by it, as we continue concentrating on intrapsychic processes—the focus of analytic activity. By introducing a rational logical approach, the patient had caused me, at least temporarily, to abandon this focus.

He wanted me to accept astrology as a scientifically valid system, equating it with the way I view psychoanalysis. His arguments were based on sound principles of scientific methodology. I felt angered by this, because he was attacking beliefs I highly value. He was making inroads into my ego-ideal by elevating astrology to the status of a science, a position I reserve for psychoanalysis. I felt he was making a travesty of both the scientific approach and psychoanalysis by wanting to replace it with astrology. He was upsetting my value system. I was not aware of any of this as it was happening. I simply felt that I should accept the patient's attitudes about astrology, and, at the same time, I had the urge to oppose him vigorously.

Now I can see that, in my mind, I was mixing up defensive adaptations with standards and values. Of course, the ego-ideal judges which adaptations are consonant with its standards, and I believed I had accepted most of his standards. I should have been comfortable with his values, because he seemed to have ideals that are similar to mine. His placing astrology in a scientific frame of reference, however, was a jarring but not obvious inconsistency to me. As long as I was unaware of this inconsistency, I was disturbed, because he was so eloquently rational that he was causing me to believe he was right. Until I was able to learn that his rational approach represented the superficial organization of a paranoid system, I found myself in an analytic quandary.

This patient's ego-ideal was able to find his paranoia acceptable, because the latter was worked out in a secondary-process fashion. My countertransference dilemma was the outcome of a conflict within my ego-ideal because I had not yet recognized the paranoia.

As I look at the patient's material now, it becomes obvious that he was being megalomanic about his various systems, especially astrology. He was, in fact, delusional about his powers of forecasting the future and his own unlimited abilities to determine the fate of a world that he had neatly divided according to the paranoid dichotomies of good and bad. He was omnipotently good and powerful, qualities that were implanted by his astrological skills, and there were external forces that are inherently evil, seeking to undermine him and to make him suffer miserably. As I present this material, it seems consistent with a basically paranoid orientation, but that is not the way he described it. His discussions were calm and carried out in a well-modulated tone that indicated sensitivity and perceptiveness. He had pulled his thoughts and feelings together so that they seemed plausible on the surface.

I am reminded of certain patients whose delusional system is rationally constructed but founded on a false premise. We call these cases *paranoia vera*. I suppose my patient had qualities similar to this rare group of patients; but, even so, there was no particular false premise serving as a foundation for a rational sequence of convictions. All of his beliefs, if toned down, could have been true, but are unprovable; there are too many gaps in our knowledge to be able to explore them. He was, in fact, discussing metaphysical principles without recognizing that he had gone beyond the scientific frame of reference. This must be the case with any rationally stated delusion.

Some of the patient's actions were based on grandiose beliefs, but this was not easily discernible. For example, he became very angry with me because I did not prevent him from having spent a night with a lesbian. They had had sexual intercourse, and he felt that once this were known, he would be disgraced. It was difficult for me to understand why he was so upset; a sexual encounter, even if it were known that his partner was a lesbian, would seem unlikely to attract much attention. The patient insisted, however, that he was ruined, and that I had not protected him.

Admittedly, the patient's family had an illustrious history; some of his ancestors had made significant contributions in learned fields, and he felt he had to live up to that tradition. Also, he belonged to an exclusive, conservative club, and this escapade might have jeopardized his membership. But even granting these considerations, the patient's intense reactions did not appear to be justified merely on the basis of this position in society.

What gradually emerged was that he felt his divinity was being threatened. Although he did not directly admit it, he believed he was the Messiah. It would be difficult, however, to attract disciples if they knew about his "human sinfulness." This delusion determined the disruptive extent of his responses and the intensity of his anger. This material came out in bits and pieces and was not easy to put together, because he always returned to "rational" elements, such as the threatened prestige of his family.

My adverse countertransference reactions were manifested by an impulse to argue with him, that is, to confront the material directly and to correct the reality distortions. From a professional viewpoint, this is as wrong as one can be. It is, in fact, tantamount to trying to argue a psychotic patient out of a delusion. I did not know this at the time, but I must have made some unconscious appraisal about what he was doing, because I felt disturbed about my need to convince him that he was wrong about astrology, and I experienced considerable guilt about not having the proper psychoanalytic attitude. I was conflicted about my analytic identity.

The patient's rational approach also created distance between me and the underlying helplessness and misery that dominated his self-representation. More obviously delusional or disturbed patients reveal their vulnerabilities, and megalomanic defensive systems are easily understood as attempts to establish overcompensatory adaptations to protect them from their terrifying helplessness. Their delusions symptomatically hold them together, and as analysts, we are in no way impelled to cruelly deprive them of what they so desperately need. In contrast, my patient's neediness was, during the phase of treatment I am discussing, hardly discernible.

Some of the people who listened to the tape-recorded interview complained about the patient's arrogance and his pontificating attitude. I do not believe any of us would have been irritated by it if we could have seen that it was connected to his inner sense of emptiness. Instead, we tended to place his all-knowing attitude alongside his actual accomplishments, which amounted to absolutely nothing. We experienced his ignoring of reality as offensive.

Again, for psychoanalysts, this would be an unusual reaction, and it is, if we are operating in a psychoanalytic frame of reference. The patient, however, had succeeded in pulling us out of the analytic context, and we were responding as any nonprofessional observer might have. He had presented his material in such a fashion that we neither recognized its defensive megalomanic overcompensating qualities nor the underlying helpless vulnerability he was defending against. As long as he succeeded in getting us into another frame of reference, which was based on his consistency, rationality, and his realistic limitations, we were no longer functioning as analysts. We felt guilty about having abandoned the analytic stance. Furthermore, standards that we valued, the content of our ego-ideal, were being threatened.

In summary, it was not necessary for me to make any interventions with this patient. Usually, when under counter-transference stress, we interpret to relieve our discomfort. I felt better toward the patient when I understood the specific way he threatened my ego-ideal. At the same time, I was better able to focus on his underlying helplessness rather than on his superficial and tenuous arrogance.

Countertransference and the Self-Representation

I am discussing countertransference in terms of what parts of the analyst's psychic anatomy are mainly affected. In the previous section I concentrated on the ego-ideal; here, I will discuss the self-representation. The following is an illustrative clinical example.

My patient, a mental health professional in his middle thirties, constantly berated psychoanalysis. He was always pointing out the excellence and effectiveness of other therapeutic orientations. He attacked psychoanalysis in general and me in particular for being ineffectual, passive, and not providing any feedback. He did not feel that I was permitting him to become "locked in" with me. He was relentless in his criticism of psychoanalytic concepts and continually stressed the benefits of physical exercise. He took judo lessons following each session, and he credited whatever improvement he achieved to these lessons. In spite of the magnitude of his depreciation, I was able to view it as a transference phenomenon. He had projected some depreciated imago into me as well as the hated, inadequate parts of himself. I did not believe that I was disturbed by the way he was relating to me.

Thus I was surprised one session when I complimented him on his sports car, which I could see from the window of my home office, and he responded with a scowl. I briefly noted my compliment, because I had seen this automobile on many other occasions and never felt inclined to say anything about it. His flash of anger, of course, impressed me.

He lay on the couch and told me that he was livid with rage. He said that I had attacked him in the session on the previous day, that I had been sarcastic, nonprofessional, and disrespectful. He acknowledged that this was out of character for me, but this did not mitigate the intensity of his anger. I was astonished, because I had absolutely no recall of having behaved in any unusual way. Still, I felt that something was definitely wrong, and I was especially curious because of my uncharacteristic remark about his sports car. I conjectured that perhaps I was feeling guilty about something. I agreed with him that something had happened that neither of us understood. I confessed that I did not remember having acted in the way he stated, but I felt that I must have done something, that in some way I had felt threatened by him, and that we should investigate it. He accepted what I said and, to some extent, felt mollified. Then we were able to reconstruct the following sequence.

He had begun the previous session in his customary fashion, extolling the virtues of another school of psychiatry. At one point in his discourse, he mentioned the name of a man who was a proponent of that particular school, and he added that he was well aware of the fact that I intensely disliked this person.

Now, this comment represented a significant reality distortion. I had no feelings whatsoever against the psychiatrist he mentioned. I did not know him personally, nor had I read anything he had written. In fact, I had never heard of him. Obviously because of transference projections, the patient was attributing something to me that was in some way related to his inner conflicts.

So I made an interpretation; I said something about his need to view me as defensively reacting to vulnerabilities that he had projected into me. It was the patient's response to this interpretation that had prompted what he remembered as my sarcastic reaction.

As the patient and I were going over this sequence of events, I had a fantasy as to what had occurred during that interpretive interaction, or, more correctly, lack of interaction. In my fantasy, I viewed the patient as if he were a tape recorder and I was listening to the playback. When I interrupted him to make my interpretation, someone shut the machine off, and the tape stopped playing. It stopped as long as I was talking. When I finished, the machine was once again turned on and continued playing. If the tape were to be played over from the beginning, there would have been no record of my intervention; there would have been no break at all in the continuity of what was being said, and a listener would not have known that there had been any pause in the narrative.

After my interpretation, according to the patient, I had become sarcastic. I still could not remember having said anything in a sarcastic tone, but I recalled feeling very uncomfortable and irritated, so I presume that he was correct.

After having established the sequence—secured the data, so to speak—we were both interested in discovering the nature of our interaction. The patient conjectured that we were facing an oedipal problem in reverse. He believed that I was being competitive with him because I was threatened by the rise of a young man in our profession upsetting my supremacy. Naturally, I had to give credence to all of his ideas, but this one did not seem to fit; at least if these feelings were there, they did not strike me as dominant. Rather, my conscious feelings toward the patient were paternal, and I found my thoughts focusing pleasantly on his achievements. I do have a son who was then pursuing a career in psychiatry and psychoanalysis, and my feelings about that situation were also pleasant and warm. I realized that these could be defensive fantasies, but I did not think so.

I waited for further associations to clarify these issues, and although it seemed that he had embarked on an entirely different track, he did, in fact, oblige me. He began by discussing his father, a person much depreciated by his mother. The patient described him as a coarse, uneducated peddler who spoke with a heavy Eastern European Jewish accent. The mother, by contrast, considered herself an educated, well-bred person, who had an aristocratic background. In fact, she came from the same Russian *Shtetl* her husband did. Nevertheless, she treated him as if he were a nonentity, as if he did not exist, and he, being a passive person, seemed content to fade into the background. The patient claimed that he was hardly aware of his presence.

Although the mother ignored the father, she extolled the virtues of her brother, the patient's uncle, whom he never saw during his early childhood. When he finally met him, the patient recalled bitterly how disappointed he was in this man who had been presented to him as an idol. His father was meek and inoffensive, but his uncle was stupid, mean, and arrogant, and turned out to be a ne'er-do-well. The father, at least, had been able to make enough money to give his son a fine education.

As the patient talked about his father being a nonentity, I recalled the pause in the tape, which had been such a key element in my fantasy. I was now able to identify my feelings. I was not experiencing anxiety based on competitive feelings, as my patient had claimed. Instead, I was experiencing something much more terrifying and elemental. I was being overwhelmed by existential anxiety. The patient had succeeded in making me feel the way his father did—as if I did not exist. Then I apparently started attacking him, presumably to defend myself from this feeling of nonexistence. My anger was a validating affect, and through it I could establish some sense of being.

There are many facets to the behavior and attitudes this patient displayed in the analytic setting. It became clear that he reviled me as his mother had depreciated his father. The various personality theories and therapies he praised stood in a similar relationship to him as his uncle did to his mother. In spite of his lavish praise at the expense of psychoanalysis, he had still chosen psychoanalysis for himself. His attitudes were defensive. It became apparent that at some point or another in his life, he viewed supportive persons and objects of identification as empty. In the analysis he idealized other systems of treatment, but this was all meaningless, because they, like the uncle, could not give him the structure and support he was seeking.

The patient also felt empty, vulnerable, and basically as if he really did not exist. He had made his mother's evaluation of his father the basis of his self-representation. He needed to rid himself of his sense of nonexistence and helplessness by projecting it into me. He was able not only to achieve this projection of his fatherlike self-representation during the session in which I was sarcastic, but he also succeeded in having me feel the pain of his existential quandary. In the following session I was able to interpret what had happened, and this episode became a central issue to which both of us referred frequently during the remainder of the treatment.

My countertransference disruption and response became the fulcrum on which subsequent analytic interactions turned. The patient was able to understand the defensive meaning of his adherence to other schools of therapy and his depreciation of the psychoanalytic approach, and he finally incorporated psychoanalytic principles as his own, finding them more compatible with his basic orientation and philosophy than he had anticipated.

In Chapter 3 I discussed the same kind of threats to the therapist's self-representation as occurred with this patient. There, I described how the patient did not cathect the analyst because of the lack of connecting bridges between primitive and advanced psychic levels. This type of patient demonstrates a lack of psychic structure, whereas the one I just discussed was manifesting compensatory defensive adaptations and projections in a better integrated psyche. The analyst, however, still experiences, in one form or another, an existential crisis.

There is also some similarity between this patient and the young man who proselytized for astrology, although there are also vast differences. Both patients threatened my ego-ideal, and I believe this is a constant factor in all countertransference responses that are potentially disruptive. The first patient presented his system in an apparently rational framework, but he did not try to get me to change my psychoanalytic perspective. He wanted me to include his ideas in my frame of reference. The second patient wanted me to change my approach entirely in favor of one of the schools he felt was superior to mine. This latter patient's psychopathology was more involved with having me give up my analytic identity than that of the first patient. The form his projections took specifically involved the psychoanalytic method. This situation can lead to very difficult therapeutic complications.

Countertransference and the Loss of Mental Representations

Often there is a direct correspondence between the intensity of countertransference disruption and the primitiveness and severity of psychopathology. The following clinical vignette illustrates how a patient with specific structural defects can stir up intense feelings in the therapist.

I discussed this patient in Chapter 7. She was the 30-year-old woman who presented me with an amorphous wooden statuette when we first started treatment. This patient demanded that I be constantly available to her, and by this she meant that she had to know when I would be out of town and where I would be staying. Actually, she did not want me to ever leave and became furious when I left for a meeting or a vacation no matter how far ahead of time I told her about it. Actually, I did not like informing her about my trips, because she would brood and dwell on them for months, and they would become the center of her distress.

This patient had an amorphous self-representation and was not able to hold any image of an external object between sessions. She had to see me daily in order to be able to retain a mental representation of me. I was intrigued when I learned that the patient's most intense upheaval did not occur with my departure; rather, it was a reaction to my return. After I left, she would lose whatever tenuous mental representation she had of me. My return was felt as traumatic because she could not integrate my presence into her psyche. I had become similar to a foreign body that could not be smoothly incorporated into her ego. That is why she went to such great lengths never to lose me. Her efforts, at times, were awesome and even uncanny.

For example, I had been seeing her six times a week when an unexpected personal emergency required that I leave the city for a 24-hour period. I saw her during her usual Saturday morning session, and was planning to leave that afternoon and to return the following evening. I had chosen not to tell her about this trip, because I could not give her any substantial notice, and, besides, it would in no way interfere with her schedule; I would be back in sufficient time for her Monday appointment. As soon as she came into the consultation room, however, she challengingly asked me where I was going and expressed resentment that I was not going to tell her about this trip. I was astonished and asked her how she knew about my leaving. She replied that I was more formally attired than usual and that I had the anticipatory look of someone who was going to do something different than the usual routine. She then went on to revile me for not having told her where I would be, and she dismissed as irrelevant my protestations that this would have no effect on our schedule, and indeed, they were irrelevant. In order to be able to maintain an internal image of me, she had to know or think she knew where I would be 24 hours a day, 7 days a week. If she could keep an image in an area familiar to her, she could retain me within her ego; otherwise, she would lose me. Then when I returned, I would be a stranger that could only be experienced as an intrusion rather than as an integrated object representation.

I have already described the statuette she gave me: The facial features were indistinct, the arms were cut halfway between the shoulders and elbows, and it generally looked like an emaciated person or a mummy. At the time, I viewed my acceptance of the statuette as accepting the patient in spite of the way she perceived herself.

After several years of treatment, I went away for two weeks, the longest period that I had been away since I first started treating her. I suppose I had become somewhat complacent about her, because she now functioned rather well. She had begun to feel alive for the first time in her life, and she had been more than competent in her daily routines, whereas prior to treatment, ever since adolescence, she had spent at least several months of the year in the hospital.

When I returned she was furious. She threatened to quit treatment and reviled me in every possible way. In view of our relatively peaceful and harmonious relationship prior to my trip, I began feeling a mounting discomfort. The patient sprang from the couch, grabbed the statuette, which was in an alcove next to my chair, and flung it into the fire that was burning in my fireplace. I was stunned and furious and shouted, "Now you've done it!" Then I stood up and told her to leave. This happened in my home office, and when she started walking out the front door of my house, I admonished her, again in a loud voice, not to slam the door. Then I realized that all I had to do was flip a switch to extinguish the fire and retrieve the statuette, because I have artificial logs and a gas fire. The base was only slightly charred, although it was broken in two. The latter was not a problem, however, because the break had occurred at the thinnest spot of the statuette, which, incidentally, happened to be at the umbilicus. I glued it together and then sat down to recuperate. In about 10 minutes I had pulled myself together and was ready to see my next patient, although my memory continued to be occupied with the highly charged interaction I had just experienced. As soon as I finished with my last appointment, the patient called me on the telephone and asked how I felt. I said in a melancholy and tired way that I felt fine. She then asked me about the statuette. I said that she was also fine and told the patient I had been able to glue her together. The patient, obviously pleased, said: "Good, I will see you tomorrow."

The patient's lack of psychic structure made it difficult, if not impossible, to retain a mental representation without the reinforcement of the external object in the outer world. In the analysis, she created a situation based on her ego defect. She presented me with a statuette, obviously a replica of her self-representation, so that I could retain a mental representation of her. The statuette was my external reinforcement, which would be constantly with me, except for when I left on trips. This paralleled her tenuous intrapsychic retention of me. Was I, in fact, exhibiting a similar lack of psychic structure? I believe that I both was and was not. I know I do not have difficulties in forming and holding mental representations. I was, nevertheless, able to create in my own mind a state that was in many ways identical to that of the patient, as she herself explained. In general, however, we were operating at different structural levels, a fact that made analysis possible.

At first, I concluded that the patient had been able to project a part of herself, the devalued, amorphously constructed self-representation, into me. She would then assume that I would have the same problem in holding a mental representation that she had. Consequently, she had to give me the statuette so that I could retain her image. She was constructing a stage that corresponded to her structural level. Apparently, I had reacted to the projection by decathecting, that is, losing her mental representation.

Still, if this were the situation, there would be no therapeutic process. At best, we would have a mutually supportive *folie à deux*. Due to the unstructured nature of the transference–countertransference relationship, she would not be able to continue

functioning in her daily life because we would be equally helpless and vulnerable. Such a level of fixation in both of us would
not enable her to use the more structured aspects of my psyche.
Projection would obliterate my more differentiated ego mechanisms.

Furthermore, the patient gave no evidence that she had
achieved the capacity to project. She did not impart her
thoughts or feelings to external objects. She related to people
only in terms of being soothed or soothing them, but the latter
was expressed in terms of primitive fusion mechanisms. They
had to be actually within her perceptual sphere, a condition that
is not required for the operation of projective mechanisms.

Rather than project, she "extruded" the parts of herself that
could neither be soothed nor nurtured. She demonstrated this
early in treatment with the following quasidelusional sequence.
I say "quasidelusional" because to this day I do not know how
concrete or metaphorical she was being. Almost as an after-
thought, during one session, she mentioned she was pregnant.
She did not elaborate. The next day she spent the whole session
moaning and groaning, because she claimed she was having
labor pains. The following session she told me that she had
delivered a baby, a most unusual child. She described him as
having a face with no features. He did not have eyes, ears, nose,
or mouth, anything that would distinguish or identify him. His
head was structureless and amorphous. The rest of his body was
peculiar. He had no arms; instead, he had two coil-type telephone cords. They could be stretched, and when released, they
would spring back into their curled-up state.

Because the baby had no mouth, nurturing him would be a
problem. At first she kept him in the refrigerator, so that he
could preserve himself, absorbing the foods there by osmosis.
The patient felt that this was not sufficient, however, so she
popped a hole in his face with a can opener and that served as a
mouth.

This baby had leprosy, which meant that parts of his body
would decay and fall off if he were placed in sunlight or otherwise received warmth. To survive, he had to be kept in the
refrigerator. After several weeks, she got tired of him, so she put
him on a sunny windowsill, where he crumbled into little pieces.

I bring up this macabre material to emphasize its primitive nature, which, to my mind, antedates the establishment of projective mechanisms. The patient had no feelings about this "delusional" baby, who had no way of taking things in or of expelling. He had no openings in his body, and he was so amorphous that he could not be a repository of projected feelings. As parts of him crumbled in decay, he seemed to be the product of a similar breaking off from his mother. The lack of a mouth, that is, of psychic structure, only permitted nurture through osmosis, rather than an interaction based on introjective and projective mechanisms.

True, she constructed a mouth for him, but this was a mutilation, not the outcome of structuralization. Consequently, whatever the mother put in him was experienced as an intrusive assault, because the mouth opening was not part of an integrated digestive system. The baby could gain some sustenance from being fed through the "gaping wound" mouth, but food did not become completely absorbed to become part of a unified body. Instead, his body remained fragmented and disintegrated.

He could not gain cohesion and sustenance from the usual modalities of relating, which, during infancy, include introjective and projective processes. In addition to not having a mouth, the baby had no arms that could hug. He could not be loved or soothed. Warmth was destructive; he survived only in a cold environment. This baby could not survive in an ordinary environment, which helps the psyche fulfill its potential for emotional development by providing nurture and soothing in the context of warm, loving object relationships. To summarize briefly, this child lacked a potential for growth, inasmuch as he had no mouth through which he could be nurtured, no arms that would allow him to hug and to be loved and soothed, and he had leprosy, which kept him fixated at a fragmented level and prevented the achievement of unity and cohesion.

Returning to our dramatic, and for me disturbing, confrontation, I repeat that I do not believe it was the outcome of mutual projection. The material involved was at a level more primitive than one that could use projection as a defensive adaptation. The patient had, by this time, progressed beyond the amorphous-baby stage. She was able to form a mental representation of me based on my ability to keep a mental representation of her. Our interaction, however, was based on different levels of psychic structure.

When she first gave me the statuette at the beginning of treatment, she lived in a world in which people could not hold mental representations. Because she could not, she could not conceive of anyone else being able to, at least in a relationship with her. She could only view me as she viewed herself, because her ability to perceive and integrate was defective.

My view of her was not based on a similar defect of my own. As therapy progressed, I found myself becoming increasingly capable of introjecting her intrapsychic state. I experienced several phases of response to her that were consequences of the therapeutic process. I will concentrate on my reaction to how I perceived her. At first, I had no difficulties in keeping her in mind, so to speak. In fact, I thought a good deal about her in between sessions, and I brought up her material frequently in various seminars. I felt harassed by her demands, and this kept me focused on her. Her material was also fascinating and memorable, and the therapeutic challenge she presented me caused me to continue concentrating on our interaction. In view of her almost total initial incapacity, her progress was an outstanding achievement. My mental orientation toward her gradually changed. As she functioned better, I became less concerned and perhaps less involved.

Now I can see that the sequence of my reactions represented a repetition of her traumatic past. They represent a re-enactment of the repetition compulsion. Furthermore, I had identified with the primitive mental state that she had initially presented to me and from which she had progressed. Inasmuch as her behavior was no longer bizarre and intense, I had decathected her, which was somewhat similar to her inability to cathect internal objects. She became threatened, because if I could not hold her mental representation, then she would lose the ability to maintain mine. Consequently, she had to create a situation in which I would again cathect her, so that she could also feel me as an internal presence. She had to make me alive for her in the same way that I was constantly aware of her at the beginning of treatment. She succeeded in evoking an intense, agitated, uncharacteristic response from me that she could use to cathect my imago, one that had become remote and lifeless. In a sense, I had behaved as crazily as she once did.

In the session following my outburst, the patient stated that I had felt the same misery she had always known, and she was quite correct. Although I had identified with her former inability to cathect internal objects, I had formed an attachment to the statuette that compensated for my loss of interest in her. This was also similar to her initial ego state, because as the statuette stood for a concrete external replica of her self-representation, it was constantly within the sphere of my perceptual awareness when I was functioning as an analyst. To have lost it faced me with the kind of loss she felt when I left on a trip. I reacted as I did because I was closely identified with her primitive ego state. She caused me to respond in such a disruptive fashion because she wanted to maintain the progress she had made and not regress back to such an early level.

In spite of my repetition of her behavior, which was based on an ego defect, I was nevertheless operating at a higher level than she was. It was this differential that enabled our interaction to be productive rather than catastrophic. I had not actually regressed to an ego state in which I could not hold a mental representation. Instead, I had identified with such a state, but the incorporation of that state occurred within an ego that was capable of forming integrated internal images. The patient was aware of this and could risk having me feel such primitive disruption because she knew I had enough ego integration to contain and survive it within a psychoanalytic context.

Countertransference and the Unreasonable Patient

The patient I have just described could be considered unreasonable. Her need to have me within the vicinity, and therefore available to her 24 hours a day, 7 days a week, represents an unrealistic demand. No analyst could or would want to live up to it. When understood as the consequence of her ego defect, however, which affected the stability of mental representations, the patient's attitude could be rationally understood, even if it were itself irrational. Because her psychopathology involved a reexperiencing of the infantile past, my simply creating an environment—we might call it a corrective environment—that she had never known would not have helped her to overcome her problems, which were based on a relative lack of psychic structure. As discussed, our interaction was complex and intense and not based on an attempt to provide her with an optimal setting to undo the effects of the traumatic past. Because my focus was on understanding the subtle and sometimes painful elements of the transference-countertransference relationship, I did not usually experience the patient's demands as oppressive and constrictive.

There are instances, however, when it is not possible or very difficult to preserve the psychoanalytic focus. I have referred to many situations in which the patient's behavior is so disruptive that it goes beyond the analyst's limits of tolerance (Giovacchini, 1979b). I have also discussed how tolerance varies from analyst to analyst. Some patients, though, would cause serious difficulties for all analysts. Immediately we can think of the violently threatening patient who would cause the therapist to fear for his safety. Obviously this is intolerable. The therapist can expect some capacity for control in a patient. We might have to demand a certain degree of conformity, realizing that, to some extent, we are hampering the patient's autonomy and suppressing the manifestations of psychopathology.

If a patient cannot meet our minimal requirements, we can only view the situation as an example of the limitations of analysis and conclude that it is impossible, at least for the time being, to provide an analytic setting. We assume that perhaps such patients will someday be able to control quantitatively the expression of their symptoms without necessarily altering their fundamental psychopathology. There is a group of unreasonable patients, however, for whom this is not possible.

One of the most disconcerting situations I can think of is the patient's refusal to leave at the end of the hour. The patient knows he is being unreasonable and intruding on someone else's time, but it makes no difference. He does not care about others, only himself. In fact, he may even resent your having given him evidence that you are not involved entirely with him, that you actually have other patients.

There are several ways in which one might respond to such a dilemma, but none is guaranteed to work. Of course, it is best to keep matters in an analytic context, but there are inherent problems in doing so. For example, if we know, we might attempt to interpret the meaning of such behavior, but we are really doing it more to seek relief for ourselves than to make an unambivalent observation about the patient's mental processes. Our interpretation will be either a prohibition or an appeal for the patient to leave. In extreme cases, I suppose one could call the police or security guards to have the patient ejected. It would be especially unpleasant to physically throw the patient out, assuming that the therapist were able to do so, but it has been done, especially with children. None of these alternatives is satisfactory, however, and some may permanently impair one's capacity to continue the analysis, although the analyst may not particularly care.

Fortunately, I have not had this problem often. My inclination has been to focus on the countertransference element, in view of the fact that I would be using interpretation about the patient's behavior to manipulate him into leaving. The first time I was faced with the dilemma I told the patient, a middle-aged woman, that I wanted her to leave so that I would not get further upset and feel that I did not want to see her on her next appointment. If she persisted in such behavior, I said, she would render me analytically useless, because I would sit there worrying about the end of the hour instead of listening to her. This patient understood and left, and I felt satisfied, because I had honestly reported what was going on in my mind.

Years later, I had a similar encounter, again with a middle-aged woman, and I said to her exactly what I had said to the previous patient. This patient completely surprised me when she sarcastically replied that she did not have any interest at all in my feelings; her only concern was her own state of mind. Furthermore, she had heard from a friend who was attending one of my seminars that I had said the same thing to another patient, so she was fully prepared for my ploy, as she put it. I felt helpless and told her so. I then added that I was leaving. The appointment was in my home office, so I could move to another section of the house. When I returned, I said, I expected her to be gone; otherwise, I would terminate treatment. The patient angrily left, but I was not pleased with myself for having threatened to break off the analysis. On the other hand, I did not know what else I could have done, and I still do not know.

I want to give another extreme example, which may or may not suggest ways of dealing with these patients, but can lead us to have better feelings toward them based on our understanding of their needs.

The patient is a single woman in her early twenties; she is being treated by a psychiatrist who comes to see me periodically for supervision. We both have considerable understanding about the patient's personality structure and psychopathology. Briefly, she is a primitively fixated person who has little in the way of adaptive techniques to relate to the external world. As is true for this group of patients, she has considerable difficulty in forming and maintaining mental representations, and her capacity to deal with her needs and environment symbolically is correspondingly limited.

She had made many demands of her therapist, but there was little substance to them, and it gradually became apparent that she needed to have constant contact with him. She called frequently, both day and night. At first this irritated him, but he was able to tell her on occasion that he did not want to talk to her any longer and to hang up. And he sometimes switched his telephone to an answering machine. In other words, he could control his feeling of being impinged on by the intrusion of her telephone calls. The patient was angered by his rejections, which did not occur often, but she learned to tolerate them.

The situation in the office was another matter. She would refuse to leave at the end of the hour. The first time this happened, there were no particular consequences, because she was the last patient of the day. The psychiatrist simply left, asking the patient to make certain the door was locked when she finally decided to go. He felt uneasy about the situation, but vainly hoped it would not happen again.

Inevitably, at the end of the next session, she again firmly stated that she wanted to remain in the office forever. This time the therapist picked her up and carried her into the hall. He did not want to do this, and felt humiliated and guilty for having abandoned his professional decorum, but he also felt anxious, helpless, and ambivalent. He felt his patient's neediness, and he wanted to treat her, but she was upsetting him to the point where he could no longer function in a therapeutic context.

The patient called him that night to express her anger. He understood her needs, but because he experienced them as unreasonable or, at best, incompatible with his own needs, the treatment was facing a serious impasse. He wanted to continue treating her, but did not see how he could in view of her demands. He devised the following unorthodox solution: He would see her in a place where he could be mobile and terminate the session without having to depend on her acquiescence. Instead of meeting in his office, they held their sessions early in the morning in a booth in the restaurant located in his office building. He was able to find a table that was relatively isolated from others, because the restaurant was not particularly full at that hour. This arrangement has been in effect several months and has turned out to be comfortable for both therapist and patient. It might be stretching the point to consider this an analytic relationship, but it is based on an understanding of the patient's needs, psychodynamics, structural defects, as well as transference demands. In any case, the treatment continues, and it seems to be progressing as it should.

These are difficult, often impossible, situations. Most therapists would not want to do what my supervisee did. They could not tolerate working outside the familiar confines of their offices. In part, the psychoanalytic process is defined by a specific ambience. With some patients, however, this may be too restrictive a definition.

Freud must have understood this, because we can read about his peripatetic analyses (Jones, 1953). His analyses of Ferenczi and Mahler occurred while he took walks with them and discussed their dreams. I do not believe my supervisee's behavior to be any stranger than Freud's, but I also realize that Freud's precedent is not sufficient to justify it. I suppose the only justification that would make sense would be a relationship characterized by a steady unfolding of the transference based on the infantile traumatic environment and the repetition compulsion. This seems to be occurring with my supervisee's patient.

Demanding that our patients see us in a particular setting can be considered a form of rigidity. I know that I have this kind of rigidity; and given that I am comfortable in my consulting room and with the types of patients I treat who accommodate themselves to the setting I provide, I do not feel at all impelled to become more flexible. I have spent many years working in this fashion, and have become a creature of habit. Furthermore, we have to realize our limitations. No one can treat all types of patients. Still, I believe it is important to recognize that some patients cannot be treated in a conventional setting, and if the therapist is not totally tied to that setting, many of these patients could have an analytic experience in surroundings where the therapist is not vulnerable to infantile demands.

The analyst's lack of vulnerability helps to create a calm, secure setting in which the patient's anxieties can be contained. The analyst maintains an observational frame of reference and does not become personally enmeshed in the content of the patient's feelings and associations. These are essential features of any analysis. The unreasonable patient's demands interfere with what we might consider these formal elements of analysis. Analytic sessions, for some patients, recapitulate certain infantile rhythms. The routine frequency of the interviews is perceived as a nurturing or soothing experience. Tension accumulates during the time between sessions. If some mental representation of the analyst can be sustained, then waiting for the next session becomes tolerable, because the patient can obtain some gratification, or at least relief, from the analytic introject and the anticipation of the next interview. The unreasonable patient finds this in-between time intolerable.

These patients' lack of psychic structure do not permit much variability of symptomatic manifestations. Freud (1915a) discussed how sexual drives can be directed toward many different objects. They have considerable flexibility, whereas the ego or self-preservative instincts do not. The latter can be expressed only in a limited fashion, and there are no substitute objects of gratification. In the treatment setting, most patients can modulate their symptoms—the expression of their psychopathology—in such a way that they can be contained in the consultation room. Patients often fear that they cannot, and may test the analyst, but usually the patient and analyst reach a compromise. The unreasonable patient often cannot modulate his symptoms and character traits so that they are compatible with analytic routine.

Patients who, because of an ego defect, cannot integrate internal objects and form mental representations require the constant presence of the nurturing or soothing person. There is no substitute for this, and these patients have not sufficiently developed the capacity for symbolization to displace their needs onto alternative objects.

Whatever the specific qualities of the infantile environment for these patients, it has been traumatic in that as children, they felt abandoned. Such children did not suffer from a total absence of object relations, but, rather, they experienced inconstant relationships, and their needs were capriciously handled. Sometimes they were met, and at other times, they were ignored or rejected. The external world is thus experienced as unpredictable, but the child's needs, because of biological rhythms, follow a predictable sequence. Inasmuch as the child does not have the security that he will be cared for, he later forms the impression that either his demands are unreasonable or that he lives in an unreasonable world.

As adults, such people demand the right to be unreasonable, which represents a defense against and compensation for an unreasonable infantile environment. They require instant and total satisfaction of needs because, otherwise, they will not have any assurance whatsoever that gratification is forthcoming. This is the only method they have to render the world predictable.

Discussion

I have touched on several difficult clinical situations that would cause varying degrees of disruption for most analysts. I have by no means exhausted the topic, however. There are as many types of transference–countertransference relationships as there are individual differences in patients. I have examined what we might consider to be general constellations of structural psychopathology as they manifest themselves in the transference, and how they evoke responses in the therapist.

I have not made reference to two major areas: the transference–countertransference relationship that might occur with patients who have considerable differentiation and whose psychopathology can be understood on the basis of intrapsychic conflicts, and, at the other end of the spectrum, the therapist's reactions to a psychotic transference.

Regarding the former, I do not believe there is much to be said. These patients may be difficult because their defenses are rigid, but disruptive feelings in the therapist usually belong in the category of idiosyncratic countertransference reactions. Although the analyst has to be in tune with the deeper unconscious elements of the patient's personality, his countertransference task in the transference context is to make the unconscious conscious; that is, he is to use his secondary process to give coherence to the patient's primary process. Of course, the analyst also uses his own primary process, but presumably in a nonconflictual fashion.

I believe that Freud (1910a) had this type of patient in mind when he warned about the dangers of countertransference and advised that it should be eliminated as soon as possible, perhaps by means of further analysis for the analyst. I agree that countertransference responses to the well-integrated psychoneurotic patient are more likely to prove detrimental than reactions to sicker patients. The deeper we go in our psychoanalytic explorations, that is, the closer we approach the most primitive levels of the psyche, the greater the tendency to stimulate characteristic responses in most therapists.

Reactions to the psychotic transference constitute a special problem that once again raises the question of treatability. Many analysts would agree that the emergence of a psychotic transference is the outcome of an error in judgment: The patient should not have been accepted for psychoanalytic treatment in the first place. Perhaps this is true in many instances, but when dealing with something as complex as the human psyche, sweeping generalizations are usually unwarranted.

The psychotic transference emphasizes an important countertransference element. Throughout this article, I have been discussing countertransference in terms of the patient's influence on the therapist. Now I want to discuss briefly the reverse situation, the therapist's effect on the patient, and the therapist's countertransference to the patient's response to him.

Analysts have to feel comfortable with their patients, at least most of the time. Some patients may be especially threatening for certain analysts, and the therapist may or may not be aware that he is feeling anxious. Because of anxiety, the therapist may respond in one of two fashions. The first I have already mentioned: The therapist may make interpretations to obtain relief by what he believes to be analytic activity. Because his primary motive in this endeavor is to calm himself, rather than to understand what is going on in the patient's mind, his interpretations are intrusive and premature. The other response would be to abandon the analytic position and to try to manage these patients' lives. The therapist's attempt may take the form of suggestions, advice, guidance, and activities supposedly designed to support the patient rather than to analyze him. These two possible responses are not mutually exclusive; the analyst may intertwine one with the other.

The patient, for his part, believes on the surface that he is having an analytic experience, but at another level, he feels assaulted or abandoned. Moreover, the patient feels confused. The analytic frame of reference is merged with reality. With patients whose reality-testing is precarious, this could become an overwhelming threat. As I have mentioned elsewhere (Boyer & Giovacchini, 1980), this situation could create a psychotic transference. The latter, however, would not be the outcome of the analytic approach having caused unmanageable regression. Rather, the abandonment of analysis would have led to a breakdown of reality-testing and the extinction of whatever self-observing function the patient might have had. If the analyst reacts to the patient's external and internal worlds as if they were the same, the patient's boundaries can only become further blurred, which may make analysis impossible.

Reactively, the analyst becomes defensive. He does not recognize his role in the patient's decompensation. In any case, the therapist's most frequent response is to abandon analysis entirely, and in extreme cases, he may have to hospitalize the patient.

I do not mean that all psychotic transferences are precipitated by the therapist's reactions to his own anxiety. I believe that there are some patients who present us with distortions of reality that will include the therapeutic interaction. These psychotic transferences can be detected at the very beginning, however, and the therapist can determine then whether analysis is feasible. The patients I have been discussing did not begin treatment with a psychotic transference; it developed later.

Patients who develop a psychotic transference create situations that therapists find painful to tolerate, and often they unwittingly react in a fashion that can make for insurmountable obstacles. Still, it helps, as usual, to understand the nature of the interaction in terms of the infantile past. For example, a married woman in her late forties developed intense and rigid paranoid ideation toward me. She accused me of loathing her, and of being the cause of all the pain and misery she had felt ever since childhood. I had only known her as an adult patient for several years, but, as is the case with paranoid thinking, logic and reality had very little influence on her.

For several months, as her depression deepened and her anxiety intensified, she was feeling increasing amounts of tension. During that period she went into business with a recently found friend, and opened a boutique. At first she was happy in her new venture, but gradually she became suspicious of her partner. She believed that her associate was cheating her by hiding the full amount of their sales. Her anger mounted, and she started attacking me for not having stopped her from getting involved in this operation. She presented me with innumerable details about her partner's misdeeds, and how she was being exploited. At the same time, her anger toward me became more acute, because I had not warned her against nor predicted what happened. Furthermore, she insisted that I should call her former friend to tell her what a vicious person she was.

I found it extremely difficult to tolerate this patient's abuse, and I did not understand my intolerance. True, she was a very difficult patient, and it was especially aggravating to listen to her attack me for something I had not done regarding activities in the external world, when I wanted to maintain our intrapsychic focus. I believed that what she was demanding was outside the psychoanalytic sphere, and I was angered by her blaming me for not having done something that I believe would have been a technical error. Nevertheless, she kept accusing me of having failed her and of being the cause of all her pain.

After one stormy session, she quit treatment, or perhaps I took the initiative in terminating our relationship. I was arguing with her and defending myself instead of analyzing her. On the other hand, the patient perceived any attempts at analysis on my part as defensive manipulations, and, to a large measure, she was correct. I was locked into a psychotic transference, and felt functionally paralyzed. I had begun to absorb some of the pain she accused me of having created, and I experienced considerable relief when she terminated.

After she left, however, and I could again enjoy a sense of calmness, I tried to examine our stormy and disruptive interaction. When she first entered treatment, she complained that she suffered from anhedonia. She did not know what a pleasurable feeling was. She felt generally numb, knowing neither pleasure nor pain. During several years of treatment she had begun to feel minimal amounts of pleasure and enthusiasm, as occurred when she first opened the boutique, but these moments were followed by bouts of intense psychic pain. So, in a sense, she was correct when she accused me, or rather the therapeutic process, of being the source of her pain.

I concluded that this patient represented an example of privation, as Winnicott (1963a) has described. She had so little capacity to feel gratified that she was not even able to feel frustrated and deprived. If there is minimal or no endopsychic registration of gratifying experiences, then the psyche does not comprehend deprivation and the ensuing pain. Once the patient was able to derive some satisfaction and pleasure, she developed the capacity to feel deprivation and pain, and the analysis was indeed responsible for this sequence of feeling states. I also concluded that the psychotic transference was the manifestation of the repetition compulsion, in which I had become the failing caretaker. By not controlling the outside world, I had left her exposed and vulnerable and was not giving her the protection she had needed as an infant but never received. Here again, I was failing her by not furnishing her with a protective shield, the *Reizschutz* that Freud (1920) wrote about.

My countertransference responses were disruptive, because I find it difficult as an analyst to accept the transference role of failing the patient. Certain patients confront us with our failures in subtle as well as in crude and overt ways. Deprecating me for not having warned her about the business involvement is an example of a crude and overt confrontation. Reviling me for not understanding her and for not appreciating her needs, in addition to her not being helped by my interpretations, stirred up resentment, and this was particularly painful when I was unaware of how infantile factors were operating. My reactions must have served only to confirm the patient's perceptions of our relationship in terms of early psychic developmental levels and object relationships. This negative feedback sequence intensified the sense of reality attached to the transference and solidified its psychotic qualities. Both the patient and I had gradually diminished our self-observing functions.

Within a year, this patient called and told me she had missed her analysis and would like to return. By this time, I had mellowed considerably toward her; my feelings had been mitigated by understanding that I was reacting against the role she had assigned me, and by so doing, accepting it. She was somewhat timid the first few minutes of her return, but then was sufficiently bold to tell me that I had failed her. She was surprised and pleased when I agreed. She next retorted that I should apologize for having failed. I refused to apologize, on the basis that failing was part of my analytic task. The patient chuckled and then began attacking me for not having protected her. Now I was amused rather than angered, because I had been able to put matters in an analytic context, and she had allowed this to happen. I had been especially heartened by her phone call, when she said that she had missed her analysis.

This was an exceptionally fortunate outcome of the effects of a psychotic transference. Most similar situations lead simply to termination of treatment, often under unpleasant circumstances, as did happen with my patient when we stopped seeing each other. As I stated, it is frequently uncertain as to whether the patient or therapist has taken the initiative in stopping therapy. Because of the primitive qualities of psychopathology, a chain reaction, so to speak, is set in motion when feelings get out of control. The patient becomes convinced of the reality of his attitudes and expectations, and the analyst, for his part, feels angry as he fights against incapacitating and paralyzing demands. If the therapist did not have such countertransference reactions, could the construction of a psychotic transference be avoided? This is a difficult question to answer.

We have learned that the essence of a psychoanalytic relationship is the handling of the transference, so we have to understand as best we can what can facilitate or hinder this task. That is why we focus so much on countertransference. Whatever we learn about the most difficult of these situations, the psychotic transference, will have extremely important consequences for the treatment of a group of patients who, for the most part, have been considered inaccessible to the psychoanalytic method.

Summary

Our current concentration on countertransference phenomena is the outcome of the expanding of clinical horizons. The deeper we delve into our patient's personality, the more we get in touch with the primitive elements of our own psyches. This can be both rewarding and painful.

I have reviewed several types of transference–countertransference relations in terms of the resonance of the patient's psychopathology with specific elements of the analyst's psyche. The analyst may feel a threat to the integrity of his ego-ideal; the cohesion of his self-representation may be disrupted; or he may absorb the patient's pain in his self- and object representations.

When the patient's psychopathology makes demands of the therapist that are at odds with the analytic procedure, the treatment situation can be threatened. I have discussed one of the most trying dilemmas of this sort—confronting the patient who refuses to leave at the end of the hour.

Some patients spend more time talking about the analytic method than about themselves (although everything they say does involve some part of their psyches). This situation develops precisely because the patient's adaptive modalities and needs clash with the analyst's observational frame of reference. Although any patient may feel some gulf between wanting his infantile needs to be gratified and the analyst's wanting them to be understood, the patients I am discussing have very little concept of what being understood means. No one has ever attempted to understand them as separate persons. Consequently what the analyst offers is incomprehensible, and all they can understand and feel is the miserable frustration raging within themselves. The analyst also feels frustrated, because the patient appears unable to recognize or to use what he has to offer.

If the analyst can control his own frustration, the patient may be able to use the calm and acceptance of the analytic setting to soothe his inner agitation. This could create a relationship in which the patient may incorporate some of the analyst's understanding orientation; I have called this process the formation of the analytic introject.

Finally, I have introduced the topic of the psychotic transference, but I have discussed it only briefly without reaching any definitive conclusions. We all know how impossible these patients can be from a therapeutic perspective, and if they are treatable there is much we have to learn. For the moment, the most we can do is to look at the various facets of our reactions to them and to the nature of their structural defects. Even though it may turn out that the majority of patients who form psychotic transferences are untreatable by the psychoanalytic method, what we learn about them and ourselves can help us to treat other patients who are also difficult, but not impossible.

Part III

Integration and Adaptation

Chapter 10

Creativity, Psychopathology, and Character Structure

Most psychoanalysts find the topic of creativity fascinating. Although psychoanalysis began as an investigative method to explore clinical phenomena, Freud soon began to apply his techniques and insights to the study of creative personages, such as Leonardo da Vinci (Freud, 1910b). He also turned his attention to those unconscious factors in the artist that determined certain unique qualities of the creative product, such as he did regarding the *Moses* of Michelangelo (Freud 1914a). These studies, which often read like detective stories, use clinical insights, but they have little to do with therapeutic issues.

Clinical studies of creative persons, that is, conclusions drawn from the analyses of patients who are creative, attract the attention and stimulate the enthusiasm of most psychoanalysts. I have noted that at meetings, both national and international,

We wish to thank the University of Chicago Press for permission to reprint parts of this chapter published (1981) in the article, "Creativity, Adolescence and Inevitable Failure," in *Adolescent Psychiatry*, 9: 35–60.

papers on creativity are always well attended and eagerly discussed. It is especially interesting that among these analysts, many of them are also actively engaged in the psychoanalytic treatment of patients suffering from primitive mental states.

At first glance, such attitudes may not seem surprising. Such interests may seem natural for psychoanalysts; why examine the matter further? If we pause, however, there is a phenomenon here: Why should the topic of creativity or the creative process have universal appeal? There must be some explanation, and perhaps one that is clinically relevent. It is not an *a priori* truism that clinicians are interested in creativity, although our inclination not to question our admiration for creative accomplishment is an indication of how deeply ingrained creativity is in our ego-ideal.

Psychoanalysts become psychoanalysts because, among many reasons, they are attracted to the study of the unconscious mind. The operations of the primary process, and its effects on behavior and productivity, are subjects that concern clinicians and our efforts to understand these processes further are the essence of our work with patients. The creative process contains many features that conform to primary-process configurations.

There are many persons who do not value creative pursuit. Among character types, the concrete, literally minded person often has little interest in art or music and has no particular inclination to be creative himself. When seen as patients, such people are often difficult to treat, because they lack psychological-mindedness, and their minds do not reveal themselves through metaphor, imagery, or symbolism. These patients have problems in getting in touch with the primitive parts of themselves, and are either unconnected (see Chapter 3) or defended against early primary-process-oriented ego states. Their surface behavior is sometimes well ordered and reality-oriented, being under the dominance of the secondary process. This is a rigid organization devoid of fantasy and imagination. Ego boundaries are firm, and the transitional space is poorly developed.

I do not wish to generalize from what clinicians have learned from concrete and difficult patients. On the whole, however, the person who is not interested in creativity is likely to be noncreative and not an advocate of psychoanalysis.

By contrast, the creative scientists I have had in treatment all seemed to have an intrinsic understanding of the psychoanalytic process and, in turn, were fascinated with unconscious ideation. They readily accepted psychoanalysis as a valid scientific discipline. This does not mean they were easy to treat; it means they understood the methods and aims of analytic treatment, and they did not question the basic premises of the procedure.

The creative personality apparently has access to various parts of the psyche when creating. Psychopathology, when it involves psychic structure, interferes with the fluidity of the psychic apparatus by isolating various segments from the main ego stream. This fragmentation is a primitive defensive adaptive splitting mechanism that is characteristic of the mental operations of primitively fixated patients. If being creative requires that upper levels of the psyche have ready access to primitive ego states (Giovacchini, 1960, 1971, 1981a), then severe psychopathology would inhibit and even abolish creative activity. This was the situation with the scientists I treated.

Though creativity is the outcome of primitive primary-process-oriented activities and thought processes, it is not related to emotional disturbances, including those that are associated with fixations at primitive mental states. As will be discussed, however, there are some similarities in the mental mechanisms involved in both creativity and psychopathology. Perhaps these similarities account, in part, for the fact that clinicians who deal with patients suffering from severe psychopathology are particularly interested in the creative process. It is fascinating to observe how a creative orientation and its characteristic mental mechanisms can degenerate into psychopathologically constrictive and defensive adaptations, and to preside over the reverse process in treatment, when the resolution of psychopathology leads to a creatively liberated person. The creative process has its focus in primitive mechanisms, as does psychopathology, but there are important differences that determine whether psychic operations are expansive or constricted.

Psychopathology is often obvious—easy to recognize and define. Creativity is much more subtle; it is not necessarily discernible. So many activities and products have been labeled creative that the concept of creativity is all but meaningless. In fact, the adjective "creative" has promiscuously crept into our language. We do not have a precise definition of what constitutes a creative accomplishment. Perhaps the only precise way of defining creativity is to identify a psychic process that is invariably associated with productivity. A process, however, is not a rigid sequence, and it is dependent on many variables that can alter different aspects of it and still not change its course or direction.

The creative product is something that did not previously exist: a realm, a new frame of reference, a better explanatory hypothesis, or a novel combination of already known factors or concepts. Our current reality is expanded by the creative product. Something has been added to it, even when the new perspective destroys some previously held and cherished beliefs.

The creative product can be thought of as an accretion to reality. Freud (1910b), quoting Leonardo da Vinci, discussed the sculptor's working according to the *via di levare*, a point also emphasized by Michelangelo. Poetically speaking, the statue is inside the marble block. The sculptor's task is to chip away the outside cover and to reveal the statue that was previously hidden in the stone. This *modus operandi* stands in contrast to the *via di porre*, the painter's perspective, in which something is added to a void, the blank canvas. The *via di porre* appears to result in an entirely new creation, whereas the *via di levare* implies a discovery, the unearthing of something that has always existed.

From a psychoanalytic viewpoint, these distinctions become blurred, if we recall that no thoughts or actions occur in a vacuum. What the painter puts on the canvas is, to a large measure, the outcome of projection. Feelings and parts of the self have been arranged in novel combinations and elaborated so that they can be visually apprehended. The sculptor works in a similar fashion: Parts of his psyche are projected and become the model that gives the statue its final form. What was previously inside the marble was the potential for a statue. The inner core of the marble block is an amorphous piece of stone, and it has the same significance and potential for the sculptor that the blank canvas has for the painter. The materials of the artist's craft serve as containers of projection, somewhat in the same manner as the blank screen does for the dream (Lewin, 1958) or the neutral analyst as the recipient of transference projections.

The creator give structure to what was previously unstructured. This also happens in the treatment of patients suffering from primitive mental states; the goal of therapy is to further ego integration and the acquisition of psychic structure. The latter are new structures that represent a differentiation of what previously had been amorphous ego states. The creation of a better-differentiated personality in treatment has some features that parallel the production of a creative product. Whether the treatment process can be considered creative is another question that might stretch the concept and definition of creativity to its limits.

Nevertheless, the creator in the act of creating furthers his emotional development and attains higher levels of ego integration. As he extends the scope of perceptual and executive systems, both the external and internal worlds become expanded. Analysts also increase the range of their psychic functioning as their patients improve within a psychoanalytic context. Here again, we can compare the creator, the therapist, the creative process, and the therapeutic process. Still, we have to be cautious not to be misled into thinking that all of these functions and roles are creative.

I believe, however, that many clinicians sense that the more they understand about the creative act, the more they will learn about psychic growth in general, and this will enhance our knowledge of the therapeutic process. Because treatment is a growth-promoting experience, the analysis of creative persons who have lost their ability to create because of psychopathology offers us an opportunity to learn something about the creative process. As the patient's ego integration reaches higher levels from the acquisition of insights gained in the transference context, he regains his capacity to create, and such activity is, in turn, instrumental to helping the patient's emotional development. The interplay of the psychic operations characteristic of creativity and the working-through process are highlighted.

I wish to investigate how character development in treatment becomes intertwined with creative activity. I emphasize again that I am not equating growing up emotionally with a creative act, no matter how awesome and wonderfully intricate and ingenious a fully developed human character is. If that were the case, most of us would be geniuses, but we would be confusing the product with the process.

Treatment also permits us to make inferences about early stages of psychic development, as this book has repeatedly stressed. The background of the creative person, as studied in the psychoanalytic setting, may lead to special insights about the growth-promoting factors of early development. Freud (1905) believed that there are in childhood impediments to drive differentiation, psychic maturation, and the unfolding of sexuality. In part, this is due to the immature state of the child's biological endowments. There are also intrinsic conflicts, such as those stimulated by the oedipal configuration, that impede the progression of a developmental impetus. The child destined to be creative often has had unique experiences and circumstances during infancy and childhood that have mitigated these inherent and environmental impediments that generally make the pathway to the achievement of autonomy and self-confidence difficult.

It would be rash and premature to assume that the special circumstances surrounding the creative child have some etiological connection with creativity. At most, we can surmise that these are favorable conditions in which a creative potential can be nourished and flourish. Some aspects of many creative person's backgrounds are traumatic, however, and it would be difficult to understand how these traumas could have any beneficial effects. Can a conflict-producing experience lead to the acquisition of certain defenses that can later be brought into the service of creative endeavor? I do not believe this happens often, although I would not exclude such a possibility entirely.

Creativity and Psychopathology

Clinical studies of scientists in psychoanalytic treatment strengthen the conviction that insanity is not associated with genius. On the contrary, mental illness inhibits rather than promotes creativity. Still, it seems to be true that many truly creative persons appear to have severe emotional problems. This is especially clear with artists and writers, but there is also a popular stereotype of the mad scientist. Regardless of the close association of psychopathology and creativity, this still does not mean that there are any process connections between the two.

As clinicians, the creative persons we see will always have emotional problems, but, as stated, we can read about many gifted and productive men and women having been schizophrenic, having severe depressions, and committing suicide. We are often overwhelmed by the amount of emotional illness we find in so many prominent innovators. Whether this is statistically significant when compared with the emotional problems found in the immensely larger group of noncreative, ordinary people is, at this time, impossible to determine. As far as I know, no one has investigated the highly gifted psychologically healthy person.

I do not wish to belabor this topic further, because there are so many obscurities that we can hardly frame relevant questions about psychopathology and creativity. To this day, our concepts about psychological health, for the most part, remain naïve.

There is still a tendency to equate early developmental ego states with psychopathology. The labeling of a psychic configuration or a mental process as primitive, in many instances, conjures a picture of an emotionally disturbed person. Regression, in a similar vein, has been thought of as an exclusively abnormal phenomenon. The study of creativity has made significant contributions to modifying this outlook, however, as exemplified by the concept of regression in the service of the ego (Kris, 1952). Consequently, although the creative process may involve primitive mental mechanisms and deal with parts of the self that relate to primitive mental states, I repeat that this does not mean that the act of creating is, in any way, associated with mental aberrations.

In Chapter 8, I discussed how a productive experience can degenerate into psychopathology. I gave one example of a young man who heard voices that purportedly helped him to play a musical instrument. At times, the voices would no longer be benign. They would revile and attack him in a typical paranoid fashion. Apparently what had been a positive, harmonious, adaptive, interaction between various parts of the self had turned into a manifestation of pathological splitting and paranoid projection. This patient had been a highly creative scientist when he was not overwhelmed by paranoid symptomatology, and he clearly demonstrated in his life in general how his creativity had been replaced by psychopathological adaptations that led to disruption rather than psychic equilibrium. Thus, what may have been an example of creative mental activity at one time, may lose some qualities that are responsible for its innovative capacities.

There are undoubtedly synthesizing elements that help the psyche to maintain a close, intimate relation with reality as well as allowing it to be immersed in primary-process-oriented early developmental levels. The primitive is placed in a coherent context, but once the latter is no longer operative, the primary process dominates, control is lost, and psychopathological defenses have to be constructed in order to regain emotional equilibrium. This sequence from creativity to emotional illness may give the deceptive appearance of a connection between insanity and creativity.

As synthesizing elements can be lost and thereby produce emotional decompensation, they can also be acquired and lead to a relatively healthy emotional equilibrium. Can they lead to creative activity? In other words, can the reverse sequence occur, in which psychopathology becomes converted into creative accomplishment? Again, this would not imply an etiological connection between psychopathology and creativity, because something would have to be added, some other variable would have to be involved, to effect such a change. The psyche will have gained some synthesizing accretion that causes it to operate in a creative and nonpathological fashion.

Futhermore, this reverse sequence does not imply that creativity has a restorative effect. Some time ago, analysts were inclined to view the creative act as a healing station on the path to mental health (Klein, 1929, Lee, 1940). Freud, for example, was known to suffer from occasional depressions, and it was postulated that he became engaged in creative activities to obtain relief from his depressive misery. Still, these are inferences made from phenomenological sequences and cannot be established without an understanding of the underlying process. Creativity leads to higher states of psychic integration, but this does not necessarily mean that it can undo the effects of psychopathology.

We can gain some insight into these questions, that is, questions about creative mechanisms and their vicissitudes, as they are related to psychopathology. My main clinical experience has been with scientists rather than with artists. Although I have seen some artists, I do not believe, however, that there are fundamental differences between the mental mechanisms of artists and scientists. Perhaps their respective skills and native endowments involve different aspects of the ego's executive system, but I am more interested in the many similarities shared by these groups. And even within the group of scientists I have had the opportunity to study, there exist many features in common, not only in terms of background, but also in terms of talents and psychopathology. It is a remarkable fact that three contemporary Nobel laureates met each other in high school when they were members of a science fiction club.

I will present clinical material to emphasize some of these similarities, and I will highlight psychic mechanisms associated with unique developmental and characterological constellations that, in my opinion, have some relevance to the creative process. Psychopathology, as is so often the case, sharpens our focus and permits us to observe psychic mechanisms that would have been otherwise unnoticeable. With scientists, their capacity to work can be correlated with the operations of various adaptations or with their breakdown. The appearance of psychopathologically constructed defenses usually leads to an inhibition of productive and creative accomplishment.

I will discuss how characterological features are involved in the creative process. I believe there are inner forces in some persons, because of native endowment and the encouragement of the infantile ambience, that propel them toward the goal of being creative. These forces are usually associated with developmental tasks. As I mentioned earlier, there are intrinsic features involved in psychic development that lead to failure in some areas, which include drives and ego structure. The truly innovative person, however, can convert what most often is experienced as inevitable failure into a higher level of psychic structure. If this does not happen, then we are confronted with a certain type of patient, many of whom I have been discussing in this book. The backgrounds of the patients I present in this chapter, however, are nowhere near as traumatic as the larger group of patients suffering from primitive mental states. They had supportive relationships and experiences (see Chapter 11).

Of course, the clinical picture some creative patients present is of a very severe character disorder or even that of an overt psychotic decompensation. Even so, as will be evident from the cases I am about to introduce, there are also salient differences that distinguish them from the ordinary, noncreative, severely disturbed patient.

I will first present a famous scientist, whom I analyzed after he had already made his mark in the world. This patient's creativity had reached fruition before entering analysis, but his psychopathology interfered with his being able to continue to perform at such high levels. Next, I will discuss an adolescent patient who, 10 years after completion of his treatment, achieved considerable renown in his area of scientific specialization. It was clear that he could not function at any level without treatment.

Clinical Material

The patient, a scientist in his late thirties, was encouraged to seek treatment by his wife and concerned colleagues. He had become moody, sluggish, and distraught, and spent long hours staring into space. He also heard voices that talked about divine missions, and at one point, he believed he was Christ. He was also tense and anxious most of the time, a marked contrast to his previous cheerful and calm manner. He always seemed distressingly preoccupied. All of these reactions occurred a week or two after the death of his father.

In spite of his distress, he talked freely. He described his childhood and adolescence as having been fairly happy. He is the second-born of three children; his two sisters adored him and, from what I gathered, still do. His father was a successful businessman who reputedly had his share of charisma. The mother, said to be a beautiful woman, apparently doted on him and immensely enjoyed his precociousness.

The patient was obviously gifted and a fast learner. His father, who was somewhat scholarly and interested in science, started giving his son private lessons when he was only two years old. He was told that he was taught arithmetic and could multiply and divide by the age of three. At four, he knew Euclidian geometry well, and was able to construct his own theorems. He was also taught geography and history, but by the time he started school, he had already outstripped his father in all of these subjects, pursuing them on his own and having developed a voracious appetite for reading books and learning.

He did not fit the stereotype of the typically bookish student—reclusive, skinny, and shy. On the contrary, he was popular with his peers, and had an extraordinary number of playmates. He recalled one particular Sunday promenade with his parents when he was six; they were astonished at the number of young children who came up to him to say hello and chat.

He was also very active physically, preferring sports that permitted the exercise of individual skills one-on-one, such as boxing and wrestling, rather than team sports. He played hard.

In school, he was rapidly advanced and graduated from elementary school at the age of nine. He was able to straddle different frames of reference successfully. In the classroom he was the youngest and smallest as well as the smartest. Nevertheless, he did not threaten anyone, even though he usually was the teacher's favorite. The bigger boys did not resent him, because, in the physical area, he was no competition. Instead, they went to him for help, or he actually did their homework for them. Because he could do it without any effort, he gladly complied. The girls thought he was "cute" and tended to mother him. He told me, with a nostalgic, wistful look, how he remembered the older girls hugging him and how he loved the smell of their perfume. Apparently his female teachers were also in the habit of hugging him, something he still thought about fondly.

Outside the classroom he played with boys his own size and

age, and he was comfortable there, too. They admired his
intellect, but because they had no competitive strivings in that
area, they were content to just give him nicknames, such as "the
genius," and let it go at that. With his peers, he was accepted
more as a teacher than as a follower, and he enjoyed the position
he was placed in.

At this point we might wonder why anyone with such a
childhood, having been so talented and engaging and loved by
everyone would, as an adult, be seeing a psychiatrist. I refer to
his adult psychopathology later. At first it appeared to be surprisingly severe, a schizophrenic decompensation, but it turned
out to be considerably less serious.

In retrospect, the patient became aware of difficulties with
his father, beginning in early childhood. He was admired by all
members of his family but he was, nevertheless, afraid of his
father. At first, he viewed him as a strong, stern character who
could easily lose his temper, but he had a tender, loving side as
well. Perhaps what disturbed the patient most was his father's
emotional lability.

By the time he was five, he reported, he had become aware
that his mother hardly ever talked about her husband. From the
mother's conversation, it seemed as if he did not exist. When the
patient moved beyond the confines of his home, and came into
contact with other adults, as happens in school, he was able to
make comparisons. He also noted that on the rare occasion his
mother or older sister did speak about his father, they were
subtly depreciating.

The patient, during the oedipal phase and early postoedipal
period, had many omnipotent fantasies, and these continued
well into adolescence, although by then they were cast in erotic
tones. During childhood he would build enormous space ships
in his mind and travel to and discover distant planets. He would
also encounter all types of obstacles that he always successfully
overcame. He would fight monsters and giants.

His dreams were especially interesting in that he had a large
number of what psychologists call lucid dreams; these are said
to occur particularly in creative persons. A lucid dream is a
dream in which the dreamer is aware of the fact that he is
dreaming. These are often pleasant dreams, inasmuch as one

can do all kinds of things—satisfy diverse needs and take unusual risks—because it is only a dream and no one can get hurt. A lucid dream this patient still remembered involved being able to fly and to lift steamships and buildings with prodigious strength. This took place before Superman became a cultural icon.

The patient began to de-idealize his father as he idealized a teacher who had become intensely involved with him. He began to see his father's shortcomings: Underneath some superficial bluster, he was passive and submissive to his wife and older daughter. He also reported that now he believes his father could not have helped being jealous of him. Still, in spite of his superior position, part of the patient was still afraid of him.

He emphasized his conflicting viewpoints. On the one hand, he was clearly the victor in the oedipal triangle. On the other hand, he had an internalized image of his father as a powerful, strong, and wise man who, in comparison to himself, made him feel inferior, a feeling he seldom overtly experienced.

He became passionately involved in science, and even in his prepuberty years, he had a reverential awe for what he was learning and the teachers who taught him. As he advanced in school, he always managed to have at least one teacher whom he idealized and who, in turn, would admire him and encourage him to fully develop his talents. These were close relationships in which confidences were shared; his mentors would reveal their own personal hopes and aspirations. The patient was especially fond of a particular instructor who spoke with almost religious fervor about a very famous scientist whose genius had revolutionized the field he specialized in. This instructor had hoped to study under the scientist's tutelage, but he was not successful enough academically to achieve this coveted position. My patient, on the other hand, did get his Ph.D. under this scientist and became almost equally famous.

Afterwards, he continued idealizing, although the objects of his idealization became increasingly more abstract. He idealized his work and the principles and goals of science, which he saw as the objective search for truth. Among the numerous books he had read, Michael Pupin's (1925) autobiography particularly impressed him given that he had the same propensity for idealizing an abstraction. Pupin, for example, believed that every American college and university could raise an invisible capital consecrated to the eternal truth and fill it with the icons of the great saints of science. The saints of science, he said, imparted their knowledge, that is, their secrets, to their "sons," the younger, eager, sincere students of science.

Compared with his childhood, my patient's adolescence was relatively unhappy. In high school and, later, at the university, he continued attracting people because of his academic brilliance as well as his personal charm. He was aware of a developmental lag however. By the time he was passing through puberty, his colleagues seemed already well established in their sexual identity and social relationships. He was no longer satisfied being cast in the role of the young ladies' "darling." Instead, he wanted a girlfriend and a sexual partner, but he could not believe that any girl would relate to him at that level. He now suffered from feelings of inadequacy and felt defeated in an area in which he believed he did not have the endowments required for success. He thought that other young men were better looking, stronger, and more appealing than he was.

As might be expected, he was extremely sensitive and easily wounded by any rebuff, actual or imagined. He tried to overcome his sense of inferiority by directly confronting what he feared. During his first year at the university, he mustered his courage and started asking numerous girls for dates. His record of success did not please him, but he managed to go out occasionally, and petted fairly heavily. He also joined a fraternity and caroused a good deal with his fraternity brothers. In summary, there was some heterosexual activity, but most of his time was spent in "bull sessions" and drinking beer. He was also aware that he was covering up for his basic sense of insecurity and that, in the sexual area, he felt very much a failure.

Academically, he continued in his usual brilliant fashion. There was no problem too difficult for him, and he soon had a reputation for being able to do anything. In this regard, there was an aura of omnipotence about him. He actually believed he could create at will.

His capacity for visual imagery was developed to the point that he could conjure pictures of pages he had read when he needed the information on them. He did not actually have a photographic memory, but he had the ability to produce eidetic images. He could also reproduce problems in his mind, no matter how complex or difficult, and effortlessly visualize the solutions. Interestingly, after adolescence, his eidetic experiences disappeared, although he is still able to have powerfully vivid visual experiences.

Again, the responses of his fellow students were not hostile, envious, or competitive. His peers apparently identified with his grandiosity, as evidenced by their enthusiasm and pride when they talked about his "miraculous" feats of intellect. They were proud to know him personally, because he was gradually becoming a legend. Equally interesting was that he was in no way arrogant or prepossessing. In spite of a megalomania that seemed to say, 'If I can see it, that is, if I can conjure it in my mind, then it exists,' he accepted this gift in a calm, unobtrusive fashion and he did not threaten others.

He endeared himself to his colleagues by being interested in their interests. There was nothing that he found dull. Though he was deeply immersed in science, he also found his other subjects, the humanities, history, art, and music fascinating. He was a good listener as well as an eloquent speaker.

Once more the reader may wonder how this scientist, with all his gifts, intellect, charisma, and sensitive, *simpatico* reactions to his peers, became a patient. How could anything go wrong? His range of activities was wide, and many of his actions and involvements seemed incongruous, such as his propensity both for riding a motorcycle, and for highly abstract intellectualism. Still, everything was not well.

As I mentioned, in the sexual area, he was very insecure. The polarities were striking. Basically he considered himself a failure. He became increasingly shy around women, and when he started graduate school, he stopped dating altogether. He became sufficiently depressed and concerned that he contacted a psychiatrist, but he stopped seeing him after several months because he did not feel any better about himself. Nevertheless, he continued doing extremely well in his work, and it was this success that sustained him.

Creative persons operate within broad spectrums, a fact

this patient illustrated in various ways. He demonstrated many of the qualities that have been considered characteristically associated with the creative process. He was grandiose but not arrogant, inquisitive and curious but not intrusive, and although he valued what he did to the degree of idealization, he could also appreciate the involvement and enthusiasm of others for areas in which he had little interest, such as economics and business. Many years ago, Roe (1953) and Stein (1953) outlined traits and qualities commonly found in the true innovator. The sense of failure, however, was not on their lists.

The clinician could easily focus on elements of this patient's past history and make speculative formulations that would explain his adolescent sense of sexual inadequacy. Freud (1905) emphasized how conflicts, including guilt as well as castration anxiety, are reawakened after the latency period during the early prepubertal period. Blos (1966) also refers to the reawakening of old conflicts during adolescence. Do feelings of inadequacy during what many authors have considered the vulnerable period of adolescence necessarily constitute psychopathology? Is this sense of inevitable failure perhaps part of the process of facing adult aspirations, such as sexual satisfaction, with the psychic equipment of childhood?

In the same context, we have to examine how the patient's creative talents were related to his dilemma. Were they simply artifacts that ran parallel to his intrapsychic conflicts, thereby leading to what seem to have been enigmatic contradictions to his characterological orientation? Certainly his good feelings about his scientific proclivities and his bad feelings about his heterosexual capacities and their social extensions did not cancel each other out; this was not a neutralizing interaction (Hartmann, 1955). Futhermore, the bad feelings did not "spoil" the good ones (Klein, 1929). Even if not peacefully, they were at least able to coexist. Again, the creative factor may be implicated, in that such an ego is able to keep separate these two aspects of the psyche; we can identify this as a special strength, a special ego capacity of our creative character structure.

From another perspective, we can consider whether creative talents or the infantile environment in which they developed lead to vulnerabilities that become manifest during adolescence and adulthood. I believe that focusing on these issues will provide us with further insights about both the creative process and its psychopathological vicissitudes. Before proceeding with them, I will present some material from an adolescent patient who was known to be gifted, but who failed to perform up to his enormous potential. In contrast to the first patient, he was so obviously disturbed during adolescence that he and his family sought intensive treatment while he was a freshman in college. In some ways, he had always been considered peculiar.

I mentioned this patient earlier. Several months after having started college at a highly academic prestigious university, his personal habits broke down completely. He stopped bathing, shaving, brushing his teeth, and ceased to function socially altogether. He just sat in his dormitory room doing nothing. Finally, his classmates took him to see the student health psychiatrist, who, at first, diagnosed him as an acute schizophrenic. However, after his parents came to visit, the patient became less apathetic and did not have the signs and symptoms of a psychosis. He gave the appearance of a frightened, confused young man who had very little self-confidence and an amorphously constructed identity sense. These, as I have made clear, are the symptoms that Erikson (1959) described as constituting the identity-diffusion syndrome. The parents, who had been in analysis themselves, questioned whether analysis might be feasible, and because the patient also seemed to show some interest in intensive treatment, he was referred to me.

The patient is an only child of a wealthy, socially prominent family. Both parents are talented, successful persons. From an early age, he showed considerable proclivity for mathematics, physics, chemistry, and biology. He was also interested in astronomy, but dealt with it simply as a fascinating hobby. His parents were very proud of him and doted on him. They bought him expensive, powerful telescopes, and during adolescence, big motorcycles and expensive cars. The patient enjoyed them, but he never felt truly happy. Something was missing, in that he could not experience a solid sense of gratification and fulfillment.

His father, highly successful in the competitive business world, did not expect his son to succeed him in the empire he had created. He prided himself about his liberal attitudes and his respect for autonomy. In view of his son's interest in biology, he had hoped that he would seek a career in medicine.

My patient quickly revealed how much he revered his parents and hated himself. The latter was based principally on his failure to live up to the expectations his parents had of him. He felt even worse because he had nothing to rebel against. He could not justifiably accuse anyone of having imposed anything upon him.

During treatment, it became slowly apparent that he had experienced the infantile environment as oppressive to his autonomy. As an adolescent, he became aware of painful feelings that he described as disruptive agitation. When he was taken to the student health clinic, he was deeply disturbed. He had withdrawn completely from the external world because he believed he could not hold himself together. He described feeling as if he would "explode," and there was nothing he could find that would calm him.

At first, I thought of rage, but it was the underlying sense of futility, misery, and hopelessness that was most impressive. He reviled himself mercilessly for his lack of accomplishment in view of the tremendous advantages and opportunities he had had all his life. He stressed his failure.

At the same time, he was not without some grandiosity. His narcissism was not totally depleted, as it might have seemed at first. In the back of his mind, he was convinced that he had the capacity to make momentous discoveries. During his treatment, he often seemed megalomanic when he would actually boast about his brilliance, his photographic memory, and how he could conduct experiments that would prove the validity or invalidity of various controversial hypotheses. At these moments, he was decidedly unpleasant, approaching obnoxiousness. He would pace up and down the consultation room, gesticulating and shouting, and loudly lamenting how stupid everyone was, including me. Though he loathed the stereotype of the rich man's son as a spoiled brat, he sometimes presented such a picture.

When he pontificated about the area of mental development and health, he was naïve and sophomoric and, for the most part, incomprehensible, so it was difficult for me to determine whether he was being delusional about his capacities. I had no inclination to challenge him, and even if I had, the other dismal picture that he painted of himself would have forced me to remain silent.

I will pursue what happened to both these patients later, because I now wish to discuss the data I have presented. I should mention that some 10 years after treatment, the second patient made various discoveries that revolutionized some aspects of industry. He also made an enormous fortune for himself.

It will be interesting to understand further some of the questions I raised regarding the first patient, namely the coexistence of grandiosity and a sense of failure. We can also profitably explore how creative ability relates to this curious clinical phenomenon.

Psychic Processes and Ego Development

To repeat, both patients could present contradictory ego states almost simultaneously. The second patient, for example, could feel megalomanic at the end of a session that had been dominated by bitter self-recriminations. This young man, because of the quantitative exaggeration of psychopathology, made clearer those processes and character traits that illustrate certain parallelisms between elements of the creative process, adolescent character consolidation, and ego development. As discussed, a mechanism that might be essential to creativity may decompensate into a pathological defense or become involved in a disintegrative, regressive current, causing it to lose adaptive and creative capacities.

I am referring specifically to dissociation, the splitting mechanisms that have been so frequently implicated in borderline psychopathology (Kernberg, 1975). This mental mechanism, however, can be taken out of the context of psychopathology and viewed in terms of its adaptive capacities: It permits the ego to continue functioning at very high levels and to reach innovative states of integration that lead to the production of creative products or consolidations. Both patients used dissociation extensively, but the first patient was able to maintain self-esteem and to function efficiently and creatively.

Is dissociation a defense for these patients, as it is for noncreative patients, allowing them to maintain psychic equilibrium? Ordinarily we think of defenses as reestablishing a balance, a compensation to counteract the decompensatory effects of psychopathology. At best, this can be considered a psychopathological equilibrium because it is a compensatory maneuver. The psyche expends a tremendous amount of energy to maintain a precarious balance and we would not expect there to be enough remaining for creative activity.

This is not true for the first patient. He was very productive as he maintained the split between those parts of his personality that bordered on the grandiose and megalomanic and those that caused him to feel inadequate and a failure. In fact, it seemed necessary to have the capacity to effect such a dissociation if he were able to continue functioning at such a high level. Later, during adulthood, he temporarily lost this capacity, and he was unable to continue with his very creative work. The second patient could not function because he could not use dissociation well enough. He had some grandiose moments, but they were not highly cathected, whereas his sense of inevitable failure was.

Eissler (1958) tells of a similar situation with Goethe, who apparently had an "encapsulated" psychosis. That is how Eissler saw it. Goethe, according to Eissler, was able to keep the creative and psychotic parts of his psyche separate. When he was unable to do so, his psychotic parts dominated and rendered him unable to function. It was part of his genius, however, that he could reinstate splitting mechanisms.

Does the concept of splitting used here correspond exactly to the dissociation we find in severe psychopathology? Inasmuch as we formulate dissociation as a mechanism in which connections within the ego are dissolved, then I believe something similar happens with my patients. This is an intraego process and involves similar levels in the psychic hierarchy. In other words, whatever splitting occurs involves the same ego subsystems. For example, in my patients, we are witnessing dissociation of the self-representation, rather than, let us say, dissociation of executive skills, which would cause a person to be very clumsy in some situations and adept in others. There can also be perceptual dissociations as well as those involving the integrative and memory systems.

For example, Norbert Wiener, the father of cybernetics and an undisputed genius, dramatically illustrates various types of dissociation. It is well known that he was so clumsy that in his classroom it was necessary for his secretary to write on the blackboard for him. He was unable to coordinate his movements well enough to move a piece of chalk along its surface. I learned from one of his students that when Wiener was doing research in a hospital in Mexico City he was a favorite among the interns. He would become involved in their two most popular pastimes, wrestling, and chess. I naturally surmised that he must have been a chess master, but an ineffectual, unskilled, and awkward wrestler. I was completely wrong; he was the best wrestler and the worst chess player of the group.

Dr. Wiener was well known for his photographic memory. He had almost total recall for practically everything he had ever read. Still, there is an apocryphal anecdote that used to be circulated at the Massachusetts Institute of Technology, where Dr. Wiener held his academic appointment. Around the noon break he is walking along and encounters a colleague. The two stop and chat for a few minutes, and then begin to move on. Before departing, Dr. Wiener asks his friend in which direction he was heading before they stopped to chat. After being told, he replies, "Then I haven't had lunch."

The dissociations discussed here are structurally similar to splitting mechanisms in general, but I believe there are fundamental differences. My first patient, at the time, and my second patient, later in life, had, if any, a minimum of dynamic interplay between the split-off parts of their egos. There was very little connection or continuity between the grandiose competent self-representation and the inadequate, failing parts of themselves. To maintain this separation, the first patient did not require large expenditures of psychic energy. His grandiosity and success did not constitute a compensatory defense against what he perceived as weakness and vulnerability. These were two states of mind that coexisted without intruding into each other. This isolation of structural configurations permitted him to make innovative discoveries, something the second patient could not do because he had not yet been able to achieve such a separation. I pursue the specific qualities of psychic processes associated with creativity further in the next chapter.

To repeat, being able to effect a dissociation was a necessary psychic activity so that my patient could be creative. According to Eissler (1958), this was also true of Goethe. Can we then state that dissociation is a defense required for creative functioning? I cannot generalize, of course, but it is necessary for some. I would question, however, whether dissociation would be part of a defensive system if its outcome is the preservation of creativity. Here, we can distinguish an adaptation that maintains the highest level of functioning possible and a defense that protects against a psychotic breakdown.

We can question whether dissociation is fundamentally involved and intrinsically related to creativity (see Chapter 11). Both my patients emphasized how they were able to make use of splitting mechanisms since childhood. As I have stated, the patients and I concluded that their ability to keep various parts of their psyches from intruding into each other was a talent, a strength associated with creative capacity. Greenacre (1956) stressed that these are ego strengths, unusual discriminatory sensitivities, that are found in creative persons, but they cannot be considered etiological factors. Still, we can ask whether there are unique and special childhood environmental configurations that are particularly conducive to the development of creative ability, as Greenacre (1957) explored, or to the development of dissociative psychic mechanisms.

Environmental Factors, Developmental Stages, and their Vicissitudes

Both patients had mothers who were unusually devoted to them. They were breast-fed beyond the usual period, well into the first year. The first patient actually had two mothers, in that the oldest sister also doted on him. Jones (1953) tells us about the devotion between Freud and his mother.

The backgrounds of both my patients differ markedly from those of noncreative, seriously disturbed patients. The latter have had very little gratification during infancy, and nurturing was deficient. They have a noticeable lack of caretaking experiences and relationships. The patients presented in this chapter were, from many viewpoints, well taken care of, even though they faced conflicts during their formative years.

I have not found one instance of parental neglect in any of the creative patients I have had the opportunity to study. On the contrary, if it is possible, some patients seemed to have a surfeit of parenting (see Chapter 11). As the first patient illustrated, he, in effect, had two mothers, a mother and an older sister. They both looked after him, giving him considerable attention. I recall three other patients who had two fathers, the second father being an uncle who lived with the family or who lived sufficiently nearby that he was constantly present. These patients were very fond of their uncles, and during early childhood, preferred them to their fathers. They also seemed to identify with and idealize them, even more so than their fathers.

I do not believe that we know enough about Freud's background to reach conclusions about the parental constellation of his childhood. It is well known, however, that for many years his wife's sister lived with him and his family. Apparently, Freud was very fond of "Tanta Minna" and spent many hours conversing with her. His wife took care of the house, children, and food, and his sister-in-law helped nourish him intellectually.

These particular family configurations might help us to understand the many-sided aspects, the numerous facets to the innovator's personality. I do not mean to indicate that to be creative, a person must have more than one father or mother, because many have been content with just one. When such a situation occurs, however, it can lead us to some insights about the dissociative process.

One of the patients who was raised by his father and an uncle revealed that he incorporated the father's prohibitive superego and the expansive uncle's ego-ideal. Consequently, he was overtly much more attached to his uncle, and directed his negative feelings toward his father. The latter, however, were not particularly intense, and he was able to make various qualities of the father his own. He had incorporated aspects of both his father and uncle in an ego-syntonic fashion, and later in life, after having become more aware of his father's benign concern for him, he could shift anger back and forth from the father imago to the uncle imago. These were separate imagos, but still could be considered subcategories of the general functional unit of paternal parent. This unique arrangement made dissociation a benign rather than a disruptive process (see Chapter 11) and facilitated the patient's propensity to idealize teachers and their capacity to achieve.

As the precocious talents of the two patients I have presented flourished, they were increasingly idealized, inasmuch as others joined the admiring throng. It would seem that they were able to incorporate life experiences, that is, integrate them into their memory systems, because they were so gratifying; and with the increased self-esteem that they produced, they were able to proceed to further accomplishments. This would, in a sense, constitute a positive feedback, and since there was so much harmony between the inner and outer worlds, there would not seem to be much need for dissociative mental mechanisms.

This is where their fathers enter the picture. The first patient emphasized his disillusionment. As he viewed his father from a more realistic perspective, he was able to see that underneath the facade of competence and self-confidence, his father was insecure and unsuccessful. His mother reinforced this picture. The second patient's father, by contrast, was indeed, successful. Still, as his son grew older he became unhappy with the materialistic attitudes that surrounded him. He wondered about his father's ethics and integrity and became less and less pleased with the gifts that his father so lavishly gave him.

When I first saw my adolescent patient, he was, as I have described, in a state of identity diffusion. In addition to having lost, relatively speaking, his sense of identity, he was in a painful quandary about his value system. He did not know what he aspired to and what he could respect. On the one hand, he regretted the crass materialism of his father's world, but at the same time, he was perceptive enough to know how pleasant and comfortable the absence of want could be. He enjoyed his sports cars, for example, but he felt that he should not.

As treatment progressed, he relived this conflict in the transference. He reviled himself for having no integrity and for being rich and privileged. This was not in harmony with his ego-ideal. As he directed his feelings outward, he would then attack me because of the way I lived, my high fees, and other qualities that he attributed to the "materialistic, greedy Establishment." These angry attitudes are not unusual during adolescence, but what distinguished my patient was his ready propensity to internalize his feelings against himself as well as directing them toward me. It became clear that he was projecting and reintrojecting his father imago.

He had been able to keep his idealization of his mentors and science dissociated from the image of the father who, during latency years, had fallen from grace. This accounted for both his self-aggrandizement and self-depreciation. The latter was the outcome of his introjected father, but as he was hating himself, he was also attacking his father.

The first patient was phenomenologically psychotic when he came to see me. He was an angel in God's entourage and at war with the Devil and his cohorts. At times, he believed he was the son of God. The split between good and evil had reached paranoid proportions, but his psychosis, if that is what it was, was colorful and even entertaining rather than grim and painful. For example, he patterned his "delusions" around the plot of Anatole France's fascinating novel, *The Revolt of the Angels*, wherein the forces of evil and the forces of good are not only juxtaposed but reversed. The protagonist's guardian angel rejected God and wanted him replaced by the Devil.

He began treatment by challenging me to analyze him, and for a long time he would not lie down on the couch. He was suspicious of me, accused me of working for the Mafia and of wanting to destroy his brain. He soon saw me as the Devil, but he also saw himself as behaving devilishly. At times, he was the guardian angel, and at other times, he was the protagonist, somewhat of an amoral libertine who preaches virtue to an angel who does not believe in God. He reenacted this interplay with me, and I must confess that some of his sessions were amusing, something I seldom feel with psychotic patients. He often told me of a particular conversation in the novel between the guardian angel and the protagonist, Maurice. The angel is arguing with Maurice and trying to enlist his aid in order to raise funds so that he can organize a cadre of angels to dethrone God and replace him with the Devil. As the angel argues more and more heatedly, Maurice, in an astonished voice, exclaims that it seems that the angel does not believe in God. The angel replies that of course he believes in God; his very existence depends upon that belief; but he protests that his is not a just God.

As long as he mixed his delusions with the plot of the novel, he was animated and comfortable, although he was totally paralyzed as far as work was concerned. As he gradually internalized the feelings attached to them, however, he began experiencing the same coexistence of grandiosity and self-debasement and confusion that my adolescent patient experienced. He also projected and reintrojected the hated parts in the transference as well as later idealizing me. Both patients carried their idealizations from my person to psychoanalysis in general.

The adolescent patient's psychopathology intensified to the point where he could not function during his teenage years, and he was not able to achieve his creative potential until late in young adulthood. It is doubtful that he would have been able to reach the heights he did without treatment. In some respects, the other patient had a difficult adolescence, but he still functioned continuously at a very high level until he had his "psychotic" decompensation.

Perhaps the relationship of these patients to their fathers was a variable that determined whether psychopathology or creativity would gain the upper hand. The adolescent patient deidealized his father, but that did not change anything. His father continued being powerful and competent. The disillusionment concerned only one facet of his character, the one that involved moral integrity. The father remained strong, whereas the other patient's father was totally discredited. Although the latter patient later developed symptoms that have been associated with severe psychopathology, he was able to cling to his grandiosity and be sustained by it more easily than the adolescent. The depreciated father did not threaten his megalomania, whereas the strength of the adolescent's father interfered with the patient's capacity to generate a level of self-esteem that would permit him to function. He was not able to maintain an effective dissociation between the valued and devalued parts (the paternal introjects) of the psyche.

I want to mention briefly what caused these patients to decompensate and to discuss the outcome of their therapy, because these are peripheral issues to the subject of creativity. The adolescent, as mentioned, could not integrate himself into his new college environment. This is a common situation with youngsters who suffer from the identity-diffusion syndrome. He found himself in an environment without the usual supports. Furthermore, his increased adolescent sexual urges and the expectations that he be successful sexually as well as intellectually were significant stresses that rendered his usual adaptations ineffective. The other patient's illness began after his father died. His megalomanic orientation overwhelmed him. Besides the guilt, which he felt at a more structured level, the omnipotence of his thoughts, or, more precisely, of his destructive feelings, received reality-validation from his father's actual death. He had to set a massive dissociation in motion to keep his hostility from invading his ego and destroying his megalomania. He devised the colorful delusions that I have already described.

As a transference object, I was alternately assigned by both patients the role of omnipotent ally or depreciated persecutor. The latter assignment, however, did not result in a grim, paranoid relationship. Both viewed me as someone benign, but because I valued creativity, I was jealous of their innovative prowess and would steal their ideas to aggrandize myself. They also playfully teased me about my inferiority. They had a need to feel sexually superior to me, but they were secure in the feeling that they could surpass me intellectually.

This material was not difficult to deal with analytically. They both understood that I was not threatened by either side of their ambivalence as I interpreted the transference projections. I let myself, on occasion, stray from the strictly analytic orientation by becoming interested and involved with some of the fascinating ideas they brought me. I knew they were trying to capture my interest, and they often succeeded in doing so.

The adult scientist gradually relinquished his delusional system in an unobtrusive manner. It seemed simply to disappear by blending with his creative thoughts. After several years of treatment, he terminated because he was offered an extremely attractive position in another city. From time to time, he sends me a postcard indicating that all is well and that he continues working with an almost hypomanic fervor.

The adolescent is now an adult, and like the other patient, is married and has children. Curiously, he is with the Establishment he so reviled, in that his creativity is in the industrial realm and has made vast sums of money for himself and his employers, including his father, a major stockholder in the company.

Omnipotence and Creativity

The truly creative product, however, whether it is tangible or an idea, constitutes something that has never previously existed. Even if its component parts are known, their combination is novel. In a sense, the creator can be thought of as producing something from nothing. Of course, the fundamental law of conservation of matter and energy does not permit such an *ex nihilo* sequence, but in the mind of the creator, this seems to be the case, and inasmuch as he has such a belief, he is being omnipotent, because reputedly, only God has achieved such a feat. *The sense of omnipotence and creativity are intrinsically related to each other.*

The scientist patient, when he had achieved considerable integration during treatment, would calmly relate how he could "will" himself to have an idea. He would describe his mind as being empty. He would then "command" himself to think of something brilliant, and there, as if by magic, it would appear. We both knew it was neither that simple, effortless, or magical, and that his training, experience, and knowledge were operating at levels below perceptual awareness.

As I have emphasized elsewhere (Giovacchini, 1965), the creative person, at least these patients, did not seem at all arrogant when they talked about this omnipotent attitude. In no way was the scientist patient offensive, and it seemed that others did not experience him that way. He was casual, and although proud of his talents, he was not prepossessing and did not depreciate others who generally did not approach his level of performance. On the contrary, he respected the efforts others made and was even naïvely accepting of ideas that on closer inspection often proved to be pedantic and sophomoric.

There was an idealistic quality to his omnipotence. Ordinarily we think of idealization as consisting of the idealization of a person, an institution, or a cause. My patient idealized his creative potential, which he considered to be a "gift from God." He had the same attitude that some very talented tenors have about their "golden" voices, such as Caruso and more recently, Pavarotti, who refer to their voices as something God gave them to keep. This is an interesting combination of megalomania and modesty. The implication is that the possessors of these talents do not deserve any special credit; they were privileged to be bestowed with these gifts by a deity for the good of mankind. They have obligations in view of this sacred trust.

Kris (1952) stressed that the creative act, in addition to the construction of something new, involves communication. The creator has to have an audience who understands what he had done. While creating he is synthesizing and integrating in such a fashion that it is potentially understandable. My scientist patient and other scientists I have treated sought analysis because, among other reasons, they possessed a gift they could not use. They felt they could not maintain contact with the external world, and this heightened their sense of painful alienation. Their psychopathology, in a sense, represented a reaction to being cut off from the external world. They communicated only with various parts of the self, and because of their withdrawal from reality, their mental orientations often appeared to be psychotic.

Inevitable Failure

Adolescence, according to some authors (Blos, 1966), is a stage of life in which some developmental tasks that could not be dealt with in childhood are confronted once again. Arnstein

(1979) questions whether crisis is a necessary factor in the quest for identity. Scharfstein (1978) emphasizes that creative activity enhances the progression on the path toward autonomy. In other words, growing up emotionally is a task that has to be completed, and there are obstacles that have to be overcome.

Freud (1905) states that the child, as his sexual instincts develop, will experience failure that will create a breach in infantile omnipotence. This will carry over as a sense of failure in the early postpubertal age of adolescence.

According to Freud (1914c), if the infantile environment has been optimally gratifying, early developmental stages from autoerotism to the secondary narcissism of beginning object relationships are characterized by a sense of omnipotence. Though there are inevitable frustrations throughout the course of development, because instantaneous gratification is neither possible nor, according to Freud, even desirable, on the whole, the child knows that his needs can be met and that he is capable of being gratified.

When the child, in early childhood, faces strong oedipal urges, there is no possibility of gratification. For the child, gratification would mean victory over the giant adult of the same sex. It would also mean that he has the somatic equipment by which he can achieve heterosexual satisfaction, and, of course, he does not. The little boy cannot successfully pursue the goal of sexually possessing his mother. At this oedipal level, failure is inevitable. Thus, the sexual instincts become associated with failure. It might also be said that there is an asynchrony between instinctual development and the acquisition of the appropriate somatic apparatus that will be incorporated into the ego's executive apparatus and enable a person to experience sexual fulfillment. From this viewpoint, instinctual precocity or a somatic lag is part of normal emotional development.

It is often very difficult to distinguish what constitutes an aspect of normal development and the manifestations of cultural norms or the outcome of psychopathology. This has been an especially hard distinction to make when we study the adolescent phenomenon. Nevertheless, it is a frequent enough occurrence that the child develops feelings of vulnerability and inadequacy during the oedipal phase and that these feelings are reawakened with the biologically stimulated sexual urges of the postpubertal period. They are then felt in a pervasive fashion as a sense of inevitable failure in the anticipation of a heterosexual relationship. Establishing a sexual relationship becomes a perplexing problem.

There has been considerable cultural support for the maintenance of the sexual mystique. From a masculine viewpoint, women can never be understood by men; they are attractive but unfathomable creatures. They represent a problem that can never be solved, and man will always remain inadequate in the face of its enormity.

These attitudes fit better with a mid-Victorian milieu, or any society in which sexuality is, to a large measure, repressed. In view of the current liberal attitudes about sex, this orientation would not be expected to be prevalent. Nevertheless, it is not an unusual one among a fair number of adolescents and some adults who are not necessarily patients seeking treatment. I have seen it invariably, however, among the creative men I have had the opportunity to analyze throughout the years.

I have discussed a scientist (Giovacchini, 1971) who avidly pursued different women and had married several because he wanted to make their behavior predictable. Otherwise, he felt inferior and a failure. He had to master a problem and this compulsion to seek solutions carried over into his creative work.

According to Freud (1905), the sexual aspect of psychic development, because of the human's long period of dependency and physical immaturity, presents inherent difficulties. The oedipally oriented ego faces inevitable failure. The task of achieving a sexually secure self-representation will remain unfinished until early adulthood, and even then, the mnemonic residues of childhood frustration will, to some extent, continue to have their effects. In some instances, creative scientists carry this sense of an uncompleted task into their work, and the impetus of a developmental lag becomes a factor in creative endeavor.

These scientists illustrate an interesting conclusion first reached by Zeigarnik (1927). A completed task does not keep a person's interest. Once the problem is solved, there is little further investment in it. For the creator, it loses its cathexis, or at least, its major force since he remains proud of his acomplishment. The act of accomplishing, however, is much more important than what is accomplished. Zeigarnick discovered experimentally that an unfinished task, that is, an unsolved problem, retains its cathexis. If abandoned, it still vividly remains in the person's mind. Even after years have passed, an incompleted action is easily remembered in contrast to completed tasks. My patients constantly had unfinished tasks even after they gained security in the sexual area.

Creativity, Precocity, and Connecting Bridges

Regardless of psychological factors, in the final breakdown, creativity is a quality found in persons with special gifts. There must be an inherent constitutional factor of which we know practically nothing. There are attributes of innate talent, however, that can be understood in terms of both emotional and psychic developmental factors. I have already presented clinical material emphasizing such elements, but now I wish to derive some generalizations from data obtained from the treatment of a larger group of patients.

The creative persons I have treated, read about, or know showed their proclivities early in childhood. They were destined for greatness. Psychoanalysts have discovered that precocity may be the outcome of psychopathology, a defensive response to a traumatic assaultive infantile environment (Bergmann & Escalona, 1949; Boyer, 1956). The patients I have reported, many of whom were creative scientists, found that their precocity helped them to maintain psychic equilibrium; whether it was primarily a defensive adaptation is difficult to determine. In view of their later creative accomplishments, it is not surprising that their talents would flourish early. Their precocity led to success.

The precociousness of the sexual instinct Freud (1905) wrote about and that of the creative person permits some interesting comparisons. Freud was referring to instinctual precocity, whereas in creative persons, I am emphasizing an early unfolding, a premature appearance of talents. The ego's integra-

tive functions and executive apparatus develop and structuralize to a degree that is further advanced than what is usual for
that particular age period. In contrast to what Freud was describing, precocity here refers to overdevelopment of certain
aspects of psychic structure relative to instinctual organization,
the reverse of his formulation in which the instinct, the sexual
instinct, is further ahead developmentally than the rest of the
psyche. To repeat, *these are two antithetical situations, two
types of precocity: (1) psychic structure outstrips instinct, and
(2) instinct outstrips psychic structure.*

The first type of precociousness is associated with creativity, whereas the second type, according to Freud, is innate to
infantile development. In the former, precociousness can become the vehicle for a successful, creative adaptation, whereas
the latter is doomed to failure. My patients, especially the scientists, demonstrated this peculiar combination of success and
failure. Is such a combination a necessary condition to activate
the creative process?

We do not know what the psychological variables are that
are involved in creativity. The psychic processes of adolescence, however, often seem to be related to creative activity.
For example, the scientist had the capacity for eidetic imagery
and a photographic memory as an adolescent, but these abilities
diminished as an adult. He did not totally lose them, but they
had reached their peak during his college years.

During adolescence, there is considerable rearrangement of
various psychic agencies that finally lead to character consolidation. With puberty, there is a biological heightening of sexual
impulses. Unlike the child, the adolescent now has the somatic
equipment to seek sexual gratification, but does not yet have the
psychic structure and orientation that would enable him or her
to have a satisfactory experience during adolescence. The oedipal failure of childhood is recapitulated.

The creative person can convert failure into success. The
heightening excitation induced by the hormonal accretions of
puberty produce a generally higher energy level, which is not
restricted to sexual urges. There is an all-pervasive zest for life in
the well-adjusted adolescent. For the creative or potentially
creative adolescent, this energy is harnessed to serve the talent
that had precociously appeared in childhood. In other words, a

320 Integration and Adaptation

connection is established between precocious psychic structure and instinctual activity. Thus, sensual urges that were associated with inevitable failure during childhood become linked with successful activities, and this begins during adolescence.

I do not mean that creativity is the outcome of sublimated sexual energy. I am purposely leaving the concept of psychic energy vague, because I do not wish to engage in what would be irrelevant controversy in the context of this discussion. Rather, I am stressing that to gratify needs and to function generally requires energy. This energy is used in many ways, both sexual and nonsexual. The task of adolescence is to acquire psychic structure so that a variety of needs, including sexual needs, can be gratified, and to use the upsurge of energy that occurs with maturation in a harmonious and efficient fashion.

Instinctual forces are associated with primitive psychic levels. During the course of emotional development, there is a structural progression that establishes a hierarchy, a psychic spectrum, as stressed in Chapter 3. The two ends of the spectrum are joined together by intermediary levels that are established as a smooth continuum. *This continuum or bridge is poorly established in the precocious psyche of childhood and during adolescence.*

During the creative act, primitive parts of the psyche governed principally by the primary process come in apposition to structured secondary-process levels. There is no bridge between the two. The continuum is temporarily relinquished. As stated, psychic structures that developed precociously become connected with instinctual elements without a modulatory bridge between the two. This lack of a bridge is characterized by what appears to be the coexistence of contradictory elements, and it seems as if the psyche is split or dissociated. This occurs during the creative act, which culminates in a synthesis and a reestablishment of a connecting bridge that serves as a continuum.

The lack of a continuum between various levels of the psyche that occurs with the precocious child and during adolescence may produce a creative person or it may lead to psychopathology, as discussed in the first section of this book. There are many factors that determine the final outcome, as my patients demonstrate.

Summary and Conclusions

The lack of rigidity in the adolescent's character structure could provide a fertile setting for the realization of creative potential. Fluidity of character structure, however, could also be an element in the production of psychopathology and the combination of creative ability and emotional illness seems to be fairly common.

Still, comparisons and combinations do not mean that there are causal connections between what is being studied. Similarities may be only at the surface level. For example, during the creative act, the creator may seem to be using primitive psychic mechanisms such as dissociation. He may also appear to be indulging in magical thinking as evidenced by megalomania. On closer scrutiny, however, it becomes apparent that he is in control of the primitive within himself as he is simultaneously operating at higher levels of integration. The creator has a tremendous amount of energy that causes him to perceive and to feel more intensely than usual.

I presented two patients. The first demonstrated psychopathology that coexisted with creative capacities. His adolescence was characterized by an ego dissociation—one part of his psyche preserving his capacities for innovation and experienced as pleasurable, associated with success, grandiosity, and high levels of self-esteem, and the other part of his psyche containing the remnants of his childhood oedipal humiliation, which he carried with him as a sense of failure and inadequacy. As long as he could maintain this dissociation, he functioned well. Later, as an adult, he could not maintain this split, and he developed symptoms that were phenomenologically psychotic, but from a diagnostic viewpoint not nearly so serious. The second patient decompensated into an identity-diffusion syndrome during adolescence, and he did not realize his creative potential until after his treatment was terminated.

Various parts of the creator's psyche are hypertrophied, such as the perceptual apparatus and the ego-ideal. Hypertrophied is not the most apt term, because it implies constriction, which is not at all the situation in creativity. I mean that these structures and functions are better developed than usual and that they are apparent earlier during the course of development. This can also be called precocity.

I discussed two types of precocity, one characterizing the creative person and the other an instinctual precocity that Freud (1905) postulated as typical of the sexual instinct. The former refers to ego functions and structures, such as the integrative system and the ego-ideal, which are advanced for the child's age, whereas the latter consist of oedipal sexual urges that are also premature in the sense that the ego does not have the apparatus to ensure their gratification. Thus, there is, on the one hand, a precocity of structure that heightens self-esteem and, on the other hand, a precocity of instinct that leads to feelings of inadequacy. Both my patients demonstrated the effects of these processes in the dissociation they experienced to a fairly intense degree during adolescence.

During the creative act, the modulating bridge that forms a continuum between the primitive and the integrated-structures parts of the personality is temporarily inoperative. During adolescence, such a bridge is in the process of being established. The talented and secure youngster can take advantage of his relatively unstructured ego and use it for creative activity. This may be a reason why so many innovators, particularly mathematicians and physicists, have flourished during their youth.

As an adult, the creator retains the capacity to reproduce an ego state in which connecting bridges and continuums are abolished. He is reproducing and reliving an adolescent ego state, a vibrancy and youthful zest which is the essence of the creative process.

Chapter 11

Primitive Mental Mechanisms and Creativity

The Creator's Early Environment

The last chapter stressed that two creative scientists had somewhat gratifying backgrounds in that they were, for the most part, loved and valued. How these early relationships contributed to their creativity is not at all understood, except that some connection between experiences that promote self-esteem and the self-confidence that is associated with creative accomplishment would make sense.

To take this further, I would like to investigate quantitative factors. Most of the creative scientists that I have had the opportunity to treat came from large families. This does not necessarily mean that they had many siblings; on the contrary, some were only children. More often than not, however, an extended family was very intensely involved with the future creator. As children, these scientists usually had many people around them, although they had their own space to which they could withdraw when they wanted to be alone. I found it interesting that those patients who were only children had four to six children of their own when they established their families.

As I did to some extent in the previous chapter, I will be making comparisons throughout this one between psychopathological factors and primitive orientations that are components of creative activities. There may be some superficial similarities between the family constellations that promote mental illness and those that foster the blooming of creative potential. Granting those similarities, there are also vast differences that may not be readily discernible on the surface.

As for resemblances, the families of many patients suffering from primitive mental states are large, and as a child, the patient was surrounded by relatives. It is not unusual for the disturbed character types seen in treatment to have had more than 10 siblings. These early settings, because of the number of people involved and the multiplicity of confused relationships, are chaotic and generate within the vulnerable child states of acute tension that cannot be soothed (see Chapter 3).

The backgrounds of my creative patients may have been noisy, and the members of the family might have been highly excitable, but they were apparently not disturbing and did not produce agitation. These scientists recalled their childhoods as tranquil, and when they were actively creating, they felt as if they were working in peaceful surroundings. From their descriptions, the atmosphere they created and in which they were immersed seems to have been anything but peaceful. It was vibrant and exciting. Still, I had the feeling that the patients were correct; their atmosphere was not disruptive. I also had the feeling that their past environment was characterized by bristling activity and involvement. It did not seem quiet or devoid of stimulation.

The differences between the infantile environments of noncreative, primitively fixated patients and those of creative patients, of course, concern early object relationships. Whereas extremely disturbed patients had chaotic, turbulent backgrounds, perhaps crowded with many people, the creative innovator has usually had many warm and loving relationships in a highly stimulating environment with considerable input. A famous mathematician of the last century did his most important work sitting in a chair in his living room surrounded by his wife, children, and grandchildren, all visiting and playing. He needed this stimulation to be able to create. As a child, he had lived in a setting with a large, extended family.

The infantile environments of many creative persons are quantitatively different from the norm in terms of nurturing relationships. Most striking were the number of patients who had surrogate fathers, but whose biological fathers were also present. In a group of nine scientists I have analyzed throughout the years, four of them had uncles living with the family until the age of puberty. Two of these patients preferred their uncles to their father during their childhood, because the former tended to indulge them, whereas the father's role was that of the disciplinarian. Later, after puberty, they held their fathers in higher esteem.

In these instances the functional aspects of object relationships were fragmented (see Chapter 10). The father represented the superego, whereas the uncle was equated with instinctual gratification and narcissistic enhancement. The latter led to a sense of optimism and confidence that were undoubtedly assets in furthering their creative endeavors. The splitting of roles was not a constricting, defensive adaptation. These scientists seemed to thrive on gratification rather than being fixated to infantile satisfactions that block emotional development and progression.

Other patients had multiple mothers, usually older sisters or aunts, but the mother still held the powerful and favored position. She remained the most important person of their childhood, although the patients felt considerable fondness for their aunts; and these scientists continued throughout their lives being close to their older sisters, from whom they currently derive considerable emotional support.

All the creative patients I have had the opportunity to study had a propensity for forming relationships that impelled others to take care of them. This ability seemed to stem from what they sometimes referred to as a successful childhood. They were able to carry over the gratifying relationships and fulfilled expectations of the past into the present. It is also interesting that those who looked after them did not feel imposed on or resent their having to minister to someone else's needs. They were fond of them and were glad to be able to treat them in either an avuncular or maternal fashion.

Potential for Soothing and Creativity

In Chapter 3, I discussed the disruptive agitation that characterizes patients suffering from primitive mental states as the outcome of defective soothing mechanisms. I discussed primal confusion, which is manifested by an incapacity to integrate and to react to external stimuli in a fashion that leads to ego synthesis. For example, these primitively fixated patients respond with displeasure and agitation to what most of us would consider comfortable warmth, whereas they might be soothed by both physical and emotional coldness. In a similar vein, quiet rooms are not conducive to relaxation, but discordant noise may have marked quieting effects. Sensory input is responded to in a paradoxical fashion, and this is manifested in their psychopathology.

By contrast, creative patients are easily soothed, although their responses, at times, appear to be paradoxical. They often do their best work in a high-decibel setting, as the mathematician I have mentioned illustrated, although some scientists demand absolute quiet. Those who find noisy settings optimal describe a harmony, a rhythm, to the sound they are immersed in, rather than cacophony. Apparently the volume of auditory stimuli, if kept within certain limits, is not the primary factor that accompanies relaxed productivity. The scientist perceives an organization to his environment even if it appears frenetic, and he feels calm, although to the observer, he may seem hyperactive. Creative involvement and activity, in many instances, imposes order on what strikes most of us as inherently disorderly and chaotic. The creative scientist is often doing something similar with his psyche.

I am describing a parallel process between the creative act, as it makes sense of some aspect of the external world that previously was unknown or did not make sense, or as it produces something new, and the mental processes of the creator while creating. Inner excitement can be organized to the extent that the creator feels soothed rather than disrupted. If the destructive effects of psychopathology interfere with the efficient functioning of soothing mechanisms, however, then the psyche feels agitated and overwhelmed. The latter was usually the reason my scientist patients sought analytic treatment.

As discussed in Chapter 3, defects in soothing mechanisms are associated with the most primitive developmental levels, which are concerned with biological, rather than mentational, modes of functioning, in which circadian rhythms are prominent. Effective soothing establishes a synchrony between the various operations characteristic of prementational states. The creative scientist seems to have an extraordinary capacity for effecting a state of harmony at this most primitive level of psychic development. He has a tremendous potential for self-soothing, although with psychopathology, it can break down.

Though I have focused almost exclusively on scientists, I wish to present some clinical material derived from an artist who was talented enough to make a living from his art, something I understand to be quite rare. I realize that it is especially difficult to assess an artist's creativity, much more so than that of a scientist, especially if the clinician has some background and familiarity with the patient's professional area. With art, the criteria are much more nebulous. My patient's works had been reviewed by two prominent art critics, however, and they were highly praised.

I will concentrate on his background to emphasize the type of nurturing and soothing he received. He was raised by three excitable women, his mother and her two sisters, all of whom, from his descriptions, sounded like hysterical character types. Apparently, the father left the house when he was three years old. To this day, he does not know whether his parents divorced or simply separated. His upbringing was mainly in the care of these three women, although two weekends a month he spent with his father.

The contrast between his home setting and the one the father provided was immense. At home, everything was disorganized and frenetic. His aunts and mother were constantly bustling around, and according to him, "making mountains out of molehills." They would become frantic over having misplaced some item that really did not matter, and might spend the whole afternoon looking for it. If the patient came home and found them in the midst of such activity, more often than not, he would locate the item immediately. In summary, they seemed to represent the epitome of inefficiency and confusion. The father, on the other hand, was calm, collected, logical, and organized. The patient saw him as the antithesis of his mother and her sisters, and he conjectured that this was the reason for their separation.

In spite of these differences in the ambience that each parent created, the patient believed in retrospect that throughout the years the two continued to be fond of each other. Neither parent ever said anything critical to their son about the other, and when they met they were cordial and affectionate. The patient conjectured that as long as they did not have to share the same roof, they could maintain a good relationship. The parents shared a mutual concern, and that was their talented son's welfare.

The patient, an only child, showed artistic talent during early childhood. He began by drawing houses and landscapes and then switched to elaborate battle scenes before he was four years old. Around five, he was a fairly sophisticated reader, and his mother and aunts reveled in the "opportunity" to bring him books that would describe the battles he wanted to draw. He started with rather simple renditions of skirmishes between cowboys and indians, but then moved on to very complex and colorful tabloids of the Gallic, Punic, and Carthaginian campaigns. He was especially fond of Scipio Africanus and Horatio at the Bridge. The women surrounding him were delighted to do his bidding and waited on him hand and foot. They encouraged his artistic pursuits and admired his works, liberally showing them off to their friends, who usually responded enthusiastically. The patient unabashedly enjoyed all this attention and produced several hundred pictures before he entered elementary school.

In school, he perfected his technique and experimented with water colors. He also continued to draw battle scenes, because they amused his classmates, but his interest had turned to drawing human faces. He sketched portraits of his teachers, all women, and they were delighted with the pictures, which he generously gave to them as gifts. In turn, his teachers gave him inordinate amounts of attention, but his classmates did not resent his favored position, as was true of the patient I described in the previous chapter. He took all of this admiration in his stride.

His mode of relating and his perception of himself were interesting and at variance with each other. Others saw him as highly excitable, constantly on the move, and always involved with some project, perhaps artistic, but not necessarily. For instance, around the age of eight, he became involved with an older companion in building a racer for a Soap Box Derby that qualified as an entry in the races, though it did not win. His teachers and friends described him as a character in a Mack Sennett movie who moved, felt, and thought at a much faster rate than average.

The patient did not understand why he was evaluated that way, because he saw nothing unusual in the pace he kept. He thought of himself as calm, serene, and at ease with most situations. He stated that he liked everyone, compared himself to Will Rogers, who said that he had never met a man he didn't like. When I first saw him at the age of 48, he reported that he had never been in a fight in his life, and that he abhorred physical violence.

He had supreme confidence in his capacity to produce good art and in the fact that through his work, he would always be self-sufficient. He derived obvious pleasure from telling stories about famous artists paying for their meals by making a small sketch. He especially liked the story (perhaps apocryphal) of the artist who did not have enough money to pay the check at a restaurant. Nevertheless, he was unperturbed and simply painted some coins on the plate, which more than satisfied the owner.

Throughout the course of treatment, he revealed various mental processes that he used to maintain psychic integration. Regardless of his "Mack Sennett" level of activity, he still felt calm and soothed. He did not lose his inner organization and capacity for integration. In fact, the latter seemed to be linked with hyperactivity and this is not surprising in view of his background.

His aunts and mother lived in a frenetic setting. Of course, they created the setting but it was one in which they apparently functioned well. They were truly devoted to the patient and lavished him with maternal care. If we can think in such terms, we might say he had an overabundance of mothering (see Chapter 10). We might also be suspicious of the idyllic qualities of his childhood world and wonder about the traumatic assaultive qualities of these early object relationships. In this regard, we have to evaluate whether his sense of calm, rather than representing a superior capacity for self-soothing, might not be indicative of a defensive adaptation serving as an insulating barrier against potentially disruptive agitation.

The fact that his energy was always channeled into productive activity and usually led to creative accomplishment speaks against the defensive qualities of his calm demeanor, because any defensive process has some constrictive qualities and inhibitory effects. He also showed enthusiasm and *joie de vivre* rather than hypomanic excitement dispersed in random and often self-destructive activity. Nor did he show schizoid withdrawal, which is commonly a manifestation of the deadening anesthesia that some patients defensively experience to protect them from a lack of or defective stimulus barrier. In these psychopathological instances, object relations are paralyzingly frightening, whereas this patient seemed to move easily into close and intimate relationships. Granted, this pattern could also have defensive elements, but all psychic orientations and behavior must have some defensive features. The question that is relevant for assessing the nature of psychopathology is how much of a defense versus a nonconstricting adaptation the patient's subjective state and behavioral expression represent.

In the previous chapter, I discussed how a scientist had subdivided the father imago into two components patterned after his relationship with his father and his uncle. Each had a different function, the father representing the prohibiting superego, and the uncle introjected as a provider of instinctual gratification. I described this intrapsychic state as an example of benign, that is, nonpathological, splitting that was later incorporated into creative activity which was based on the tolerance of ambiguity and the capacity to sustain antitheses. Disparate elements, for the creator, are not necessarily incompatible, as evidenced by the patient's talent for dealing with conceptual oxymorons and for splitting father figures into opposing components, such as id and superego.

What I have just referred to, the capacity to tolerate and to harbor disparate elements in an intrapsychic construct such as a parental imago, has the beneficial effect of producing tolerance for what the noncreative person might experience as painful intrapsychic conflict. The creator uses splitting mechanisms to facilitate psychodynamic balance and to maintain intrapsychic harmony. This level of calm is derived from higher intrapsychic levels than what I have been discussing as the increased capacity for self-soothing, which I believe is characteristic of the creative personality.

The artist demonstrates similar phenomena that stem from an earlier developmental level. Rather than forming an imago containing diverse components, he was able to internalize different environments that had both nurturing and soothing elements. The women that surrounded him with care maintained a frenetic pace, which, in some ways, might have contributed to the picture of perceptual activity that he presented. The setting the father provided, however, was calm and quiet, as well as methodical and organized. He described how pleasant and secure he felt as a child when he was with him. Apparently, the father was able to construct a peaceful, protective atmosphere, and the patient pleasurably anticipated the weekends he spent with him. The time spent with the father produced a sense of well-being.

The two overtly different settings, that of the mother and aunts and that of the father, were harmoniously internalized. I believe the endopsychic registration of these ambiences contributed to the formation of soothing and regulatory mechanisms. As stated, the differences in these two environments were overt, but they each provided nurture and soothing, and within the psychic realm, they blended rather than clashed with one another. One setting supplemented the other, although, on the surface, it would appear as if they would be at variance, and as if the beneficial effects of one would be cancelled out by the other, for example, the father's calming influence, by the aunt's and mother's disorganization and frenetic activity.

This hyperactivity was a superficial element of the child's relationship to his mother and maternal surrogates. Underneath all the bluster and confusion were warm and nurturing feelings, and today he still speaks fondly of these three women as being "kooks with good hearts." He derived considerable succor from this part of his life, and in his current adaptations revealed its influence along with his father's. I refer again to how his surface behavior was similar to his mother's and aunt's in that he appeared hyperactive to his colleagues, and I also experienced him as being an intense person. By contrast, even his seemingly high emotional pitch was directed to constructive and well-organized activities. The father's calming propensities became evident in his rational and deliberate behavior as well as in his subjective state of inner harmony.

The early environment can be considered to be a split environment in the same manner that certain object relationships are viewed as being the outcome of dissociative or splitting mechanisms. Unlike the splitting of objects, however, which always leads to the formation of polarities, the split environments became imbricated and complemented each other. This enhanced the functioning of homeostatic-producing mechanisms. Still, this was not altogether successful and devoid of some psychopathological consequences. Again, I must remind myself and the reader that this artist, in spite of certain optimal adaptations, was still a patient, which indicates that he must have had some problems. I have stressed the harmony of the maternal and paternal ambience, but at other levels, they created difficulties, especially when the patient tried to discover segments of the outer world that were compatible with these two infantile worlds, a process that I have repeatedly referred to as externalization.

His conflicts became evident in his relationships with women. He sought treatment because his third marriage suffered the same fate as the previous two. Each wife left him for another man: his third wife wanted to return, but the patient was no longer interested in continuing the relationship.

All three of his wives were excitable women, although as far as I could tell, they were somewhat different in terms of their character structure and psychopathology. The first wife was obviously schizophrenic, delusional at times, and actively hallucinating. The second and third wives seemed to have many hysterical features and to be fairly well connected to reality. They were, however, unpredictable and emotionally labile and often presented themselves as extremely helpless and vulnerable. Early in the courtship, the patient found their helplessness charming and he was attracted by their need to be protected and taken care of. Problems arose when each wife's behavior and dependent attachment to him became inconstant and erratic. Apparently none of them had the capacity to sustain an object relationship for any period of time. In contrast to him, they were unable to be soothed, although he needed to minister to their needs to be able to achieve calm satisfaction. They could not integrate the ambience he tried to create, and eventually they had to establish chaotic extramarital relationships.

During the course of treatment, we learned that he was trying to work out some of the covert disruptive elements of his relationship with his mother and aunts. Though, as I have emphasized, he derived many benefits from his mother and aunts, he had also developed some anxiety about intimate attachments to women. At one level, he was able to be soothed by them, but the highly charged electric atmosphere they created caused him to feel unconsciously anxious and insecure.

These anxieties surfaced during the analysis when he was in the midst of a maternal transference. He was extremely gratified as to how calm he could feel after a session, even when he had been quite agitated at the beginning. He had also cut down considerably on his alcohol consumption, because, as he stated, he did not require a drink in order to relax. On the other hand, he did not trust my reliability and psychic strength. He was afraid that because of the pressures of analytic work, I might collapse and not be able to continue taking care of him. What he was most afraid of was that this might occur when he least expected it, that is, when he could not prepare himself against this contingency. He viewed my strength as transient and my behavior as unpredictable.

It was interesting how an infantile ambience that was soothing and gratifying affected current object relationships with women, and interfered with establishment of a stable, intimate, heterosexual attachment. He found stability in his relationships with men, friends and colleagues, and in his work. Later in analysis, when he had more confidence in my constancy and consistency, he was reacting to me in terms of a paternal attachment.

I am reluctant to draw inferences about where the content of his paintings belongs in the clinical picture. It is tempting to view them as manifestations of characterological configurations and adaptations, but there is always the danger of making them fit into a Procrustean bed, to read meanings into the artist's product to support preconceived formulations that have been speculatively constructed from the clinical interaction. Nevertheless, during childhood, the patient's drawings and paintings moved from colorful battle scenes to portraits and finally to landscapes that dominate his current output. The latter seem to have a soothing effect on the viewer.

Control, Confidence, and Success

The fear of loss of control is associated with primitive, vulnerable ego states. To some measure, it is an upward extension of defective soothing. To be soothed and calmed is to feel protected, and this leads to a sense of inner harmony and control. Needs can be experienced as pleasant rather than becoming painfully intense as regulatory mechanisms fail. Similarly, external stimuli are modulated so they can be smoothly integrated within the ego sphere, and add to, rather than disrupt, a pleasurable level of excitement. The fear of loss of control is associated with psychopathology at these very early developmental stages.

The unprotected, easily overwhelmed ego constructs defenses to protect against the loss of control. I have discussed several types of psychopathology that utilize defenses to maintain a false sense of control. Here, I will simply mention the extreme instance in which dependence on external reality and even the existence of inner needs is denied, as occurs in patients suffering from anorexia nervosa. As briefly discussed in the first section of the book, these patients have a false sense of omnipotent autonomy because they feel themselves to be totally self-sufficient. If a person does not need nurture, then that person is in complete control of his or her destiny. Obviously, this denial of inner and outer reality is a psychopathological defensive adaptation often designed to protect against loss of control, which is preceived as a terrifying disintegration of the psyche.

The creative person is usually quite confident about being able to maintain control, even or especially when he is experiencing intense feelings. This self-confidence is characteristic of the well-compensated creator, but it can break down under certain circumstances that recapitulate the traumatic elements of the infantile environment. I recall a particularly prominent scientist (Giovacchini, 1960) who had a schizophrenic breakdown, but rather quickly recovered. He then told how he enjoyed exciting situations. He would talk of a sense of inner exhilaration as one might experience on a roller coaster, or while watching fireworks. Many external stimuli could produce states of ecstasy with or without erotic overtones, but when the patient was mentally sound he found such excitement totally nonthreatening.

The same combination of excitement, pleasure, and the secure feeling of being able to keep his emotions within certain boundaries carried over to his work. He felt intense exhilaration when working out a problem, something he usually did with ease and with complete confidence that he would find the correct solution, which he inevitably did. His apparent schizophrenic breakdown, however, was ushered in by his losing control of his thoughts, as he explicitly stated, while being on the brink of having unravelled a very knotty theoretical dilemma. When he became once again stabilized, he had no difficulty whatsoever in making an immediate breakthrough.

The mental processes I have been discussing are further examples of psychic mechanisms that represent psychopathological primitive defenses, such as denial and the need for control, found in patients suffering from anorexia nervosa, as well as the psychic characteristics that are found in the creative personality and are instrumental to creative accomplishment. As in all other adaptations found both in psychopathology and creativity, their similarities apply only to their surface qualities and not to their basic interactions at deeper levels of the personality. The creator has supreme confidence in his ability to maintain control. Patients suffering from primitive mental states are rigid in what amounts to a complete preoccupation with being on top of every situation, and they cannot relinquish any interaction or ritual that keeps them in a dominant position. In Chapter 5, I discussed how some vulnerable and narcissistic patients could not permit themselves to lie on the couch for fear of losing their position of superiority.

The various clinical examples I have presented in these two chapters abundantly demonstrate that the creative characterological configuration can regress to a psychopathological organization. The confidence the creative person displays is both nonoffensive and nonintrusive, whereas with emotional illness, it is experienced as reactive, defensive, and painful. It is this loss of what appears to be rational confidence that distinguishes the creative personality from its psychopathological counterpart. If the creator becomes concerned about issues of control, he is, most likely, in the midst of a regressive, ego-disintegrating process that may later stabilize itself by forming a neurotic or psychotic constellation.

A brilliant graduate student in his middle twenties had had visions of Christ and some of the Apostles. He could not discuss this with anyone, because he was afraid that others would believe he was insane and either hospitalize him or "lock him up" in an asylum. He had become afraid that he would be seized while asleep and dragged away. He saw himself as vulnerable and basically undefended. Consequently, he had to be vigilant and on top of every situation, otherwise he would be overwhelmed.

At the beginning of our relationship, he insisted that I be quiet. It was his session and he was going to do all the talking. My role, according to him, consisted of sitting still and just listening. I was not to interrupt him or make any demands. The latter meant that he would not lie on the couch, no matter what I felt about it facilitating the treatment interaction. What I believed did not count. He was going to fill the consultation room and be completely dominant.

He lamented his lost creativity and the loss of his ability to retain vast amounts of information. He wistfully described how he had been able to take over an experiment and his colleagues and assistants were always in tune with his needs. They would faithfully follow his directions, not questioning his decisions and giving him total control. They apparently were willing to have him as their leader, and gladly gave him complete control. I learned that this was not a retrospective falsification of the past. The referral source, a senior member of the patient's department, spoke with pride of this graduate student's "genius" at quickly grasping the essence of a problem and how to resolve it. According to his mentor, he generated enthusiasm, rather than resentment, in both his colleagues and his subordinates.

The atmosphere in my consultation room was not so felicitous, however. I felt immobilized by the patient's need for control and dominance. He was telling me exactly how I had to react, and he alone was determining how the therapeutic setting should be constructed. Clearly, he was defending against feelings of helplessness and vulnerability, and he needed omnipotent control to maintain psychic equilibrium. His hallucinations were the expression of a similar defensive need, an appeal to divine intervention to protect him from unmanageable, disruptive, destructive inner forces. The need for control had reached a peak when he was unable to function professionally.

I do not believe it is necessary for the theses I am discussing to go into much detail about the reasons for his decompensation. It suffices to point out that he had experienced several humiliating and frustrating situations, all involving, for a person as sensitive as he was, considerable loss of self-esteem. Because a proposal had been poorly written by a colleague, he did not get a grant that he had counted on. Furthermore, his girlfriend had shown what seems to have been a mild interest in the colleague who had written the ill-fated proposal. Previously, everything had gone well in his life; he had known only a series of successes, and admiration and praise. At least that is how he remembered his past. I will return to the loss of ego integration in creative persons later in this chapter.

A further distinction between creative personalities and patients whose psychopathology leads to constrictions and diminished functioning is the degree of success they have achieved. This observation, in a sense, is a tautology, because what it basically expresses is that the creative person succeeds in creating, whereas the emotionally ill noncreative person does not; but clearly, this is a useful distinction to keep in mind in a clinical situation. For example, I have seen many patients who could easily be classified as borderline or narcissistic personalities who talk endlessly about what they are going to do. They describe grandiose projects that will come to fruition because of their unique talents. Even in the early stages of organization, the therapist can sense how impractical or unrealistic the proposal is. In fact, the project hardly ever goes beyond an endless early stage of organization. In brief, these are the writers who do not write, the painters who do not paint, and the students who never get a degree.

By contrast, creative persons such as those I have described in the clinical examples have a history of success. They get things done without any fanfare. Theirs is a soft Midas touch that is considered a mode of functioning rather than anything unusual. True, the creator is very proud of his abilities, but he also takes them for granted. He has set up standards for himself that he does not expect of others. He remains within the framework of his ideals, and he has little need to make others aware of his superior abilities. He believes they will be self-evident.

What I have just described was true of most of the creative persons I have seen, but I realize there must be numerous exceptions to such calm, nonobtrusive, self-confidence. In our educational journeys through universities and graduate schools, we are all familiar with bright, arrogant, obnoxious students whose special talents include an incredible capacity for getting others to hate them. Nevertheless, the question remains as to how truly creative these students are. The outstanding examples that have been reported had rather mundane futures. It is difficult to determine whether these unpleasant, intrusive prodigies were innately creative and whether they were able to sustain or exercise it as they matured. The further question that naturally follows is whether such characteristics can be compatible with a creative orientation. It would be naïve to believe that all great scientists and artists are pleasant and charming persons. There are too many examples that point in the opposite direction. Nevertheless, this does not mean that the undesirable aspects of their personalities are connected to their creative orientation. Many scientists feel that the act of creating is an ennobling experience (Pupin, 1925).

The group that is always striving to create but never does causes us to wonder further about the significance of the creative act for psychic economy. Most of the patients I had the opportunity to study were obsessed with creative strivings. They valued creative accomplishment to the same extent as the creative scientists I have seen, but they differed in that they constantly failed. Their obsession with creativity was obviously defensive and not part of their true selves. It was not integrated into their psyches in a smooth ego-syntonic fashion. Rather it was part of a false self that was desperately trying to appease both the inner and outer worlds. Under these energy-drawing circumstances, they could not help but fail. Failure, however, was not just a natural consequence of defensive processes that could not be converted into goal-directed productive behavior. It had a purpose of its own for maintaining psychic equilibrium that can be contrasted with the role of success for the creator.

As repeatedly discussed, for whatever reasons, the caretakers of the child destined to be creative related intensely to his accomplishments. There was an active involvement based on a series of productions by the child that brought him admiration and gratification. The child learned early in life that his talents could bring considerable narcissistic gratification and pleasure. This sequence of production and reward, a reward that soon became a constant feature of the infantile environment, later became equated with success. The child may not have known he was being successful in the abstract meaning of the word, but he learned that he had some inborn attributes others did not have that were instrumental in bringing him pleasure. Because some parts of himself could regulate the production of pleasure, he achieved a significant degree of control that maintained psychic equilibrium. Success became an adaptive character trait that brought soothing and satisfaction.

The degree of ego-syntonicity of success as a character trait is an important factor, among others, that determines the stability of the creative configuration. As my patients demonstrated, there are impediments to and conflicts about the total integration of success in the ego's adaptive and executive systems, and these led to emotional illness and inhibition of creativity. By contrast, the patient who usually fails or never can complete a task has had considerable difficulty in absorbing an introject of success, so to speak, into the main ego current. In the most disturbed cases, failure has become a dominant adaptive modality.

Again, I am describing a spectrum that contains stabilized creativity at one end and repeated failure at the other. Failure also has a purpose of its own, in that it helps to preserve psychic balance, even though it is a psychopathological balance. In many instances, depending on the severity of psychopathology, the patient is not aware of the fact that his life has been punctuated by a series of failures. In these instances, failure has become truly ego-syntonic, and it is difficult to determine whether or not the patient actually has any creative potential. In other instances, the patient is very much aware and disturbed by his propensity for nonachievement; failure then is more of a symptom than an ego-syntonic character trait, and is often the main motive for seeking treatment.

Most of the creative patients I have treated have been able to make success part of their personality, but not entirely. If they had, I doubt that they would have needed treatment. This partial instability of the creative configuration, as determined by some lack of integration of success into the psychic fabric, may explain some of the idiosyncrasies that some geniuses have prominently displayed. Leonardo da Vinci and Michelangelo immediately come to mind. Both were notorious for their propensity not to finish certain major works of art. Even the unfinished product is a masterpiece, proving that their creativity was nevertheless quite active, but they occasionally could not bring it to final fruition. Undoubtedly, there were unconscious rebellious attitudes operating, but it is also likely that total success as a characterological adaptation was not completely integrated in their psyches.

At the other end of the spectrum, I recall nonproductive patients who at some time in treatment revealed that they were comfortable with their failures. This, of course, was not absolutely true, because they felt sufficiently frustrated by not achieving their creative aspirations that they felt miserable. Other patients were really not genuinely interested in innovative accomplishments or becoming involved in intellectual challenges. They felt they should be, as an aspect of their false selves, but bascially they were more interested in appearances than in actually working in their professed area of expertise.

I have described two different types of patients who are unsuccessful. The first group may possess talents that could emerge once they worked through their conflicts about or their inability to integrate success. Failure would then no longer be used in the service of adaptation. The second group never really valued creativity, and it was not an integral facet of their value system. Basically their true self-representation did not include creativity.

To build up self-esteem and as a narcissistic overcompensation, however, they constructed a false creative self-representation in order to solidify a shaky identity sense. The role of artist or scientist established a firm sense of identity that served as an anchor around which they could organize their relationships in the external world. A patient who had made considerable progress in treatment referred to a book *Home is the Sailor* by the Brazilian author Jorge Amado to best describe his psychic state before he entered treatment. In this novel, the protagonist is a young, rich, charming bachelor who travels with a close-knit circle of friends. Their lives consist of a series of pleasures, playing cards, attending the theater and opera, regular visits to their brothel, as well as having various affairs. Except for our hero, every member of this group has a solid professional identity. One is a lawyer, another a doctor, still another a naval officer; they represent the professions, the military, and the world of commerce. By contrast, the hero is just a dilettante without any area of expertise.

The protagonist becomes depressed, and his friends rally to

his aid. They ask him what is bothering him, and he confesses that whereas all of them are solidly entrenched in a vocation or profession, he has nothing. He is a nobody, having nothing to define him. He lacks an identity, except for that of a wastrel. They can play around all they want because these activities are a diversion, a subsidiary aspect of their lives, whereas, for him, it is all he has. So in spite of their constant company, he feels lonely and isolated.

His naval officer companion hastens to reassure him and responds that this is no problem; it can be remedied easily enough. If all he were seeking was an identity by establishing himself in a profession, then that could be arranged. He would become a captain in the merchant marine. All they had to do was to hire someone to take the exam for him so he could get his papers. This being done, the protagonist buys uniforms, spyglasses, quadrants, and all the paraphernalia that are the identifying possessions of a captain in the merchant marine.

It is not necessary to pursue this story, which led to a hilarious sequence of events. The patient was emphasizing the "phony" qualities of the main character's identity. It was a false self-representation designed merely to impress the world, but it did not have any connections to the core of the protagonist's psyche. It was just a matter of appearances that led to a precarious emotional stabilization. In the novel, the hero was satisfied, although he had to face some conflictful moments when he was nearly revealed as a fraud. In real life, the patient was not able to sustain himself indefinitely on a similarly constructed identity based on the appearance of success.

Isolation and Withdrawal: The Maverick Orientation

One of the popular stereotypes of the creative scientist and artist is that of the loner. In extreme instances, they have been viewed as schizoid personalities, and, as is usually the situation when examining creative persons, we can find numerous examples to support the stereotype. This is another instance, however, in which what appears to be a primitive defensive adaptation on the surface is not at all what it seems. If an artist or scientist operates on the basis of schizoid mechanisms—Gaugin, for example—we are witnessing a psychopathological imbalance that contributes nothing to the capacity to create. At the most, it can be said that *their connection to the creative process is based on the possibility that they are the outcome of a regressive degradation of an ego function involved in creating.*

It follows that the isolation of some creative personalities is markedly different from schizoid withdrawal. I have already pointed out that some creative persons, such as the late nineteenth-century mathematician I have discussed, work best surrounded by people. They are calmed by the excitement and bustle. On the other hand, there are creators who require silence and, if need be, have to separate themselves from others in order to reach their goals. They have to shut out all external distractions to get in touch with their inner feelings and let their inspirations develop. In some instances, they require isolation that goes beyond physical surroundings. They may have to work apart from colleagues and institutions.

They may appear alienated or rebellious, and this is often true. Society is known for rejecting innovative ideas or unfamiliar artistic styles. If what is produced represents an extension or a valid replacement of some aspect of an area of knowledge, however, it will eventually be incorporated into the system. There may be tragic examples where this has not happened, but there are also many recorded instances of an initial violent rejection finally being overcome and the greatness of the discovery being recognized. The theories of evolution and psychoanalysis are prominent examples of the latter. Mendelian genetics is another. The theory or discovery may have been ahead of its time, perhaps because the surrounding world was not sufficiently sophisticated to use it or to recognize its worth.

In our clinical work, we can become easily confused when some of our patients present themselves as frustrated geniuses who have been unfairly treated. They complain about how their work has been ignored, and this helps them to justify their withdrawal from the scientific community. They accuse their colleagues and the community at large of being insensitive, crass, and in extreme cases, stupid. The truth of the matter is often difficult to evaluate, because sometimes the patient's arguments seem valid, and most of us know enough about academic communities to believe that injustices can occur and that new ideas, especially in such settings, can be threatening. I have often wondered whether I was dealing with paranoia or being faced with reality, although the two are by no means mutually exclusive. I recall two patients whose ideas were later accepted and who finally became recognized as brilliant and creative persons, but this occurred only after many years of struggle and bitterness.

To some degree, we could believe that a certain amount of paranoia and withdrawal might be appropriate in the risky attempt to present new ideas, and perhaps to shatter old, cherished beliefs. Freud felt this keenly when he "disturbed the sleep of the world" by introducing his theories concerning the power of the unconscious over the conscious mind and sexuality, and especially concerning infantile sexuality. He withdrew from the scientific community during the years "of splendid isolation."

Is a new paradigm, as Kuhn (1962) calls a novel conceptual system, intrinsically threatening to the older and ruling generation, which clings to the current model? Kuhn believes that acceptance occurs only with the generation to follow. Thus, it would seem that the more impressive the innovation, the stronger the rejection and the creator, being human, reacts with bitterness and withdrawal.

Of course, some new ideas are easily and readily accepted, which confronts us with another familiar dilemma: How do we establish gradients of creativity? Were the ideas that shook the world incorporated into science without a struggle? The heliocentric theory of astronomy, the theory of evolution, relativity theory, psychoanalysis—these certainly were not. Once a theory had gained a degree of acceptance, then further discoveries by the creator might have been warmly received, but this was not true initially. And the discoveries that have not met opposition— are they in the same class as the ones I have just mentioned? They do not seem to be. These are questions, however, not answers.

The natural response of the creator to the rejection of or opposition to his work may be to feel isolated. This reaction would thus represent something other than a defensive withdrawal. In a sense, the appearance of similarity at one level to a schizoid orientation would be an intrinsic characteristic of the creative orientation. This comparison is misleading, however, because a schizoid orientation is always viewed in the context of psychopathology, whereas creativity must be placed in a frame of reference that is outside the realm of emotional illness. Still, in our clinical practices, the creative persons we see do suffer from psychopathology; and conversely, many persons who have aspirations to be creative and who view themselves and their productions as highly innovative are, in fact, paranoid persons who have withdrawn into their shell, often to protect themselves from realizing that they lack talent, and that their accomplishments are insignificant and mediocre. Of course, as my clinical examples indicate, we also see creative patients who have withdrawn for reasons that are intrinsic to their work, and to preserve a psychic equilibrium that is threatened by the internal disruption that characterizes their psychopathology.

Once again, I wish to separate attributes of a psychopathological defensive process from those that are intrinsic to the creative process. I have extended the definition of the word "intrinsic" to include the creator's responses to the reactions of the external world to the creative product. It must be understood that a particular quality found to characterize the creative activity of one person is not necessarily universal. Nevertheless, there are orientations that we often find in creators—in my experience, creative scientists—that merit special attention. I am referring to the orientation of a maverick.

Mavericks are characterized by being different from the norm. In spite of differences, they do belong to the herd, but they are usually found on the periphery. They are not outcasts, nor are they rebellious enough to leave or be ostracized.

The creator is often a maverick, but not only in terms of his innovations being ignored or rejected by the larger group. Like the maverick in a herd, the creator is a maverick even before he has "disturbed the sleep of the world." He is different, and this is recognized early in his life; but, as some of the clinical examples I have presented indicate, he is not ostracized from the group. He is not fully accepted either, but is considered generally likable, and is usually admired because of his intelligence and ingenuity.

The maverick presents us with an interesting paradox. The group has a natural tendency to shun persons who either overtly or covertly urge its members to examine themselves and their orientations. The group values conformity, and its members tend to identify, to some extent, with each other as well as with their leader (Freud, 1921). The maverick is by definition a nonconformist, yet he achieves a certain degree of acceptance and sometimes idealization.

Some years ago, there was a popular television Western series called "Maverick," in which the eponymous hero was a delightful, charming drifter who always achieved his ends through his cunning and wiliness. His cause was usually noble, but at times it was achieved by outswindling swindlers. Bret Maverick was a gambler by profession, and he was not above cheating on occasion when it might be considered appropriate, given that he was dealing with scoundrels. He frequently gained the admiration of the townspeople, and there was, as a rule, a romantic interest. Although Maverick got the girl, however, he did not establish roots, and moved from adventure to adventure without much continuity.

Maverick's main attractions were his charm and ingenuity. He constantly emphasized the superiority of brain over brawn, and instead of being scorned in a rough Western society where men survived because of their physical strength and their agility with guns, he was hospitably incorporated in the group. He did not remain very long, though, because he could not allow himself to settle down to a conventional homesteader's or rancher's life. He was a nonconformist involved in a peripheral occupation, gambling. He was liked, perhaps envied, but he did not suffer resentment. He had no position in the community, and he was never offered any, but he would not have accepted anything permanent if it had been offered. To repeat, he was a nonconformist, but he fought to uphold the standards of the group, and he had incorporated much of their moral sense.

I focus on this fictional character because he offers us a splendid example of a situation in which it is difficult to distinquish psychopathology from talent.

According to one dictionary definition, a "maverick" is an unbranded calf. This could have a double meaning. The first and most obvious is that the calf is not officially or even legally recognized as part of the herd. It does not bear an *imprimatur*. The second inference we can draw is that, in a sense, mavericks are more fortunate than their contemporaries, because they are not subjected to the process of branding, and thus they start life unblemished and without pain. I am discussing cattle, and perhaps we cannot transfer too many of these observations and speculations to human beings; but I believe some comparisons are intriguing.

The creative person begins life with some advantages that may contribute to his not being fully accepted by the group. Similar to the maverick, he is not outside the herd; at the most, he is on the periphery. In the scientific or academic community, he is usually a member in good standing of the organizations that represent his profession, but he is not part of the "in group" unless he has become famous. In this case, his productions will have been so innovative that they have made a tremendous, if belated, impact in his lifetime. Even then, he may have little political prestige or administrative authority. In this connection, it is interesting how little influence Freud's ideas about the training of lay analysts had in the United States.

Not all creative persons are mavericks, but many are, and I believe all creators share a character trait that is integral to the creative process. They possess a particular type of freedom that may be associated with being "unbranded." From an adaptive viewpoint, this means that they do not feel constrained by being a member of a group, a group that requires a specific type of external world to support it. The creator derives support from within, without considerable reinforcement from external objects.

In the first section of this book, I described externalization as a mechanism in which the ego attempts to find a world that will support its defenses and adaptations. The degree of mental health is determined by how much congruence exists between the inner world of the psyche and the external world of reality. The creative person changes the external world through his creativity. He adds segments to it or changes our perceptions of and beliefs about certain segments of the surrounding world. His productions solidify the relationship between the internal and the external. Before he has made his mark on the world, however, (an apt way of expressing his endeavors, given that he is altering the status quo), his mode of relating, although different, is effective, even if it is not entirely in accord with the conventional way of doing things. The amount of externalization that is required for the maverick is much less than what is ordinarily required for the noncreative ego to function. These are, of course, impressionistic assessments. Exact quantitative determinations are outside the scope of studies based exclusively on the gathering of clinical data.

The maverick scientist stays within the accepted conceptual framework, and this is a factor in determining how he can maintain some degree of harmony with his colleagues and feel at home in the professional organizations to which he belongs. Because of his intrepid individuality, however, he can create his own system, which may at first be rejected, because he seems to be undermining the pillars and foundations that support the prevailing scientific system. The creators that I have treated had no such intentions. Usually, they respected and defended the basic premises of their field, seeing their works as merely an extension and modification of some of the surface elements of a common frame of reference.

A Titan such as Einstein may have shaken our view of the world by postulating the General Theory of Relativity, but he had no intention of destroying Newtonian physics, nor did he, in fact, do any damage to these early and fundamental principles. Within certain boundaries, Newtonian mechanisms remain a pragmatic way of dealing with a variety of phenomena. Einstein's frame went beyond these boundaries, but it is possible to conceptualize a continuum between Newton's and Einstein's frames. It will not, however, be a smooth continuum. The intermediary steps between psychoanalysis and its antecedents are much easier to trace (see Ellenberger, 1970).

The maverick must have a tremendous amount of self-confidence in order to maintain his convictions and to continue pursuing his work. The external world does not usually support him. He invariably prompts the envy of colleagues who have to labor long hours to accomplish what their more talented peer seems to accomplish effortlessly. His elders may feel threatened by his inventiveness and creativity and may even do their best to discredit his work and to hold back his professional advancement. The maverick may learn that only the conformists, those who "do not make waves," as one patient put it, succeed in getting ahead in certain institutional settings. Another scientist, not a patient, who was a Nobel Laureate, often maintained that rewards went to the mediocre, and he often quoted Anatole France's epigram, *Les savants ne sont pas curieux* ("Scholars are not curious"). This scientist had been virtually ignored and passed over until he became famous by winning the Nobel prize. Such scientists are mavericks, and although they were always on the periphery, they remained undaunted and continued activities that contributed to their peripheral position in the group and caused them to be unpopular, although at the same time, they are usually well liked. They have a firm belief in what they are doing, a belief that is able to sustain them in spite of the professional disadvantages they may have to endure.

Apparently, the gratifications of early childhood and the position of having been the favorite is able to sustain these creative persons in their professional endeavors. They seem to have developed a backlog of self-esteem and self-confidence that gives them an internal sense of security that they can project into that part of the external world that is occupied by their work. They are able to externalize their infantile environment into that segment of reality that represents the professional arena. Because the early environment was so supportive, these scientists create their own world, which helps them to maintain faith in their principles and strivings.

In writings about mavericks, I have confined myself to scientists, because I have had considerably less clinical experience with artists. I suspect, however, that much of what I have concluded about scientists also applies to artists. The professional environment of the artist may not be as stratified or as structured as that of the scientist, but these may be just quantitative distinctions. The psychic process and object relationships involved undoubtedly have many similarities to those I have just discussed.

Inner Turmoil and Internal Objects

I have already stressed the remarkable capacity of the creator to maintain control of internal feelings that in other persons may cause agitation, disruption, and, in some instances, ego dissolution. As the various clinical examples illustrate, this can also happen to a creative person, but such an event is always accompanied by a breakdown of creative functioning. Obviously, then, there is a connection between the creative process and emerging inner feeling states that threaten to get out of control. The psychic mechanisms involved in creative production are synthesizing and integrative processes; they serve to tame inner psychic states that, by themselves, could cause ego disintegration and fragmentation.

The creator, as I have emphasized, also has an extraordinary ability for self-soothing. This means that inner turmoil is only temporary, and psychic equilibrium can be quickly reestablished. Undoubtedly, to a large measure, this is accomplished by the psychic processes involved in their innovative work. Still, the creative person's character contains what we might call soothing introjects, endopsychic registrations of infantile soothing experiences, that can be cathected during moments of inner turmoil. It is reasonable to assume, however, that the creative act involves a distribution of psychic energy that leads to a reactivation of these introjects.

I believe that the soothing potential of creative activity, as it reproduces calming infantile relationships, represents a special ego quality that is disturbed by psychopathology. It also accounts for the quasimystical and quasireligious elements that are often incorporated in the creative act. To be soothed is a positive experience that is accompanied by a satisfaction and integration characteristic of early developmental stages. This is not a clearcut situation, because distinctions between early, primitive ego stages and later, advanced, sophisticated ego states become blurred in creative endeavor. I am referring to a nirvana state that includes expanded ego boundaries as well as differentiated ego systems, synthesized with one another and operating harmoniously.

The calming effect of creative activity has been frequently noted by all of my creative patients, and they have commonly used religious metaphor to describe this experience, although none was religious in a formal sense. Einstein stated, "God does not play dice," believing in a higher force that regulated the universe; but he did not see this beyond an abstraction. My patients had no particular conviction of a personal superior being, a cosmic morality, or an afterlife. I believe these orientations of quasireligious, cosmic conceptions and a sense of inner peace are further examples of ego states that cannot be placed in the usual hierarchy proceeding from amorphous organizations to well-differentiated, well-functioning, reality-attuned intregations. *These configurations characteristic of creative functioning can be conceptualized as supraordinate states that perhaps belong in a different frame of reference than the sequence of stages of emotional development.*

Yet, patients emphasize that this kind of peace is very much a part of them; it pervades their entire being and is in no way felt as alien or fragmented. As one patient expressed it, it felt as if all the good feelings and persons inside of him had swelled up and were dominating his body cavity, which extended from his head to his toes. He further described it as an "energetic calm," illustrating the casual use of the oxymoron that is characteristic of creative persons and their mode of thinking, as described in the previous chapter.

With psychopathology, these soothing interactions are made apparent by their malfunctioning. The good and valued introjects swelling within, that is, dominating the ego current, can also be threatened by destructive, malignant introjects. I recall a patient, a highly talented commercial artist, who attacked and reviled me for many months after the beginning of treatment. He also filled the consultation room with a stench that was offensive to the patients who followed him. I finally had to insist that he bathe before he came to his appointments, which he did. He continued attacking me, but he valued our sessions, and had a deep respect for me and the treatment relationship. It became apparent that he was projecting, as part of the transference, what he considered to be the hated and damaged parts of himself into me. This gave him considerable relief, and he felt soothed after each session.

Gradually, his surface attitude toward me changed. He was grateful because I had survived the worst he could "dump" on me. He saw me as a source of strength, invulnerable and constant, and able to construct a relationship that made him feel safe. He was, of course, idealizing me, but in an interesting and unique fashion. For example, his good feelings caused him to view me as an expert art critic. He asked me questions about how I would evaluate a particular stylistic pattern of a school of painting. He wanted to know how I would compare one school with another. I was quite surprised, because it was apparent that he was endowing my judgments with an expertise that he, in fact, possessed. It became clear that he was attributing to me qualities that belong to his artistic orientation and skills.

Unlike the more common transference interaction, this patient was projecting the valued parts of himself into me. This was abundantly clear in his dreams and associations. He depicted me as a safety deposit vault in which he could keep and protect his valued belongings. His earlier attacks and debasement of me served to test how strong and impervious to damaging influence this vault could be. Once he ascertained that it was capable of withstanding his onslaughts, he felt safe in "depositing" his good internal objects.

As is true of all the creative patients I have seen, their imagery is rich, and their metaphors are especially relevant and instructive. There is a poetic style to their associations and their descriptions of their moods and feeling states. Often they depict complex psychic processes in dramatic but understandable terms.

This patient was emphasizing that he could not contain both good and bad objects within himself. He had to first project what he considered to be his bad parts into me. This gave him considerable relief of inner tension. He felt calmed after each session. Then, having been reassured that he had not destroyed me, he could allow himself to let me "keep" his valued parts for him. He had much more faith in my ability to keep good internal objects separate from bad ones than in his own. Just as I had survived his attacks, I would not let the valued objects be destroyed.

In a sense I had become his caretaker, and he felt secure in handing me the responsibility for maintaining his internal organization. I now was his protector, and by identifying with my superior capacity to separate bad from good internal objects, he could avoid experiencing the tension and agitation that would have followed a clash between these introjects. Instead of needing to soothe himself, he felt that our relationship led to a sense of inner harmony.

This is another clinical example that illustrates how primitive mental processes are involved in talent, creativity, and psychopathology. The polarities of good and bad internal objects were dominant in determining psychic functioning and the establishment of defensive adaptations. The latter were chiefly organized around projective and splitting mechanisms (see Chapter 10). I have stressed some of the unique qualities of the transference, because whereas the projection of destructive and disruptive introjects is a fairly common occurrence in the treatment of patients suffering from character disorders, the projection of valued parts of the self is a relatively rare phenomenon and more likely to occur during the therapy of creative persons.

Even though this patient was suffering from psychopathology, there were unique qualities of character structure that illustrated a wide spectrum of psychic functioning. He could become extremely concrete, as illustrated by the distinct features of good and bad that he could assign to internal objects. On the other hand, he illustrated the ability to perceive and to express himself in a rich, poetic, and sensitive fashion, with an incisive use of metaphor. He demonstrated a fluidity and expansiveness of ego boundaries that, I believe, is typical of creative persons. When he was in good psychic equilibrium, he moved from higher to lower ego levels with ease, maintaining a calm, confident balance. His relationships with internal and external objects were flexible and nonthreatening as he moved in and out of fusion states. This was amply illustrated when he made me into a "safety deposit box" for his valued internal objects.

Fantasy and Transitional Phenomena

This book has placed considerable emphasis on the role of the transitional space and the transitional object in the production of psychopathology. As Winnicott constantly reminds us, the transitional space is the area of creative accomplishment; this, too, suggests that there are similarities between psychopathological and creative processes, but, to repeat, it does not imply any etiological connections. I have discussed the creative aspects of the transitional space in some detail when covering the areas of working through and the therapeutic process (Chapter 8).

The perception of reality as grim and dangerous changes to an illusion of danger once perceptions are examined in the transitional space. The creator, in a similar but reverse sequence, first creates an illusion, which then becomes transformed into reality. The illusion is constructed in the transitional space and may involve a manipulation of objects therein, over which the creator maintains control. Earlier in this chapter, I discussed how important the feeling of control is for the creative act. I am now pointing out that the construction of fantasy occurs in a setting that, from one viewpoint, is considered part of the creator's psyche rather than a part of the external world. This accounts for the creator's feeling of mastery and dominance over the content of the fantasy, a situation that also occurs in lucid dreams (Chapter 10), because the dreamer is aware that he is dreaming and that he is in no real danger. Part of the creator's calm is based on feeling safe in the midst of the stimulation of turbulent feelings.

The manipulation of objects in the transitional space refers to objects in the broadest sense. I am referring not only to personal and part-objects, but to functions, such as nurture, soothing, and other gratifying and integrative transactions, as well as to concepts belonging to a higher order of abstraction. The creator, as does the child with the transitional object, plays with these various elements in the transitional space.

Both creative scientists and artists have particular attitudes about the creative product that emphasizes how innovative activity occurs in the transitional space. While working, the creator believes he is the sole possessor of the content of his innovative preoccupation. In science, the problem belongs to the investigator. He feels that it is part of the self, and as discussed earlier, under his complete control. Winnicott (1953, 1969) described the exact same circumstances existing between the child and objects existing in the transitional space. Only when they move outside that space into the external world does the infant feel they are not part of the self and outside the sphere of inner control. Winnicott calls the beginning of the process that leads to the construction of the transitional object, and later to the external object as a separate entity, primary psychic creativity. Although he was writing about a developmental sequence, he recognized that the processes he was describing were also in some way linked to creative productivity.

It is a very common phenomenon for the scientist and artist to lose interest once they have been successful in a project. They value their productions, but somehow the intense fervor they previously had is gone. When they are involved, they are totally immersed in their work, but once the results have materialized, there is a significant lowering of cathexis. They acknowledge their work, but they do not feel bound to it as they did when they felt it was part of themselves. What they have produced is now part of the external world; perhaps, as sometimes occurs in science, it has replaced a segment of reality.

From this viewpoint, the creator has to lose a part of the self while creating. Instead of the ego perceiving itself as having lost something, however, it has gained a higher order of integration, inasmuch as it has established another contact with the external world. Some writers have compared the creative process to the act of giving birth. As a metaphor depicting a detachment from the self or body as the production of a valued entity or person in the outside world, it is an apt comparison. The process of creating, however, involves the construction of fantasy that is worked over by complex psychic mechanisms and intellectual processes. The production of a baby is also complex, but remains primarily in anatomical and physiological frames of reference.

Fantasy activity is a prominent feature of the creative act, but it need not be conscious or well-organized fantasy. All of my creative patients had many fantasies and tended to make up stories about even the most mundane events. Their thinking was predominantly visual, and they seemed to be fantasying practically all the time. They frequently saw things in their "mind's eye," and this often led to making interesting connections that proved to be instrumental in solving the problems they were currently pursuing.

Poincaré (1952) gives two examples illustrating how fantasying and playing with visual images led to momentous discoveries. One of them refers to himself. One day, while taking a walk, he apparently had a vision of different colored balls and blocks whirling around. He juxtaposed them in different combinations and finally was to establish a branch of mathematics known as *Fuchsian* functions. The other example concerns a famous chemical discovery. It is the often-discussed dilemma of Kekulé when he was trying to discover the formula for benzene. He struggled and struggled with the problem, until one night he had a dream in which a snake was rolling down a hill with its tail in its mouth. When he awakened, he is said to have had the solution in his mind. What he had been unable to grasp was that he had to place the carbon molecules in a ring configuration, as was concretely depicted by the snake.

On other occasions, the fantasy process is not obvious. One of my patients told me about a colleague, a Nobel Laureate, who had become a legend in his own time. He was a jokester and a prankster whom everybody indulged because of his impressive talents. For example, his confreres would present him with a problem that had eluded them for weeks on end, and he would come up with an immediate answer that was invariably correct. When asked how he did it, he could not tell them; he was aware of repeating the crucial questions over and over again in his mind, and then the answer would suddenly emerge. He claimed that he had no idea how he did it.

It was not possible to study the mental processes of this famous scientist, but, I recall a patient who could, on occasion, experience a similar phenomenon, which he called intuitive hunches. After such a satisfying episode, I would ask him to free associate specifically to what might have been going on in his mind at the time he was able to evoke a solution to the problem. Without fail, he would recall thoughts and fantasies that had gone through his mind so quickly that he was unable to retain them; so at the time it had seemed that his conclusions sprang from nowhere. In my consultation room, he described what might be called primary and secondary fantasies. The former refer to the fleeting and, at the time, forgotten impressions he had when he was having his "hunches." The latter were, in fact, associations that he had while on the couch; they represented secondary fantasies about the primary fantasies. They also depicted various transference feelings, given that my "deviation" from analysis to explore any interest in creativity could not help but have some influence on the course of the analysis. I do not wish to dwell on this technical issue, which involves what could be considered a clash between a therapeutic perspective and a research interest. I will simply mention that it did not seem to create any particular obstacle that impeded the course of the analysis.

To find a solution to a problem that has never been solved before, perhaps never even been previously articulated, represents an accretion to reality. This is a creative accomplishment, which, in the case of the scientist I have just been discussing, occurred without any conscious awareness of the mental process operating at the time. His primary fantasies were concrete representations of his thought processes, as Freud (1900) described when he wrote about Silberer's "functional phenomena." My patient reported images of being underground and digging deep tunnels, breaking through the surface, and being flooded with sunlight. He also saw numbers spinning furiously in whirlpools that dragged him back into the earth. This was an exhilarating rather than a frightening, nightmarish experience, but he emphasized again that he was not aware of any of these feelings and images during the short time he was working on a problem. He was somewhat cognizant of a vibrant feeling that he attributed to the excitement of seeking a solution.

In association to the creative, intuitive state, he thought of Maury's dream, described in Chapter I of the *Interpretation of Dreams* (Freud, 1900). Maury, who lived during the French revolution, had an involved dream in which he was found guilty by a tribunal, taken out of his cell, and driven in a cart to the guillotine. There were many incidents and details in the dream, which ends when Maury feels the blade hit his neck as he is being executed. He then awakened from the dream to find that the headboard of the bed had fallen on his neck and awakened him. Freud concluded that the dream stimulus was the somatic impact of the falling headboard, and that the lengthy, involved dream occurred in a fraction of a second. There were many reasons the patient described Maury's dream. Some point to transference issues, such as wanting to be my collaborator as he indicated an interest in psychoanalysis. He was also pointing out how the unconscious, and this includes unconscious mental activity, is not bound to the passage of time. Freud has emphasized the timelessness of the unconscious, and the patient was stressing how quickly fantasy and images can occur and, therefore, be glossed over. He had little difficulty, however, in recalling them during our sessions.

The fantasies he had when immersed in problem-solving mental processes were pictorial, concrete representations of complex, abstract thought operations. They undoubtedly were concerned with primary-process factors as well (see Giovacchini, 1960). A fantasy is so constructed that it includes images and perceptions, sometimes stimuli, from the outer world. As just stated, in addition, it is based on structures, activities, and processes that belong to the inner world of the mind. Thus, a fantasy is the product of the inner and outer worlds. This in-between characteristic of straddling two worlds would, from a conceptual viewpoint, properly locate fantasy production in the transitional space. The fantasies of creative persons, whether perceived or not at the time, are the manifest content of a latent creative process. We do not know very much about these underlying innovative activities, but, as the fantasies indicate, they contain many primary-process elements that are subjected to integrative processing, a secondary-process operation. Here, again, we have a combination of activities that are directed toward both the inner and outer worlds, stressing the importance of the transitional space.

Summary and Conclusions

The basic source of creativity still remains a mystery and is perhaps outside the realm of psychoanalytic exploration. Still, there is much about the psychic operations and character structure of creative persons that can teach us considerably about innovative processes. If we have the opportunity to treat such persons, there is also much that we can learn about the unique features of their psychopathology. Somewhat ironically, this enables us to illuminate psychopathological factors that are generally found in character disorders and mental breakdown, conditions that are rarely associated with creative functioning.

The backgrounds of creative scientists and artists often differ from those of patients suffering from primitive mental states. The environments of the former seem to be gratifying and soothing, rather than depriving, destructive, and disruptive. Some of the scientists I have studied seem to have had an abundance of mothering and, in some instances, have had two fathers, that is, in addition to the biological father, had another man in the house who related to the patient in a fatherly or avuncular fashion.

Most of the scientists I treated could be considered mavericks. They belonged to the herd, so to speak, but they remained on the periphery. They retained some of the values and standards of the group, but they did not allow themselves to be constricted by convention. This freedom was a factor in determining their bold ventures in seeking new conceptual systems.

During regressed periods, creative patients may fear that their valued internal objects may be destroyed by disruptive inner turmoil. In order to feel safe and once again achieve calm, the patient may project his good parts, those that contain his creative talent, into the analyst. He places them there for safe keeping, trusting in the therapist's greater capacity to keep good and bad separated.

The creative patient has a special adeptness for using metaphor and producing fantasies. Some seem to be fantasying all the time, whereas others solve problems by making intuitive hunches without being aware of any conscious thought processes or fantasies. There are, nevertheless, fleeting fantasies. One patient had very little difficulty recalling them later during a session, and revealed how fantasies that were not perceived at the time of problem solving were instrumental to his creative endeavors.

The use of fantasy in the creative process highlights the importance of the transitional space. The creator works in this area, and fantasies, similar to transitional objects, have elements of both the inner and outer world. The creative process relies heavily on the primary process, and some of its operations superficially resemble psychopathological adaptations. The operations of the mind in the in-between transitional space involve processes that contain both elements of the self and of the outer world, and may lead to mental breakdown or to creative integration.

The study of the mind at its highest level of functioning reveals the breadth of the mental apparatus from its structured integrative levels to the depths of the personality. The latter contain the focal elements of psychopathology, which, alongside creative activity, can occupy the transitional space. Although, as has been often emphasized, there are no etiological connections between creativity and emotional illness, the maladaptations that are characteristic of disturbed primitive mental states can be dealt with in a creative fashion in a psychotherapeutic setting.

References

Alexander, F. (1961). *The Scope of Psychoanalysis*, New York: Basic Books.
Arnstein, R. (1979). The adolescent identity crisis revisited. In *Adolescent Psychiatry*, S. Feinstein and P. Giovacchini, eds., pp. 71–84. Chicago: University of Chicago Press.
Balint, M. (1968). *The Basic Fault*. London: Tavistock.
Bateson, G. (1951a). Conventions of communication. In *Communication: The Social Matrix of Psychiatry*, J. Ruesch and G. Bateson, eds., pp. 212–218. New York: W. W. Norton.
——— . (1951b). Information and codification. In *Communication: The Social Matrix of Psychiatry*, J. Ruesch and G. Bateson, eds., pp. 168–212. New York: W. W. Norton.
Beatrice, J. (1985). Narcissism, object relatedness and drive-conflict. In *Yearbook of the Society for Psychoanalytic Psychotherapy*, R. Langs, ed., 1:247–273. Hillsdale, N.J.: Newconcept Press.
Bergmann, P., and Escalona, S. (1949). Unusual sensitivities in very young children. In *The Psychoanalytic Study of the Child* 3 & 4: pp. 333–352. New York: International Universities Press.

Bertin, C. (1982). *Marie Bonaparte*, San Diego, New York & London: Harcourt, Brace and Jovanovich.

Bion, W. R. (1957). Differentiation of the psychotic from the nonpsychotic personality. In L. Grinberg, *Second Thoughts*, pp. 43-64. London: Heineman, 1967.

Blos, P. (1966). *On Adolescence*. New York: International Universities Press.

Boyer, L. B. (1956). On maternal stimulation and ego defects. In *The Psychoanalytic Study of the Child*, 11:236-256. New York: International Universities Press.

―――. (1983). *The Regressed Patient*. New York: Jason Aronson.

Boyer, L. B.,and Giovacchini, P. L. (1967). *Psychoanalytic Treatment of Characterological and Schizophrenic Disorders*. New York: Jason Aronson.

―――. (1980). *Psychoanalytic Treatment of Schizophrenic, Borderline and Characterological Disorders*. New York: Jason Aronson.

Brazelton, T. B. (1963). The early mother–infant adjustment. *Pediatrics*, 32:931-938.

Breuer, J., and Freud, S. (1895). Studies on Hysteria, *Standard Edition*, 2:1-252.

Bullard, D. (1984). *The concept of psychotic regression*. Presented at the Colloque International Psychoanalyse: Adolescent Psychoses, Paris, May, 1984.

Byschowski, G. (1952). *Psychotherapy of Psychosis*. New York: Grune & Stratton.

Dorpat, T. (1976). Structural conflict and object relations conflict. *Journal of the American Psychoanalytic Association*, 24:855-874.

Eisnitz, A. J. (1981). The perspective of the self-representation. *Journal of the American Psychoanalytic Association*, 29:309-337.

Eissler, K. (1953). The effect of the structure of the ego on psychoanalytic technique. *Journal of the American Psychoanalytic Association*, 1:104-143.

―――. (1958). Goethe and science. In *Psychoanalysis and the Social Sciences*, W. Muensterberger and S. Axelrod, eds., 5:51-89. New York: International Universities Press.

Ellenberger, H. (1970). *The Discovery of the Unconscious*. New York: Basic Books.

Emde, R., Goensbauer, T., and Harmon, R. J. (1976). *Emotional Expression in Infancy*. New York: International Universities Press.

Emde, R., and Robinson, J. (1984). The first two months: recent research in developmental psychobiology and the changing view of the newborn. In J. Noshpits & J. Call (Eds.), *Basic Handbook of Child Psychiatry.* New York: Basic Books.

Epstein, L., and Feiner, A. H. (1979). *Countertransference.* New York: Jason Aronson.

Erikson, E. H. (1959). *Identity and the Life Cycle.* New York: International Universities Press.

Federn, P. (1952). *Ego Psychology and the Psychoses.* New York: Basic Books.

Feinsilver, D. (1980). Transitional relatedness and containment in the treatment of a chronic schizophrenic patient. *International Review of Psycho-Analysis,* 7:309–318.

———. (1983). Application of Pao's theories to the case study of the use and misuse of medication. *Psychoanalytic Inquiry,* 3 (No. 1): 125–145.

Flarsheim, A. (1975). The therapist's collusion in the patient's wish for suicide. In *Tactics and Techniques in Psychoanalytic Therapy, Vol. II: Countertransference,* ed., P. Giovacchini, pp. 155–195. New York: Jason Aronson.

Fox, R., Sheas, S., and Dumas, T. (1980). Stereopsis in human infants. *Science,* 207:323–327.

Fraiberg, S. (1969). Libidinal object constancy and mental representation. *The Psychoanalytic Study of the Child,* 24: 48–70. New York: International Universities Press.

Freeman, D. (1971). Genetic influences on development of behavior. In *Normal and Abnormal Development of Behavior,* G. B. A. Stoelings and J. J. Van der Werff Ten Bosch, eds., Leiden: Leiden University Press.

———. (1979). The sensory deprivations. *Bulletin of the Menninger Clinic,* 43: 29–68.

Freud, A. (1951). Observations on child development. *The Psychoanalytic Study of the Child,* 6: 18–30. New York: International Universities Press.

Freud, S. (1900). The interpretation of dreams. *Standard Edition,* 4–5: 1–629. London: Hogarth Press, 1964.

———. (1905). Three essays on the theory of sex. *Standard Edition,* 7: 122–243. London: Hogarth Press, 1964.

———. (1909a). Five Lectures on psycho-analysis. *Standard Edition,* 11: 1–56. London: Hogarth Press, 1964.

———. (1909b). Notes upon a case of obsessional neurosis. *Standard Edition,* 10: 151–251. London: Hogarth Press, 1964.

———. (1910a). The future prospects of psycho-analytic therapy. *Standard Edition,* 11: 139–153. London: Hogarth Press. 1964.

———. (1910b). Leonardo da Vinci and a memory of his childhood. *Standard Edition*, 11: 59–139. London: Hogarth Press, 1964.

———. (1911). Psychoanalytic notes on an autobiographical account of a case of paranoia (dementia paranoides). *Standard Edition*, 12: 1–82. London: Hogarth Press, 1964.

———. (1912a). The dynamics of transference. *Standard Edition*, 12: 97–109. London: Hogarth Press, 1964.

———. (1912b). Recommendations to physicians practising psycho-analysis. *Standard Edition*, 12: 109–121. London: Hogarth Press, 1964.

———. (1914a). The Moses of Michelangelo. *Standard Edition*, 13: 209–237. London: Hogarth Press, 1964.

———. (1914b). Observations on transference love. *Standard Edition*, 12: 157–172. London: Hogarth Press, 1964.

———. (1914c). On narcissism. *Standard Edition*, 14: 67–102. London: Hogarth Press, 1964.

———. (1914d). Remembering, repeating and working through. *Standard Edition*, 12: 145–157. London: Hogarth Press, 1964.

———. (1911–1915). Papers on technique. *Standard Edition*, 12: 85–175. London: Hogarth Press, 1964.

———. (1915a). Instincts and their vicissitudes. *Standard Edition*, 14: 103–140. London: Hogarth Press, 1963.

———. (1915b). Repression. *Standard Edition*, 14:141–159. London: Hogarth Press, 1963.

———. (1915c). The unconscious. *Standard Edition*, 14: 159–215. London: Hogarth Press, 1963.

———. (1916). Some character types met with in psycho-analytic work. *Standard Edition*, 14: 309–337. London: Hogarth Press, 1963.

———. (1916–1917). Introductory lectures on psycho-analysis. *Standard Edition*, 15–16: 13–481. London: Hogarth Press, 1964.

———. (1920). Beyond the pleasure principle. *Standard Edition*, 18: 3–66. London: Hogarth Press, 1964.

———. (1921). Group psychology and analysis of the ego. *Standard Edition*, 18: 65–143. London: Hogarth Press, 1964.

———. (1923a). The ego and the id. *Standard Edition*, 19: 1–60. London: Hogarth Press, 1964.

———. (1923b). The infantile genital organization: an interpolation into the theory of sexuality. *Standard Edition*, 19: 141–149. London: Hogarth Press, 1964.

———. (1924a). The loss of reality in neurosis and psychosis. *Standard Edition*, 19: 183–191. London: Hogarth Press, 1964.

——. (1924b). Neurosis and psychosis. *Standard Edition*, 19: 149-153. London: Hogarth Press, 1964.

——. (1926). The problem of anxiety. *Standard Edition*, 20: 75-177. London: Hogarth Press, 1964.

——. (1937). Analysis, terminable and interminable. *Standard Edition*, 23: 209-255. London: Hogarth Press, 1964.

——. (1938). Splitting of the ego in the process of defence. *Standard Edition*, 23: 129-271. London: Hogarth Press, 1964.

Fromm-Reichman, F. (1959). *Psychoanalysis and Psychotherapy*. Chicago: University of Chicago Press.

Giovacchini, P. (1958a). Mutual adaptation in various object relationships. *International Journal of Psycho-Analysis*, 39: 1-8.

——. (1958b). Some affective meanings of dizziness. *Psychoanalytic Quarterly*, 27: 217-225.

——. (1960). On scientific creativity. *Journal of the American Psychoanalytic Association*, 8: 407-426.

——. (1965). Some aspects of the ego ideal of a creative scientist. *Psychoanalytic Quarterly*, 34: 79-101.

——. (1967). Frustration and externalization. *Psychoanalytic Quarterly*, 36: 571-583.

——. (1969). Treatment of marital disharmonies: The classical approach. *Character Disorders and Adaptive Mechanisms*, pp. 221-253. New York: Jason Aronson, 1984.

——. (1971). Characterological factors and the creative personality. *Journal of the American Psychoanalytic Association*, 19: 524-542.

——. (1972). *Tactics and Techniques in Psychoanalytic Therapy, 1*. New York: Jason Aronson.

——. (1975a). *Psychoanalysis of Character Disorders*. New York: Jason Aronson.

——. (1975b). *Tactics and Techniques in Psychoanalytic Therapy. Countertransference*. New York: Jason Aronson.

——. (1977). A critique of Kohut's theory of narcissism. *Adolescent Psychiatry*, 5: 213-235.

——. (1979a). The sins of the parents: the borderline adolescent and primal confusion. *Adolescent Psychiatry*, 7: 213-233.

——. (1979b). *The Treatment of Primitive Mental States*. New York: Jason Aronson.

——. (1980). *A Clinician's Guide to Reading Freud*. New York: Jason Aronson.

——. (1981a). Creativity, adolescence and inevitable failure. *Adolescent Psychiatry*, 9: 35-60.

——. (1981b). Countertransference and therapeutic turmoil. *Contemporary Psychoanalysis*, 17: 565-595.

——. (1984). *Character Disorders and Adaptive Mechanisms*. New York: Jason Aronson.

Giovacchini, P., and Boyer, L. B. (1975). The psychoanalytic impasse. *International Journal of Psychoanalytic Psychotherapy*, 4: 25-27.

——. (1983). *Technical Factors in the Treatment of the Severely Disturbed Patient*. New York: Jason Aronson.

Gitelson, M. (1958). On ego distortion. *International Journal of Psycho-Analysis*, 39: 243-275.

Glover, E. (1930). Grades of ego differentiation. *International Journal of Psycho-Analysis*, 11: 1-12.

Greenacre, P. (1956). Experience of awe in childhood. *The Psychoanalytic Study of the Child*, 11: 9-30. New York: International Universities Press.

——. (1957). The childhood of the artist. *The Psychoanalytic Study of the Child*, 12: 47-72. New York: International Universities Press.

Greenson, R. (1969). *The Technique and Practice of Psychoanalysis*. New York: International Universities Press.

Grolnick, S., Barkin, L., and Muensterberger, W. (1978). *Between Reality and Fantasy: Transitional Objects and Phenomena*. New York: Jason Aronson.

Guttman, S., Jones, R., and Parrish, S. (1980). *Concordance to the Psychological Works of Sigmund Freud*. Boston: G. K. Hall.

Hartmann, H. (1939). *Ego Psychology and the Process of Adaptation*. New York: International Universities Press.

——. (1950). Comments on the psychoanalytic theory of the ego. *The Psychoanalytic Study of the Child*, 5: 74-96. New York: International Universities Press.

——. (1955). Notes on the theory of sublimation. *The Psychoanalytic Study of the Child*, 10: 9-29. New York: International Universities Press.

Held, R. (1981). Development of visual acuity in infants with normal and anomalous visual experience. In *Development and Visual Perception*, 3, eds., Aslin et al., pp. 63-96. New York: Academic Press.

Herrick, E. J. (1956). *The Evolution of Human Nature*. Austin: University of Texas Press.

Jacobson, E. (1964). *The Self and the Object World*. New York: International Universities Press.

Johnson, A. M., and Szurek, S. (1952). The genesis of antisocial acting out in children and adults. *Psychoanalytic Quarterly*, 3: 323–335.

————. (1964). Etiology of antisocial behavior in delinquents and psychopaths. *Journal of the American Medical Association*, 154: 814–817.

Jones, E. (1953). *The Life and Works of Sigmund Freud, I*. New York: Basic Books.

Kernberg, O. (1975). *Borderline Conditions and Pathological Narcissism*. New York: Jason Aronson.

Klaus, M., and Kennell, J. (1982). *Parent–Infant Bonding*. St. Louis: Mosby.

Klein, M. (1929). Infantile anxiety reactions reflected in a work of art. *International Journal of Psycho-Analysis*, 10: 436–444.

————. (1946). Notes on some schizoid mechanisms. *International Journal of Psycho-Analysis*, 27: 99–110.

Kohut, H. (1971). *The Analysis of the Self*. New York: International Universities Press.

Kris, E. (1952). *Psychoanalytic Explorations in Art*. New York: International Universities Press.

Kuhn, T. S. (1962). *The Structure of Scientific Revolutions*. Chicago: University of Chicago Press.

Lee, H. B. (1940). A theory concerning creativity in the inventive arts. *Psychiatry*, 2: 229–293.

Levine, H. (1979). The sustaining object relationships. *Annals of Psychoanalysis*, 7: 203–231.

Lewin, B. D. (1958). *Dreams and the Use of Regression*. New York: International Universities Press.

Lindon, J. (1967). Panel on regression. *Psychoanalytic Forum*, 2: 295–317.

Lipton, S. (1977). The advantages of Freud's techniques as shown in the analysis of the rat-man. *International Journal of Psycho-Analysis*, 58: 255–273.

Loewald, H. (1960). On the therapeutic action of psycho-analysis. *International Journal of Psycho-Analysis*, 41: 16–33.

Mahler, M. (1952). On child psychosis and schizophrenia: autistic and symbiotic infantile psychoses. *The Psychoanalytic Study of the Child*, 7: 286–305. New York: International Universities Press.

————. (1963). Thoughts about development and individuation. *The Psychoanalytic Study of the Child*, 13: 307–324. New York: International Universities Press.

————. (1972). A study of the separation-individuation process and its possible application to borderline phenomena in the psychoanalytic situation. *The Psychoanalytic Study of the Child*, 27: 403–424. New York: International Universities Press.

Martin, P. (1975). The obnoxious patient. In *Tactics and Techniques in Psychoanalytic Therapy. Vol. II: Countertransference*, ed., P. Giovacchini, pp. 196–205. New York: Jason Aronson.

Masterson, J. (1976). *Treatment of the Borderline Adult: A Developmental Approach*. New York: Brunner/Mazel.

Meltzoff, A. N., and Moore, M. K. (1977). Imitations of facial and manual gestures by human neonates. *Science*, 198: 75–78.

Modell, S. (1968). *Object Love and Reality*. New York: International Universities Press.

Noy, P. (1979). The psychoanalytic theory of cognitive development. *The Psychoanalytic Study of the Child*, 34: 385–421. New York: International Universities Press.

Pao, P. N. (1979). *Schizophrenic Disorders*, New York: International Universities Press.

Piaget, J. (1937). *The Construction of Reality in the Child*. New York: Basic Books, 1954.

————. (1952). *Language and Thought of the Child*. London: Routledge & Kegan Paul.

Poincaré, H. (1952). *Science and Method*. New York: Dover.

Poland, W. S. (1984). On the analyst's neutrality. *Journal of the American Psychoanalytic Association*, 32: 283–301.

Pupin, M. (1925). *From Immigrant to Inventor*. New York: Charles Scribner & Sons.

Racker, H. (1968). *Transference and Countertransference*. New York: International Universities Press.

Reichard, S. (1956). A re-examination of "Studies in Hysteria." *Psychoanalytic Quarterly*, 25: 155–177.

Rinsley, D. (1982). Object relations theory and psychotherapy, with particular reference to the self-disordered patient. In *Treatment of the Severely Disturbed Patient*, eds., P. Giovacchini and L. B. Boyer, pp. 187–215. New York: Jason Aronson.

Roe, A. (1953). *The Making of a Scientist*. New York: Dodd, Mead.

Roth, D., and Blatt, S. J. (1975). Ego structure, psychopathology and spatial representation. In *Tactics and Techniques in Psychoanalytic Therapy: Vol. II: Countertransference*, ed., P. Giovacchini, pp. 281–292. New York: Jason Aronson.

Ruesch, J. (1951). Communication and mental illness. In *Communica-*

tion the Social Matrix of Psychiatry, eds., J. Ruesch, and G. Bateson, pp. 50–94. New York: W. W. Norton.

Sandler, J., and Rosenblatt, B. (1962). The concept of the representational world. *The Psychoanalytic Study of the Child*, 17: 128–145. New York: International Universities Press.

Schafer, R. (1984). The pursuit of failure and the idealization of unhappiness. *American Psychologist*, 39: 389–406.

Scharfstein, B. (1978). Adolescents and philosophers: A word in favor of both. *Adolescent Psychiatry*, 6: 51–58.

Schur, M. (1958). The ego and the id in anxiety. *Psychoanalytic Study of the Child*, 13: 190–223. New York: International Universities Press.

Searles, H. F. (1975). The patient as therapist to his analyst. In *Tactics and Techniques in Psychoanalytic Therapy, Vol. II: Countertransference*, ed. P. Giovacchini, pp. 95–151. New York: Jason Aronson.

——. (1976). Transitional phenomena and therapeutic symbiosis. *International Journal of Psychoanalytic Psychotherapy*, 5: 145–204.

Shapiro, T. (1984). On neutrality. *Journal of the American Psychoanalytic Association*, 32: 269–283.

Spitz, R. (1945). Hospitalism: An inquiry into the genesis of psychiatric conditions in early childhood. *The Psychoanalytic Study of the Child*, 1: 53–74. New York: International Universities Press.

——. (1957). *No and Yes*. New York: International Universities Press.

——. (1965). *The First Year of Life*. New York: International Universities Press.

Stein, M. (1953). Creativity and culture. *Journal of Psychology*, 32: 311–322.

Sterba, R. (1934). The fate of the ego in analytic therapy. *International Journal of Psycho-Analysis*, 15: 117–126.

Szajnberg, N. (1983). Visual maturation and part-object mental representations in the first half year of life. *Mental Health Journal*, 4: 83–94.

Tausk, V. (1919). On the origin of the influencing machine. *Psychoanalytic Quarterly* (1933) 2: 519–550.

Tustin, F. (1981). *Autistic States in Children*. London: Routledge & Kegan Paul.

Valenstein, A. F. (1983). Working through and resistance to change: Insight and the action system. *Journal of the American Psychoanalytic Association*, 31: 353–375.

Wallerstein, R. (1981). The bipolar self. *Journal of the American Psychoanalytic Association*, 29: 377–394.

——. (1983). Defenses, defense mechanisms and the structure of the mind. *Journal of the American Psychoanalytic Association*, 31: 201–227.

Winnicott, D. W. (1952). Psychosis and child care. In *Collected Papers: Through Pediatrics to Psycho-analysis*, pp. 219–228. New York: Basic Books, 1958.

——. (1953). Transitional objects and transitional phenomena. In *Playing and Reality*, pp. 1–26. London: Tavistock, 1971.

——. (1956). Primary maternal preoccupation. In *Collected Papers: Through Pediatrics to Psycho-Analysis*, pp. 300–315. New York: Basic Books, 1958.

——. (1960). Ego distortion in terms of the true and false self. In *The Maturational Processes and the Facilitating Environment*, pp. 140–153. New York: International Universities Press, 1974.

——. (1963a). The development of the capacity for concern. In *The Maturational Processes and the Facilitating Environment*, pp. 73–83. New York: International Universities Press, 1974.

——. (1963b). The mentally ill in your case load. In *The Maturational Processes and the Facilitating Environment*, pp. 217–230. New York: International Universities Press, 1974.

——. (1967). The location of the cultural experience. In *Playing and Reality*, pp. 95–103. London: Tavistock, 1971.

——. (1969). The use of an object and relating through identification. In *Playing and Reality*, pp. 86–95. London: Tavistock, 1971.

——. (1971). *Playing and Reality*. London: Tavistock.

Zeigarnek, B. (1927). Das behalten erledigter und unerledigter handlung. *Psychologische Forschung*, 9: 1–85.

Zetzel, E. (1956). Current concept of transference. *Journal of the American Psychoanalytic Association*, 1: 526–537.

Subject Index

Acting out
  as resistance, 218
  vs. working through, 218–220
Amnesia, childhood, 9, 208
*Analysis Terminable and
  Interminable*, 180
Analyst
  Freud's view of, 1–3
  function of, 3, 11
  impact of schizophrenic
    patient on, 172
  neutrality of, 125–126, 128–129
  optimal fusion of, with
    patient, 24
  responsiveness of, 198
  self-representation of, 207
  as supportive of delusions in
    schizophrenia, 168–171
  as transitional object, 28

Analyst-patient relationship, 4,
  34, 232–235
  symbiotic transference in, 24–
    25
Analytic neutrality. *See*
    Neutrality, analytic
  countertransference vs., 244
  projection and, 226
Analytic setting
  components of, 223
  disruption of, 220–228
Anger
  soothing effect of, 53, 67
  as soothing mechanism, 67
Animate object constancy, 106
Anorexia nervosa, 155–156
Anxiety
  apathetic terror and, 112
  Freud's view of, 141

Double-bind message, 149–150
  effect of, an ego, 151
  psychic death and, 153
Drives
  conflicting, 103
  Freud on, 103
  and structural conflicts, 103

Early mentation stage
  description of, 40
  ego boundaries in, 41
  ego organization in, 40–41
  preobject state of, 41
Ego
  drive conflict with, 104
  executive functions of, 64
  self-representation as
    subsystem of, 104
  self vs., 104
Ego boundaries, 20, 25
  of borderline patient, 76, 108
  effect of trauma on formation
    of, 32
  loss of, 107
  of patient treated as
    transitional object by
    mother, 81
  in psychotic patient, 153–154
  in schizophrenia, 39–140, 138,
    154
Ego psychology
  contribution of, to
    psychoanalysis, 5
  id and, 102
  object relations theory and,
    102
Emotional development, Freud's
  model of, 5, 19
Environment mother, 200
Erotic transference, 206
Evocative memory, 105, 106

mental representations in, 105
and object constancy, 130
Executive ego system, effect of
  defective self-representation
  on, 141
Externalization, 58–59
  analytic setting disruption by,
    227
  corrective emotional
    experience vs., 227–228
  nature of, 223
  projection vs., 226

False-self, 8, 25, 46
  as adaptive mechanism in
    schizophrenia, 159
  character neuroses and, 45–46
Fantasy, 209
  primary vs. secondary, 356
  transitional phenomena and,
    353–358
Fixation, 38
  and object constancy, 110
Fragmentation, 46, 99
  in borderline patient, 86
  See also Splitting
Free association
  borderline patients and, 94–98
  deterrants to, 4–5, 206
  Freud's view of, 3
  pressure technique in, 178
  resistance to, 4
Functional phenomena, 357
Fusion
  fear of, 113–118
  in schizophrenia, 154

Genius. *See* Creativity
Good enough mother, 80, 81
Grandiosity, 185, 228

Name Index

Alexander, F., 90, 227
Arnstein, R., 315–316

Balint, M., 20
Barkin, L., 79
Bateson, G., 149, 150
Beatrice, J., 21
Bergmann, P., 318
Bertin, C., 2
Bion, W. R., 139
Blatt, S. J., 41
Blos, P., 302, 315
Boyer, L. B., 20, 44, 46, 77, 88,
    113, 133, 223, 245, 278
Brazelton, T. B., 17
Breuer, J., 2, 3, 110, 178, 195, 207
Bullard, D., 150
Byschowski, G., 112

Dorpat, T., 103
Dumas, T., 41

Eisnitz, A. J., 104
Eissler, K., 93, 306, 308, 123
Ellenberger, H., 134, 348
Emde, R., 17
Epstein, L., 247–248
Erikson, E. H., 91, 303
Escalona, S., 318

Federn, P., 25, 104, 112
Feiner, A. H., 247–248
Feinsilver, D., 28, 236, 238
Flarsheim, A., 68
Fox, R., 41
Fraiberg, S., 34, 88, 105